When Will These Things Happen?

A Study of Jesus as Judge in Matthew 21-25

PATERNOSTER BIBLICAL MONOGRAPHS

A full listing of titles in both this series and
Paternoster Theological Monographs
appears at the end of this book

PATERNOSTER BIBLICAL MONOGRAPHS

When Will These Things Happen?

A Study of Jesus as Judge in Matthew 21-25

Alistair I. Wilson

Foreword by Simon J. Kistemaker

Wipf & Stock
PUBLISHERS
Eugene, Oregon

Wipf and Stock Publishers
199 W 8th Ave, Suite 3
Eugene, OR 97401

When Will These Things Happen?
A Study of Jesus as Judge in Matthew 21–25
By Wilson, Alistair I.
Copyright©2004 Paternoster
ISBN: 1-59752-727-0
Publication date 6/5/2006
Previously published by Paternoster, 2004

This Edition Published by Wipf and Stock Publishers
by arrangement with Paternoster

Paternoster
9 Holdom Avenue
Bletchley
Milton Keyes, MK1 1QR
PATERNOSTER Great Britain

Series Preface

One of the major objectives of Paternoster is to serve biblical scholarship by providing a channel for the publication of theses and other monographs of high quality at affordable prices. Paternoster stands within the broad evangelical tradition of Christianity. Our authors would describe themselves as Christians who recognise the authority of the Bible, maintain the centrality of the gospel message and assent to the classical credal statements of Christian belief. There is diversity within this constituency; advances in scholarship are possible only if there is freedom for frank debate on controversial issues and for the publication of new and sometimes provocative proposals. What is offered in this series is the best of writing by committed Christians who are concerned to develop well-founded biblical scholarship in a spirit of loyalty to the historic faith.

Series Editors

To Jenny

Contents

Foreword

In the last two decades, scholars have studied the cultural setting of the historical Jesus and with reference to him have reappraised the topic of eschatology. Much of their research on Jesus has been published, and of late this research has been dubbed the Third Quest for the Historical Jesus

One notable contributor to this body of research is Marcus Borg. He has written on Jesus as, among other things, *sage and prophet*, arguing for a 'non-eschatological Jesus'. But the question must be asked whether his writings adequately represent Jesus as the eschatological judge. Alistair Wilson carefully examined this theme in the light of Matthew 21-25 and concluded that an independent study on Jesus as judge is warranted in regard to the nature of judgement, the time of judgement, and Jesus' role in judgement. He set out to write a dissertation titled *Matthew's Portrait of Jesus as Judge*, of which the present book is a minimally revised form. He learned that Matthew has composed his gospel as a coherent message and pursued the goal of presenting a faithful account of Jesus' life and message. The theme of judgement is part and parcel of that gospel.

Wilson concludes that Jesus is a prophet with a prophetic ministry and authority. This authority exceeds that of the prophets, for Jesus not only pronounces judgement but also enacts it, and by doing so he assumes the role of Yahweh. Thus, as Jesus pronounces judgement on those who sin willfully he portrays himself as judge. By means of parables, he teaches that those who have rejected God even while enjoying his blessings would have to appear before the judge of all nations. Jesus' judgement extends beyond the prediction of Jerusalem's destruction and includes an eschatological trial that is universal.

Recently some scholars, including Marcus Borg and John Dominic Crossan, have rejected the teaching that Jesus is an eschatological judge. They depict him as a Jewish rabbi who challenged the societal structure of his day. They set forth the teaching that Jesus filled two models of prophet and sage that are complementary but not mutually exclusive. For example, Borg thinks that Jesus believed in a Day of Judgement but he rejects the teaching that Jesus preached an imminent end. Wilson points out that Matthew in his gospel regarded Jesus not merely as a temporal judge but as an eschatological judge, who will return to judge all nations. Chapters 21-25 indicate that Jesus passed judgement on his religious contemporaries and predicted a universal judgement that would take place at the end of time. Indeed Jesus is the judge of both Israel and the nations.

Alistair Wilson has written a study that reveals first-class scholarship. He demonstrates that he is fully abreast of issues that are currently being discussed. In his interactions he is tactful, serene, and persuasive. While applauding the view of others, he nevertheless shows his difference from them by carefully demonstrating on the basis of Matthew's Gospel that Jesus indeed is judge both in the first century and at the consummation. This book is an excellent addition to evangelical research that champions a high view of Scripture.

Simon J. Kistemaker,
Reformed Theological Seminary, Orlando, Florida, USA

Acknowledgements

This book is the result of a long process of study and writing through which numerous people have enabled me to persevere. I am pleased to have the opportunity to record my thanks to the following people:

To Mr Jeremy Mudditt of Paternoster for his willingness to accept my work into the Biblical Monograph Series and for his patience when the finished product took longer to appear than any of us would have wished.

To Rev. Dr Anthony Cross who has been particularly helpful throughout the process of preparing the manuscript for publication. I am grateful both for his careful scrutiny of my work and for his warm encouragement to persevere.

To Professor I. Howard Marshall, the supervisor of my doctoral studies, whose gentle yet firm direction, incisive comments and great patience made possible completion of the thesis, of which this book is the published form.

To the 'Anonymous Benefactor' who generously provided the financial resources to fund my postgraduate research without any expectation of personal thanks. I am grateful for this person's willingness to use their money in furthering Christian scholarship, and I trust that this book brings them some degree of satisfaction.

To my colleagues at the Highland Theological College, both teaching and non-teaching staff, whose friendship, support, illuminating comments and words of encouragement are appreciated far more than they can know.

To my parents, Iain and Edna Wilson, who have supported me in every way throughout my lengthy process of education.

To my Mother-in-Law, Daphne Spraggett, whose appreciation of both the joys and frustrations of writing have enabled her to offer wise counsel on numerous occasions during the writing of this book. My late Father-in-Law, Roy Spraggett, provided me with a model of diligent study of the scriptures used in service of the Church of Christ. I am glad to acknowledge his substantial impact on my life.

To my wider circle of family and friends, who have prayed for me and shown interest in my work, of which this book has been a part.

To my wife, Jenny, whose love, friendship, and companionship are great gifts from our Father in Heaven. It is a joy to serve him together..

To my children, Rachel, Bethany and Stephen, who while too young as yet to appreciate what Daddy has been writing all these years, nonetheless, by their love and affection, put the significance of this book in proper perspective. They have enabled me to maintain my sanity by providing appropriate distractions from study at regular intervals, and for that I am deeply grateful, even if I did not show it at the time. I pray that they will grow up knowing and trusting the Jesus who is the subject of this book.

Abbreviations

AB	Anchor Bible
ABD	*Anchor Bible Dictionary* D. N. Freedman, ed. (New York: Doubleday, 1992)
ABRL	Anchor Bible Reference Library
BAG	*A Greek-English Lexicon of the New Testament*, Edited by W. Bauer, W. F. Arndt and F. W. Gingrich (Chicago: University of Chicago Press, 1957).
BBR	*Bulletin for Biblical Research*
BDB	Brown, F., S. R. Driver and C. A. Briggs, *A Hebrew and English Lexicon of the Old Testament* (Oxford, 1907)
BECNT	Baker Exegetical Commentary on the New Testament, edited by M. Silva (Grand Rapids: Baker)
BETL	Bibliotheca ephemeridum theologicarumlovaniensium
BGBE	Beiträge zur Geschichte der biblischen Exegese
BJRL	*Bulletin of the John Rylands Library*
BLG	Biblical Languages: Greek
BZNW	Beihefte zur Zeitschrift für die neutestamentliche Wissenschaft
CB	Coniectanea Biblica
CBQ	*Catholic Biblical Quarterly*
DJG	*Dictionary of Jesus and the Gospels*, edited by J. B. Green, S. McKnight and I. H. Marshall (Leicester: IVP, 1992)
DPL	*Dictionary of Paul and his Letters*, Edited by G. Hawthorne and R. P. Martin (Leicester: IVP, 1993)
DLNT	*Dictionary of the Later New Testament and Its Developments* Edited by P. H. Davids (Leicester: IVP, 1998)
EDNT	*Exegetical Dictionary of the New Testament*, edited by H. Balz and G. Schneider (Edinburgh: T&T Clark, 1990-1993)
EKK	Evangelisch-Katholischer Kommentar zum Neuen Testament
ExpT	*The Expository Times*
FS	Festschrift
FOTL	The Forms of the Old Testament Literature
GP	Gospel Perspectives
HBT	*Horizons in Biblical Theology*
IBC	Interpretation: A Bible Commentary for Teaching and Preaching
ICC	International Critical Commentary
IRT	Issues in Religion and Theology
JETS	*Journal of the Evangelical Theological Society*
JBL	*Journal of Biblical Literature*

JSNT	*Journal for the Study of the New Testament*
JSNTS	Journal for the Study of the New Testament Supplement Series
JTS	*Journal of Theological Studies*
LXX	Septuagint
MBS	Message of Biblical Spirituality
NAC	New American Commentary (D. S. Dockery, General Editor)
NCBC	New Century Bible Commentary (R. C Clements, Old Testament Editor; M. Black, New Testament Editor; Grand Rapids: Eerdmans)
NSBT	New Studies in Biblical Theology
NWNTI	*Noncanonical Writings and New Testament Interpretation*, C. A. Evans (Peabody: Hendrickson, 1992)
NICNT	New International Commentary on the New Testament, (Edited by G. D. Fee; Grand Rapids: Eerdmans)
NICOT	New International Commentary on the Old Testament (Edited by R. L. Hubbard; Grand Rapids: Eerdmans)
NIDNTT	*New International Dictionary of New Testament Theology*, Edited by C. Brown (Carlisle: Paternoster, 1975-78)
NIDOTTE	*New International Dictionary of Old Testament Theology and Exegesis*, Edited by W. Van Gemeren (Carlisle: Paternoster, 1996)
NIGTC	New International Greek Testament Commentary Edited by I.H. Marshall & D. A. Hagner (Grand Rapids: Eerdmans)
NovT	*Novum Testamentum*
NovTSup	Novum Testamentum Supplement Series
NT	New Testament
NTG	New Testament Guides
NTS	*New Testament Studies*
OT	Old Testament
OTL	Old Testament Library
SBJT	*Southern Baptist Journal of Theology*
SBLMS	Society of Biblical Literature Monograph Series
SBT	Studies in Biblical Theology
SJT	*Scottish Journal of Theology*
SNTSMS	Society for New Testament Studies Monograph Series
SOTBT	Studies in Old Testament Biblical Theology
Str-B	Strack, H. L., and P. Billerbeck, *Kommentar zum Neuen Testament aus Talmud und Midrasch*, 6 vols. (Munich, 1922-61)
TANZ	Texte und Arbeiten zum neutestamentlichen Zeitalter
TDNT	*Theological Dictionary of the New Testament*, Edited by G. Kittel (Grand Rapids: Eerdmans)

TDOT	*Theological Dictionary of the Old Testament*, Edited by G. J. Botterweck, H. Ringgren and H. J. Fabry (Grand Rapids: Eerdmans)
TNTC	Tyndale New Testament Commentary Series
TOTC	Tyndale Old Testament Commentary Series
TrinJ	*Trinity Journal*
TWOT	*Theological Wordbook of the Old Testament*, Edited by R. L. Harris, G. Archer, B. Waltke (Chicago: Moody Press, 1980)
TynB	*Tyndale Bulletin*
UFHM	University of Florida Historical Monograph
WBC	Word Biblical Commentary
WTJ	*Westminster Theological Journal*
WUNT	Wissenschaftliche Untersuchungen zum Neuen Testament
ZNW	*Zeitschrift für die neutestamentliche Wissenschaft*
ZTK	*Zeitschrift für Theologie und Kirche*

CHAPTER 1

Introduction

The following book is a study of Matthew's portrayal of Jesus as *the judge*, who has authority to pronounce and enact judgement on his Jewish contemporaries and, equally, on all the nations at the great eschatological Day of Judgement. The primary focus of this study is Matthew 21-25. The topic was prompted in particular by the work of one American author, Marcus Borg, and the reasons for this should now be explained.

In 1984, Marcus Borg published a revision of his doctoral thesis entitled *Conflict, Holiness and Politics in the Teachings of Jesus*.[1] This work falls into the category of studies now commonly known as the 'Third Quest for the Historical Jesus',[2] in that it takes a fairly positive attitude towards what can be known of Jesus (primarily from the synoptic tradition) and, most importantly, in that it seeks to understand Jesus in the context of first-century Palestine. The ethos of this scholarly endeavour is summed up in much-quoted words from E. P. Sanders:

> The dominant view today seems to be that we can know pretty well what Jesus was out to accomplish, that we can know a lot about what he said, and that those two things make sense within the world of first-century Judaism.[3]

---

[1] M. Borg, *Conflict, Holiness and Politics in the Teachings of Jesus* (New York: Edwin Mellen Press, 1984). The book has recently been reprinted (Harrisburg: TPI, 1998) with a new Foreword by N. T. Wright. Unfortunately, the pagination in the most recent edition is different from the original. Since the recently published edition is far more accessible, I will use page numbers from this edition.

[2] It is interesting that N. T. Wright has recently described Borg, when his work is viewed as a whole, as 'a bridge' between the 'New Quest renewed' and the 'Third Quest', though he had previously classed him as a representative of the latter stream of study. See his *Jesus and the Victory of God* (London: SPCK, 1996), 75 and particularly n. 215. Some scholars have been sceptical of such distinctiveness within this latter body of scholarship to justify the terminology of 'Third Quest'. See the recent discussion in S. E. Porter, *The Criteria for Authenticity in Historical-Jesus Research* (JSNTS 191; Sheffield: Sheffield Academic Press, 2000), 28-59.

[3] E. P. Sanders, *Jesus and Judaism* (London: SCM Press, 1985), 2. Sanders mentions *inter alia* M. Hengel, J. Jeremias, C. H. Dodd, G. Vermes and A. E. Harvey as representatives of this stream of scholarship. For a critical analysis of recent literature

N. T. Wright, who coined the term 'Third Quest',[4] and who was, like Borg, a doctoral student of Professor George B. Caird at Oxford, greeted Borg's work with enthusiasm. He notes how Borg sets Jesus' message in an atmosphere of conflict, and brings out the essentially *political* nature of what Jesus taught. He then goes on,

> It is in his study of Jesus' language about the future that Borg makes his most striking contribution. Developing Caird's insights about the nature of apocalyptic language, he argues extremely forcefully that the warnings are not about the end of the world, but about the end of the present world order, focusing on the 'imminent and yet contingent destruction of Israel' (p. 202). The command for hasty evacuation (Matt. 24:15-22) hardly envisages the end of the whole world. If this is correct - and Borg's is one voice among a growing number urging similar points - then the time is ripe for a major reappraisal of New Testament eschatology as a whole.[5]

In work which follows up this important book, Borg expends a considerable amount of energy in arguing for a 'non-eschatological Jesus'.[6] Borg seems to be arguing that we should abandon the eschatological scholarly consensus, developed since the work of J. Weiss[7] and A. Schweitzer,[8] and move towards an understanding of Jesus which is much more focused on political and social factors. However, Borg's understanding of what 'non-eschatological' means with reference to Jesus is not entirely transparent, and the question might well be

---

associated with this strand of scholarship, see particularly B. Witherington III, *The Jesus Quest* (Carlisle: Paternoster, 1994) and M. A. Powell, *The Jesus Debate* (Oxford: Lion, 1998). For a topical survey, the reader should consult the essays in B. D. Chilton and C. A. Evans (eds), *Studying the Historical Jesus: Evaluations of the State of Current Research* (Leiden: Brill, 1994).

[4] S. Neill and T. Wright, *The Interpretation of the New Testament 1861-1986* (Oxford: Oxford University Press, [1964] 1988), 379.

[5] Neill and Wright, *Interpretation of the New Testament*, 389-90.

[6] Particularly notable are: 'A Temperate Case for a Non-Eschatological Jesus' *Foundations and Facets Forum* 2.3 (1986), 81-102; 'An Orthodoxy Reconsidered: The "End-of-the-World Jesus"' in L. D. Hurst and N. T. Wright (eds.), *The Glory of Christ in the New Testament* (Oxford: Clarendon, 1987), 207-17; 'Reflections on a Discipline: A North American Perspective' in B. D. Chilton and C. A. Evans (eds), *Studying the Historical Jesus: Evaluations of the State of Current Research* (Leiden: Brill, 1994), 9-31.

[7] J. Weiss, *Die Predigt Jesu vom Reiche Gottes* (Göttingen: Vandenhoeck & Ruprecht, 1892). ET: *Jesus' Proclamation of the Kingdom of God* Translated and edited with an introduction by R. H. Hiers and D. L. Holland (London: SCM Press, 1971).

[8] A. Schweitzer, *Vom Reimarus zu Wrede* (1906). ET: *The Quest of the Historical Jesus* (London: A&C Black, 3rd edn 1954). The first English translation of Schweitzer's substantially expanded second German edition of *Quest of the Historical Jesus* (1913), was published by SCM Press in 2000.

raised in response to this as to whether 'eschatology', properly defined, plays a much greater and more influential part in the thought and message of Jesus than Borg allows.

In this present work I intend to start from Borg's insights and try to go further in the light of other contemporary studies of Jesus and the gospels. I shall gladly concur with Borg in his setting Jesus in an environment of conflict; I shall applaud his attempt to understand Jesus in terms of the culture of his day; and I shall take up his understanding of the interpretation of 'apocalyptic' language.[9] However, I intend to argue that Borg has failed to take his work far enough. He offers a number of valuable insights into Jesus' ministry but he does not integrate into his work the understanding of the authors of the gospels that Jesus is the coming Judge. In seeking to set Jesus in a Palestinian milieu, and by interpreting his words in terms of Jewish understanding Borg has certainly taken the correct methodological steps. He has failed, however, to treat all the evidence consistently in this way, and goes astray by reverting to a sceptical use of critical methodology in the case of certain crucial texts (particularly the 'coming Son of Man' sayings) and to a fundamentally *non-Jewish* reading of these texts.

It should be stated clearly that I recognise that Borg's phrase 'non-eschatological' does not mean 'non-judging'. Borg states quite explicitly that 'Jesus did speak of history as having a general resurrection and final judgment as its boundary.'[10] However, he does not seem to have appreciated *Jesus'* role as judge, and this failure seems to be intimately related to his conviction that Jesus did not have an 'eschatological' message, in the sense of a message about the culmination of God's plans. Instead Borg appears to regard God as the judge, and to understand that God's judgement will take the form of a final catastrophe. In this he appears to stand remarkably close to Schweitzer, even though he places the timing of this event in the indeterminate future rather than the immediate future.

In a candid moment in his book, Borg admits that his thesis does not fit well with all the evidence of Matthew's gospel. He examines what he calls the 'threat-warrant tradition' of the gospels. He claims that the 'threats', found in various forms (parables, pronouncement stories, comparisons, laments, proverbs), have in common 'warning of a future consequence that flows out of present behaviour.' Most of these threats have a 'warrant' attached, defined as 'an indication of the action that will lead to the actualization of the threat.' He poses two key questions which require to be dealt with:

---

[9] Despite Wright's unqualified use of the term 'apocalyptic' in the citation on the previous page, I place this term in inverted commas here because its significance is controversial in contemporary scholarship. The question of the propriety of this term as a description of the language that Wright and Borg have in mind will be discussed later in this book.

[10] Borg, *Conflict*, 221.

First, are the threats really seen as consequences of the quest for holiness, or are they the consequences of something else, e.g., individual transgressions or sinfulness? For this question, the contents of the *warrants* are crucial. Second is the major question: what is the nature of the threatened consequences? Here primary attention centers on the contents of the *threats*.[11]

It is interesting that Borg finds Matthew's witness uncomfortable in relation to his thesis here. He writes,

> If Matthew's special material alone served as the basis for making a judgment, the answers to both the above questions would be straight-forward: individual sinfulness warrants the threat of eternal condemnation. Matthew's *warrants* consistently point to generalized sinfulness...Most frequently the *threats* peculiar to Matthew point to the eternal fate of the individual...though in two cases the threat consists of ecclesiastical discipline...The exceptions to this pattern are found, strikingly, in the parables peculiar to Matthew. But this pattern, as regards both threats and warrants, diverges remarkably from that found in the rest of the synoptic tradition...For this reason, special Matthew will not be included in the following analysis, though the Matthaean parables (Mp) will.[12]

On the basis that any thesis should account for as much evidence as possible, there are two fundamental questions which must be raised against Borg's work. First, is it really the case that material that is distinctive to Matthew's gospel (and therefore, presumably, representative of Matthew's views) is unconcerned about the 'Politics of Holiness' and the consequences of that worldview? And, as a corollary of this, does Borg's approach to the material in Matthew require that Matthew has presented an incoherent account which betrays different perspectives on judgement? Secondly, is Borg's political view deficient in omitting the threat of future, personal judgement in the teaching of Jesus? Clearly we are raising issues which have relevance both to the study of the gospel of Matthew and to the 'Quest of the Historical Jesus'.

In this study I wish to focus on the theme of judgement which is prominent throughout the gospel of Matthew, but is particularly developed in chapters 21-25 of Matthew. These chapters also include a significant proportion of the material designated 'special Matthew' by Borg[13] and thus provide us with an opportunity to examine Borg's specific assertion relating to that material, as well

---

[11] Borg, *Conflict*, 214.

[12] Borg, *Conflict*, 215.

[13] In fact there are five portions of text that are special Matthew material (M), but Borg designates three of these 'parables' (Mp) and thus includes them in his analysis. The pericopae are 21:28-32 (Mp); 22:11-14 (M); 23:33 (M); 25:1-13 (Mp); 25:31-46 (Mp). While 25:14-30 is similar in several respects to the narrative in Lk. 19:11-27, there are sufficient substantial differences to cast doubt on the view that this portion of Matthew is 'Q' material. See D. A. Hagner, *Matthew 14-28* (WBC 33B; Dallas: Word, 1995), 733 for discussion.

as the character of Matthew's account taken in its own right. I do not intend to respond directly to Borg's contention that Matthew's special material has a different character to the rest of the material in his gospel (though I shall bear that claim in mind and comment on it when appropriate). Rather I will concentrate attention on a portion of Matthew which I perceive to have an internal coherence, and interpret each pericope in that broader context.

Many commentators have noted the presence of the theme of judgement in Matthew in brief compass, but there is only one monograph (in French) which examines the theme in the whole of Matthew from the perspective of redaction criticism with the result that emphasis on redactional changes carried out by Matthew obscures the literary coherence of Matthew's narrative.[14] The recent volume by Sim[15] is concerned with the related, but broader, issue of 'apocalyptic eschatology', but, in fact, Sim's treatment is much more concerned with reconstructing the social setting of the Matthean community than with the theological themes in Matthew's account, or how Matthew's account relates to the teaching of Jesus.

Thus, no previous study has examined Matthew's portrayal of Jesus as judge as a literary whole, apart from reference to the other Evangelists. Further, no previous study has attempted to demonstrate the coherence of the particular section of Matthew taken up in this book as a sustained presentation of Jesus the judge. Finally, another neglected question must be asked: how does Matthew's presentation of Jesus the judge relate to the reality of Jesus' ministry?

In dealing with this theme I wish to focus particularly on Matthew's perception of the *nature* of the judgement which Jesus preached; the *time* of the judgement; and *Jesus' own role* in judgement, and I will elaborate on these points briefly. Firstly, Borg's work faces us with the question of whether Jesus was only interested in judgement at the end of the world, a spiritual judgement by which individuals receive reward or punishment on the basis of spiritual criteria, or whether he was also concerned for the social, religious and political situation in the first century and prepared (and authorised) to pronounce social, religious and political judgement on the people and structures which were out of step with God's will. Secondly, if Jesus was proclaiming judgement on people and/or structures, when did he anticipate this judgement to be effected? It could be that he treated his own words and actions as present judgement, or it might be that he believed that all wrongs would be rectified on the final day, or it might be that he expected some judgement in the imminent future, or perhaps he anticipated a combination of these forms and times of judgement. Perhaps, indeed, he had no idea when or how judgement would take place. These possibilities need to be addressed. Finally, did Jesus leave judgement in the hands of

---

[14] D. Marguerat, *Le Jugement Dans L'Évangile de Matthieu* (Geneva: Labor et Fides, 1981).

[15] D. C. Sim, *Apocalyptic Eschatology in the Gospel of Matthew* (SNTSMS 88; Cambridge: Cambridge University Press, 1996).

his God, or did he consider himself to be in a position not only to proclaim judgement but also to exercise it?

Matthew's treatment of this theme will be examined as an important subject in its own right, as we try to ascertain the reasons for the prominence of judgement material in the first gospel. But we will also be looking to Matthew's account of Jesus' teaching with a view to its significance for the 'historical Jesus', and therefore as a possible basis for offering a critique of several modern views of Jesus, and so we will have come full circle from Borg's volume. In order to carry out this study of Matthew I will adopt some of Borg's work as a helpful starting point, modifying his positions at various points where I believe he has not done justice to the New Testament evidence. But before we can begin work on Matthew we must survey the work of Borg and other significant modern scholars in greater detail.

CHAPTER 2

Survey of Literature

Introductory Remarks

In order to understand and respond to Borg's position on the theme of judgement, it is important to have some appreciation of the broader field of literature within which his work stands. This task is complicated somewhat because a complete response to Borg on this issue demands that we survey two distinct types of literature, namely eclectic studies of Jesus which draw on material from each of the synoptic gospels, and studies of the canonical text of Matthew's gospel.

We have noted that Borg's work stands in the stream of the 'Quest of the Historical Jesus', or, more precisely, the so-called 'Third Quest'. It is necessary, therefore, to examine other volumes from that stream of research that deal with the theme of judgement to a greater or lesser extent. However, Borg's rejection of significant Matthean material requires that we probe into Matthew's view of judgement, and therefore that we also survey some of the range of secondary material relating to synoptic and Matthean scholarship.

Until quite recently, there had been relatively little material in the latter category, *i.e.* volumes written specifically on the theme of judgement in Matthew's gospel. Much more effort had been expended on discussing the view of Jesus on this theme, as reconstructed through the application of critical methodology to the three synoptic gospels. This survey will, therefore, fall into two parts.

The first part will involve a discussion of works concerned with 'the historical Jesus' which draw on the whole synoptic tradition, although particular attention will be paid to discussions of Matthew, even if these form only a small part of a larger study.

The second part of the survey will deal with several important works, mostly published in the last fifteen years, which focus particularly on Matthew's gospel. These studies make no claim to say anything about Jesus' views, but simply analyse Matthew's perception of Jesus, and Matthew's purposes in recording the material he does.

Studies of Jesus' View of Judgement

Was Jesus a preacher of judgement? The contemporary fascination with the teaching and life of Jesus of Nazareth is perhaps matched only by the frustration that is experienced in trying to make sense of all the various accounts of these subjects which have been written in recent years.[1] The fundamental problem facing researchers is that none of these accounts can be verified by reference to anything that comes firsthand from Jesus himself. He left no writings. We have access to his teaching only through the four (though a small minority of scholars would claim more[2]) gospels; a fact which raises numerous complex issues of methodology. This difficulty has in no way inhibited scholarly endeavour, however, and we will now survey several works which seek to bring

---

[1] A sense of the diversity of views on Jesus is given by the title and content of the book (and BBC television series) by Mark Tulley entitled *Lives of Jesus* (London: BBC Books, 1996). Witherington, *The Jesus Quest*, provides a survey in this field up to 1994. Several significant volumes have since been published, particularly the important volume by Wright, *Jesus and the Victory of God*, which also provides a very useful survey of recent scholarship. Wright's book is itself the subject of a book-length critical review: C. C. Newman (ed.), *Jesus and the Restoration of Israel* (Downers Grove: IVP, 1999). A rather more recent survey of the scholarly literature is provided by Powell, *The Jesus Debate*.

[2] A number of scholars have argued for the priority of the *Gospel of Thomas*, the *Gospel of Peter* and a reconstructed Q as sources for our knowledge of Jesus. This claim is made particularly strongly by representatives of the 'Jesus Seminar' (including notably J. D. Crossan, *The Historical Jesus* [Edinburgh: T&T Clark, 1991]). An open, though rather more cautious, approach is taken by G. Theissen and A. Merz, *The Historical Jesus* (London: SCM Press, 1998), 37-50. However numerous scholars representing quite different theological perspectives have been strongly critical of such views. One of the fullest discussions is found in J. P. Meier, *A Marginal Jew* Vol 1 (ABRL; New York: Doubleday, 1991), 112-41. Meier concludes his thorough discussion as follows (140): 'I do not think that the rabbinic material, the *agrapha*, the apocryphal gospels, and the Nag Hammadi codices (in particular the *Gospel of Thomas*) offer us reliable new information or authentic sayings that are independent of the NT.' Similarly, J. H. Charlesworth and C. A. Evans, 'Jesus in the Agrapha and Apocryphal Gospels' in Chilton and Evans (eds), *Studying the Historical Jesus*, 479-533, conclude (533): 'Despite the wealth of materials, not a great deal can be gleaned from the agrapha and apocryphal writings that appreciably aid [*sic*] in the effort to construct a picture of the historical Jesus.' See also R. E. Brown, *An Introduction to the New Testament* (ABRL; New York: Doubleday, 1997), 822, 829. In common with these latter scholars, I do not accept the view that Thomas is an early independent source of Jesus tradition. While I will refer to 'Q' as an effective shorthand device to indicate material common to Matthew and Luke, but absent from Mark, this should not be taken to imply a commitment to Q as a single written document. Also, I explicitly repudiate the view that Q reflects a theological perspective in conflict with that of Mark. (See E. P. Meadors, *Jesus the Messianic Herald of Salvation* [Peabody: Hendrickson, 1997].)

us the teaching of Jesus, focusing particularly on studies which describe the portions of the source documents which relate Jesus to the theme of judgement.

Since it is the work of Marcus Borg that stimulated this piece of research, and since he is probably the most significant modern representative of the 'non-eschatological' perspective on Jesus, we will devote a major amount of space to a thorough exposition of, and response to, his work. However, in order to give some sense of the progression of the debate, consideration of his writings will be placed in the context of a broadly chronological survey of scholarship.

Some studies, which are considered below, do not have extensive discussions of judgement *per se*, and instead concern themselves with the question of the imminence of the *Parousia* (understood as the visible return of the resurrected and ascended Jesus). We have included these discussions in our survey because the link between the *Parousia* and the Day of Judgement is so strong (founded on the OT concept of the *Yom Yahweh*[3]) as to make a concern for one subject almost indistinguishable from a concern for the other.[4]

Jesus Proclaims that Eschatological Judgement Lies in the Imminent Future

J. WEISS AND A. SCHWEITZER

These scholars are largely responsible for the view, in broad terms, which Borg regards (no doubt, correctly) as the dominant image of Jesus since the turn of the century. Their foundational significance is so widely recognised and so well documented that we will do little more than note their work here.[5] In 1892, J. Weiss published his ground-breaking work, *Die Predigt Jesu vom Reiche Gottes*.[6] He argued that Jesus' message of the kingdom of God was not, as Harnack and Ritschl had believed, concerned with a present spiritual experience. Rather, Jesus proclaimed an apocalyptic kingdom which lay entirely in the future. Following on from Weiss, A. Schweitzer claimed that Jesus expected the kingdom of God to be ushered in by the imminent coming of the 'Son of Man', a figure which, according to Schweitzer, Jesus understood to be other than himself. This

---

[3] *NIDOTTE*, 2:419-24; *TDOT*, 4:7-32, 6:7-32; *NIDNTT*, 2:887-95.

[4] See G. E. Ladd, *The Presence of the Future* (Grand Rapids: Eerdmans, 1974), 8.

[5] See, for example, N. Perrin, *The Kingdom of God in the Teaching of Jesus* (London: SCM Press, 1963), 16-23 and 28-36; C. Brown, 'The Parousia and Eschatology in the NT' in *NIDNTT*, 2:901-31; *idem*, 'Historical Jesus, Quest of' in *DJG*, 326-41; Wright, *Jesus and the Victory of God*, 18-21; Porter, *Criteria for Authenticity*, 36-47. For biographical details and bibliography, see Donald K. McKim (ed.), *Historical Handbook of Major Biblical Interpreters*, (Leicester: IVP, 1998).

[6] Göttingen: Vandenhoeck & Ruprecht. ET: *Jesus' Proclamation of the Kingdom of God* Translated and edited with an introduction by R. H. Hiers and D. L. Holland (London: SCM Press, 1971).

view had its foundation in Schweitzer's understanding of Matthew 10:23,[7] and so it can be seen that Matthew's gospel has been an important influence from the earliest stages of the modern discussion.[8]

It is remarkable that the next author we will examine writes some fifty years after Schweitzer's work was first published. This great gulf reflects the effectiveness of Schweitzer's book in stopping the 'Quest' in its tracks. Wright comments,

> He demolished the old 'Quest' so successfully - and provided such a shocking alternative - that for half a century serious scholarship had great difficulty in working its way back to history when dealing with Jesus.[9]

Though Bultmann's lack of interest in the historical Jesus was a significant force in scholarship for several decades,[10] the 'New Quest', instigated by Käsemann in 1953,[11] opened up new avenues for historical investigation of Jesus. Yet, Bultmann's mark was left on German scholarship, and it was not long before the rather existentialist efforts of Bultmann's pupils were overtaken by scholars rediscovering the heritage of Schweitzer.

W. G. KÜMMEL

Kümmel's important book[12] may be included in this section of the survey only with a certain degree of qualification. Kümmel's perception of an imminent *Parousia* is not that of Schweitzer. Kümmel accepts that Jesus anticipated a delay of a generation before the end. Yet this appears to be a matter of difference in extent rather than difference in nature.

---

[7] *Quest of the Historical Jesus*, 357-58. Schweitzer claims that Mt. 10:23 is the key text for understanding Jesus' expectations, and the history of Christianity in the light of the 'delay of the Parousia'.

[8] Brief excerpts from the work of Weiss and Schweitzer (along with other significant figures in the history of the 'Quest') may conveniently be found in G. W. Dawes (ed.), *The Historical Jesus Quest: Landmarks in the Search for the Jesus of History* (Louisville: Westminster/John Knox Press, 1999), 172-184, 185-212.

[9] Wright, *Jesus and the Victory of God*, 21

[10] 'I do indeed think that we can now know almost nothing concerning the life and personality of Jesus, since the early Christian sources show no interest in either, are moreover fragmentary and often legendary; and other sources about Jesus do not exist,' R. Bultmann, *Jesus and the Word* (London: Collins, 1934), 14.

[11] The New Quest was sparked off by E. Käsemann's famous lecture 'The Problem of the Historical Jesus', presented to a group of Bultmann's former pupils, and published in *ZTK* 51 (1954), 125-53. [Reprinted in *Essays on New Testament Themes* (SBT 41; London: SCM Press, 1964), 15-47.] See Wright, *Jesus and the Victory of God*, 23-24.

[12] *Promise and Fulfilment* (SBT 23; London: SCM Press, 1957). See the comments of Ladd, *Presence*, 29-30. See also Kümmel's article, 'Eschatological Expectation in the Proclamation of Jesus,' reprinted in B. D. Chilton (ed.), *The Kingdom of God* (IRT 5; London: SPCK, 1984).

Kümmel begins with the question of the imminence of the eschatological events, focusing on the terms ἐγγύς and the cognate verb ἐγγίζειν. Against Dodd[13] he argues that they can only mean 'to come near'. They cannot refer to something that has already come. Following on from this he investigates the key text Mark 9:1. This he understands to mean that some of Jesus' disciples will not die because the kingdom will come in power. However, he rejects Schweitzer's view that Jesus expected that the kingdom would come within his own lifetime, basing his argument on the fact that only 'some' of those standing there would see the coming kingdom. From this and other texts, Kümmel deduces that Jesus expected the coming of the kingdom to be a future event that would occur within the generation of his hearers. The fact that Kümmel does not accept that Mark 9:1 is in its original context is a severe disadvantage to gaining a correct interpretation of the verse. That the verse stands immediately before the dramatic account of the transfiguration clearly indicates that the evangelist, at least, saw a direct fulfilment of Jesus' words in the event he was about to describe. Kümmel deals with various objections to his thesis, particularly that a long delay is required by texts such as those which speak of preaching to a wide audience. It is also unfortunate that certain texts which might be detrimental to Kümmel's thesis are disallowed as not being authentic words of Jesus.

In the second part of his work, Kümmel discusses Jesus' relationship to Jewish apocalyptic literature. He notes that 'Jesus adopted the preaching of John the Baptist with regard to the immediately impending judgment and he announced it himself,' and points to M. Werner as a representative of the view that Jesus and the authors of the various apocalyptic works do not differ in principle.[14] He admits that there is what he describes as 'an extensive apocalyptic text' found in Mark 13 and parallels, but he is not happy to rest on this text given the disputes over its textual history and so he looks elsewhere for features of apocalyptic. Kümmel refers to several synoptic texts which refer to the resurrection followed by the judgement, and devotes several pages to an extensive discussion of Matthew 25:31ff. in particular. He concludes that, though Jesus shares certain apocalyptic conceptions with the Jewish apocalypticists, the thrust of Jesus' eschatological language does not lie in apocalyptic instruction but in promoting change of life in the present. Yet he does not seem

---

[13] C. H. Dodd, *The Parables of the Kingdom* (London: James Nisbet & Co, 1935). A revised edition was published by Fontana books in 1961, from which edition I draw my citations. In this published version of his 1935 Shaffer Lectures at the Divinity School of Yale University, Dodd identifies his debt to the work of Schweitzer with respect to eschatology and then expounds his famous 'realised eschatology' view. On the summary of Jesus' teaching found in Mark 1:14-15, Dodd argues on the basis of usage in the LXX that the form of the Greek verb ἐγγίζειν found in Mark 1:15 should be rendered 'has come' rather than 'has drawn near' (36-37).

[14] Kümmel, *Promise*, 88.

to regard Jesus as doing more than proclaiming a future judgement in prophetic fashion. What is more, he believes that Jesus anticipated this final climactic judgement to take place within a single generation. The text which stands as a possible contradiction to this is Mark 13. According to F. Busch, Mark 13 is a farewell discourse concerning the suffering Messiah. Kümmel summarises his view that Mark 13,

> is not intended to describe the sequence in time of the final events, but to enjoin patience in the final tribulation, the termination of which through the parousia, though near, is unknown.[15]

Kümmel argues that this is completely wrong. He claims,

> It is incontrovertible that Mark 13 as a whole is intended to be a prediction of the events immediately preceding the end and of the end itself.[16]

This interpretation is consistent with the earlier conclusion that the end would be after a short delay but within the generation of Jesus' audience. Kümmel believes that Mark understood the destruction of the temple to be inextricably linked with the end. At the same time as claiming that Mark 13 is thoroughly eschatological, Kümmel also wants to avoid the view that Mark 13 comes from Jewish apocalyptic literature. He again acknowledges the apocalyptic language employed but claims that this simply shows the common ideas shared by Jesus. However, where he believes that elements of apocalyptic literature can be traced, he ascribes these verses to the later Jewish-Christian tradition brought into service by Mark.

Though Kümmel believes that the inbreaking of the kingdom of God is a future event for Jesus, he also argues that Jesus understood the kingdom of God to be effective in his own person. Thus,

> men are distinguished decisively by their acceptance or rejection of the Son of Man in action even now, yet expected to be fully effective in the near future; thus the fundamental presupposition for the future eschatological judgment was created already in the present, in which Jesus was the determining factor.[17]

This is seen in texts such as Mark 2:19a; 8:38; Matthew 19:28; Luke 12:32; 17:20f.; 24:26. It is very clear in the account of the controversy over Jesus' exorcisms found in Matthew 12:28 (and pars). Here Jesus points to his exorcisms and claims that they prove that the kingdom has arrived (ἔφθασεν). The aorist verb refers to an event of which the consequences can already be felt, and so it cannot be regarded as a synonym of ἤγγικεν (as K. W. Clark attempted to

---

[15] Kümmel, *Promise*, 96-97.
[16] Kümmel, *Promise*, 98.
[17] Kümmel, *Promise*, 105.

prove).[18]

Kümmel points to the healing activities of Jesus as evidence of the present experience of the eschatological kingdom. In particular, he notes the reply given to the disciples of John the Baptist when they enquired whether Jesus was 'the coming one', claiming that allusion is made to the eschatological expectations in Isaiah 29:18f.; 35:5f.; 61:1. In his response, Jesus points to himself as the one in whom these expectations are realised. He is the messenger of the coming kingdom.[19] Kümmel also finds evidence for Jesus' understanding the kingdom to be present in the cleansing of the temple, the last supper, and the saying about the kingdom suffering violence (only a present kingdom can presently be assailed). The various parables of the kingdom speak more about the coming of the kingdom than of its present realisation, and Kümmel is not prepared to understand the Christian community as an expression of the kingdom; that was true of Jesus only.[20]

What of Jesus' use of apocalyptic language? Kümmel offers his interpretation as follows:

> Now at last it can be fully and finally understood why Jesus speaks of future eschatological events and makes use of several conceptions of apocalyptic, but nevertheless does not offer apocalyptic teaching, but an eschatological message; the intrinsic meaning of the eschatological event he proclaims does not lie in the end of the world as such, but in the fact that the approaching eschatological consummation will allow the kingdom of that God to become a reality who has already in the present allowed his redemptive purpose to be realized in Jesus.[21]

Kümmel concludes that there is no interest in revealing apocalyptic secrets found in the teaching of Jesus.[22] Any use that Jesus makes of the language of apocalyptic is purely in the service of pointing to the coming kingdom which finds its proleptic realisation in himself. Kümmel seems particularly concerned to point out that Jesus' message is not invalidated by the fact that there was no imminent end to the world. But this still leaves us with the question of why Jesus used apocalyptic language at all. Did he intend to predict the course of future events, or do the images of apocalyptic refer to present realities? Can we allow for such a sharp disjunction between apocalyptic and eschatology that the first can be found to be false and the latter may still be said to be valid? There is also the fact that Kümmel is very insistent that the eschatological message cannot be limited to a present significance; the future element, the promise which is the counterpart of fulfilment, is essential. Yet, in effect, he boils every-

---

[18] Kümmel, *Promise*, 106, n. 6, citing an article (no title is provided) by K. W. Clark, *JBL* 59 (1940), 374ff.

[19] Kümmel, *Promise*, 111.

[20] Kümmel, *Promise*, 140.

[21] Kümmel, *Promise*, 154.

[22] So Ladd, *Presence*, 30.

thing down to an existential experience of faith:

> So for the believer the question is not whether he will accept the correctness of an
> apocalyptic prediction or of an interpretation referring to the present of that which
> relates to the beyond, but whether he will respond to the divine mission of *that*
> Jesus who could promise us the reign of God, because it was already being
> fulfilled in him.[23]

But this seems to be an unfortunate dichotomy. It is the fact of the outworking of the kingdom in Jesus' ministry that provides foundation for his message
concerning future events. The words of Jesus regarding the events of the future
may not simply be disregarded, but are rather given their authentication in his
earthly ministry. Thus though experience might lead a gospel reader to question
whether there was to be a *Parousia*, the partial realisation of the promise of the
kingdom found in Jesus gives assurance that what Jesus said will indeed happen. This being the case, we do well to try to find an interpretation of Jesus'
words which does not require postulating a drastic error.

C. K. BARRETT

C. K. Barrett's short study on Jesus also emphasises the note of imminence in
Jesus' eschatological expectations, thus standing in the tradition of
Schweitzer.[24] Barrett's attitude to the future expectations of Jesus is that the
evangelists have introduced material to deal with the reality of the non-event of
the *Parousia*. He believes that the tradition concerning the mission to the Gentiles, a key plank in the argument against an imminent *Parousia*, is not authentic. He cites Jeremias who concludes 'that Jesus limited his activity to Israel
and imposed the same limitation upon his disciples.'[25] However, when we consider Matthew's account of the final judgement, we find that Jesus spoke of
being judge, not solely of Israel, but of the nations (Matt. 25:32). This belief
that the nations would be accountable before him would suggest that he expected them to be faced with the challenge of discipleship. In fact, Barrett's
approach suffers, along with so many works from that era, from the influence
of the criterion of dissimilarity.[26] This means that significant texts are too easily

---

[23] Kümmel, *Promise*, 155.

[24] Barrett, *Jesus and the Gospel Tradition* (London: SPCK, 1967), 8, writes, 'It is
   doubtful whether anyone today would accept all Schweitzer's conclusions, but the
   main point stands; the story as a whole is controlled by eschatology, and eschatology
   is theology.'

[25] Barrett, *Jesus and the Gospel Tradition*, 72, citing Jeremias, *Jesus' Promise to the
   Nations* (London: SCM Press, 1959), 55.

[26] Barrett comments (*Jesus and the Gospel Tradition*, 73-74), 'We have already seen that
   the gospels as they stand do look forward to an interval between the resurrection and
   the coming of the Son of man - inevitably so, since they were written within this
   interval. We have to enquire whether the time-scheme that was forced upon the

passed over, and a more robust study of the texts as they stand is required.

Barrett responds to a key argument against an imminent *Parousia* raised by Kümmel and Beasley-Murray who point to the suffering which is forecast for the disciples.[27] Barrett claims that the gospels were written during a period of suffering which is reflected in certain of the gospel sayings, and, at any rate, Jesus expected that his disciples would suffer along with him.

This response is only satisfactory if one accepts that Matthew intended to incorporate the history of his community into his gospel; it is not so effective if Matthew distinguishes 'the past of Jesus'[28] from the events of his own time.[29]

Barrett also rejects Beasley-Murray's claim that the world evangelisation of Mark 13:10 must occur before the return of Jesus. He believes that this refers to an apocalyptic proclamation. In sum, Barrett does not consider the position of Kümmel and Beasley-Murray to be tenable:

> It cannot (in my opinion) be said that a case has been made out for the view that Jesus looked forward to an interval between his death and resurrection on the one hand, and, on the other, the establishing of the kingdom of God in power, or the coming of the Son of man.[30]

He continues with a well-placed criticism of the views of these two scholars:

> evangelists by the unrelenting course of events was shared by Jesus himself, and this is a delicate inquiry, because it was inevitable that his utterances, whatever they may originally have been, should be, if not consciously altered, at least understood and reinterpreted in the light of passing years. It may fairly be said that any sayings ascribed to Jesus which agree with the evangelists' viewpoint will have to be looked at with some suspicion, and that special attention ought to be given to any which appear to disagree.'

[27] Barrett, *Jesus and the Gospel Tradition*, 74, responding to G. R. Beasley-Murray, *Jesus and the Future* (1954) and *A Commentary on Mark Thirteen* (1957) - now available in a revised and combined edition in *Jesus and the Last Days* (Peabody: Hendrickson, 1993) - and Kümmel, *Promise and Fulfilment* (1957).

[28] See the recent work of E. E. Lemcio, *The Past of Jesus* (SNTSMS 68; Cambridge: Cambridge University Press, 1992). Having studied various aspects of Matthew's presentation of Jesus, Lemcio concludes, 'The evidence marshalled above leads to the conclusion that Matthew maintained the distinction between before and after in a thoroughgoing, comprehensive manner. Nuances of terms typical of the post-resurrection narrative but foreign before are not commonly projected backwards. Vocabulary characteristic earlier is not projected forwards' (72), and again 'I conclude that the messages intended for the Matthean community were anchored firmly in a narrative of Jesus earthly ministry whose "pastness" was conveyed in an idiom appropriate to the time yet intelligible by the reader/listener' (73).

[29] See the comments in chapter 3, on methodology.

[30] Barrett, *Jesus and the Gospel Tradition*, 76.

Indeed, Dr Beasley-Murray and Dr Kümmel seem to get the worst of both worlds, for though they find room in Jesus' thought for an interval before the *parousia* they believe that he expected this interval to last no more than a generation, so that even on their view the accuracy of Jesus' forecast is not saved.[31]

In place of this interpretation of the gospel material Barrett stresses the likelihood of Jesus having made predictions of his vindication after the Passion.[32] He contends that the *Parousia* sayings served as *alternatives* to resurrection predictions in pointing to this future vindication. Both kinds of saying are not found together.[33] This is an important claim, and can be accepted to some extent, in that Barrett has highlighted the fact that several sayings which have been regarded as *Parousia* predictions can more acceptably be read as predictions of vindication.[34] However, Barrett goes too far in effectively replacing the hope of the *Parousia* with the reality of the resurrection. In so doing, he has apparently not sufficiently recognised the important distinction, as well as the important relationship, between the imminent event of the resurrection and the future events of the *Parousia* and final judgement.

His view also demands that Paul drastically misinterprets the Jesus tradition, in that he holds tenaciously to the conviction that the resurrection is an indispensable foundation of Christian faith (1 Cor. 15), yet also emphasises the certainty of the future *Parousia* of Jesus.

R. H. HIERS

Some years later, in the face of many critics of Schweitzer, R. H. Hiers[35] attempted to rehabilitate Schweitzer's *konsequente Eschatologie*. That Hiers' position has been unusual and distinctive in the modern theological climate has been noted by NT scholarship.[36] However, Hiers has stated his case forcefully, and deserves more of a hearing than he has been given up till now. Hiers believes that Schweitzer's thesis that Jesus expected an imminent eschatological event is largely correct.[37] His argument is that Jesus stands in continuity with

---

[31] Barrett, *Jesus and the Gospel Tradition*, 76.

[32] Barrett, *Jesus and the Gospel Tradition*, 76.

[33] Barrett, *Jesus and the Gospel Tradition*, 81-82.

[34] See the discussion of the 'coming Son of Man' sayings, below.

[35] R. H. Hiers, *The Kingdom of God in the Synoptic Tradition* (UFHM 33; Gainesville: University of Florida Press, 1970), *The Historical Jesus and the Kingdom of God* (UFHM 38; Gainesville: University of Florida Press, 1973) and *Jesus and the Future* (Atlanta: John Knox Press, 1981).

[36] G. E. Ladd, for instance, identifies Hiers as a notable exception to the general consensus of opinion which has regarded the work of Schweitzer and Weiss as being in need of substantial modification. G. E. Ladd, *A Theology of the New Testament* (Cambridge: Lutterworth Press, 2nd edn 1994 [1974]. Revised by D. A. Hagner.), 56.

[37] This is not to say that he is uncritical of Schweitzer, or that he thinks that Schweitzer said all there is to be said. Hiers does raise various criticisms against Schweitzer's

the apocalyptic thought of Judaism which, he claims, expected an imminent end
to the current state of affairs. The whole of Jesus' ministry was geared towards
calling people to repentance in the face of the imminent judgement which was
the focal point of Jewish apocalyptic literature.[38] Thus we must now appreciate
that Jesus was in error in his expectation of an imminent end and must apply his
words today in the full knowledge of that fact.[39]

Hiers' discussion of the judgement is of particular importance for his argument. He claims that,

> despite its important place in Jesus' preaching and the great mass of related
> synoptic passages, the Judgment generally has been mentioned only incidentally
> in studies of Jesus' message and the gospels.[40]

Though he mentions notable exceptions in Jeremias,[41] Manson[42] and Kümmel,[43] Hiers finds a widespread neglect of the judgement in New Testament
scholarship. Where reference is made to judgement, it appears as a very vague
concept, and few people seem to expect a literal fulfilment of Jesus' teaching
concerning the judgement. Hiers attributes much of this neglect to the theological climate of the modern era. The optimistic view of God and man held by
liberal theologians found room only for the message of eternal life. The advo-
cates of 'realised eschatology' had no need of a future judgement. Hiers mentions that Bultmann believed the radical call to obedience would be degraded if

---

work, in particular his failure to deal with the significance of Jesus' exorcisms, his
'proposal that Jesus intended to hasten the coming of the Kingdom through the
repentance aroused by his (and his disciples') preaching,' and 'his contention that
Jesus deliberately provoked the Jewish authorities to bring about his suffering and
death so that he, himself, might thereby bear the tribulations prerequisite to the coming
of the Kingdom of God.' Hiers, *Historical Jesus and the Kingdom of God*, 3.

[38] The imminent judgment demanded strong measures, and so the ethics of Jesus are
'interim ethics', Hiers, *Historical Jesus and the Kingdom of God*, 19-24.

[39] Hiers suggests that the reluctance to accept that Jesus was in error or the belief that his
teaching requires reinterpretation for a modern readership (both founded on
theological rather than historical grounds) are the most significant reasons for the
widespread rejection of Schweitzer's interpretation. See Hiers, *Jesus and the Future*,
ix, 4-18.

[40] Hiers, *Jesus and the Future*, 19.

[41] J. Jeremias, *New Testament Theology* (London: SCM Press, 1971), 122ff.

[42] T. W. Manson, *The Teaching of Jesus* (Cambridge: Cambridge University Press, 1931),
269-77. Note the comments of Ladd, *Presence*, 12-13, to the effect that the final
consummation is not vital to Manson's understanding of the Kingdom: 'there is no
need for a realistic eschatology to accomplish the final victory of God's Kingdom. It
will be accomplished not by the Parousia of Christ but by the victory of the church in
the world.'

[43] W. G. Kümmel, *Promise and Fulfilment*, 43-48.

Jesus had involved concepts of reward or punishment.[44]

Hiers goes on to examine the synoptic references to the judgement, beginning with Mark and moving on to Q, M and L.[45] He is by no means particularly
sceptical regarding the authenticity of the material he surveys, and points to the
fact that at least references to the judgement are found in all the strands of tradition. Hiers points out the importance which both Matthew and Luke in particular attach to the judgement, evidenced by many references in the Q material.[46]
He comments on the data he has surveyed as follows,

> These numerous Marcan, "Q", "M", and "L" traditions about the coming
> Judgment constitute a substantial portion of the synoptic material. They can
> scarcely be dismissed as of little consequence to the evangelists or the early
> church. Together, they present a fairly consistent pattern of understanding: the
> Judgment will take place soon, in the lifetime of at least some of those who
> themselves had heard Jesus' message...Although some of the particular features
> that appear, for instance, only in "M" or "L" might be of questionable
> authenticity, there is no apparent reason to doubt that this basic understanding was
> shared by Jesus himself.[47]

Assuming this fairly positive assessment of authenticity, the cumulative effect of the evidence that Hiers has amassed does appear to be an unequivocal
indication that Jesus expected a *dénouement* at which all the nations would be
judged and in which the Son of Man would assume the decisive role of Judge.

What is not so clear is that Jesus was concerned *only* with a future, eschatological Day of Judgement. Hiers claims that even if there are certain texts
which may be understood as saying that the kingdom is already present, there
are no sayings which suggest that the judgement is in any way realised. However, Hiers concedes that Jesus does at times pronounce judgement on those

---

[44] Hiers, *Jesus and the Future*, 19-21. The reference for Bultmann's view is *Jesus and the Word*, 78ff.

[45] Hiers, *Jesus and the Future* 22-38. In Mark, Hiers identifies 6:7-11; 8:35-38; 9:43-48; 10:17-31; 13:33-37; 14:62. The Q passages are Mt. 3:7-12 = Lk. 3:7-9; Mt. 5:3-12 = Lk. 6:20-23; Mt. 5:25f. = Lk. 12:57-59; Mt. 6:19f. = Lk. 12:33; Mt. 7:1f. = Lk. 6:37f.; Mt. 7:13f. = Lk. 13:23f.; Mt. 7:24-27 = Lk. 6:47-49; Mt. 8:11f. = Lk. 13:28f; Mt. 9:37f.; 10:5-8, 15 = Lk. 10:2, 9, 11b, 12; Mt. 10:32 = Lk. 12:8f.; Mt. 11:21-24 = Lk. 10:13-15; Mt. 12:38-42 = Lk. 11:29-32; Mt. 19:28 = Lk. 22:28-30; Mt. 23:34-36 = Lk. 11:49-51; Mt. 24:37-41 = Lk. 17:26f., 30; Mt. 24:43f. = Lk. 12:39f.; Mt. 24:45-51 = Lk. 12:42-46; Mt. 25:14-30 = Lk. 19:12-26. The relevant sections of Matthean special material (M) are 5:5, 7-10; 7:21-23 (Cf. Lk. 6:46; 13:26f. Could this be Q material?); 10:23; 11:23b-24 (perhaps Q material); 12:36f.; 13:24-30; 13:36-43; 13:47-50; 16:27f.; 18:23-35; 22:13; 25:1-13; 25:31-46. The L pericopae are 12:47f. 12:49; 13:1-5; 13:6-9; 14:12-14; 16:1-9; 16:19-31; 17:28-30; 18:1-8; 21:34-36; 23:27-31.

[46] Hiers, *Jesus and the Future*, 24-25.

[47] Hiers, *Jesus and the Future*, 38.

who reject his ministry,[48] and this must surely raise a question about whether there is any kind of proleptic realisation of the events of the final judgement. Were Jesus' words of condemnation simply the expressions of his own religious perspective? Or were they true acts of judgement in themselves which would find their realisation in the final Day of Judgement?

The accuracy of Hiers' assertion that Jesus' expectation was of an imminent judgement is also highly debatable.[49] That the language which he uses stresses urgency is beyond question, but we shall see that it is far from clear that Jesus gave any indication that the final judgement would occur in the immediate future, particularly in the light of texts which may be interpreted to mean that he expressly indicated that there could be no such setting of a timetable of events.

Hiers is hesitant to decide on whether Jesus himself expected to be the Judge on 'that day', though he notes that Luke indicates this to be the case.[50] We might add that Matthew clearly shares the same view (e.g. Mt. 7:21).

Having discussed the theme of judgement in the inter-testamental literature, Hiers goes on to say

> This world-view, with its expectations and exhortations, is not fundamentally different from that which is attributed to Jesus in the synoptic gospels.

However, he does immediately add the caveat: 'Certainly there are some differences.'[51] Hiers has, no doubt, performed a valuable service to his readers in pointing them to the Jewish literature which would have been familiar to Jesus and his contemporaries. Yet his caveat is an important one; the teaching of Jesus and the teachings of the writers of 'apocalyptic' literature are different in substantive ways. The nature of these differences and the reasons for them are questions that Hiers' work leaves us with, and which we must address in this book.

D. C. ALLISON

An important voice in the recent discussion is that of Dale Allison, co-author of perhaps the most significant critical analysis of Matthew's gospel in English.[52] Allison's recent book on the historical Jesus unabashedly presents itself as a reclaiming of the heritage of Weiss and Schweitzer.[53]

---

[48] Hiers, *Jesus and the Future*, 40.

[49] Hiers, *Jesus and the Future*, 129, n. 83, offers evidence for this contention from all three synoptic gospels and all four sources: Mk. 8:38-9:1; 13:29f. and parallels; Mt. 12:38-42 = Lk. 11:29-32; Mt. 23:35f. = Lk. 1:50f.; Mt. 10:23; Lk. 18:7f.; 21:43, 36.

[50] Hiers, *Jesus and the Future*, 41 and 129, n. 100.

[51] Hiers, *Jesus and the Future*, 48.

[52] W. D. Davies and D. C. Allison, *Matthew* (ICC; Edinburgh: T&T Clark, 1988-97).

[53] Allison, *Jesus of Nazareth: Millenarian Prophet* (Minneapolis: Fortress, 1998), 34: 'Many of us have, since Johannes Weiss and Albert Schweitzer, been persuaded that Jesus was an eschatological prophet with an apocalyptic scenario.' See further the

Allison has some important remarks on method in his book, presenting a potent challenge to some contemporary researchers with respect to their methods for evaluating sources. In particular, he forcefully rebuts the value of statistical analyses of the sort employed fully by J. D. Crossan.[54] The second chapter of Allison's book is devoted to Jesus' eschatology, and here he responds directly to scholars such as Borg who proclaim that a new consensus on the non-eschatological Jesus has arrived. Allison notes that Borg chooses between apocalyptic prophet and subversive sage as two incompatible models for Jesus, and then asks,

> Why can we not think that Jesus' subversive wisdom and the threat of imminent judgment went hand in hand because they functioned similarly, namely to deny the validity of the status quo?[55]

Allison's comment, I believe, points in the right general direction, but takes the wrong avenue. His reference to imminent judgement indicates that he regards the 'apocalyptic' language in the teaching of Jesus to be fundamentally literal in its significance, and is quite comfortable with the tensions that this interpretation produces in the gospel narratives.[56] He looks to a bringing together of the prophetic and the sapiential despite the inconsistencies between the two options. In typically memorable and provocative fashion, Allison writes,

> Eschatological thinking is not (maybe about this Albert Schweitzer was wrong) *Konsequent* or consistent about anything. Jesus the first-century eschatological prophet was not a systematic thinker akin to Aristotle. His parables, warnings and imperatives appealed first to religious devotion and feeling, not to the intellect. And his poetic mind roamed in a mythological world closely related to that of the Dead Sea Scrolls, a world alive with fabulous stories such as those in *Ahikar* and fantastic images such as those in Daniel. That world did not celebrate logical consistency as a virtue.[57]

While this might appear to be an eminently reasonable position at which to

---

substantial response to Allison's book in the recent volume by Ben Witherington III, *Jesus the Seer: The Progress of Prophecy* (Peabody: Hendrickson, 1999), 254-69.

[54] See the appreciative remarks on this section in Witherington, *Jesus the Seer*, 255-260.

[55] Allison, *Jesus of Nazareth*, 114.

[56] Allison explicitly challenges metaphorical readings of such language, particularly that of George B. Caird, in *The End of the Ages Has Come* (Fortress, 1985).

[57] Allison, *Jesus of Nazareth*, 115. Allison appears to be playing with the German word 'Konsequent', and its common English translation 'consistent', in that he addresses the issue of logical consistency which is not what is meant by the German word (which should be translated 'thorough-going'). In the following critical remarks, I address his comments about lack of logical consistency without reference to his dubious use of the German term.

arrive, in fact it leads to hermeneutical despair. While any speaker or author may be proven to be inconsistent by means of an accumulation of incontrovertible evidence, it is not appropriate to turn inconsistency into a virtue to be applauded. Allison also appears to equate the claim that Jesus 'was not a systematic thinker' with a verdict of logical inconsistency. It is very difficult to see how one would substantiate a claim regarding the manner of Jesus' thinking, given that we only have access to selected recorded elements of his teaching. However, the broad sweep of Jesus' carefully crafted teaching, which incorporates a resounding emphasis on the kingdom of God, a challenge to the religious establishment of his day combined with acceptance of the marginalised who would come to him, and a high ethical calling, does not lead naturally to the conclusion that Jesus was 'not consistent about anything'.

With respect to the theme of judgement, Allison has a brief section on 'The Final Judgment'[58] in which he notes that a number of Jesus' sayings indicate a future reversal of injustice.[59] He then offers a general analysis of such sayings, as follows,

> The sayings in the Jesus tradition about judgment are naturally sorted into at least three categories, each of which has a different aim. Some function primarily as exhortation, others as consolation, still others as rebuke.[60]

These are helpful categories, but we may ask whether the category of 'rebuke' is strong enough for some of Jesus' sayings regarding judgement. We contend that there are a number of occasions, at least, where Jesus' words are a 'declaration of judgement' which will certainly come about. In the ensuing discussion, Allison focuses his attention on various other eschatological issues, including the imminence of whatever catastrophic event is awaited and the use of 'eschatological' or 'apocalyptic' language. On the former issue he is adamant that Jesus did expect the 'eschatological kingdom of God':

> As historians we must not confuse our convictions with Jesus' creed. And regarding the latter, eschatological imminence was part and parcel.[61]

Following on from this conviction, Allison rejects the attempts of recent interpreters to read 'apocalyptic' language in non-literal ways. He regards these efforts as expressions of a typical phase of the existence of a millenarian movement – coming to terms with the disappointment of expectations which are not fulfilled.[62]

---

[58] Allison, *Jesus of Nazareth*, 131-36.
[59] Allison, *Jesus of Nazareth*, 133-34. Allison is sceptical about the dominical origin of the account in Mt. 25:31-46, indicating that he regards it to be drawing on *1 Enoch*.
[60] Allison, *Jesus of Nazareth*, 135.
[61] Allison, *Jesus of Nazareth*, 151.
[62] Allison, *Jesus of Nazareth*, 152-69, especially 167.

In the end, Allison stands firmly on the side of Schweitzer. Jesus anticipates the imminent arrival of the kingdom of God, and all the associated events.

M. REISER

One of the most significant volumes to be published in recent years on the subject of Jesus' view of judgement is that of M. Reiser, entitled, in English translation, *Jesus and Judgment*.[63] Reiser's volume is divided into three main parts. In the substantial first part he considers the theme of judgement as found in the literature of second temple Judaism. A brief discussion of the Hebrew Bible leads on to consideration of other early Jewish literature. Reiser concludes this investigation with the conviction that these documents

> reveal, as their *basic eschatological model*, the expectation of a judgment that leads to the damnation of some and the salvation of others.[64]

After a brief discussion of the proclamation of John the Baptizer, Reiser indicates that John stands firmly within the tradition of early Jewish eschatology, and particularly 'within that tradition that starts from the perspective, not of a contrast between Israel and the Gentiles, but of a division between sinners and righteous within Israel.'[65] Thus Reiser argues for a robust doctrine of eschatological judgement within Judaism.

In turning to Jesus, Reiser recognises the paucity of thorough study on the theme of judgement highlighted also by this study. The only significant treatments that he highlights are those of T. W. Manson,[66] and J. Jeremias.[67]

However, Reiser's study almost completely bypasses the material found in Matthew 21-25, with which we are concerned in this book.[68] Thus, while Reiser provides a valuable discussion of Jewish background material, and useful discussion of several important synoptic texts, his work will have very limited bearing on the discussion in this book.

---

[63] M. Reiser, *Jesus and Judgment* (ET translated by L. M. Maloney; Minneapolis: Fortress, 1997). German edition is entitled *Die Gerichtspredigt Jesu: Eine Untersuchung zur eschatologischen Verkündigung Jesu und ihren frühjüdischen Hintergrund* (Münster: Aschendorff, 1990).

[64] Reiser, *Jesus and Judgment*, 144.

[65] Reiser, *Jesus and Judgment*, 191.

[66] *The Teaching of Jesus.*

[67] *New Testament Theology.*

[68] The only exception is Mt. 22:2-14, though in fact Matthew's text is only included on the grounds of a possible parallel with Lk. 14:16-24, which is dismissed as 'rather improbable' in the first few lines of discussion. The remainder of the discussion draws almost entirely on the Lukan material. See Reiser, *Jesus and Judgment*, 241-45.

Jesus Does Not Proclaim Future Eschatological Judgement

Though Borg may be correct in saying that the Schweitzerian 'apocalyptic prophet' has been the dominant image in NT studies this century, it would be going too far to say that it has been the only one. There are several scholars who have come to the conclusion that Jesus did not teach that he would return in the future in order to judge the world, and, as a corollary to that, that he did not focus on future judgement to any great extent in his preaching.

C. H. DODD

Although Dodd is famous for his 'realised eschatology' view, this position does not prevent him from recognising that several parables, especially some of those recorded in Matthew's gospel, contain 'a warning to be ready for something which has not yet happened,'[69] and he devotes a chapter of his book to these parables.[70] However, for Dodd, the crucial question is, What is that 'something'? In answering that question, Dodd rejects the authenticity of the occurrences of '*Parousia*' in Matthew 24 on the basis that they are unique to Matthew, and favours instead the Lukan phrase 'the days of the Son of Man' (Luke 17:26). He then comments,

> The coming of the Son of Man, in its aspect as judgment, is realized in the catastrophes which Jesus predicted as lying immediately in store – the persecution of Himself and His disciples, the destruction of the Temple and of the Jewish nation. These catastrophes He regarded as an immediately imminent development of the existing situation. Thus the care-free people eating and drinking at ease like the ante-diluvians are the men and women whom Jesus saw about Him, stupidly unaware that the judgments of God were in the earth, and destined at any moment to be overwhelmed with disaster.[71]

Dodd is not unaware, however, that certain parables seem to point inescapably towards eschatological judgement. Yet he is not willing to regard such future orientated material as authentic:

> It seems possible, therefore, to give all these 'eschatological' parables an application within the context of the ministry of Jesus. They were intended to enforce His appeal to men to recognise that the Kingdom of God was present in all its momentous consequences, and that by their conduct in the presence of this tremendous crisis they would judge themselves as faithful or unfaithful, wise or foolish. When the crisis had passed, they were adapted by the Church to enforce

---

[69] Dodd, *Parables*, 126.
[70] Dodd, *Parables*, 115-30. The chapter is entitled 'Parables of Crisis'. See the discussion of Dodd's views in Ladd, *Presence*, 17-20.
[71] Dodd, *Parables*, 126-27.

its appeal to men to prepare for the second and final world-crisis which it believed to be approaching.[72]

Thus, for Dodd, Jesus does not proclaim future judgement except in the events between his death and resurrection and the fall of Jerusalem in AD 70. His parables are intended to point his hearers to these imminent events, and where the parables appear to point to something else, there Dodd finds evidence of the Church's moulding of the traditional material. Allison regards Dodd as the forerunner of the more recent attempts to reinterpret eschatological language.[73]

T. F. GLASSON

In his discussion of the belief in the *Parousia* of Jesus,[74] T. F. Glasson similarly holds that Jesus did not predict his imminent future return,[75] but that this expectation was developed and retained in the early church,

> partly because of its association with the Last Judgment, and partly because it provides a denouement to mark the victorious consummation.[76]

This comment shows that, though the main focus of Glasson's work is belief in the *Parousia* of Jesus, this is inextricably linked to the issue of judgement.

Indeed, in the course of his study, Glasson devotes an entire chapter to the theme of judgement, and begins by identifying the particular concern with the judgement to be found in Matthew, while at the same time admitting his scepticism of the authenticity of that concern.

> In Matthew the Parousia is linked with the Judgement, and we must therefore make some reference to this subject as it appears in the teaching of Jesus. Some authorities have held that He never spoke of Himself as Judge, and it is

---

[72] Dodd, *Parables*, 129-30.

[73] Allison, 'Jesus and the Victory of Apocalyptic' in Newman (ed.), *Jesus and the Restoration of Israel*, 130, with reference to Dodd, *Parables*, 81. Cf G. B. Caird, *The Language and Imagery of the Bible* (London: Duckworth, 1980), 252-54.

[74] T. F. Glasson, *The Second Advent* (London: Epworth, Third edn 1963 [1945]).

[75] Glasson, *The Second Advent*. In his Preface to the third edition, Glasson indicates his specific intention to provide a response to A. Schweitzer's views. He writes, 'Though very few scholars would now sponsor his thesis, and "consistent eschatology" has few supporters, his main point that Jesus lived and worked in an expectation of an imminent and catastrophic "end of the world" is still very widely accepted, particularly on the Continent.' Our earlier survey of books by Hiers and Allison illustrates how premature Glasson's comments on followers of Schweitzer were. See Moore, *The Parousia*, 51-52.

[76] Glasson, *The Second Advent*, 209

noteworthy that references to this effect are confined (among the Synoptic Gospels) to Matthew.[77]

Glasson accepts that Jesus spoke of 'man's accountability to God's judgement' but believes that 'for the most part the statements are general and lack pictorial details.' They lack reference to Jesus as judge or to a great Day of Judgement. Yet it is exactly these details which are found in Matthew. For this reason, Glasson believes that the stress on judgement found in Matthew is due to Matthean redaction and does not echo the teaching of Jesus. Matthew 25:31-46 is understood to be a 'Matthean construction', simply 'an expansion of such teaching as is found in xiii. 40-3, Matthew's explanation of the Tares parable' (though Glasson does acknowledge that the passage has 'at its heart genuine words of Jesus similar to sayings found elsewhere,' citing 10:40-2 as an example).[78] For Jesus, judgement was much more a present reality. 'Jesus had a message for communities as well as individuals. He believed in a judgement of God which runs through history.'[79]

J. A. T. ROBINSON

A similar view is reached by J. A. T. Robinson,[80] whose work is subtitled, 'Did the early church misinterpret the original teaching of Jesus?' The answer, according to Robinson, is, 'Yes'! In discussion, for example, of Matthew's use of the term '*Parousia*' he speaks of it as,

a term which is clearly editorial on its first appearance (24.3) and which evidently betrays the usage of the Church.[81]

Robinson makes his point more fully a few pages later when he writes,

what fails is the evidence that Jesus thought of the messianic act as taking place in two stages, the first of which was now shortly to be accomplished, the second of which would follow after an interval and must in the meantime be the focus of every eye and thought. For we have now reviewed all the sayings about the coming of the Son of man, whether in vindication or in visitation. And in them we have found nothing requiring us to suppose that Jesus envisaged a second such moment of the Son of man, beyond and separate from the culmination of the ministry which he came to fulfil. We are far from saying that he could not have done so - merely the evidence fails that he did. In all the decisive cases his words have a more natural application, not to a future advent, but to those climactic events in which he himself stood; though it is equally natural that the Church,

---

[77] Glasson, *The Second Advent*, 127.
[78] Glasson, *The Second Advent*, 130.
[79] Glasson, *The Second Advent*, 129.
[80] J. A. T. Robinson, *Jesus and his Coming* (London: SCM Press, 1957). Robinson acknowledges his debt to Glasson's volume on pages 13-14.
[81] Robinson, *Jesus and his Coming*, 78.

which did not stand in these events, should later have adapted the teaching to its own hope.[82]

This is not to say that Robinson does not accept that Jesus held a belief in eschatological judgement. In fact, he states quite plainly that

> Like every Jew, Jesus visualized history as bounded by the final judgement, 'that day' of traditional expectation (Matt. 5.21-30; 7.22; 10.15; 11.21-4; 12.36, 41 f.; Luke 10.12-15; 11.31 f.), which would be marked by a general resurrection (Mark 12.25-7 and pars.; Luke 14.14) and a final separation of saved and lost.[83]

Moreover, Robinson is prepared to acknowledge that there are passages 'which leave no doubt that [Jesus] saw himself as intimately connected with it.'[84] Yet, Robinson does not regard the role of Jesus as judge to be a theme in Jesus' teaching.

Both Glasson and Robinson provide an important precedent for the approach adopted by Borg to the interpretation of the apocalyptic language found in the OT, and yet they also, in my opinion, provide a corrective to his work, in that they interpret the language of Daniel 7:13, not as a prediction of the *Parousia* of Christ (the view Borg takes, inconsistently in my view), but as a picture of enthronement and vindication.[85]

M. BORG

Borg entered the arena of Jesus Research with two significant books in the 1980s. First, there was a scholarly volume entitled *Conflict, Holiness and Politics in the Teachings of Jesus*. This was a substantially revised version of his doctoral thesis, produced in the early seventies under the supervision of George Caird. The second work, *Jesus: A New Vision*,[86] is a more popular treatment of the issues surrounding who Jesus was, although it builds on the insights of his previous book. Both books have demonstrated themselves to be worthy of serious attention. In addition to these works, Borg has published several articles which follow on from, and develop, his thesis.[87] Borg has become known for his presentation of a 'Non-Eschatological Jesus', and since this has had such a significant impact on contemporary thought, we will devote more space to consideration of his views.

Borg highlights two 'images' of Jesus. Firstly, according to Borg, the image generally accepted by the Christian community is found in the exalted Christology of John's gospel and in the theological developments reflected in the ecu-

---

[82] Robinson, *Jesus and his Coming*, 81-82. See Moore, *The Parousia*, 52-53.

[83] Robinson, *Jesus and his Coming*, 37.

[84] Robinson, *Jesus and his Coming*, 38.

[85] See Glasson, *The Second Advent*, 64; Robinson, *Jesus and his Coming*, 44-45.

[86] M. Borg, *Jesus: A New Vision* (London: SPCK, 1993 [1987]).

[87] See the bibliographical details in footnotes 1 and 6 in Chapter 1.

menical creeds of the early Christian church.[88] Yet Borg acknowledges that this popular image is largely unacceptable to the academic community. Secondly, there is the academic image of Jesus, dominant since the work of Schweitzer and Weiss, as an eschatological prophet who expected the coming of the kingdom within his own lifetime.[89] Since that event evidently did not happen, we are left with the sad portrait of a Jesus who got it wrong.[90] This image, however, appears to have no relevance for ordinary Christians who are outside the academic community. Thus the two main images of Jesus are separated from each other by a great chasm which seemingly cannot be bridged.[91]

Borg proposes a third image, which, he claims, has far more relevance to the present day, while still being true to the principles of historical scholarship. He does not dwell on matters of method, but his brief comments broadly echo those of Sanders cited earlier:

> Though it is true that the gospels are not straightforward historical documents, and though it is true that every saying and story of Jesus has been shaped by the early church, we can in fact know as much about Jesus as we can about any figure in the ancient world. Though we cannot ever be certain that we have direct and exact quotation from Jesus, we can be relatively sure of the *kinds* of things he said, and of the main themes and thrust of his teaching. We can also be relatively sure of the kinds of things he did: healings, association with outcasts, the deliberate calling of twelve disciples, a mission directed to Israel, a final purposeful journey to Jerusalem.[92]

Borg's work examines Jesus under the two broad headings of 'Spirit' and 'Culture', but within these bounds he suggests four categories which help us to understand Jesus. Thus, according to Borg, we are to regard Jesus as a 'healer', a 'sage', a 'prophet', and a 'revitalisation movement founder'.[93]

Borg claims that Jesus was 'a Spirit-filled person in the charismatic stream of Judaism.'[94] It is at the beginning of his public ministry that Jesus demonstrates himself to be within the charismatic stream of Judaism. From the time of his baptism by John and the vision of the Spirit descending on him as he came out of the Jordan, Jesus' ministry was characterised by Spirit. Spirit was the source of his ministry and is evident throughout the ministry in the form of visions, prayer (the particular intimacy of *Abba* is noted), and the way in which Jesus spoke of himself and reacted to others.

---

[88] *New Vision*, 2-4.

[89] *New Vision*, 11-12; 'Reflections', 11-12.

[90] Borg, *New Vision*, 12, says of Schweitzer's Jesus: 'Jesus was mistaken; the end did not come, and he died perhaps realising his mistake.'

[91] *New Vision*, 12-14.

[92] *New Vision*, 15.

[93] *New Vision*, 14-17. These themes are in evidence in Borg's earlier work also, primarily in his concluding chapter. See Borg, *Conflict*, 239-71.

[94] Borg, *New Vision*, 25.

For Borg, the most obvious mark of Jesus' Spirit-filled life was the miracles (or 'mighty deeds') which he performed.[95] Borg dissents from the scholarly tendency to dismiss the historicity of the miracle accounts and to see them rather as part of the church's *story* of Jesus. While arguing for the validity of the latter view, he believes that it is not exclusive of the former approach, claiming that 'the tradition that Jesus was a "wonder-worker" is historically very firmly attested.'[96]

As part of the *history* of Jesus, Borg draws particular attention to acts of exorcism and healing. The accounts of these events are regarded as generally reliable since they are well attested in early sources and find abundant parallels in first century religion. Even Jesus' opponents agreed that he performed mighty deeds, though they attributed his power to demons.[97] It is noted that first century Jews distinguished between healings and exorcisms,[98] and that others at that time also practised exorcism. What characterised the exorcisms which Jesus performed was *power,* demonstrated in an authoritative command (Mark 1:23-27), and often resulting in convulsions and cries from the person being liberated. The people who witnessed these exorcisms responded in various ways. Some regarded them as manifestations of the power of God, but the religious authorities challenged Jesus as a sorcerer (Mark 3:22-30).[99] Jesus responded by claiming to be empowered by the Spirit of God.

Jesus was known as a healer, even more than as an exorcist. Borg notes the many, if sometimes summary, accounts of healings in the synoptic gospels and the various ways in which they were accomplished. Sometimes Jesus spoke a word (Mark 3:5), sometimes he touched the person (Mark 1:40-42) and sometimes he used physical means such as saliva (Mark 8:22-26). In all these situations, Jesus was drawing on spiritual power. Borg draws a parallel between Jesus and the Jewish charismatic Hanina ben Dosa in his healing at a distance (Matthew 8:5-13). This places Jesus, yet again, firmly in the charismatic stream of Jewish religion. Borg's understanding of Jesus as a charismatic figure stands in the line of Geza Vermes' *Jesus the Jew*.[100] Vermes also understood Jesus to be in the stream of other contemporary charismatic figures such as Hanina ben

---

[95] Borg, *Conflict*, 88. It is interesting to note that Borg refers the reader to a number of volumes relating to shamanism, including one entitled *The Shaman's Doorway* (New York: 1976).

[96] Borg, *New Vision*, 59.

[97] Borg, *New Vision*, 61.

[98] Borg, *New Vision*, 61-62. Borg is to be commended for making this distinction. Contrast the tendency to blur these categories in C. A. Evans, *Luke* (Peabody: Hendrickson, 1990), 77, 82.

[99] This understanding of Jesus' activities is reproduced in modern times by Morton Smith, *Jesus the Magician* (San Francisco, 1978). For a brief but useful discussion of the applicability of the category of magic to Jesus miracles, see Theissen and Merz, *The Historical Jesus*, 304-06.

[100] G. Vermes, *Jesus the Jew* (London: SCM Press, 1973).

Dosa and Honi the Circle Drawer.[101]

One of the distinctives of Borg's work is his understanding of Jesus in the context of 'conflict'. In an important chapter in *Jesus: A New Vision*, he describes Jesus' 'social world' by which he means not only the religio-political environment in which Jesus lived but also the shared convictions of the time.[102] He sets the scene of Judea under Roman rule, describing the situation as a crisis. In examining how this situation arose, Borg first identifies the 'conventional wisdom' which lay at the root of the Judean social world. This had its source in the folk wisdom which gave guidance for living day by day, and, more importantly, in the *Torah* which God had given to his people. The *Torah* was interpreted by the 'sages' or 'teachers of wisdom' and so Borg can describe Israel's conventional wisdom as largely '*Torah* wisdom'.[103] Borg also says that the conventional wisdom regarded reality as based around reward and punishment. Thus to choose the path of wisdom was to bring blessing to one's life. The corollary of this was that lack of blessing indicated punishment. A third element of this conventional wisdom was that it was the primary means of giving identity. This was accomplished by means of establishing boundaries between various groups. The fundamental boundary was between Jews (the 'children of Abraham') and Gentiles, but there were also many boundaries drawn within the Jewish community which formed a social structure. Borg writes,

> It [conventional wisdom] also conferred more particular social identities with well-defined expectations and limitations: landowner, priest, husband, wife, father, oldest son, rich, poor, noble, peasant, man and woman. The different degrees of status associated with these categories produced a hierarchical order in the society. Moreover these boundaries and hierarchies were quite rigid, firmly ingrained in the tradition (for example, the different roles given to men and to women, the different status accorded to oldest son and younger sons, the distinction between Jew and Gentile). Thus, to a large extent, both identity and social structure were "given" by conventional wisdom.[104]

Particularly important in Jewish society, according to Borg, were the categories of 'righteous' and 'wicked'. Those who lived according to conventional wisdom were given the identity of the 'righteous' and those who failed to do so were 'wicked'. Borg suggests that this situation could have continued in perpetuity but for the presence of the Romans.

Roman rule brought severe economic pressure. The *Torah* required tithes of the people which amounted, according to Borg, to 'slightly over 20 percent per year.'[105] On top of this, the Romans required taxation on land and crops as well

---

[101] See Evans, *NWNTI*, 232-38; Theissen and Merz, *The Historical Jesus*, 307-08.

[102] Borg, *New Vision*, 79.

[103] Borg, *New Vision*, 82.

[104] Borg, *New Vision*, 83.

[105] Borg, *New Vision*, 84.

as other sundry taxes. This led to a total tax burden of around 35 percent (to say nothing of the 'commission' which unscrupulous tax collectors might add). Since many farmers could not pay such taxes a dilemma arose. The Roman taxes had to be paid (they were legally enforceable) but the Jewish taxes could be neglected, at the sole cost of not obeying *Torah*. Since many were in danger of losing their land, they had no real choice; they did not pay the Jewish taxes and so a class of 'non-observant' Jews came into being.[106]

Non-observance threatened the whole structure of Jewish society and so there had to be a response. That response is identified by Borg as the 'Politics of Holiness'.[107] This was a theme developed from the 'holiness code' of the Old Testament, understood in terms of separation from everything unclean. This addressed both the requirement to be faithful to a God who required holiness, and also the need to survive in a hostile environment. This was seen in intensified form in the renewal movements of the first century: the Pharisees, the Essenes and what Josephus calls the 'fourth philosophy'.

The Pharisees responded to non-observance with a call to be 'a kingdom of priests'. That is, they imposed on themselves the purity standards of the temple. Their sanction against those who did not follow the same path was ostracism.[108] They were 'the most visible manifestation of the Politics of Holiness,'[109] but were peaceable, and were seemingly resigned to the fact of Roman occupation. Far less resigned were the Essenes and those engaged in the resistance against Rome, sometimes referred to as Zealots.[110] These groups all tried in different ways to respond to the Roman occupation in terms of the 'Politics of Holiness'. The outcome was that many people found themselves outside the boundaries of these various groups. So people became 'sinners' and 'outcasts', distinct social groupings who were caught up in a complex system of politics beyond their control. In all this, the Jews were heading ever closer to confrontation with the Romans, so that the shadow of war hung over the people of Jesus' day. The reasons, according to Borg, were twofold. Firstly, the people were aware of real injustice in the land from which they longed to be released. And secondly, the people were committed to a life of holiness (even if that was variously under-

---

[106] Borg, *New Vision*, 85.

[107] Borg, *New Vision*, 86-87.

[108] D. A. Neale, *None But The Sinners* (Sheffield: JSOT Press, 1991), 43-44, points out that E. P. Sanders has stated that this ostracism was not crippling to those who were non-observant since (a) the Pharisees did not exert any great control over religious life in Israel, and (b) they did not consider non-Pharisees to be *lost*, but simply *non-haberim* (those who were members of an association for observation of strict religious purity). See Sanders, *Jesus and Judaism*, 174-211.

[109] Borg, *New Vision*, 89.

[110] Borg points out the danger of using any term which suggests a coherent group, since whether or not such a group existed is far from certain. He suggests that we speak of a 'current of resistance' rather than a movement, *New Vision*, 90.

stood) which was incompatible with Roman rule.[111]

This context of conflict in which Jesus conducted his ministry is reflected in the gospel accounts in the New Testament. B. Witherington, in a discussion of the 'Q' logion found in Matt 11:12-13/Luke 16:16 ('the kingdom of heaven suffers violence'), judges that it gives 'substantial support to M. Borg's contention that "there is much in the gospels that suggests conflict as a context for interpreting the teaching of Jesus." '[112]

How did Jesus respond to the 'Politics of Holiness'? Borg's first answer to this question is that he challenged the Jewish conventional wisdom in his role as a *Sage*.[113] This, for Borg, means that he taught a 'way' (as opposed to ethics or doctrines); a way of transformation. Borg brings to our attention the methods of teaching employed by Jesus, particularly proverbs, parables and lessons from observation of nature. All these formed 'an invitation to see differently.'[114] His teaching formed a critique of the four key themes of conventional wisdom: wealth, family, honour and religion. He taught about a gracious God, filled with compassion and this was to be the foundation of his alternative to the 'Politics of Holiness'. And he spoke of the need of dying to a self-centred way of life, of placing one's confidence in God and of radical inward change. But he did not simply undermine the existing attitudes; he offered a different way.

As Borg points out in an essay, the model of Jesus as sage has been warmly grasped by several scholars in contemporary Jesus research.[115] However, he also shows his awareness that the notion of 'sage' can be very different from one scholar to another, some favouring a 'cynic' sage model,[116] and most denying an eschatological element to this Wisdom teaching.[117] His own model of a 'teacher of subversive and alternative wisdom'[118] appears to depend partly on comparative studies of major figures in world religions such as Lao Tzu and the

---

[111] Borg, *New Vision*, 92-93.

[112] B. Witherington, *The Christology of Jesus* (Minneapolis: Fortress, 1990), 46-47, citing Borg *Conflict* 24. In a footnote to page 47, Witherington adds, 'In general, I agree with Borg on Jesus' conflict with his context, but I find the attempt to de-eschatologize Jesus unconvincing.' We will turn to this latter aspect of Borg's work shortly.

[113] Borg, *New Vision*, 97. The recent work of Ben Witherington, *Jesus the Sage* (Edinburgh, 1994), is a major treatment of the theme of Wisdom as a key to understanding Jesus.

[114] Borg, *New Vision*, 99.

[115] 'Reflections', 17. Borg writes, 'This is the stroke in a sketch of the historical Jesus about which there is greatest consensus.' This may be rather too optimistic.

[116] Notably the work of F. G. Downing and J. D. Crossan. See the discussion of G. A. Boyd, *Cynic Sage or Son of God?* (Wheaton: Bridgepoint, 1995).

[117] See the discussion in Witherington, *Jesus the Sage*, 118-41; Boyd, *Cynic Sage or Son of God?* 145-50.

[118] 'Reflections', 17. The model is developed in *New Vision*, 97-124.

Buddha.[119] Borg understands Jesus' role as sage to mean that,

> He affirmed another vision and another way. He taught an alternative way of being and an alternative consciousness shaped by the relationship to Spirit and not primarily by the dominant consciousness of culture.[120]

As one reads these words, the question arises whether this is the language of comparative religion more than the language of faith in the God of Israel.

As to the second way in which Jesus responded to the 'Politics of Holiness', Jesus, we are told, was a 'revitalization movement founder'.[121] This is not to say that Jesus was political in the sense of being a revolutionary, but he was political in the sense that his teaching was intended to shape the community of Israel as they lived in history. This new movement was in continuity with its roots in Jewish religion, but also recognised that the situation in which Israel found herself required a new and radical approach. This movement was (a) intended for Israel in particular, (b) charismatic in the sense that it displayed the power of the Spirit, (c) itinerant and (d) marked by joy as it centred on Jesus and developed in his presence.[122] The movement had one supreme distinctive, and that was compassion. Jesus practised the 'Politics of Compassion' which negated all the boundaries established by the various groups in Israel. Thus Jesus and his followers ate with outcasts[123] and associated with women. They offered good news to the poor and they lived in peace, to the extent that Borg can call them the 'Peace Party' of Palestine.[124] They also focused on the spiritual significance of many concepts which had previously been understood in physical terms, such as the temple and the notion of 'Israel' itself. Borg summarises this section by claiming that Jesus intended to establish an alternative community, characterised by compassion, inclusiveness, love and peace, and, through that community, to criticise his own culture and call it away from its present path. In this sense Jesus' message was 'emphatically "political".'[125]

There can be little doubt that Jesus' ministry is characterised by the formation of a community of disciples, but it is not clear that Borg's presentation of Jesus as a 'revitalisation movement founder' does justice to the nature of Jesus' ministry. At the most obvious level, it leaves us with a failure, since Jesus was not successful in turning national Israel to his way. I am inclined to the view that any aspects of Jesus' ministry which might fit this model are better under-

---

[119] *New Vision*, 97.

[120] *New Vision*, 116.

[121] Borg, *New Vision*, 125.

[122] Borg, *New Vision*, 126-29.

[123] See Neale, *None But The Sinners*, 60-67, for the Rabbinic regulations regarding table fellowship, and for discussion of the relevance or otherwise of these regulations to the first century situation.

[124] Borg, *New Vision*, 137.

[125] Wright, *Who Was Jesus?* 15.

stood as part of the complex of activities which form Borg's next model for Jesus – the prophet.

'Of all the figures in his tradition, Jesus was most like the classical prophets of Israel.'[126] His prophetic role is particularly seen in the warnings of coming judgement. In the past, scholars have interpreted these warnings as predictions of an imminent end of the world. Thus, as we have already mentioned, Schweitzer could understand Jesus as a visionary who 'got it wrong', and who is finally bewildered at being abandoned by God. Borg argues that, while some of the sayings attributed to Jesus do indeed have a note of imminence, most of the judgement sayings refer to a coming national catastrophe, namely the destruction of the temple. In the OT, the people of Israel had become complacent in the conviction that God would never abandon his own chosen dwelling-place. Such 'Zion theology' was the target of the preaching of prophets such as Jeremiah and Ezekiel. Borg argues that Jesus' message carries on this theme of warning and that the warnings only make sense when seen in this historical, non-eschatological light.

It is one of the most significant of Borg's theses that Jesus was not an eschatological preacher but rather spoke to his own time with a view to changing the culture in which he lived. As Borg points out in an article for George Caird's memorial volume, this understanding is very much in tune with that of his mentor. In discussing several elements of Caird's work which influenced him (as Caird was his mentor), Borg writes

...he frequently called into question one of the prevailing orthodoxies of New Testament scholarship in this century: the widely shared conviction that Jesus proclaimed the imminent end of the world...

adding,

Professor Caird never tired of sparring with this view...[127]

Borg develops the thesis of his book in this article by incorporating three elements into his argument:

The first element is drawn partly from the work of Gerd Theissen on the 'Jesus movement' of AD 30-70. Theissen argues that the Jesus movement was one of several movements of the time which offered responses to the social issues of the day. This is in accord with Borg's thesis that what Jesus intended to accomplish was 'the transformation of Israel, not the preparation of a community ready for the imminent end of the world.'[128] This argument is not conclusive, as

---

[126] Borg, *New Vision*, 150.

[127] M. J. Borg, 'An Orthodoxy Reconsidered: The "End-of-the-World Jesus"' in Hurst and Wright (eds.), *The Glory of Christ in the New Testament* (Oxford: Clarendon, 1987), 208. Also, 'Reflections', 12.

[128] Borg, 'The "End-of-the-World Jesus"', 210-11.

Borg admits. The force of this argument is cumulative when combined with others.

The second argument is an attack on the exegetical base for the eschatological understanding of Jesus' preaching. Borg reports that the 'coming Son of Man' sayings are increasingly being regarded as inauthentic. Borg clearly welcomes this development, pointing to the work of G. Vermes as evidence against a titular use of the phrase.[129] Interestingly, Borg is not concerned with the idea that Jesus expected an eschatological Day of Judgement. Referring to Luke 10:12, 13-14 and Luke 11:31, 32, he writes,

> These sayings indicate that there is a "cosmic" strain in Jesus' eschatology: he did see history as having a final judgement at its boundary; like many of his contemporaries, he believed in the resurrection of the dead and the last judgment.[130]

What he wishes to stress is that these sayings do not contain any note of imminence. Even the view of many in the early Christian church that there would be an imminent end of the world does not, claims Borg, require that that is what Jesus taught. Rather, this belief stemmed from the 'Easter event'.

Moving on from these first two arguments, Borg offers the portrait of Jesus, which we have already discussed, as a *'Gestalt'* which 'provides us with a fuller picture, one which more comprehensively incorporates what we find in the synoptic texts themselves.'[131] It is the coherence of this *Gestalt* that Borg offers as his third argument.[132] However, many scholars have reacted to Borg's 'new vision' with scepticism, seeing his Jesus as only one more product of a tendentious reading of the New Testament.[133]

We must return to this issue a little later for fuller evaluation, but it must be said at this stage that Borg has really only presented one substantive argument for a non-eschatological Jesus. His first and third arguments are simply alternative presentations of the evidence which do not in fact deal with the presence of the various eschatological texts. These texts stubbornly remain to disturb Borg's view of Jesus and his community, unless they are done away with on the basis of the second argument. Thus Borg's argument stands or falls with the

---

[129] Borg, 'The "End-of-the-World Jesus"', 211.

[130] Borg, 'The "End-of-the-World Jesus"', 213.

[131] Borg, 'The "End-of-the-World Jesus"', 217.

[132] These arguments are similarly expounded in Borg's article, 'A Temperate case for a Non-Eschatological Jesus,' *Foundations and Facets Forum* 2.3 (1986), 81-102, though this article does not significantly advance Borg's case.

[133] While praising the sensitive use of social-scientific analysis, Ben Meyer accuses Borg of insensitivity to 'the solid evidence of non-metaphorical eschatology in the gospels', 'Jesus' Ministry and Self-Understanding' in Chilton and Evans *Studying the Historical Jesus*, 339. See also Meyer's rather dismissive remark in Wansbrough (ed.), *Jesus and the Oral Gospel Tradition*, 428-29.

issue of the authenticity of the 'coming Son of Man sayings'.[134] Yet Borg does no serious exegesis of these sayings. Astonishingly, he relies heavily on the findings of G. Vermes, with little apparent awareness that other views have been expressed. D. C. Allison lists several contemporary scholars, including J. Collins, U. Luz, M. Reiser and E. P. Sanders, who believe that at least some of the coming Son of Man sayings may be traced back to Jesus.[135] In more recent writings, Borg has drawn on J. D. Crossan's analysis to demonstrate the frailty of the coming Son of Man tradition, but Allison has rebutted Crossan's use of sources and shown that 'one can do anything with statistics'![136] These sayings thus take on such a significant role in Borg's argument that it is vital that we re-examine them later on in the course of this book.[137]

However, I consider Borg's broad analysis of Jesus' ministry to be largely persuasive *as far as it goes and with several reservations*.[138] I believe that he has highlighted some important facets of Jesus' ministry through the use of the categories of charismatic, sage, prophet, and revitalisation movement founder. This multi-faceted approach to understanding Jesus in particular is a significant advance over many previous studies which had frequently attempted to fit Jesus into a single mold.[139] Nonetheless, I believe that his focus on Jesus' temporal ministry, along with his *religionsgeschichtlich* methodology, has blinded him to the fact that none of these categories are sufficient to explain Jesus' words and works. Significantly, Borg rules out any conception in Jesus' self-consciousness of his being the Messiah. He writes,

> In all likelihood, the pre-Easter Jesus did not think of himself as the Messiah, or in any exalted terms in which he is spoken of.[140]

---

[134] So also Witherington, *The Jesus Quest*, 94. In fact, Meier (*A Marginal Jew*, 2:350) claims that even should these sayings be inauthentic, Borg's case is still not proven: 'Even if one were to judge all the Son of Man sayings inauthentic, this decision would in no way negate the fundamental insight we have gained in this chapter. Jesus' message of future eschatology and a future kingdom does not rise or fall with Jesus' statements about the Son of Man – a point some critics fail to grasp.' The footnote at the close of the quote refers to Borg's *Jesus: A New Vision*.

[135] Allison, *Jesus of Nazareth*, 114-15 n. 81.

[136] Allison, *Jesus of Nazareth*, 116.

[137] See the discussion in Chapter 5.

[138] For published assessments of Borg's work, see Witherington, *The Jesus Quest*, 93-108, Wright, *Jesus and the Victory of God*, 75-78, Powell, *The Jesus Debate*, 111-22.

[139] Powell, *The Jesus Debate*, 121, notes that 'Borg's view is more comprehensive than many.'

[140] 'Portraits of Jesus' in H. Shanks (ed.), *The Search for Jesus* (Washington: Biblical Archaeological Society, 1994), 87, cited by Powell, *The Jesus Debate*, 122. Borg appears to be somewhat more cautious in his *New Vision* where he writes (50), 'We cannot know if Jesus made these [messianic] associations himself.'

This is remarkable since 'Messiah' is such a fundamentally Jewish category, which other Jews were not shy to adopt.[141] In fact it seems that Borg's Jesus is not quite Jewish enough.

Particularly, I believe that the theme of judgement against Jesus' contemporaries, which Borg finds so important, only truly has bite when the one who pronounces this judgement is correctly identified, and it is recognised that he has the authority to carry out what he proclaims.

J. D. CROSSAN

A very different tack which nonetheless yields similar results is taken by the stimulating and provocative author, J. D. Crossan, who is a fellow-member with Borg of a group known as the 'Jesus Seminar'. Crossan is important to our survey because he represents an emphasis on Jesus as sage which leads him to dismiss the eschatological and judgement elements from Jesus' ministry. This is particularly due to the fact that the model of sage adopted by Crossan is the Hellenistic Cynic sage, which is then applied to the Jewish Jesus. Crossan is probably the most high-profile author who takes this position, although he is taken as a representative of several other scholars, including, notably, F. G. Downing. Crossan's recent and massive work bears the characteristically bold title 'The Historical Jesus', but is sub-titled somewhat more humbly, 'The Life of a Mediterranean Jewish Peasant'.[142] Crossan's Jesus is a very human figure, as the sub-title suggests, who is not at all interested in the issues of eschatology. Crossan does believe that Jesus once,

> must also have accepted John's apocalyptic expectation, must have accepted John as the Prophet of the Coming One.[143]

However, Crossan understands Jesus to have 'changed his view',[144] and in concluding his discussion of the apocalyptic texts from the gospels which are influenced by Daniel 7:13 he writes,

> this whole stream of tradition, far from starting on the lips of Jesus, began only after his crucifixion with a meditation on Zechariah 12:10, then moved on to combine Daniel 7:13 with that prophecy, and finally left only the barest vestige of those beginnings in the perdurance of the *see* verb for the apocalyptic judge.[145]

This is despite the fact that Crossan acknowledges the very high level of at-

---

[141] So also Wright, *Jesus and the Victory of God*, 77. Messianic pretenders are identified in both Josephus and the NT (see Acts 5:36-37; 21:38).

[142] J. D. Crossan, *The Historical Jesus* (Edinburgh: T&T Clark, 1991).

[143] Crossan, *The Historical Jesus*, 237.

[144] Crossan, *The Historical Jesus*, 237.

[145] Crossan, *The Historical Jesus*, 247.

testation for such tradition.[146] This is due in part to his acceptance, following in the footsteps of Borg, of Vermes' arguments for a generic, non-titular use of *bar nasha* which is incompatible with the view which holds that Jesus drew on the Daniel 7 tradition.[147]

The Jesus we are left with is 'a peasant Jewish Cynic', living an itinerant life of philosophising among 'the farms and villages of Lower Galilee,' whose strategy, far from announcing the eschatological kingdom, 'was the combination of *free healing and common eating*.'[148] There is no place for Jesus the judge in Crossan's presentation.

Studies of Matthew's View of Jesus and Judgement

Having seen the range of views concerning Jesus' expectations of judgement, we now want to focus our attention on Matthew's presentation of Jesus' preaching on this subject. The latter should certainly bear a very close relationship to the former, but it needs to be recognised that there is a significant difference in perspective. Matthew is writing some thirty or more years after the death of Jesus. If, as Schweitzer claimed, Jesus thought that the kingdom of God would come dramatically after the briefest period of time, Matthew clearly knows that such an expectation was not fulfilled, and therefore must reinterpret Jesus' words for his own time. On the other hand, of course, the fact that Matthew records words of Jesus which might appear to recent scholarship to have remained unfulfilled may be an indication that we should rethink our interpretation of these words.

Several works have dealt with this subject matter, more or less directly, and I will briefly discuss the most important of these.

G. BORNKAMM

Without doubt, the essay by G. Bornkamm entitled, 'End-Expectation and Church in Matthew',[149] and particularly the first portion of that essay, broke new ground in the study of the theme of judgement in Matthew. For the first time, the theme of future judgement was clearly seen to pervade the whole of the gospel as a central theme and to provide an important motivation towards discipleship for the church to which Matthew was writing. Bornkamm surveys the several discourses of the gospel, identifying the consistent emphasis on the end, particularly in the conclusions of the main discourses: the discourse of the Baptist (3:1-12); the Sermon on the Mount (5-7); the Missionary Discourse (9:35-10); the Parables of the Kingdom (13). Here he points out particularly

---

[146] Crossan, *The Historical Jesus*, 243.
[147] Crossan, *The Historical Jesus*, 238-43.
[148] Crossan, *The Historical Jesus*, 421-22.
[149] In G. Bornkamm, G. Barth and H. J. Held, *Tradition and Interpretation in Matthew* (London: SCM Press, 1963), 15-51.

how the two parables of the tares and of the dragnet emphasise Matthew's view of the church as a mixed community which will be separated at judgement. Moving on to the so-called Discourse to the Congregation (18), he notes that verse 1 immediately sets the eschatological tone. He continues through the Parables of the Vineyard and Marriage Feast, the Woes on the Pharisees, and the Apocalyptic Discourse. In the introduction to the latter, Bornkamm contends, Matthew has altered the somewhat exclusive character of this discourse as it is found in Mark. In Matthew's gospel, the discourse is not solely for a few but for 'the disciples'. In concluding his survey, Bornkamm writes,

> This short analysis of Matthew's Gospel has shown us the close linking of conception of the Church and end-expectation there, but it has also repeatedly revealed wherein the link between the two consists, namely in the understanding of the law and thereby of the new righteousness, which distinguishes the disciples of Jesus from the Pharisees and the scribes and is at the same time the standard by which the members of the Church are to be judged by the coming judge.[150]

The key strength of Bornkamm's work is, unfortunately, also its weakness. Employing the methodology of redaction criticism, Bornkamm does more than simply describe the various aspects of judgement in Matthew's gospel; he sets out an overall interpretation of this material, indicating its *function* as a part of the literary whole, written to a community of believers. This makes Bornkamm's essay particularly valuable, and his approach has been followed, to some extent, by many subsequent interpreters.

However, in dealing primarily with the *changes* which he believes Matthew has effected on his sources, Bornkamm does not take sufficient notice of the material which Matthew has preserved in much the same form. Thus what Bornkamm isolates is Matthew's distinctive details, not necessarily the most significant ones. This means that there is little emphasis on Matthew's narrative as a whole.

In addition, the connection he makes between eschatology and ecclesiology gives the impression that eschatological teaching is intended to have a purely parenetic function, and so the question of the significance of the teaching on judgement for our understanding of future events is left on one side.

D. MARGUERAT

The next significant treatment of judgement in Matthew was the mammoth thesis by D. Marguerat, *Le Jugement dans l'Évangile de Matthieu*.[151] Marguerat's work is an exhaustive redaction-critical study, and leaves no doubt as to the importance of the theme of judgement in the first gospel.[152] The book is divided

---

[150] Bornkamm, 'End-Expectation', 24.

[151] Marguerat, *Le Jugement dans l'Évangile de Matthieu*.

[152] Judgement, says Marguerat (*Le Jugement*, 3) is 'un thème théologique de première importance pour l'évangéliste Matthieu.'

into five parts. The first part picks up introductory issues such as terminology and the rhetorical function of the proclamation of judgement.[153] According to Marguerat, Matthew presents Jesus as the one who possesses eschatological authority as he concludes Jesus' major discourses (as well as other references) with eschatological teaching. Human beings in general are faced with the threat of judgement, and two groups in particular – the disciples and the Jewish people (represented primarily by their leaders).[154] Particularly important for Marguerat is the relationship between judgement and the law in Matthew, which he expounds in the second main section of his book.[155] He writes,

> Un regard jeté sur les autres synoptiques prouve enfin que nous rencontrons ici, dans l'accentuation du thème du jugement et son lien avec la thématique de la Loi, une originalité du premier évangile.[156]

Judgement then, for Matthew, is based on fidelity to the words of Jesus as he gives final interpretation to the law. Marguerat devotes some attention here to the phrase 'the Son of Man'.[157] The third section of Marguerat's book deals with the failure of Israel, and so deals with important sections of Matthew (such as portions of chapters 21 and 23) which will be examined in the present book also. These accounts form a warning to the church not to follow the example of the Jews. This leads to a consideration of the church under judgement (focusing largely on Matthew 18-20) in the fourth part, while the fifth section deals with the eschatological discourse (chapters 24-25) under the heading of 'être vigilant'. In these latter sections, Marguerat particularly emphasises the importance of the threat of judgement as an incentive to faithfulness for the church. However, although Marguerat treats a substantial portion of the material in Matthew 21-25 in various places, he does not bring out the coherence of chapters 21-25 as a unit of Matthew's gospel. Perhaps this is partly due to the redaction-critical methodology which he employs, since he understands Matthew to have made little attempt to draw together material from his sources into a coherent presentation of judgement (although he does give careful attention to the finished text as it stands also). Further, Marguerat concentrates his attention on the issue of eschatological judgement. Hence he writes,

> Sur les 148 péricopes que l'on dénombre dans l'évangile, pas moins de 60 traitent du jugement eschatologique ou s'y réfèrent.[158]

It is my contention that Matthew's interest in Jesus as the bringer of judge-

---

[153] *Le Jugement*, 13-63.
[154] *Le Jugement*, 45-48.
[155] *Le Jugement*, 65-236.
[156] *Le Jugement*, 563.
[157] *Le Jugement*, 69-77.
[158] *Le Jugement*, 563.

ment is broader than simply future judgement. In this respect, the work of Borg provides a helpful corrective, although Marguerat is closer to the mark in recognising the pivotal significance of Jesus himself in determining the judgement of each person. Thus we believe that, though there is much to be learned from Marguerat's important monograph, it is not the final word and there is still room for further elucidation of this portion of Matthew.

B. CHARETTE

We move on to consider B. Charette's published doctoral thesis, which examines *The Theme of Recompense in Matthew's Gospel*.[159] Although dealing with a somewhat broader subject area than we are concerned with, it encompasses a significant discussion of judgement in the gospel. Charette sets the scene for both blessings and curses in Matthew with a discussion of the OT covenant, particularly as that entails an inheritance for the covenant keepers and being cut off for the covenant breakers. This is a commendable approach in that it looks to the OT for a hermeneutical key to appreciate the teaching of Matthew's gospel - clearly a wise decision given Matthew's known reliance on the OT Scriptures. Charette argues that the threats of judgement in Matthew are intended to be powerful incentives for faithful discipleship, and thus joins Marguerat in the tradition of Bornkamm in appreciating the parenetic function of the judgement material. In so doing, while benefiting from that strength, he is also subject to the same caution - that the eschatological events are not given sufficient significance for their own sake. We believe, also, that there is scope for developing beyond Charette's work in that he focuses on the final judgement, and does not give much attention to the theme of temporal judgement, or to the relationship between temporal and final judgement.

However, he makes a notable advance on Bornkamm at a methodological level in that he chooses 'Composition Criticism' as his preferred methodology. He points out that the method is a variation of redaction criticism which focuses on the final form of the text. He continues,

> Composition criticism is the product of a recent trend in redaction criticism which, admitting the limitations of earlier forms of the method, recognizes that the concerns of an Evangelist are to be found not merely in the study of the changes he has made to his sources but also in the study of the completed work he has produced.[160]

As we wish to examine a substantial portion of Matthew's gospel to appreciate the way in which Matthew brings out the theme of judgement, this methodology seems to offer a refinement of that used by Bornkamm and Marguerat, and so will encourage more sensitivity to the literary unity of the section. Cha-

---

[159] B. Charette, *The Theme of Recompense in Matthew's Gospel* (JSNTS 79; Sheffield: Sheffield Academic Press, 1992).

[160] Charette, *The Theme of Recompense*, 17.

rette actually distinguishes this methodology from narrative criticism,[161] but while we appreciate his reasoning we believe that Composition Criticism will allow us to take more account of the literary coherence of one portion of Matthew's gospel. We will take up this discussion again in the chapter on methodology.[162]

Finally, there are two comments made by Charette which I must refer to. In his introduction, Charette makes clear a fundamental presupposition:

> the present examination is interested solely in the teaching on recompense as it is presented in Matthew. Thus the question as to what the 'historical Jesus' may or may not have taught on the subject lies beyond the purview of this enquiry.[163]

Moving then to the very end of his book we find that he picks up that comment,

> It was noted in the introduction that the present study would not attempt to determine the extent to which the Gospel of Matthew accurately reflects the teaching of the 'historical Jesus' on the subject of recompense. It is possible that the teaching presented in the Gospel bears, to a remarkable degree, the stamp of the Evangelist himself. Yet, inasmuch as Matthew purports to be giving an account of the teaching of Jesus and since most of what can be known about Jesus' teaching on recompense is contained in his Gospel, *it is imperative that future attempts to delineate the teaching of Jesus treat seriously the representation that obtains in Matthew.*[164] (My emphasis.)

He continues,

> In this area of enquiry dogma has exerted an unreasonable influence. A responsible description of Jesus' teaching on this subject requires the equitable evaluation of all the relevant evidence.[165]

While it is disappointing that Charette himself did not pursue this course a little further, his comments concerning the need to take Matthew seriously in considering the 'historical Jesus' reflect my own concerns in this book, and are in tune (as I understand them) with the intentions of my methodology chapter where I attempt to bring Matthew's gospel to bear on our understanding of the 'historical Jesus'. Charette should be applauded simply for calling for an end to unwarranted dismissal of Matthew's evidence with respect to an historical approach to Jesus.

---

[161] Charette, *The Theme of Recompense*, 18-19.
[162] See Chapter 3.
[163] Charette, *The Theme of Recompense*, 11.
[164] Charette, *The Theme of Recompense*, 168.
[165] Charette, *The Theme of Recompense*, 168.

D. C. SIM

The most recent, and a particularly important, contribution to our discussion comes from D. C. Sim, whose University of London PhD thesis has been published as *Apocalyptic Eschatology in the Gospel of Matthew*.[166] Sim's distinctive contribution to the debate is that his is the first full-scale treatment of what he regards as the 'apocalyptic' material in Matthew which attempts to take account of the social setting of Matthew and his community as a key to understanding the purpose of the apocalyptic material. After a discussion of the characteristics of apocalyptic literature, Sim goes on to examine the social setting in which apocalypticism arises, and the function of apocalyptic eschatology. He argues that apocalypticism arises in a situation of severe crisis, whether real or perceived, and that apocalyptic eschatology,

> is a response to the situation of crisis and resultant alienation experienced by the author and his circle and encapsulates their efforts to deal with it...By emphasising that the world is composed of only two groups whose boundaries are clearly marked, and that the beliefs and practices of the apocalyptic community alone meet with God's approval, apocalyptic eschatology both identifies and legitimates the community which resorts to it.[167]

The second part of Sim's book focuses particularly on the use of such apocalyptic eschatology in Matthew's Gospel. This section picks up the analysis of part 1 and Sim proceeds to analyse numerous passages in Matthew's gospel, indicating how he understands the dominant themes in apocalyptic literature to relate to Matthew's gospel. Sim concludes that Matthew has adopted this particular world-view in its totality. He writes,

> His interest in this religious perspective is apparent from his redaction of his Christian sources, his adoption of certain Jewish sources and his outright creation of important apocalyptic-eschatological pericopae (e.g. 13:36-43, 49-50).[168]

The third and final major section, and the most distinctive portion of the work, is an effort to understand and reconstruct the social setting of the Matthean community. However, this issue is not of primary significance to the concerns of this study and so we will not comment further on this last section of Sim's book.

Sim's work is to be welcomed in that it devotes intensive investigation to a theme of great significance to Matthew. At the same time, there are several areas which leave a sense of dissatisfaction. Firstly, Sim's discussion of apocalyptic literature and language does not sufficiently allow for the use of symbol-

---

[166] D. C. Sim, *Apocalyptic Eschatology in the Gospel of Matthew* (SNTSMS 88; Cambridge: Cambridge University Press, 1996).

[167] Sim, *Apocalyptic Eschatology*, 69.

[168] Sim, *Apocalyptic Eschatology*, 175.

ism and other literary devices. It appears to assume that whatever is said in the apocalyptic literature is what was believed would happen. This does not allow for sufficient literary sophistication in the apocalypticists. Secondly, the claim that Matthew adopts the world-view of apocalypticism wholesale does not do justice to the fact that Matthew has broken away from his Jewish roots in a quite astonishing way, in that he now finds in Jesus the fulfilment of the Scriptures (5:17-18). Sim has failed to take sufficient account of the significant differences between the apocalyptic works of second temple Judaism and Matthew's gospel. Thirdly, in focusing on the social setting of the Matthean community and the supposed way in which that setting gave rise to the adoption of the world-view of apocalyptic-eschatology found in the gospel, Sim has, I believe, misrepresented the genre of the gospel. The impression given by his study is that the gospel is written very much to legitimate the existence of a particular, exclusivistic Christian sect, and that the gospel offers the opportunity to understand that community in some detail. However, R. A. Burridge has recently shown that the motivation which lay behind the gospel was primarily,

> a general desire to tell others about Jesus, who he was, what he did and what happened to him in the end.[169]

Sim is so involved in discovering details about the Matthean community that he does not take sufficient time to reflect on what Matthew records of Jesus' teaching. On this point, the comments of D. E. Garland are apposite,

> Since the text contains so little unambiguous information that helps to specify its setting and date, one needs to be cautious in deciding what occasion may or may not have generated its production. One should not spin off some hypothetical context and then read it into the interpretation of the text or assume that the Gospel was drafted solely to address burning issues for a limited group.[170]

Unfortunately, it seems to me that this is just what Sim has done, and that his whole thesis is affected by the decision. This is not to say that we can learn nothing of Matthew and his church from his gospel; only that this was not his main aim and interpreters must be cautious to avoid drawing undue inferences from a story which is *about Jesus*.[171]

Chapter Summary and Conclusion

My contention is that the positions surveyed in this chapter do not exhaust the

---

[169] R. A. Burridge, *What Are the Gospels? A Comparison with Graeco-Roman Biography* (SNTSMS 70; Cambridge: Cambridge University Press, 1992), 214

[170] D. E. Garland, *Reading Matthew* (London: SPCK, 1993), 4-5.

[171] As is argued in the important volume edited by R. Bauckham, *The Gospels for All Christians* (Edinburgh: T&T Clark, 1998).

range of possible options. Though they exhibit considerable diversity in their conclusions as to Jesus' view concerning immediate and future judgement, we may nonetheless observe a certain pattern.

Several authors (e.g. Crossan and Sim) share the understanding that the 'coming Son of Man' sayings relate to Jesus' return at the end of the world, and also that the language of cosmological catastrophe refers to the end of the world.

Others, including Glasson, Robinson and Borg, recognise that there may be more to such language than a prosaic account of coming events. However, they fail to find coherence in Matthew's presentation of Jesus' preaching of the final judgement, and have to resort to declaring several important texts inauthentic.

Several studies (Bornkamm, Marguerat, Charette) recognise the literary skill demonstrated by Matthew in using the theme of judgement, but only Charette comes close to considering what that implies about Jesus' preaching. I believe that there is a need for a study which

(i)   recognises the literary skill of Matthew, and therefore seeks to bring out a coherent message from his gospel without resorting to the claim of incoherence. This demands that we take careful note of the way in which Matthew has arranged his material, and allow him to tell his story in his way.

(ii)   recognises the subtleties of language employed by ancient authors, and therefore does not neglect the possibility of metaphorical significance for phrases which are difficult to understand on a literal reading. This will require sensitivity to the allusions to other literature that may be found, and careful consideration of the most likely background to the use of particular words and phrases.

(iii)   recognises the significance of Matthew's narrative for understanding the 'Historical Jesus' and seeks to take it seriously as a means of better appreciating Jesus' ministry in the context of his first century Jewish setting.

(iv)   provides a corrective both to Weiss and Schweitzer and their heirs and to Borg and his colleagues.

The purpose of this book is to make a contribution to this task.

CHAPTER 3

Problems Raised and Methodology

Problems to be Tackled

Our survey of the literature, and particularly our review of the work of Borg, has brought several problems to light:

1. In Matthew's view, was judgement a key theme in Jesus' preaching? This is a crucial question to ask, as we must beware of emphasising an aspect of the gospel that was never intended to be especially significant. So this question requires that we note the prevalence of the judgement theme in Matthew's gospel.[1] Attention must be given, then, to the sayings that relate to judgement, but we must also look beyond the sayings to the activities of Jesus that Matthew records for us.[2] We do not have to choose between the two groups - sayings and actions; both are significant for our investigation. In pursuing this investigation it will be important to take note of the use of specific terms for judgement, but it is equally important to recognise that the concept of judgement may be conveyed without the use of cognates of the verb 'to judge'. We must be careful, at this point, not to assume that the importance or otherwise of the theme of judgement is reflected in the quantity of pericopae devoted to the subject. Matthew might well have invested great significance in only a few words.

2. What kind of judgement did Jesus speak of, according to Matthew? The possible answers to this question are legion, and so care must be taken to avoid making unwarranted assumptions. Was Jesus speaking of divine judgement or the natural judgement of fate? Were his words of warning directed towards individuals, or the nation, or both?

3. What role did Jesus envisage for himself in judgement? As we discuss the ministry of Jesus as a preacher of judgement, we must ask questions about the perspective of the preacher. What led Jesus to preach judgement? What

---

[1] This is the task of the next chapter.

[2] It is a distinctive characteristic of the most recent work on the historical Jesus that scholars have moved beyond the preoccupation with the sayings of Jesus found among the 'new questers' of the 1950s and 1960s, to a fuller appreciation of the significance of his actions as well. This attitude is exemplified by Sanders in the words cited at the beginning of this book.

lay behind the unusual authority of his preaching? Did Matthew intend to convey anything in particular about Jesus in his development of this theme?

4.   Did Jesus expect an imminent final judgement? Is the idea of a final Day of Judgement important for Matthew's portrait of Jesus? Was he looking to a far-off Day of Judgement, or was his sight set close at hand? Were Jesus' expectations influenced (significantly, or less so) by the literature belonging to the apocalyptic stream of Judaism?

5.   How did Jesus' proclamation of judgement relate to the totality of his message? Is there coherence to his ministry, or do tensions remain?

In examining these questions, I will adopt Marcus Borg as my primary conversation partner, because of his significance as a contemporary NT scholar and more particularly because of his significance in stimulating the topic of this thesis through his provocative work. I hope to utilise the best of Borg's insights, along with those of others, to account for the evidence, not only of the individual pericopae that are sifted through the scholars' net, but also of the complete narrative of one of the early witnesses to the life of Jesus. However, I will not use Borg's work uncritically, and so the thesis should provide, not only a coherent account of a portion of Matthew's work, but also a critical review of a representative sample of Borg's writings.

Methodology: Introductory Remarks

These questions will be investigated in the course of this study, but first we must establish a methodology on which basis we can proceed. This is a delicate task as we are attempting to discuss the literary work of the first Evangelist *and* the teaching of the 'historical Jesus' in the course of a single study. These two areas of research have tended to employ quite different, and one might even say incompatible, methodologies. Can they be brought into meaningful conversation?

G. Maier has recently discussed the question of method at length in his book *Biblical Hermeneutics*,[3] and, in line with others before him, has demonstrated that 'there is no presuppositionless exegesis or biblical research.'[4] J. P. Meier,

---

[3] G. Maier, *Biblical Hermeneutics* (Wheaton: Crossway, 1994).

[4] Maier, *Biblical Hermeneutics*, 42-43. Cf R. Bultmann, 'Is Exegesis Without Presuppositions Possible?' in S. Ogden (trans. and ed.) *New Testament and Mythology* (London: SCM Press, 1985), 145-53. Bultmann declares, 'no exegesis is without presuppositions, because the exegete is not a *tabula rasa* but approaches the text with specific questions.' See also E. V. McKnight, 'Presuppositions in New Testament Study' in J. B. Green (ed.), *Hearing the New Testament* (Grand Rapids: Eerdmans/ Carlisle: Paternoster, 1995), 278-300, who discusses the presuppositions held by various interpreters, and K. J. Vanhoozer, 'The Reader in New Testament

acknowledging that objectivity is never entirely possible, and recognising the need for various checks on one's position, has written,

> In a sense, though, the most important hedge against rampant subjectivism is an honest admission of one's own personal stance, one's own point of view and background.[5]

It is right, therefore that I acknowledge my conviction that the biblical texts are not 'merely' historical documents, artefacts of human civilisation, but are the revelation of God.[6] The corollary of that conviction is that I expect them to be reliable in all that they relate and not to mislead. Thus I do not come to the biblical texts with methodological doubt or a 'hermeneutic of suspicion' but with a predisposition to accept their testimony. While it is probably safe to say that this position is not dominant in New Testament studies, there is a substantial body of scholars who take a similar position.[7]

It is also important, however, to state that such a position does not require that perplexing phenomena be overlooked. I seek to be both a consistent believer and a competent historian and interpreter. As Mark Allan Powell points out, some scholars will regard any 'believing' predisposition towards the text as an intrusion into the historian's domain which immediately invalidates the resulting research, and yet others disagree and are prepared to recognise that the historian cannot dissociate himself from the subject matter under scrutiny.[8] Respect for the biblical texts and thorough scrutiny of these same texts are not incompatible. Openness to the authoritative voice of the biblical text is, in my opinion, essential, but it may be, indeed must be, combined with methodological rigour.[9]

Interpretation' in Green (ed.), *Hearing the New Testament*, 301-28, who considers the philosophy of reading.

[5] Meier, *Marginal Jew*, 1:5.

[6] See Maier, *Biblical Hermeneutics*, *passim*, for discussion of those interpreters who have made precisely the opposite position one of their presuppositions.

[7] Scholars who have declared their confidence in the biblical texts as revelation, while remaining committed to the task of scholarship include R. H. Stein, *Jesus the Messiah* (Leicester: IVP, 1996), 17-24; Powell, *The Jesus Debate*, 10-15.

[8] Powell, *The Jesus Debate*, 11-13, 190-93.

[9] See the essay by A. Schlatter, 'Die Bedeutung der Method für die theologische Arbeit,' *Theologischer Literaturbericht* 31 (1908), 5-8. An English translation is found in R. W. Yarbrough 'Adolf Schlatter's "The Significance of Method for Theological Work": Translation and Commentary,' *SBJT* 1.2 (1997), 64-76, in which Schlatter writes (67), 'the historian in his historical work can never deny himself in such a way, can never annihilate his convictions – and also should not – in such a way that they do not determine his historical observations and judgements. Attempts to make of oneself a lifeless mirror, which only picks up and passes on life that is foreign to itself, are fruitless and both logically and ethically wrong.'

Methodology: Matthew's Gospel

With regard to our study of the gospel of Matthew, we will be concerned primarily with the final form of the canonical text, and will employ what has been termed *'Composition Criticism'*.[10] The particular nuance of this term is brought out well by B. Charette in his recent monograph, *The Theme of Recompense in Matthew's Gospel*.[11] He writes,

> In composition criticism the attention of the exegete is concentrated on the final or extant form of the text. Thus the method is well suited to the task of analysing one aspect of the Evangelist's thought in terms of the Gospel as a whole. Inasmuch as composition criticism undertakes to elucidate the theology of the Evangelist, it shares much in common with redaction criticism, to which it is closely related. In fact, the method may aptly be described as a holistic variation of redaction criticism. Yet the two methods are distinct from each other as regards their respective points of departure when attempting to uncover the theological perspective of the Evangelist. Whereas redaction criticism seeks to discover the distinctive emphasis of the evangelist by means of a thorough examination of his redactional activity, composition criticism begins with the finished work of the Evangelist, the final point of this editorial activity, and treats this as an intelligible whole.[12]

This method does not ignore the possibility (indeed the probability) that Matthew has made use of sources, and that he has made changes to these sources which are significant for understanding his purposes.[13] It simply takes a

---

[10] The origins of this term are unclear, although it is now used by commentators (such as R. H. Stein, in his commentary on Luke [NAC; Nashville: Broadman, 1992] 57) without substantial explanation. In their introduction to *Treasures New and Old* (Atlanta: Scholars Press, 1996), D. R. Bauer and M. A. Powell trace the roots of 'composition criticism' to the 1970s, but only provide examples of 'composition-critical' studies, including J. D. Kingsbury, *Structure, Christology, Kingdom* (Minneapolis: Fortress, 1989 [1975]). M. Parsons of Baylor University has suggested (on his Luke-Acts discussion web site) that the fundamental methodology, if not the precise terminology, may be traced to Charles H. Talbert. S. D. Moore, *Literary Criticism and the Gospels* (New Haven: Yale, 1989), 4, claims that the terminology originates with E. Haenchen (see *Der Weg Jesu: Eine Erklärung des Markus-Evangeliums und der kanonischen Parallelen* [2ed, Berlin: Walter de Gruyter, 1968], 24). There is no discussion of a methodology by this name in a recent 'state-of-the-art' volume [Green (ed.), *Hearing the New Testament*], but this does not invalidate the essential validity of the method.

[11] See the discussion of Charette's book in chapter 2.

[12] Charette, *The Theme of Recompense*, 16-17.

[13] Bauer and Powell, *Treasures New and Old*, 3, explain that 'Composition critics emphasised the total editorial achievement of the evangelist; they focused on the overall "product" of the evangelist's editorial work, rather than the minute "process" according to which the evangelist brought about changes, omissions, and additions to his *Vorlage*.'

more cautious approach to the situation, recognising two important facts:

(i) It acknowledges one of the most valuable insights of redaction criticism, *viz.* the Evangelists were not simply cut-and-paste compilers of traditional material, but were creative (in a qualified sense) authors of a literary unit. It does the Evangelist and his document more justice to treat it as a whole, noting with appreciation elements such as literary devices and structure.

(ii) Composition Criticism marks an advance over the older forms of redaction criticism in that it does not depend substantially on a comparison of the gospel with its sources (known or hypothetical) for its results.[14] This is a highly significant advance because:

(a) The scholarly consensus that once held to the simplest form of the two-source hypothesis of synoptic relationships has now largely broken down.[15] This is not to say that the majority of scholars have abandoned the priority of Mark or some variation of the two- (or four-) source hypothesis of literary interdependence. Such a view would be patently inaccurate. However, there is generally less dogmatism found in recent scholarly discussions of gospel relationships.[16] This state of affairs can be seen in the continued strenuous support of W. Farmer for a modified form of the Griesbach Hypothesis on relationships between the synoptic gospels,[17] and from a different and somewhat more isolated position, the work of J. M. Rist, who argues for the independence of Matthew and Mark.[18] However, it is particularly due to the

---

[14] No doubt, some redaction critics will feel that this is somewhat of a caricature of redaction criticism in that they are concerned about the way in which the individual Gospel is constructed. However, it seems fair to say that the distinguishing mark of redaction criticism, particularly in its classical expressions, is the focus on editorial changes of source documents.

[15] D. A. Carson, 'Redaction Criticism: On the Legitimacy and Illegitimacy of a Literary Tool' in D. A. Carson and J. D. Woodbridge (eds), *Scripture and Truth* (Leicester: IVP, 1983), 124.

[16] See the helpful discussion in R. E. Brown, *An Introduction to the New Testament*, 111-16. Cf. M. Bockmuehl, *This Jesus* (Edinburgh: T&T Clark, 1994), 18-19: 'Today, many of the pertinent questions are in a greater state of flux than at any other time this century, with several major models vying for acceptance...As long as this two-source hypothesis is not seen as the 'solution' to the so-called synoptic 'problem' (the question of the relative priority of the first three Gospels), it can offer one way of recognizing some of the key interrelations between these accounts.'

[17] W. R. Farmer, *The Synoptic Problem* (Macon: Mercer University Press, 1964), *Jesus and the Gospel: Tradition, Scripture and Canon* (Philadelphia: Fortress, 1982), *The Gospel of Jesus: The Pastoral Relevance of the Synoptic Problem* (Louisville: Westminster/John Knox Press, 1994).

[18] J. M. Rist, *On the Independence of Matthew and Mark* (SNTSMS 32; Cambridge: Cambridge University Press, 1978). See also the rather trenchant views of E. Linnemann, *Is There a Synoptic Problem? Rethinking the Literary Dependence of the First Three Gospels* (Baker, 1992).

impact of ongoing research into the oral transmission of the gospel tradition. It now cannot be assumed without question that similar accounts in both Matthew and Mark indicate a literary dependence from Mark to Matthew, nor that Matthew's account is later than Mark's.[19] Research has opened up the very real possibility that Matthew may have had access to several sources (oral tradition or written notes,[20] to say nothing of the very real possibility of eyewitness[21] memory) which could have preserved slightly different forms of the same sayings or events.[22]

(b) It recognises that Matthew's distinctive theology is found in his *complete literary work*, not solely in the alterations that he has made to his sources.[23] Thus it avoids the rather naive attempt to find theological significance in *every* change of vocabulary or word order between the gospel and its supposed source document. This is not to say that significant changes are not noted; simply that they are only a part of the whole story.[24]

The decision to work primarily with the final canonical form of the text of Matthew should, as we have already indicated, in no way blind us to the way in which the various evangelists, and for our purposes Matthew in particular, have responsibly moulded the traditional material in order to present their particular

---

[19] D. A. Carson, D. J. Moo and L. Morris, *An Introduction to the New Testament* (Leicester: Apollos, 1992), 42-43.

[20] See pp. 55-57 on the 'Scandinavian School'.

[21] Even as conservative a mainstream scholar as R. E. Brown too easily gives up the possibility of eyewitness authors, *An Introduction to the New Testament*, 109. He appears to assume that eyewitnesses would produce virtually identical accounts, despite what we know of the significance of personal perception for the shape of testimony. Also, he appears to be quite comfortable with the statement of Luke (1:2) that he relies on eyewitness testimony, although it is hard to see the difference between the author of a gospel providing a firsthand eyewitness account (as might be claimed for Matthew's gospel, for example) and providing second-hand eyewitness testimony (as is suggested by Lk. 1:2, and the tradition which traces Mark's account to the recollections of Peter) unless he is prepared to say that Luke (or Mark) felt free to substantially alter such eyewitness accounts. Is firsthand testimony more or less 'objective' than second-hand testimony? My argument is not that the Gospels are demonstrably eye-witness testimony; merely that this possibility cannot be ruled out, and that the early testimony of, for example, Papias should not be too easily dismissed. See now S. Byrskog, *Story as History – History as Story* (WUNT 123; Tübingen: Mohr Siebeck, 2000).

[22] Carson, 'Redaction Criticism' in Carson and Woodbridge (eds), *Scripture and Truth*, 124.

[23] Charette, *The Theme of Recompense*, 17. It is good to see Brown, *Introduction*, 171, encourage this view as he writes, 'we cannot afford to lose sight of Matt's highly effective narrative because of attention to comparative details.'

[24] Carson, 'Redaction Criticism', 125-26.

perspective. The work of Bornkamm, Barth and Held[25] in applying the methodology of Redaction Criticism to Matthew's gospel was received with enthusiasm by many in the scholarly community, and the value of much of their work for appreciating the particular perspective of the first Evangelist cannot be denied. However, in its most extreme form, redaction criticism assumes that Mark is the gospel which best preserves the authentic Jesus tradition and the other Evangelists modify his account to serve their theological interests. The fact that this approach has significant problems inherent in it has been helpfully discussed by D. A. Carson,[26] and recognised by many other scholars, so we will not develop the discussion here. Suffice it to say that while Composition Criticism is a methodology that is distinguishable from redaction criticism, it does not preclude a responsible and cautious use of redaction criticism where literary dependence can be demonstrated with a high degree of probability.

Related to the issue of redaction criticism is the matter of the primary interpretive background of the author in writing his gospel. Does Matthew intend his work to be read in the light of his own late first-century setting, or does he intend it to be read as an account of what happened several decades earlier? Much has been written concerning the way in which Matthew has taken the traditional material of his sources and modified it, sometimes dramatically, in order to make it relevant to his community. The particular *Sitz im Leben* which, it is frequently claimed, is in view is a Jewish church living post-AD 70, only recently and painfully separated from the Jewish synagogue.[27] Thus portions of Matthew's text may either be dismissed as unhistorical (being the creation of Matthew) or interpreted without reference to the pre-AD 30 situation of the characters involved in his narrative (since the text is 'really' speaking to the Matthean community).[28] Whether one prefers a pre-AD 70 or post-AD 70 date for the final composition of Matthew is of little consequence for this particular question, as either temporal setting is completely different from that presented in the pages of Matthew's gospel.

It is beyond dispute that Matthew was concerned that his gospel would be of value to the Christians of his own day, and he was no more interested in 'brute facts' than was any other author of a New Testament document. However, we are led to ask what Matthew's *primary* intention was in writing his gospel. Though Matthew does not explicitly spell out his intention, we may argue that the fact that his work belongs to the same genre as the work of Luke and ap-

---

[25] *Tradition and Interpretation in Matthew.*

[26] 'Redaction Criticism', 119-42, 376-81.

[27] See, for example, Sim, *Apocalyptic Eschatology*, 182-92.

[28] An example of this latter view is found in Stanton's useful volume, *A Gospel for a New People* (Edinburgh: T&T Clark, 1992), 200, where he contends that 'those who are urged to pray [a reference to Matt 24:20], however, *are* to be identified with the disciples to whom the whole discourse is addressed - the implied readers of the gospel.'

pears to display a measure of interdependence justifies our treating Luke's stated intentions (Luke 1:1-4) as at least reflective of Matthew's general intentions. On this basis, we must argue that Matthew was concerned to describe the dramatic and most significant events of Jesus' life and death in an accurate and orderly way (cf. Luke 1:3), so that his contemporaries would then be able to see the *implications* of these events for themselves (cf. Luke 1:4). Thus when we hear Jesus speak in Matthew, our first concern must be for what his words meant to the listeners as portrayed in the gospel account whether they be the disciples or the crowds or the religious authorities. Only once the meaning of Jesus' words in their original context has been ascertained can the significance of his words for later generations of Christians be determined.

There are obvious similarities between 'Composition Criticism' and 'Narrative Criticism',[29] particularly in respect of the interest in the final form of the text, but the two methods should not be confused.[30] In particular, 'Composition Criticism', at least as understood in the context of this thesis, maintains a concern for the historical referents which lie behind the narrative of the biblical text. Thus, while Matthew's literary skill is appreciated, and clear literary markers are identified and followed, matters of character and plot are not emphasised to the exclusion of historical questions.[31]

Methodology: The Historical Jesus

Having decided on a method for our study of Matthew's gospel, we must now think about the aspect of our study that attempts to relate Matthew's narrative to the 'historical Jesus'. Axiomatic to the whole task of studying the 'Historical Jesus', as it is generally conceived, is the need for sifting inauthentic material in the gospels from what truly goes back to Jesus himself, and so a comment about the method of determining the authenticity of particular pericopae is in order. The issue of authenticity has become a standard feature of all discussions

---

[29] See M. A. Powell, 'Narrative Criticism' in Green (ed.) *Hearing the New Testament*, 239-55; Bauer and Powell, 'Introduction' in *Treasures New and Old*, 6-13.

[30] Moore, *Literary Criticism*, 4, explains that composition criticism is 'a method aligned with *narrative criticism* but in the last analysis clearly distinguishable from it' (Moore's italics). Moore's whole discussion of narrative criticism in pages 3-68 is very valuable.

[31] Moore, *Literary Criticism*, 7: 'Whereas composition criticism extends the tradition of redaction criticism by reason of an overriding interest in the evangelists' theologies, narrative criticism represents a break with that tradition in the sense that the focus is no longer primarily on theology.' A good recent example of Composition Criticism being employed in the interpretation of Matthew's Gospel is found in Garland, *Reading Matthew* in the 'Reading the New Testament' series, edited by C. H. Talbert, who himself has been associated with this approach to the biblical text.

of the synoptic witness to Jesus.[32] Initially developed by Bultmann and the form critics out of a radical scepticism concerning the trustworthiness of the gospels,[33] the criteria for authenticity betray an inherent tendency to assume inauthenticity unless authenticity can be demonstrated.[34] France draws attention to the fact that even where more conservative scholars avoid the excesses of those who favour the notorious criterion of dissimilarity, they still are obliged, at least tacitly, to assume inauthenticity and argue for authenticity unless they challenge the underlying assumptions of more sceptical critics.[35]

This leads us on to discuss the wider framework of our methodology. Our survey began with works which attempt to identify the eschatological views of the so-called 'historical Jesus' by drawing material from each of the synoptic gospels and making critical judgements on whether any given pericope may be authentic or inauthentic.[36] For the purposes of this thesis, however, we will be examining only Matthew's gospel, and in its final form. Some scholars might object that to treat Matthew as if it were a presentation of the historical Jesus is an illegitimate leap to make; that we cannot treat a document which is quite clearly the product of the theological reflection of mid to late first century Christians as if it were a reliable record of the words and actions of an historical figure. In response to this, it may be relevant to make a general observation about the nature of the particular field of research of which Borg's work is one representative part. There is a significant problem inherent in the language of the 'Quest of the Historical Jesus' that is found in Borg's work, as in that of many others. While Ladd's comment that the 'historical Jesus' is 'a hypothesis reconstructed from the gospels by the use of the historical-critical method on the basis of naturalistic presuppositions'[37] does not do justice to the many

---

[32] There is a great deal of literature on the various criteria. A helpful summary can be found in Meier, *A Marginal Jew*, Vol 1, 167-95. See also the essay by R. H. Stein, 'The "Criteria" for Authenticity,' in *Gospel Perspectives* 1 (Sheffield: JSOT, 1980), reprinted in *idem, Gospels and Tradition* (Grand Rapids: Baker, 1991), 153-87. A thorough discussion of existing criteria, plus several suggestions of further criteria is to be found in Porter, *Criteria for Authenticity*.

[33] Porter, *Criteria for Authenticity*, 63-67.

[34] R. H. Stein ('An Early Recension of the Gospel Traditions?', *JETS* 30 (1987), 169) indicates the scepticism that lay behind the methodology by citing Käsemann's remark, 'The work of the Form Critics *was designed to show* that the message of Jesus as given to us by the Synoptists is, for the most part, not authentic but was minted by the faith of the primitive Christian community in its various stages' (Käsemann's italics).

[35] R. T. France, *Jesus and the Old Testament* (London: Tyndale Press, 1971), 18-22. Much the same point is made by Carson, 'Redaction Criticism', 138-39.

[36] A further striking example of this approach is found in the multi-volume work of J. P. Meier, *A Marginal Jew*.

[37] Ladd, *A Theology of the New Testament*, 175-76. Meier, *A Marginal Jew*, 1:31, speaks of the 'fragmentary, hypothetical reconstruction of him by modern means of research'.

scholars who attempt to do careful historical research from a position of faith, it does highlight the potential danger of using critical tools. C. S. Evans[38] has taken issue with this use of the term 'historical'. He contends that not only does it stand in the face of the way such language is used in everyday conversation,[39] but also that it gives a measure of objectivity to *accounts* of a person's life. A more accurate description of the various scholarly proposals for the character of Jesus' life and ministry, Evans suggests, would be 'the historians' Jesus'.[40] Borg writes of the 'popular image' of Jesus found in the Fourth Gospel and in the creeds of the church - that of the divine Son who comes into the world to save sinners - in the following way: 'as an image of the historical Jesus - of what Jesus was like as a figure of history before his death - the popular image is not accurate. Indeed, it is seriously misleading.'[41] As Borg rightly points out, such a critical understanding of the popular image of Jesus is a 'bedrock con-clusion of mainstream New Testament scholarship,'[42] and is the result of an historical-critical method taught right across the denominational spectrum.[43] However, the self-evident fact that this approach to the data of the gospels is widespread does not by itself justify that approach. The development of 'Jesus Research'[44] is to be welcomed as it seeks to understand Jesus in the context of his social and religious environment, i.e. that of first century Palestine. How-ever, the assumption that the historical Jesus is substantially other than the Je-sus presented to us in the gospel narratives raises questions concerning the competence or integrity of the authors of the gospels which are quite unwar-ranted by the evidence.[45] In fact, C. S. Evans attributes the modern distrust of the gospel narratives to a philosophical mindset – 'modernity'.[46] If Evans is

---

[38] C. S. Evans, *The Historical Christ and the Jesus of Faith* (Oxford: Oxford University Press, 1996).

[39] In 'ordinary' (by which Evans appears to mean day-to-day, non-academic) language use 'to say that an account given of some event is historical is not merely to say that it occurs in a narrative given by a modern historian, but that the event really occurred' (Evans, *The Historical Christ*, 8-9).

[40] Evans, *The Historical Christ*, 8-11.

[41] Borg, *New Vision*, 4.

[42] Borg, *New Vision*, 4.

[43] Borg, *New Vision*, 17, n. 5.

[44] The terminology preferred by Charlesworth rather than 'The Quest of the Historical Jesus'. See his *Jesus Within Judaism* 9, 26-27.

[45] See especially the discussions in C. L. Blomberg, *The Historical Reliability of the Gospels* (Leicester: IVP, 1987) and I. H. Marshall, *I Believe in the Historical Jesus* (London: Hodder, 1977). It is notable that many contemporary scholars who still hold reservations about the authenticity/historicity of certain gospel pericopae can nonetheless draw encouragingly positive and constructive conclusions about Jesus. See, for example, Theissen and Merz, *The Historical Jesus*.

[46] Evans, *The Historical Christ*, 13. See the brief discussion of the same issue in Powell, *The Jesus Debate*, 56.

correct then the term 'assumption' in my previous sentence is particularly appropriate. The distrust of the gospel narratives found in some contemporary scholarship is not, then, the inevitable conclusion of a process of historical analysis (if that were the case then the many scholars who through painstaking research come to the conclusion that the gospel narratives are in fact highly reliable would simply not have come to that conclusion!); rather, it is the result of coming to the texts and to the task of historical research with one set of presuppositions rather than another set.[47] The words of M. Hooker are pointed:

> For in the end, the answers which the New Testament scholar gives are not the result of applying objective tests and using precision tools; they are very largely the result of his own presuppositions and prejudices. If he approaches the material with the belief that it is largely the creation of the early Christian communities, then he will interpret it in that way. If he assumes that the words of the Lord were faithfully remembered and passed on, then he will be able to find criteria which support him. Each claims to be using the proper critical method. Each produces a picture of Jesus – and of the early church – in accordance with his presuppositions. And each claims to be right.[48]

Hooker identifies correctly the fundamental assumptions of each interpreter who comes to the biblical text, although what remains unsaid in her statement is that every presupposition may be and must be scrutinised and assessed with respect to its validity in the light of available evidence.

This is not to say that the biblical texts do not, in fact, throw up some puzzling phenomena, which require serious thought and intense scrutiny.[49] However, it is the contention of this thesis that it is an entirely appropriate stance, in the light of what the gospels claim to be, to treat the gospel accounts as reliable witnesses to the historical events of Jesus' life and ministry, and our discussion to this point indicates that such a stance of trust is no more harmful to the task of biblical interpretation than is any other presupposition.

The validity of this approach has been supported by the work of the scholars associated with the 'Scandinavian School', namely H. Riesenfeld and B. Gerhardsson on transmission of traditional material in Judaism, although their work was subjected to some stringent criticism, to the effect that they had made anachronistic use of Rabbinical material to establish their thesis. The recent republication of Gerhardsson's two early works with a foreword by J. Neusner[50] offers an intriguing insight into the thinking of one such critic – Neusner himself.

---

[47] So Evans, *The Historical Christ*, 20.

[48] M. Hooker, 'On Using the Wrong Tool', *Theology* 75 (1972), 581.

[49] Evans, *The Historical Christ*, 22.

[50] B. Gerhardsson, *Memory and Manuscript with Tradition and Transmission in Early Christianity* (Grand Rapids/Livonia: Eerdmans/Dove, 1998).

After a fascinating account of how Neusner initially followed his mentor, Morton Smith, in dismissing Gerhardsson's work, only to later retract his views (and submit Smith to some typically scathing criticism), he writes of Gerhardsson's approach that it,

> simply treats each set of sources [that is, the Rabbinic literature and the Gospels] as a free-standing portrait of a system that sets upon its own foundations an example, a possibility, an occasion for comparison and contrast. What can be wrong with that?[51]

More recently, work done by other scholars, particularly R. Riesner[52] and K. E. Bailey,[53] has refined the position of the Scandinavians, relying less on the contested Rabbinic material, but all of these scholars indicate that the transmission of traditional material in settings similar to that of the gospel narratives was subject to controls (whether these were formal, in the sense of memorisation[54] and/or written notes,[55] or informal[56]) such that widespread deviation from the true account was not permitted by the community within which the tradition was held.[57]

W. D. Davies, a strong critic of Gerhardsson in several ways, still offers this positive assessment:

> This means, in our judgment, that they [Gerhardsson and Riesenfeld] have made it far more historically probable and reasonably credible, over against the scepticism of much form criticism, that in the Gospels we are within hearing of the authentic voice and within sight of the authentic activity of Jesus of Nazareth, however much muffled and obscured these may be by the process of transmission.[58]

It is a pity that Davies felt the need to add the final qualification to his assess-

---

[51] In the preface to the reprint of Gerhardsson's books, *Memory and Manuscript with Tradition and Transmission in Early Christianity*, xlvi.

[52] R. Riesner, *Jesus als Lehrer* (Tübingen: J. C. B. Mohr, 1981).

[53] K. E. Bailey, 'Informal Controlled Oral Tradition and the Synoptic Gospels' *Themelios* 20.2 (1995), 4-11.

[54] See Gerhardsson, *Memory*, 122-56, 163-70.

[55] On the use of written notes among the Rabbis, see H. Schürmann, 'Die vorösterliche Anfage der Logientradition,' in H. Ristow and K. Matthiae (eds), *Der historische Jesus und der kerygmatische Christus* (Berlin: Evangelishe Verlaganstalt, 1960), 342-70. See also Gerhardsson, *Memory*, 157-63, 195, 201-2.

[56] See Bailey, 'Informal Controlled Oral Tradition', 4-11, for a valuable discussion of formal and informal control of transmission.

[57] For a recent book that draws on Gerhardsson and Riesner with particular reference to Matthew's Gospel, see Byrskog, *Jesus the Only Teacher* (Stockholm: Almqvist & Wiksell, 1994).

[58] W. D. Davies, *The Setting of the Sermon on the Mount* (Cambridge: Cambridge University Press, 1966), 480.

ment, because the work of the Scandinavians has helped us towards precisely the opposite assessment of the transmission process. It is because the teaching of Jesus was presented in memorable form; because the disciples may well have been encouraged to memorise his teaching *verbatim*, and perhaps even take written notes;[59] because Jesus was apparently regarded as the Messiah who was expected to be a teacher of great, indeed unique authority, that we can be confident that the gospel narratives are *not* the result of a process which muffled and obscured the words and actions of Jesus.

In his book, *Jesus of Nazareth*, D. C. Allison makes positive use of some of Gerhardsson's findings, but urges caution in the claims made for pre-Easter tradition:

> It should be stressed that to find pre-Easter tradition is not necessarily to find Jesus. Not only must the miracle stories have been subject to exaggeration and distortion from the first, but we have no reason to believe that the disciples did not make their own contributions and alterations. Gerhardsson's idea of a "holy word" being memorised is implausible. Recall that already in the lifetime of St. Francis his rule was being changed and even moved in directions he did not like, and that some of the Sioux disciples of Wovoka wrongly added a militant note to his message.[60]

While we take Allison's cautionary point in his first sentence, it is disappointing to find him making sweeping statements in what follows. Why 'must' the miracle stories have been exaggerated and distorted?[61] And why should we assume that the disciples would feel at liberty to modify the facts of what they saw, unless we have evidence to the contrary. It is true that it is common for religious tales to accumulate dramatic details over time and through repeated telling. However, this tendency does not constitute demonstration of such changes in the case of the Jesus tradition. It seems that Allison's comparative examples lead him to his erroneous conclusions. I have no knowledge of Wovoka's claims, but St. Francis certainly never made the claims to authoritative pronouncement and activity that Jesus reportedly made. The awe and perplexity of the disciples (as, admittedly, portrayed in the gospel narratives) does not lead me to conclude that they considered themselves to have a mandate to be substantially creative with the things they heard and saw.

Recently, K. E. Bailey has proposed the model of 'informal controlled' transmission of tradition, which, he suggests, accounts for the variations in the

---

[59] Stein points out that this is a possibility that Gerhardsson failed to develop, despite the fact that he himself had raised the likelihood of written notes. Stein notes the value of R. Riesner's work in this regard.

[60] Allison, *Jesus of Nazareth*, 72, n. 273.

[61] For a recent study that takes seriously both historical and theological aspects of the miracle accounts, see G. Twelftree, *Jesus the Miracle Worker* (Downers Grove: IVP, 1999).

narratives of the canonical evangelists and also maintains the integrity of their narratives.[62] N. T. Wright assesses Bailey's proposal as having 'the smell of serious social history about it.'[63] Wright continues,

> It allows for different shaping of material within a framework. It enables us to explain, without as yet having recourse to complex theories either of synoptic relationships or of a freely expanding tradition, the way in which again and again the story comes out slightly differently, but the sayings remain more or less identical. It shows that the narrative form is unlikely to be a secondary accretion around an original aphorism: stories are fundamental... It enables us, in other words, to understand the material before us, without invoking extra epicycles of unwarranted assumptions. These are great strengths. Until it is shown that the process Bailey envisages is historically impossible, I propose that it be taken as a working model.[64]

The difficulty with Wright's adoption of Bailey's position is that he proceeds on the basis of an assumption. (A point he surely recognises as he speaks of '*extra* epicycles of *unwarranted* assumptions.') It is virtually impossible to demonstrate conclusively that the numerous portions of oral tradition concerning Jesus' words and actions were transmitted from their first witnesses to the canonical written texts in one way rather than another. All that can be done is to provide analogy.[65] Thus Bailey's proposal will always be subject to challenge on the basis that the analogy does not work. However, the difficulty with this latter position is that it also must work on certain assumptions which can no more be demonstrated conclusively than can Bailey's. Also, the counter-claim may be made that Bailey's analogy works better than is claimed – this is essentially Wright's position. Thus the matter is methodologically in stalemate, yet it is impossible to move forward to evaluation of the narrative of Matthew without making some (at least implicit) judgement on the issue.

That being the case, we contend that it is legitimate to claim that Bailey's proposal does justice both to the character of the synoptic traditions as we have them in the three canonical synoptic gospels (ie as narratives, filled with memorable sayings and images) and to the integrity of the evangelists and that it therefore provides an appropriate provisional model for understanding the gospel narratives as carefully crafted written narratives founded on material transmitted orally. This reconstruction of the transmission of early Christian tradition will be cautiously assumed.

Thus, along with R. T. France,[66] I will assume the essential reliability of the record that Matthew (along with the other Evangelists) has left us, unless there

---

[62] See the bibliographical details of the article provided above.

[63] *Jesus and the Victory of God*, 135.

[64] *Jesus and the Victory of God*, 135-36.

[65] As has also been done by both Gerhardsson and Riesner, though in somewhat different ways.

[66] *Jesus and the Old Testament*, 22.

is significant *prima facie* evidence to the contrary. Ladd helpfully sums up this position as he describes his own method:

> while we must frequently note points where interpretation has obviously affected the form of the text, the author conceives it to be his primary task to interpret the Gospels as they stand as credible reports of Jesus and his preaching of the Kingdom.[67]

Thus, while the various criteria of authenticity will occasionally be discussed, they will be regarded as means of *confirmation* of (or raising caution over) the authenticity of the text rather than as trials to establish the authenticity of suspicious texts. Texts that conform to the various criteria may be regarded as having a particularly strong claim to be heard; texts that do not conform, however, are not for that reason to be rejected as valid witnesses to Jesus' life and teaching. It is a false logic which argues that because a saying cannot be proved to be authentic, it must be rejected as inauthentic, especially when these sayings are found in documents which consistently portray a deep concern for what is true and which purport to be accounts of historical events. This is particularly the case when, by the standards of the majority of contemporary critics, the gospels contain a significant amount of material which *is* 'demonstrably' authentic. Material which falls beyond the confirmation of the various criteria should, therefore, be given the benefit of the doubt, with the burden of proof falling on those who would seek to reject it, unless there are significant grounds for re-examining the issues.[68] Standing against the flow of much scholarship originating from his own nation, M. Reiser writes,

> I start from the assumption that it is not the assertion of authenticity, but its denial that requires proof, and that a saying or parable, in the oldest form that can be reconstructed, may be regarded as authentic, at least in its content, if that content fits within the rest of Jesus' preaching and nothing speaks against its authenticity. In my opinion, no other attitude is possible for a historian. Every historian must presume that his or her sources report reliably, within the limits of their possibilities, and to the extent that their unreliability either in detail or as a whole has not been proven. It is not the genuineness of a document that must be proven, but its falsity.[69]

While his determination to find the 'oldest form that can be reconstructed' raises the fundamental question of how one determines such a form, Reiser's

---

[67] Ladd, *The Presence of the Future*, xiv.

[68] Stein, 'The "Criteria" for Authenticity' in *Gospels and Tradition*, 154-56.

[69] Reiser, 204. Reiser cites in support of his position N. J. McEleney, 'Authenticating Criteria and Mark 7:1-23' *CBQ* 34 (1972), 431-60, among others. Compare also Jeremias' statement, *New Testament Theology*, 37: 'In the synoptic tradition it is the inauthenticity, and not the authenticity, of the sayings of Jesus that must be demonstrated.'

approach provides a positive model of constructive analysis of ancient texts which is adopted in this thesis.

It is important to note briefly why this matter is so important. If the gospels (Matthew, in this case, but also Mark, Luke, and for that matter John) are never read as coherent documents which seek to present a figure of history to us, then we will never truly hear the voice of the authors who claim to present this figure to their readers. It is, of course, important to read with discernment, but if the gospels are used simply as quarries for isolated nuggets of information, then they are not being treated on their own terms, which raises questions about whether one can ever claim to have understood a document unless it has been read in some sympathy with the author's implied intentions.

Methodology: Matthew and Jesus

Although composition criticism treats the canonical text as a narrative with its own dynamic, this perspective does not rule out an appreciation of the gospels as historical documents. F. Watson has helpfully discussed this matter in a recent essay.[70] Watson begins by asserting that,

> The four gospels are historical documents, in the sense that they preserve traces of past events, acts and utterances circumscribed by a particular set of spatio-temporal coordinates. They are also narratives: they tell a story with a beginning, a middle and an end related to one another in linear, teleological fashion. The gospels may therefore be studied as historical documents from which may be obtained various types of information about the origins of Christianity; or one may focus on the formal means by which the gospel narratives are constructed.[71]

Watson's words provide us with a good starting point for working out an approach to using Matthew's gospel as a narrative to be heard on its own terms, and also as a source of information about the 'historical Jesus'. However, Watson is well aware that the standard methodological approaches employed by interpreters of the NT do not encourage the reader to regard the gospels as both literary and historical documents at the same time. Watson's comment on the typical assumptions regarding methodological distinctness reflect closely our own concerns when he writes,

> It is assumed that history and narrative must go their separate ways: for those with historical interests, various historical-critical strategies are available, while for those with a more literary orientation, ahistorical literary-critical analysis is a fruitful possibility.[72]

---

[70] 'The Gospels as Narrated History' in *Text and Truth: Redefining Biblical Theology* (Edinburgh: T&T Clark, 1997), 33-69.

[71] 'The Gospels as Narrated History', 33.

[72] 'The Gospels as Narrated History', 34.

One then has a choice to make:

> between a historical Jesus qualitatively different from the gospel narratives, and the fictional Jesus of the narratives themselves.[73]

Such methodological dichotomy as has been described leads to an impoverishing of the testimony of the gospel narratives:

> In the customary opposition between the Jesus of history and the Christ of faith, 'history' is taken to be synonymous with reality, whereas 'faith' is identified either with illusion or, at best, with an ungrounded non-rational conviction. There is therefore a qualitative difference between the stratum within which historical Jesus research operates and that in which redaction criticism identifies the faith and the theology of the evangelists. There is the real Jesus, and there are the Jesuses of Matthew, Mark, Luke and John. The real Jesus is indeed to be found only within the gospel narratives, and yet he must be painstakingly reassembled from authentic fragments partially concealed in a mass of 'late' and therefore historically worthless material.[74]

Watson notes that underlying this approach to the gospels is a reaction to 'difference', where difference between two accounts is read as a signpost to error. He rejects this 'interpretative paradigm' and calls for 'an alternative understanding of historical research which takes seriously both the gospels' historiographical claims and the critical problem of difference.' Watson, however, seeks to relate the two sets of concerns by treating the gospels as 'narrated history'.[75]

Watson's proposal is helpful in approaching a gospel to hear its own distinctive voice through attention to literary features, yet maintaining an interest in what historical referents it purports to describe.

I do not wish to advance a position which claims that the gospel accounts (and Matthew's in particular) are merely photographic records of uninterpreted history, adopting, as it were, Von Ranke's phrase *'wie es eigentlich gewesen ist.'*[76] A more helpful analogy than the photograph is the painted portrait, and

---

[73] 'The Gospels as Narrated History', 37. Watson, in fact, draws attention to the similarities between his plea and that of M. Kähler in his famous essay 'Der sogennante historische Jesus und der geschichtliche biblische Christus' ('The Gospels as Narrated History', 64, n. 5). See also Byrskog, *Story as History – History as Story*, 1: 'To read narrative texts both as "mirrors" reflecting self-contained worlds and as "windows" opening up to extrafictional and diachronic levels of history is often considered to be a violation of proper hermeneutical conduct.'

[74] 'The Gospels as Narrated History', 38.

[75] 'The Gospels as Narrated History', 41.

[76] L. von Ranke, *Geschichten der romanischen und germanischen Volker von 1494 bis 1514* in *Sammtliche Werke* (Leipzig, 1874) Vol 33, *vii*. The citation is conveniently found in Marshall, *I Believe in the Historical Jesus*, 52, n. 12.

this has been adopted by several recent scholars[77] as a means of illustrating the diversity of the gospel accounts while, at the same time, reinforcing the fact that they each have a concern to communicate the same subject matter in a way which maintains a close relationship between their work and the reality which they portray.

This understanding of the nature of the gospels is not intended to hide the real questions that remain about the relationship between the four gospels. Rather, it is intended to protect the integrity of the Gospel writers, and Matthew in particular, in their attempt to produce an honest and historically credible account of Jesus' ministry, while still allowing for the individuality of expression and selection of material which is so obviously characteristic of each of the gospels. Clearly, each pericope in Matthew, along with the other gospels, has been challenged as to authenticity, and likewise others have provided cogent responses.[78] The value of adopting the model of the portrait is that it gives us a starting point which does not demand an extended justification of every portion of Matthew's gospel, which is instead assumed to reflect accurately the events which really happened, until clear and compelling evidence is produced to lead us to question this assumption.[79] (And, in passing, we do wish to assert that there is an objective reality - 'what really happened' - to which every 'portrait' adheres more or less closely. The problem, of course, is that all modern scholars are in the same position of having no *immediate* access to that reality whereby to test the validity of the portrait of Matthew or anyone else. In fact, Matthew may well have been one of the few people to construct a portrait of Jesus based on just that immediate access which we lack.)

At the beginning of a study that relates to both the gospel of Matthew and the 'historical Jesus', I simply wish to claim that it is not illegitimate to move from a discussion of 'historical Jesus' studies to a discussion of Matthew's gospel, and *vice versa*, since the various volumes which claim to offer us 'the historical Jesus' are, in fact, only able to offer *portraits* of Jesus ('images' of Jesus, to use Borg's preferred term), constructed by a particular individual. These portraits of Jesus painted by the various 'Questers' are *at least* as influenced by theological and methodological bias as is the portrait of Jesus offered

---

[77] Cf. R. A. Guelich, *The Sermon on the Mount* (Waco: Word, 1982) and R. A. Burridge, *Four Gospels - One Jesus?* (London: SPCK, 1994). Most recently, this model is employed by Brown, *An Introduction to the New Testament*, 105-7.

[78] See, for example, Blomberg, *The Historical Reliability of the Gospels*, on the gospels in general, and D. A. Carson, 'Matthew' in the *Expositor's Bible Commentary* Vol 8 (Grand Rapids: Zondervan, 1984), for detailed exegesis of Matthew in particular.

[79] This may be regarded by some as 'uncritical', but see the strong words of the ancient historian H. Botermann who claims that 'If ancient historians used their sources as "critically" as most theologians, they would have to close the files on Herodotus and Tacitus.' Cited in M. Hengel and A. M. Schwemer, *Paul Between Damascus and Antioch* (London: SCM Press, 1997), 322, n. 5.

to us by Matthew.[80]

There are, in fact, several reasons why a fair approach to the gospels should lead to a high regard for their trustworthiness as historical sources; or, to put it another way, why they should be seen as quality portraits of Jesus.

1) Literary. The gospels purport to be historical accounts of Jesus' ministry. They are peppered with temporal and geographical references, which give the overwhelming impression of recounting events that actually happened in time and space. To return to the painting analogy, no-one who has gazed at an abstract painting by Picasso expects to find someone with a face that looks just like the painting; the genre of the painting allows us to modify our expectations of finding a recognisable referent. However, we might well expect to look at one of Constable's landscapes and then be able to visit the location depicted, while recognising fully that Constable has invested the painting with his own personality. The gospels should be allowed literary integrity, unless it is clear that they have misled us.

2) Temporal. The authors of the gospels, whatever the precise date we assign to their works, are closest in time to the subject of their work. There is a strong case for the position that Matthew was one of the disciples of Jesus, and that his work contains eyewitness accounts,[81] although the point is not substantially affected if the author was not an eyewitness.[82] In any case, we have no extant sources earlier than Mat-

---

[80] It is interesting to read E. P. Sanders' candid explanation of his religious affiliation in the preface to *Jesus and Judaism*, where he describes himself as a liberal Protestant, presumably so that his readers will be able to make sense of his presentation of Jesus. R. E. Brown also appears to recognise that 'the Historical Jesus' can 'never be purely objective'. Meier, *A Marginal Jew*, 1:4, writes, 'Even the most careful contemporary scholars have left their own lineaments on the portraits of Jesus they painted. How could it be otherwise.' Crossan, *The Historical Jesus*, xxvii, writes of the 'positive indignity' of historical Jesus research, which is: 'the number of competent and even eminent scholars producing pictures of Jesus at wide variance with one another'. He goes on to mention examples of such works and concludes: 'that stunning diversity is an academic embarrassment' (*ibid*. xxviii). Allison, *Jesus of Nazareth*, 35-36, writes, 'As historians of the Jesus tradition we are storytellers. We can do no more than aspire to fashion a narrative that is more persuasive than competing narratives, one that satisfies our aesthetic and historical sensibilities because of its apparent ability to clarify more data in a more satisfactory fashion than its rivals.'

[81] For strong arguments, see the commentaries by D. A. Carson, R. T. France and R. H. Gundry. Gundry's volume contains a particularly useful discussion (*Matthew: A Commentary on His Handbook for a Mixed Church Under Persecution* [Second Edition, Grand Rapids: Eerdmans, 1994] 609-22).

[82] This latter point is patently obvious when one considers that the traditional ascription of authorship of the Gospel of Luke is to one who makes no claim to be an eyewitness, yet who can still affirm the authenticity of his account on the grounds that he has utilised tradition passed down by those who were eyewitnesses of the events recounted

thew, Mark and Luke for substantial detail about Jesus.[83] The author of
Matthew almost certainly shared the same linguistic and cultural heritage as Jesus.

3) Social. The gospel accounts were first circulated at a time when eyewitnesses, both supportive and hostile, could have challenged the accounts.
The fact that they were well received indicates that no-one was able to
present convincing evidence that they were false records.

4) Historical. Luke claims that his gospel was the product of careful research (Luke 1:1-4). Since Matthew and Mark are closely related to
Luke, and since their work provides ample evidence of careful and skilful arrangement, it is fair to argue that they too were based on such careful work.[84]

5) Comparative. Though differences are certainly observable, the three
synoptic gospels still provide accounts of Jesus' ministry which, on a
sympathetic reading, can be shown to be fundamentally coherent and
compatible.

6) Traditional. We have already made reference to the work of Gerhardsson *et al* who have argued forcefully for a large measure of accuracy in
the process of transmission.

Although there is inevitably some overlap with the discussion in section C
above, what I seek to establish in this section of the argument is not simply that
Matthew preserves historical details accurately, but that his complete presentation has a legitimate claim to be understood as a coherent work of historical
narrative on the grounds that he has presented an account of Jesus' life and
teaching which is no more selective and affected by personal circumstance than
any contemporary contributor to 'Life of Jesus' research.

Chapter Summary and Conclusion

This discussion of methodology may be summed up briefly as follows. In the

---

(Lk. 1:1-4). Typical dating of Matthew's Gospel among mainstream critical scholars
(ca. AD 80-90) still places it within a generation of most of the events that are
narrated. See Brown, *An Introduction to the New Testament*, 172.

[83] The letters of Paul, of course, are all probably earlier compositions than any of the
Gospels. However, even the most positive studies find only a limited number of facts
relating to the earthly Jesus in these letters (e.g. D. Wenham, *Paul: Follower of Jesus
or Founder of Christianity?* [Grand Rapids: Eerdmans, 1995], J. D. G. Dunn, 'Jesus
Tradition in Paul' in Chilton and Evans (eds), *Studying the Historical Jesus*, 154-78,
B. F. Meyer, *Aims of Jesus*, 75), and many scholars find little or nothing.

[84] In Luke's carefully crafted Prologue he emphasises eyewitness testimony, careful
investigation and accurate, orderly presentation. While these words relate specifically
to Luke's own work, they are indicative of the purpose of any work belonging to this
genre. See D. L. Bock *Luke 1:1-9:50* (BECNT; Grand Rapids: Baker, 1994), 51-67.

course of this study I will come to the text with certain presuppositions, as I believe does every interpreter, and I will enumerate them briefly below.

1. Matthew has written what is ostensibly an account of events which actually happened. Thus, while he is concerned to make his account relevant to a particular readership, his primary goal is to set out a faithful account of the life and message of Jesus of Nazareth. We should attempt to understand the words and actions of Jesus, as portrayed by Matthew, in a *Sitz im Leben Jesu* before seeking their relevance for those who first read Matthew's gospel (particularly since any reconstruction of the 'Matthean community' must be hypothetical, based on gleaning information from Matthew's narrative).

2. Matthew has certainly moulded his sources in various ways in order to produce his own distinctive theological work. However, it is not unreasonable to give his integrity the benefit of the doubt and seek to interpret his gospel so that his understanding of a portion of text is not held to be in radical discontinuity with the interpretation held by the author of his source. A harmonious interpretation should be sought and, where it can be found, should be given preference.

3. Matthew demonstrates significant skill and creativity as a literary craftsman in his presentation of material in his gospel. That being the case, we should avoid interpretations which require that Matthew placed incompatible sayings next to each other, or that he has failed to edit his sources thoroughly. We must take the harder route of trying to find an interpretation which resolves the apparent contradiction, and so makes sense of both the particular text and the gospel as a whole.

On the basis of these presuppositions, I will treat the text of Matthew as it stands in its final form. I will assume, unless there is clear evidence to the contrary, that it is a faithful account of historical events and that it makes sense on its own terms. I will treat it as a coherent whole unless incoherence can be clearly demonstrated.

CHAPTER 4

Matthew 21-25: The Limits of the Text and the Context of the Gospel

Introduction

In the following chapters we will examine a portion of Matthew's gospel (chapters 21-25) which, it will be argued, contains a coherent portrayal of Jesus as agent of judgement. In using the term 'agent' we wish to point out that Jesus' judgmental activity is not confined to his words but is also evident, very significantly, in his actions. In this way, we believe that we are able to develop one of the very helpful emphases of the 'Third Quest', *viz.* on the actions of Jesus, which though often neglected in the past in preference to his sayings, tells us a great deal about who Jesus thought himself to be, and what drove him to do what he did.[1] The use of the term 'agent' allows us to explore the way in which Jesus did not simply *speak* of judgement but actually carried out judgement in some way or other.

This means that it is not adequate to attempt to study the theme of judgement in Jesus' ministry simply by locating references to the terminology of judgement. Such terminology is indeed important, but it is not the whole story. As we shall see, the terminology of judgement is surprisingly scarce in chapters 21-25 of Matthew, yet it cannot be said that the theme of judgement is absent.

In looking at this overall theme, we will also see how Jesus' activity as agent of judgement is helpfully highlighted by the use of two of the categories favoured by Marcus Borg – the prophet and the sage. This will demonstrate that Jesus cannot be understood one-dimensionally, but must be viewed from several different perspectives to be accurately understood. However, in accepting the value of Borg's use of these categories, we will also challenge his insistence that Jesus cannot move beyond the constraints of these categories.

Before we come to the key exegetical work on these chapters, however, there are some preliminary matters which must be addressed.

---

[1] See the comments of E. P. Sanders cited at the beginning of this book.

Is Matthew 21-25 a Unit?

Our first task is to justify the decision to regard chapters 21 to 25 as a unit. The issue of the structure of Matthew has been in dispute.[2] Some commentators follow the pattern of B. W. Bacon in noting the repeated formula Καὶ ἐγένετο ὅτε ἐτέλεσεν ὁ Ἰησοῦς (7:28; 11:1; 13:53; 19:1; 26:1). This pattern confirms 25:46 as the conclusion of a unit, but challenges the decision to place the opening of the unit at 21:1. However, several recent commentators have adopted the arguments of Kingsbury[3] for paying particular attention to the phrase ᾿Απὸ τότε ἤρξατο ὁ Ἰησοῦς (4:17; 16:21) as indicative of transition between major units of material.[4] Kingsbury's structure has much to commend it, but because it is so broad it inevitably requires subdivision. Yet it also frees us to consider less obvious ways in which sections of text may demonstrate coherence, and that is what we will attempt to do in this discussion.

In discussions of the eschatological discourse in Matthew it is common for the commentators to treat chapters 24 and 25 as a distinct unit, despite recognition of connections between these chapters and what has gone before. Thus France, for example, writes,

> As judgment was also a key theme of ch. 23, it is sometimes argued that chs. 23-25 form a single discourse on judgment. Certainly there is a continuity of theme, as we shall see on 24:1-2; but the two passages are differently conceived, ch. 23 as public teaching in opposition to the scribes and Pharisees, chs. 24-25 as private teaching to the disciples. The pronounced change of scene and of audience in 24:1-3 indicates that Matthew saw chs. 24-25 as a separate discourse. Jesus' public teaching is now finished; this (like all the five great discourses, with the partial exception of ch. 13) is instruction for disciples only.[5]

We must agree with France to the extent that Matthew has clearly made 24:1

---

[2] See D. R. Bauer, *The Structure of Matthew's Gospel* (Sheffield: Almond, 1988); J. D. Kingsbury, *Matthew: Structure, Christology, Kingdom* (Minneapolis: Fortress, 1975), 1-39.

[3] J. D. Kingsbury, *Matthew: Structure, Christology, Kingdom*, 7-25, drawing consciously on earlier work by N. B. Stonehouse, *The Witness of Matthew and Mark to Christ* (London: Tyndale, 1944), 129-31.

[4] See particularly Garland, *Reading Matthew*, vii-viii, 9, although Garland takes Stanton's cautionary note that Matthew may not have worked with any clearly defined structure; C. L. Blomberg, *Matthew* (NAC; Nashville: Broadman, 1992), 22-25, 49, though Blomberg draws from and develops both Bacon and Kingsbury, as he follows Kingsbury for his main divisions and Bacon for his sub-divisions.

[5] France, *Matthew*, 333. A similar recognition of the connection between chapter 23 and the discourse in chapters 24-25 is found in Marguerat, *Le Jugement*, 479-80. Marguerat argues that the differences in addressees 'permettent de distinguer les deux discours' but also that 'le motif du jugement présente un facteur essentiel de continuité' (480).

a transitional text that distinguishes chapters 24 and 25 as a distinct unit.[6] I wish
to argue, however, that there is great advantage for interpretation in taking
chapters 21 to 25 as a wider, over-arching unit, with chapters 24-25 as a sub-
unit. A few recent authors have already followed this unit division. U. Luz, in
his recent work on Matthew's theology[7] links these chapters under the heading
'The final reckoning with Israel and the judgement of the community.' The link
Luz sees, however, is primarily geographical, as Jesus enters Jerusalem for the
final stage of his ministry, and so he does not go on to develop a common
theme running through the section, even though his chapter title indicates a
fruitful way forward. Instead he follows the typical pattern of treating chapters
24 and 25 as 'the Matthean Eschatology' without reference to the preceding
chapters.[8] Hagner recognises that 'Jesus' arrival in Jerusalem is an important
dividing point in the Gospel' and recognises that Matthew carefully constructs
his narrative in chapters 21-23,[9] yet he does not draw out continuities with the
'eschatological discourse' which he treats independently.

On further examination of these chapters it becomes clear that there are very
significant links which go beyond the simple location of the events described.[10]
In contrast to most scholars, D. B. Howell has recognised the significance of
this unit for Matthew's *narrative*.[11] However, Howell's brief comments do not

---

[6] Having said this, Matthew's use of ἱερόν in 24:1 serves to link the discourse of
chapters 24 and 25 with the events of chapter 21 (see 21:12, 14, 15, 23).

[7] U. Luz, *The Theology of the Gospel of Matthew* (Cambridge: Cambridge University
Press, 1995). In his EKK volume (*Das Evangelium nach Matthäus 18-25* [Zürich:
Benziger/ Neukirchen-Vluyn: Neukirchener, 1997], 172), Luz also recognizes the
possibility of regarding chapters 23-25 as a coherent unit ('Man könnte sie ja auch mit
Kap. 24-25 verbinden und als ersten Teil der letzten der fünf großen Reden Jesu
verstehen.'). E. Schweizer, *The Good News according to Matthew* (London: SPCK,
1975), 401-403, also seems to regard the geographical location as the dominant point
of coherence, though, like Luz, he does see parallels between the fate of the hypocrites
in chapter 23 and the possible fate of the community in chapter 24.

[8] Luz, *Theology*, 125-32. L. L. Morris, *The Gospel according to Matthew* (Leicester,
IVP, 1992), 517, also treats chs 21-25 as a unit, but again this is on the basis of
location rather than theme. The same is true of Aland's *Synopsis Quattuor
Evangeliorum* which begins a major section at 21:1 with the heading, 'Letzte
Wirksamkeit in Jerusalem' or 'The Final Ministry in Jerusalem' (365). F. W. Beare,
The Gospel According to Matthew (San Francisco: Harper and Row, 1981), 411,
identifies 21:1-22:46 as a coherent   unit, yet he does not develop the literary
connections within this section, nor identify possible connections with the following
texts.

[9] Hagner, *Matthew 14-28*, 591.

[10] Davies and Allison, *Matthew*, 3:128, comment that, '21.1-11 is not just the entry into
Jerusalem: it is also the entry into the remainder of the narrative.' It is strange
therefore that they do not appear to recognise the particular links with 21:12-25:46.

[11] D. B. Howell, *Matthew's Inclusive Story* (JSNTS 42; Sheffield: JSOT Press, 1990),
149-54.

clearly establish why these chapters should be regarded as a unit, and fail to draw out the significant verbal and thematic connections that exist. Further, Howell's claim that the theme of these chapters is the *rejection* of Jesus (that is, Jesus is passive and the object of the actions of others) does not, I believe, do justice to the note of deliberate action found throughout these chapters.

Though we argue that recognition of chapters 21-25 on the grounds of geographical location alone is inadequate, that is not to say that the geographical indicators in the text are irrelevant. Ch. 21 begins with the approach to Jerusalem and the events that follow do indeed occur in and around this *theologically* significant city.[12] In the same verse, Matthew brings us to the Mount of Olives, which plays such an important role in understanding biblical eschatology.[13] Can it be pure coincidence that ch. 21 begins here and chapters 24-25 also are set on this mountain (compare 21:1 and 24:3)?[14]

A vital piece of evidence regarding chapters 21-25 as a unit, seldom adequately recognised,[15] is the theme of the coming king in 21:1-11 and 25:31-46. The quotation of Zechariah 9:9 in 21:5 indicates the humble circumstances and attitude of the coming king; this contrasts with the majesty of the coming king in 25:31, and forms an *inclusio* around the unit. Davies and Allison give their discussion of 21:1-11 the title, 'The Prophet-King Enters Jerusalem',[16] thus drawing attention to the use of ὁ βασιλεύς, an important term for Matthew,[17] found in both 21:5 and 25:34. Yet they do not emphasise that connection in their discussion of 25:31-46,[18] favouring the 'Son of Man' motif instead. They further comment that,

> 21:1-11 par. is one of many texts that recount the triumphal arrival (*parousia*) of a ruler or military hero.[19]

---

[12] See particularly P. W. L. Walker, *Jesus and the Holy City: New Testament Perspectives on Jerusalem* (Grand Rapids: Eerdmans, 1996).

[13] See Zechariah 14:4: 'On that day his feet shall stand on the Mount of Olives, which lies before Jerusalem on the east; and the Mount of Olives shall be split in two from east to west by a very wide valley; so that one half of the Mount shall withdraw northward, and the other half southward.'

[14] Kingsbury, *Matthew: Structure, Christology, Kingdom*, 56.

[15] Kingsbury, *Matthew: Structure, Christology, Kingdom*, 98-99, recognises this motif in both passages, but does not draw conclusions about the unity of the portion of Matthew.

[16] Davies and Allison, *Matthew*, 3:111.

[17] See Mt. 2:2; 5:35; 18:23; 21:5; 22:2, 7, 11, 13; 25:34, 40; 27:11, 29, 37, 42.

[18] They do recognise the link between 21:5 and 25:34 (3:424); they simply do not develop it. Likewise, Keener, *Matthew*, 489, entitles the same section 'Jerusalem's King Enters Her Gates' but fails to develop the king motif in 25:31-46, despite the repetition of the term ὁ βασιλεύς.

[19] Davies and Allison, *Matthew*, 3:112.

There can be little doubt that 25:31 is also a report of such a *Parousia*, since we find several of the distinctive characteristics of such a report in the text: the verb of arrival ("Οταν δὲ ἔλθη), the attendant crowd (καὶ πάντες οἱ ἄγγελοι μετ᾽ αὐτοῦ), the acclamation of the king (ἐν τῇ δόξῃ αὐτοῦ).[20] Davies and Allison fail to recognise the parallels between the beginning of chapter 21 and the end of chapter 25, perhaps because they are reluctant to identify the Son of Man (25:31)/king (25:34) with Jesus. There can be little doubt that this identification should be made, however, and they seem to recognise this fact in their concluding discussion (p. 433).

The cries of the jubilant crowd should also be noted in establishing the unity of chapters 21-25. In 21:9 the crowd shouts, 'Blessed is he who comes in the name of the Lord!' (Εὐλογημένος ὁ ἐρχόμενος ἐν ὀνόματι κυρίου) quoting Ps 118:26 [LXX 117:26]. This same quotation occurs once more at 23:39, which would appear to indicate an *inclusio*, establishing a relationship between chapters 21-23. There is great irony in the fact that Jesus speaks these words to the city which was guilty of the rejection of his message though some of its inhabitants had been hailing him only days earlier.[21] But the latter occurrence of the quotation appears in the context of Jesus' prophecy of judgement on the temple (v. 38: 'Your house is left to you desolate') and his implicit promise that they would see him again (v. 39: 'you will not see me again *until...*'; λέγω γὰρ ὑμῖν, οὐ μή με ἴδητε ἀπ᾽ ἄρτι ἕως ἂν εἴπητε κτλ) both of which themes are developed in chapters 24 and 25.

We may further note the theme of judgement on the temple (seen in the incident with the moneychangers in 21:12-13) which finds its counterpart in the predictions of judgement on Jerusalem found in chapter 24. It is significant that the fig-tree (συκῆ) is mentioned in Matthew only in 21:18-22 (where it is intimately linked to the turning of the moneychangers' tables as a symbolic act of judgement on the temple), and in 24:32 where (I will argue) it concludes Jesus' prophecy of the destruction of Jerusalem. Related to the theme of judgement on the temple, yet distinct from it, is that of judgement on the Jewish religious leaders. While we might look to chapter 23 in particular for development of this theme, it is pervasive throughout chapters 21-22 also, in the various parables and responses of Jesus. Indeed, condemnation of the religious leaders is the dominant theme from 21:23, and even occasionally in the earlier part of chapter 21. This theme is taken up again, particularly, in 25:14-30.

---

[20] For discussion of the elements of a parousia see M. R. Cosby, 'Hellenistic Formal Receptions and Paul's Use of APANTESIS in 1 Thessalonians 4:17' *BBR* 4 (1994), 15-34, and the response by R. H. Gundry, 'A Brief Note on 'Hellenistic Formal Receptions and Paul's Use of APANTESIS in 1 Thessalonians 4:17' *BBR* 6 (1996), 39-41. See also the thorough study of the background, and Pauline use, of 'parousia' in J. Plevnik, *Paul and the Parousia: An Exegetical and Theological Investigation* (Peabody: Hendrickson, 1997).

[21] Hagner, *Matthew 14-28*, 591.

I conclude, then, that it is legitimate and indeed beneficial to recognise a literary and thematic coherence in chapters 21-25, and this will be the main object of our study in this work.

The Broader Context of Judgement in Matthew

It should be clear, even from the brief summary above, that Jesus' judgement is an important theme in chapters 21-25 of Matthew's gospel. However, this theme is not confined to this section of the gospel. What I am claiming, rather, is that chapters 21-25 of Matthew's gospel represent the most intensive and coherent expression of the full range of the judging activity of Jesus. These chapters must, however, be understood in the context of the expression of the theme of the judgement of Jesus throughout the whole gospel. Before looking at chapters 21-25 in depth, therefore, we must first examine the extent to which the theme of judgement is important to Matthew throughout his whole gospel. S. Travis notes, 'In comparison with Mark and Luke, Matthew heightens the emphasis on judgement, reward and punishment.'[22] The truth of this statement can be seen by examining the many instances of 'judgement' vocabulary in Matthew.[23] However, as indicated earlier, it is not necessary to restrict our investigation to those pericopae where the terminology of judgement is employed. We may, and indeed must, also take into account pericopae where the theme of judgement is expressed less directly. We shall see that this theme pervades Matthew's gospel.[24]

Building on the analyses of R. Hiers[25] and M. Reiser,[26] we may identify the

---

[22] S. H. Travis, 'Judgment' in *DJG*, 411. See also B. Charette, *The Theme of Recompense in Matthew's Gospel.*

[23] The verb κρίνω is used of future judgement in 7:1-2; and its compound κατακρίνω is similarly used in 12:41-42. In 19:28, κρίνω is used with regard to the future activity of the disciples. The noun κρίσιν is used of future judgement in 5:21-22; 10:15; 11:22, 24; 12:36, 41-42; 23:33. It is not clear whether the occurrence of the noun in 12:18 refers to the proclaimation of 'justice' or judgement'. Both translations are possible and appropriate. Cf. Davies and Allison, *Matthew*, 2:325. The noun ὁ κριτής is used in 5:25 in a way which is open to either a mundane or an eschatological interpretation. Blomberg (*Matthew*, 108) is probably right to regard the latter view as having priority on the grounds of the eschatological context of 5:21-22. It is notable that while judgement vocabulary is common in Matthew as a whole, it is generally absent from chapters 21-25. There is no ready explanation for this fact, but it must be emphasised that the absence of particular terms in no way indicates the absence of a concept, as we will seek to demonstrate.

[24] Marguerat, *Le Jugement*, 3, speaks of 'un thème théologique de première importance pour l'évangéliste Matthieu.'

[25] Cf. Hiers' list of relevant pericopae, itemised in the discussion of Hiers' work in Chapter 2 above.

[26] Reiser, *Jesus and Judgement*, 303.

following pericopae (outwith chapters 21-25) that contain references to some aspect of judgement.[27] While Reiser's analysis is valuable, it is limited in its appreciation of the scope of judgement in Jesus' proclamation. It is our contention that Jesus can be seen to embody judgement as well as to declare it. It is important that we appreciate the pervasive presence of this theme in Matthew. Reiser's particular concern is the teaching of Jesus, and so he also excludes references to judgement by John the Baptist, which means that his survey of texts fails to demonstrate the continuity of the theme between John and Jesus, and also fails to present the full extent of Matthew's interest in the subject. I have therefore provided additional references, which are marked in bold type.

3:7 (Q)	flee from the coming wrath
3:10 (Q)	the axe at the root of the tree/ fruitless tree cast in fire
3:11-12 (Q)	baptism with fire/ threshing floor/ unquenchable fire
5:4 (M)	those who mourn will be comforted
5:7 (M)	the merciful will be shown mercy
5:19 (M)	law-breaker will be called 'least'
5:22 (M)	angry words will be judged
5:25-26 (Q)	settle matters quickly before the judge sends to prison
5:32 (Q)	declaration of adultery (implied judgement)
5:46 (Q)	what reward for loving those who love?
6:1 (M)	you will have no reward from your Father
6:2 (M)	they have received their reward in full
6:5 (M)	they have received their reward in full
6:16 (M)	they have received their reward in full
7:1-2 (Q)	do not judge, or you will be judged
7:13-14 (Q)	the broad gate leads to destruction, the narrow to life
7:19 (M)	the tree that does not bear good fruit is cut down
7:21(M)	saying 'Lord, Lord' to Jesus is not enough
7:22-23 (Q)	depart from me, you evildoers
7:24-27 (Q)	houses in the storm
8:11-12 (Q)	subjects of the kingdom thrown out of the banquet
8:29 (M)	'Have you come to torture us?'
10:1, 7-11, 14 (Mk)	disciples given authority to drive out demons
10:15 (Q)	more bearable for Sodom and Gomorrah
10:23 (M)	you will not finish the cities of Israel until Son of Man comes

---

[27] See also the chart in Marguerat, *Le Jugement*, 31. I have identified each pericope according to the standard model of synoptic relationships. I present these classifications with general confidence in Markan priority but with caution regarding the precise relationships between the synoptic gospels.

10:28 (Q)	be afraid of the one who can destroy both soul and body in hell
10:32 (Q)	whoever disowns me before men, I will disown him
10:39 (Q)	whoever finds his life will lose it
11:6 (Q)	blessed is the man who does not fall away on account of me
11:21-24 (Q)	woe to you Korazin/Bethsaida... more bearable for Sodom
12:27 (Q)	they will be your judges
12:32 (Q)	whoever speaks against the Holy Spirit will not be forgiven
12:31-32 (Mk)	blasphemy against the Holy Sprit will not be forgiven
12:36-37 (M)	you must give an account for every careless word
12:41-42 (Q)	men of Nineveh will stand up at the judgement...and condemn
13:24-30 (M)	parable of weeds
13:36-43 (M)	explanation of parable of weeds
13:47-50 (M)	parable of net
15:13 (M)	every plant not planted by my heavenly Father shall be uprooted
16:27 (M)	Son of Man will come in the glory of his Father
18:23-25 (M)	parable of the unforgiving slave
19:28 (Q)	in the regeneration when the Son of Man shall sit on his throne
26:64 (Mk)	you will see Son of Man sitting at the right hand of the Power[28]

Two points should be clear from the list above. Firstly, that there is a significant body of material found throughout Matthew which relates to the broad theme of judgement. Secondly, it may be noted that a number of the above references relate to positive reward rather than to condemnation.[29]

It should now be clear from the discussion above that judgement is a prominent theme throughout Matthew's narrative. Particular attention might be drawn to the prominence of the motif in chapters 5-7 (which discourse, in fact, concludes with one of the most explicit references to Jesus' activity as judge in the whole gospel: 7:21-23) and in the collection of 'parables' found in chapter 13.

---

[28] There is no clear reference to judgement in this text. The relevance of this text to the above list depends on the interpretation of the 'Son of Man' text, so we include it here for the sake of completeness, but note that it may not be concerned with the issue of judgement.

[29] See particularly Charette, *The Theme of Recompense.*

Who is the Judge?

An important aspect of this theme is the question of who Matthew understands the judge to be. This is important to our argument because there is little doubt that Jesus anticipated a final judgement at which time God would declare his judgement. This was a generally accepted (if perhaps little emphasised) Jewish belief.[30] However, any evidence that suggests that Jesus took upon himself the role of judge (whether eschatological or temporal) would be significant for the outcome of this thesis. Study of a selection of passages in Matthew reveals that several answers may be given to this question:

UNSPECIFIED, BUT GOD IS IMPLIED

The judgement of the 'coming wrath' and the axe at the root of the tree (3:7, 10) are not linked by John to any particular figure.[31] John's proclamation of coming judgement provides an important backdrop to Jesus' preaching on this theme.[32] Particularly common is the use of the so-called 'divine passive'. We might cite 5:7 as an instance of this form. 'They will be shown mercy' is a cir-cumlocution for 'God will show them mercy' (though it is possible, given the words in 7:21-23, that Jesus is here referring to the mercy that *he* will show). Other instances of the divine passive are (apart from other possibilities among the beatitudes) 5:19, 29-30; 7:1-2; 8:12; 11:23; 12:31-2, 36-7.[33]

We might also include in this category passages such as 5:25-6 which appear to speak of more than a mundane event, but which couch the event of God's judgement in the language of a parable.[34] Several of the parables in chapter 13

---

[30] See G. F. Moore, *Judaism in the First Centuries of the Christian Era: The Age of the Tannaim* (3 volumes in 2; Peabody: Hendrickson, 1997 [1927, 1930]), 2:338-39, 385. E. P. Sanders, *Judaism: Practice and Belief 63BCE-66CE* (London: SCM Press, 1992), 272-75. See C. A. Evans, 'Parables in Early Judaism' in R. N. Longenecker (ed.), *The Challenge of Jesus' Parables* (Grand Rapids: Eerdmans, 2000), 51-75, in which he discusses the theme of judgement in the rabbinic parables.

[31] Compare Ezekiel 31:12-18 and Daniel 4:23 where judgement is expressed in terms of a tree cut down. See also Psalm 80:16 and Jeremiah 11:16 where the image is of a burned tree.

[32] See R. L. Webb, *John the Baptizer and Prophet* (JSNTS 62; Sheffield: Sheffield Academic Press, 1991), 219-60. *Idem*, 'John the Baptist and his Relationship to Jesus' in Chilton and Evans (eds), *Studying the Historical Jesus*. Also, McKnight, *A New Vision*, 4.

[33] See M. Reiser, *Jesus and Judgment*, 266-73, for an excursus on the *Passivum Divinum*. See also D. B. Wallace, *Greek Grammar Beyond the Basics* (Grand Rapids: Zondervan, 1996), 437-38 and, briefly, S. E. Porter, *Idioms of the Greek New Testament* (Sheffield: Sheffield Academic Press, 1992), 65-66 for cautions regarding the over-interpretation of this idiom.

[34] It is not entirely clear whether Jesus is pointing to an eschatological reality, or simply reflecting the draconian character of ancient justice. See Keener, *Matthew*, 185. See also Jeremias, *Parables*, 43-44.

appear to indicate final judgement where God is judge.[35]

There are also instances where the one who rewards is unspecified, such as 5:46, where the context indicates that God is in view. Somewhat different are the references to 'having their reward in full' (6:2, 5, 16) where the reference is not to a future judgement but refers to the immediate judgement.

The rather opaque reference in 10:28 to 'the one who can destroy both soul and body in hell' is still clearly to be understood as a reference to God.[36] The only real alternative is Satan,[37] but it is clear from Scripture that Satan can only operate within the constraints God allows (see Job) and believers are never called to fear Satan. A similar thought is found in non-canonical Jewish literature,[38] and Garland notes the following Rabbinic passage concerning Johanan ben Zakkai who was found by his disciples weeping on his death bed. When they asked him why he was weeping he answered:

> If I were taken today before a human king who is here today and gone tomorrow in the grave, whose anger if he is angry with me does not last forever, who if he imprisons me does not imprison me forever, and who if he puts me to death does not put me to everlasting death, and whom I can persuade with words and bribe with money, even so I would weep. Now that I am being taken before the supreme King of Kings, the Holy One, blessed is He, who lives and endures forever, whose anger, if He be angry with me, is an everlasting anger, who if He imprisons imprisons me for ever, who if he (*sic.*) puts me to death for ever, and whom I cannot persuade with words or bribe with money - nay more, when there are two ways before me, one leading to Paradise and the other to Gehinnon, and I do not know by which I shall be taken, shall I not weep?" They said to him, "Master, bless us." He said to them, "May it be [God's] will that the fear of heaven shall be upon you like the fear of flesh and blood.[39]

The 'woes' of chapter 23 and 26:24 should probably be regarded as indicating that the people concerned must face the judgement of God.[40]

---

[35] D. A. Hagner, 'Matthew's Parables of the Kingdom (Matthew 13:1-52)' in Longenecker (ed.), *The Challenge of Jesus' Parables*, 102-24. Hagner identifies the parables of the weeds and the grain (24-30, 36-43) and the net (47-50), and comments (118), 'in rounding out his collection of parables in chapter 13, Matthew returns to one of his favorite themes: the judgment of the unrighteous. And the stress here, as it was earlier, is on the occurrence of judgment only "at the end of the age" (v.49; Cf. V.40).'

[36] So Hagner, *Matthew 14-28*, 286; Carson, *Matthew*, 254. See also I. H. Marshall, 'Uncomfortable Words: VI. "Fear him who can destroy both soul and body in hell" (Mt 10.28 RSV).' *ExpT* 81 (1970), 276-80.

[37] This view is supported by a number of scholars including Olshausen, Stier, Grundmann, Stendahl, and Meier. See Davies and Allison, *Matthew*, 2:207 n. 31.

[38] 2 Macc. 6:26; 4 Macc. 13:14-15.

[39] *bBerakot* 28b quoted in Garland, 116-17. Garland also points to *bBerakot* 61b.

[40] See the discussion of chapter 23 in chapter 5.

GOD IS SPECIFIED

The Father is the one who must 'forgive our debts' (6:12) and who may with-hold such forgiveness (6:14-15). In the case of reward, the Father is identified on several occasions as the one who rewards.[41]

JESUS IS IMPLIED

The first instance we may cite is the statement of John that the 'coming one' (ὁ ἐρχόμενος) would clear his threshing floor with the winnowing fork (3:11-12).[42] The parable of the wise and foolish builders (7:24-7) may indicate that Jesus is the judge. What is clear is that (a) it follows directly the direct claim of Jesus to fulfil that eschatological role and (b) hearing and doing Jesus' words is what will make the difference in the storm which is clearly a parabolic representation of judgement. It is not explicitly said, however, who brings the storm about.[43]

In the account of the demoniacs, the demons apparently recognise in Jesus the one with whom they will deal at 'the appointed time' (8:29). While this is not explicitly stated, if correct it also has implications for the other exorcisms of Jesus which may be seen as proleptic acts of judgement.

The references to reward in 10:40-2 may be read in line with the previous reward references as implying God as judge. However, the fact that the passage speaks so pointedly about the response to Jesus, and the very clear link between 10:42 and 25:35, 40 suggests that here, perhaps, Jesus is seen in the role of judge.

JESUS IS SPECIFIED

While 3:11-12 may have given a hint of Jesus as the judge, the first explicit claim from Jesus himself (7:21-23) is striking in its clarity. While verse 21 on its own might be understood to be a simple claim of discipleship to the earthly Jesus, the following verse, linked to v. 21 so plainly by the repetition of 'Lord, Lord' plainly brings us to the scene of final judgement. The phrase 'that day' echoes the OT concept of the Day of Yahweh, which was an integral part of Jewish hope for centuries up to Jesus' own day. On that Day, Yahweh would finally act decisively to vindicate his own people and to destroy their enemies.[44] Here, in a radical reinterpretation of that hope, Jesus stands as the central fig-ure. The picture is one of personal conversation (as opposed to some kind of impersonal act of judgement) and the criterion of acceptance or rejection is knowledge of Jesus himself.

The account of the paralytic is very important to our understanding of Jesus as judge. First it includes the specific claim of Jesus to be able to forgive sins

---

[41] See 6:1, 4, 6, 18. See Marguerat, *Le Jugement*, 67-69.

[42] See the discussion in Keener, *Matthew*, 127-31.

[43] Gundry, *Matthew*, 133-36. Hagner, *Matthew 1-13*, (WBC 33A; Dallas: Word, 1993), 189-92.

[44] Ladd, *The Presence of the Future*, 64-70. Reiser, *Jesus and Judgment*, 26-28.

(9:2) and even more than that, to have authority (ἐξουσία) on earth to forgive sins (9:6). Secondly, it clearly shows the interpretation of Jesus' words and actions made by the Jewish leaders. They saw clearly that here Jesus was claiming one of the prerogatives of God and so could only conclude that he was blaspheming (9:3).

In 10:32-33 Jesus tells his disciples that their response to him will determine his response to them before his Father. A judgement scene is clearly envisaged but it is not absolutely clear who is regarded as judge. It may be that Jesus is seen in terms of a witness giving an account of his followers before the Father-judge. However, since it is Jesus who determines the reception of the disciples, it may be more accurate to see him as the judge, that task having been appointed for him by the Father. This may be confirmed by 10:34-6 where Jesus speaks of the separation which he causes by his call to commitment. This may be regarded as a proleptic indication of the separation which will occur at the judgement.

The very difficult verses 16:27-8 clearly refer to the judgement which Jesus will execute. What is not clear is how to reconcile an apparent imminent end with other passages which imply a considerable period of time before the end.

DISCIPLES ARE SPECIFIED

In 19:28 Jesus tells his disciples that 'you who have followed me' will sit on twelve thrones and judge the twelve tribes of Israel. Scholars debate whether this is an exclusive reference to the Twelve, or whether Jesus was indicating a role for every disciple in the judgement. Whichever position we may take, the reference to the παλιγγενεσία appears to put it beyond dispute that future judgement is in view.[45] Though the idea is unique in Matthew, the fact that it appears elsewhere in the New Testament (Lk 22:30; 1 Cor 6:2) indicates that it is worthy of note. It must also be noted that the judging role of the disciples is derived from the role of judge which Jesus exercises. Thus this passage serves to reinforce the theme, recurrent in Matthew, that Jesus is the judge.

In the light of the preceding discussion, we may say that judgement is a particularly pervasive eschatological theme in Matthew's gospel, and that there are several texts in various portions of the gospel which clearly indicate that Jesus exercises the role of judge. It will be no surprise, therefore, if Matthew makes this theme dominant in a substantial portion of his work.

The Structure of Matthew 21-25

A possible structure for the unit composed of chapters 21-25 is set out below. We have attempted to indicate how the question of Jesus' authority to exercise judgement is central to Matthew's concerns throughout. It will be clear that the

---

[45] See D. C. Sim, 'The Meaning of παλιγγενεσία in Matthew 19:28', *JSNT* 50 (1993), 3-12.

structure utilises the categories proposed by Borg in his various pieces of work. Thus there is the overarching theme of the 'Politics of Holiness' in collision with Jesus' 'Politics of Compassion' which leads to an atmosphere of conflict throughout the section. I have also adopted the two categories of prophet and sage as particularly helpful in approaching the unit of text. The validity or otherwise of these categories will be demonstrated by exegetical analysis of the biblical text. However, it will also become clear from the detailed treatment of these chapters that I regard Borg's understanding of these roles as defective in several significant ways, and I go beyond Borg in understanding all of these roles to be modified by the profoundly eschatological perspective which Jesus had.

I propose the following outline for Matthew 21-25, which is composed of three major sections relating firstly to Jesus' prophetic acts of judgement against the temple, secondly to his condemnation of the Jewish leaders and thirdly to his predictions of future judgement, both imminent and eschatological.

(i)   Prophetic Acts of Judgement

21:1-11		Entrance into Jerusalem - prophetic action – The Coming King.
21:12-17		Prophetic action signifying judgement on temple
	12-13	Judgement of 'Politics of Holiness'
	14	Practice of 'Politics of Compassion'
	15-17	Jesus' authority questioned
21:18-22		Judgement of temple
	18-20	Prophetic action symbolising judgement on temple
	21-22	Saying (*mashal*) on faith
21:23-27		Judgement of Leaders
	23	Jesus' authority questioned.
	24-27	Challenge in form of *mashal* concerning John the Baptist's authority

(ii)   Meshalim of Judgement of Jewish Leaders

21:28-32		Judgement of Leaders
	28-31a	*Mashal* of two sons
	31b-32	Judgement of 'Politics of Holiness'
21:33-46		Judgement of Leaders
	33-44	*Mashal* of Tenants
	45-46	Conflict.
22:1-14		Judgement of Leaders
	1-14	*Mashal* against 'Politics of Holiness'
22:15-22		Judgement of Leaders
	15-22	*Mashal* of coin challenging 'Politics of Holiness'
22:23-33		Judgement of Leaders

	23-33	*Mashal* of levirate marriage
22:34-40		Judgement of Leaders
	34-40	Challenge to 'Politics of Holiness'
22:41-46		Judgement of Leaders
	41-46	Provocative *mashal*: Whose Son is the Christ?
23		Judgement of Leaders
	Passim	Judgement on leaders couched in language and form of prophetic woe/*meshalim*.
23:37-39		Judgement of temple
	37-39	*Mashal* of mother hen

(iii)   Prophetic Proclamation of Future Judgement

24:1-35	Judgement on temple and Jerusalem
24:36-25:13	Return of Jesus
25:14-30	*Mashal* of Judgement
25:31-46	Final Judgement - The Coming King

Blomberg, in his outlines, correctly recognises the theme of judgement running through chapters 21-25, but prefers to see the theme begin at 19:1 on 'The Road to Jerusalem'.[46] While there may be something to be said for this decision, I believe that it loses the sense of total coherence which is recognised when account is taken of the theme of the coming king in chapters 21 and 25, and so I differ from him here even where I build on his work.[47]

From my suggested outline we can see that Matthew's portrayal of Jesus in the whole section is dominated by the theme which forms an *inclusio* at beginning and end, *viz.* Jesus is the coming king, who has all authority (cf. Matt 28:18), regardless of whether that is recognised in his ministry on earth or not (see 21:23-27). Although the first event in chapter 21 has no explicit relation to judgement, the overall context of these chapters suggests that it is relevant. The coming of a king would mean that he was coming either to bring blessing or to bring judgement. It is his authority as king that enables him not only to pronounce judgement but also to enact judgement, both in the context of his earthly ministry (chapters 21-23), in the immediate future (i.e. in the fall of Jerusalem, 24:4-35) and in the final universal judgement (25:31-46).

This authority to be judge is worked out in terms of two main complementary roles. Jesus performs the dramatic actions and speaks the challenging and predictive words which bring to the people the message of God (Prophet) and he speaks in riddles, startling sayings and parables which confront his hearers with God's concern for justice and with impending judgement in the tradition

---

[46] See his outlines in Blomberg, *Matthew*, 286, 338, where he clearly displays the dominant theme of judgement.

[47] See the discussion of the limits of the section above.

of the teacher of Wisdom (Sage).[48]

Chapter Summary and Conclusion

On the basis of the previous discussion, we may conclude that there is evidence to suggest that chapters 21-25 of Matthew's gospel form a distinctive block of material which coheres by means of several literary and thematic connections. The connections will become more obvious, we trust, as more detailed exegetical work is done in following chapters.

We may also conclude that the theme of judgement is characteristic of Matthew's gospel, yet is not developed in such a consistent manner in other portions of the gospel. Thus, our chosen theme is not a minor concern for Matthew, yet neither is this concern so widespread throughout the gospel so as to make our chosen portion of text unremarkable.

Finally, we have presented an outline of this section which highlights both the theme of judgement, and its two-fold application – to the present time of Jesus and to the future eschatological event. We have drawn on the models of prophet and sage, favoured among others by Borg, and so now we must defend this choice by looking at how these roles are developed in this present section of Matthew. We will deal with the themes in roughly the order in which they are dominant in the section. Material will however be drawn together from the whole of the section under consideration, and, because there is a certain element of overlap in the classification used, certain passages from the section may be discussed under more than one heading.

---

[48] Witherington, *Jesus the Seer*, 246: 'no one title or label adequately explains a figure as complex as Jesus. Multiple complementary models are required to deal with the man who fits no one formula, as E. Schweizer once called him.'

CHAPTER 5

Jesus the Judge in Matthew: As Prophet

Introduction

In the next two chapters, we will examine the theme of judgement against the backdrop of the Wisdom tradition and of the prophetic tradition. There are three main reasons for this. The first is that these two traditions account for a very substantial portion of the OT scriptures which were formative for the world-view of Jesus and his contemporaries. Secondly, the prophet and the sage are the two most promising models employed by Marcus Borg in his portrayal of Jesus, and so the contrast between his portrait of Jesus and mine will be clearer if we use these two categories. Thirdly, issues relating to the characteristics of both a prophet and a sage lie at the heart of contemporary debate regarding Jesus and his eschatological expectations. It will become clear from our discussion that, according to Matthew, Jesus reflects aspects of both of these traditions in his ministry, and that he does so in a coherent and holistic manner. It is necessary, therefore, to justify our decision to examine the two traditions separately.

The fundamental reasons for this decision are two-fold. Firstly, this method of analysis allows us to highlight the distinctive character of each tradition, and thus enables us to see more clearly how characteristics of the tradition are exemplified in Jesus. Secondly, it is vital to highlight the importance of the Wisdom tradition in particular for our investigation, as that tradition has been cited by several modern scholars, including Borg and Crossan, as the foundation for a non-eschatological reading of Jesus' ministry. Having said this, it will also become clear (e.g., in our discussion of *meshalim*) that there is some degree of overlap between the prophetic and Wisdom traditions with respect to mode of expression and significant imagery. Yet, the decision to treat each tradition distinctly is valid so long as no hard and fast division is drawn between them. We begin with a study of Jesus the judge in the light of the prophetic tradition.

Jesus and the Title of 'Prophet'

Jesus is described explicitly as a prophet only three times in Matthew.[1] The earliest occasion is recorded in 16:14. Jesus asks the disciples what the people are saying about him and they respond,

> Some say John the Baptist, but others Elijah, and still others Jeremiah or one of the prophets.

The other two instances are found in chapters 21-25, indeed both are found in chapter 21. Both of these instances are unique to Matthew, suggesting that he has a particular interest in this motif. At the end of the account of Jesus' entry into Jerusalem, Matthew records the words of the crowds: 'This is the prophet Jesus from Nazareth in Galilee' (21:11). Later, the Chief Priests and the Pharisees were incensed by Jesus' parable of the wicked tenants, and Matthew records that,

> They wanted to arrest him, but they feared the crowds, because they regarded him as a prophet (21:46).

Though these references are infrequent, they present a consistent testimony. The disciples' words in 16:14, in particular, indicate that each of the several opinions concerning Jesus commonly held during his ministry (at least, those reported by the disciples – John the Baptist, Elijah, Jeremiah, 'one of the prophets') linked Jesus to the prophetic ministry.[2] That Borg should describe Jesus as a prophet is, therefore, not particularly controversial. Although Matthew never records the disciples using the term 'prophet' of Jesus, nor uses it himself in redactional comments, neither does he ever indicate that the description is inappropriate. It would appear to be a designation for Jesus that Matthew was prepared to countenance. The questions that remain, however, are, What kind of prophet does Matthew portray Jesus to be? Is Jesus a foreteller of the future?[3] Is he a social prophet? Or is there more still to this man?

B. Witherington, in his fine study of prophecy, claims that Matthew does not regard Jesus as a prophet:

---

[1] In addition to the two texts identified, there are a number of instances where words of Jesus might be understood as self-reference in terms of a prophet. Jesus speaks of his own experience in 10:41 and 13:57, but in both cases it seems likely that he is citing traditional sayings which need not be understood as a direct claim to the status of prophet. See Witherington, *Jesus the Seer*, 247; Aune, *Prophecy*, 156.

[2] Such reports of popular opinion should not, of course, be understood to mean that popular opinion was necessarily correct or adequate. So Witherington, *Jesus the Seer*, 247.

[3] Theissen and Merz, *The Historical Jesus*, 240-80, appear to equate Jesus' designation as 'Prophet' largely with his words about the future.

In Matthew Jesus is Emmanuel, Wisdom, the Davidic Messiah, God's Son, the Son of Man, but there is hardly a mention of Jesus as a prophet. 'Prophet' does not seem to have been seen by this evangelist as either a christological or an eschatological term.[4]

However, a number of factors suggest that this is a premature statement. Firstly, Witherington makes this judgement in comparing Matthew's gospel with Luke's, which he believes makes much more use of the prophetic model. While it is true that Luke does emphasise this model in ways different to Matthew,[5] this does not mean that the model is unimportant to Matthew. In fact, it would raise significant questions about the accuracy of Luke's portrait with reference to the true characteristics of Jesus' ministry if Matthew did not reflect something of the same concerns. Secondly, the fact that Matthew records the opinion of the Jewish people to the effect that Jesus is some kind of prophet suggests that Matthew, at the least, is not concerned to remove that motif from his work. Thirdly, the lack of frequency of one particular term does not imply that Jesus is not presented as a prophet to Matthew's readers by other means.[6] Fourthly, Matthew's presentation of Jesus includes prophetic elements (such as the actions associated with his entry to Jerusalem and the woe oracles of chapter 23). It seems best to recognise that Matthew does not emphasise the language of the prophet in his gospel, but at the same time to consider *all* forms of evidence before coming to a conclusion about the significance of the prophet model for Matthew's presentation of Jesus.

If 'prophet' is indeed an appropriate designation for Jesus, then it follows that the OT documents that give accounts of the activities of the prophets of Yahweh, or that were written by the prophets of Yahweh, must provide a significant proportion of the background material for understanding the words and actions of Jesus.[7] Likewise, the more Jesus clearly stands in continuity with the prophets of Yahweh as described in the OT, the more we will recognise the validity of the designation 'prophet' as a description (if not necessarily an exhaustive description) of Jesus. We will draw heavily on these texts in the following study.

Jesus *the* Prophet?

Deuteronomy 18:18-19 established an expectation among the Jewish people that a great prophet would one day make his appearance.[8] Is Jesus hailed as '*the*

---

[4] Witherington, *Jesus the Seer*, 339.

[5] See Witherington's discussion, *Jesus the Seer*, 335-40.

[6] Particularly by means of activities associated with the prophets. See the discussion below.

[7] Of particular value in this regard is the first half of Witherington's *Jesus the Seer*.

[8] Compare 1QS 9:10-11: 'They shall govern themselves using the original precepts by which the men of the *Yahad* began to be instructed, doing so until there come the

prophet'? O. Cullmann argues that the reference in 21:46 is not particularly important, being simply a reference to Jesus as one of a class of prophets to which others also belonged (προφήτης is without the article).[9] On the other hand, the use of ὁ προφήτης in 21:11 is understood by Cullmann to be, probably, a reference to the eschatological prophet anticipated in Deuteronomy 18:18-19, and thus places Jesus in a unique category.[10] This view is resisted, however, by more recent authors such as R. Horsley[11] and N. T. Wright.[12] Hagner is representative of many when he comments,

> The title "the prophet" (ὁ προφήτης) is probably only a title of great respect here (*cf.* v 46) rather than an evaluation of Jesus as *the* prophet in the absolute sense, *i.e.*, the eschatological prophet of Deut 18:15 (cf. John 6:14; 7:40). Hence it is not simply "the prophet" or "the prophet to come," but rather "Jesus the prophet from Nazareth of Galilee".[13]

Given the lack of theological development of the theme of 'the prophet like Moses' in Matthew (and the other synoptic gospels for that matter) and the rather equivocal response of the people to Jesus in chapters 21-25, it seems most plausible to accept that this is not an explicit confession that Jesus is the long expected eschatological prophet, but that the words might well reflect that

---

Prophet and the Messiahs of Aaron and Israel.' For a discussion of a keen expectation of 'the prophet' within the Dead Sea Scrolls, see C. M. Pate, *Communities of the Last Days* (Leicester: Apollos, 2000), 122-25.

[9] O. Cullmann, *The Christology of the New Testament* (London: SCM Press, 2nd edn, 1963), 31. See Wallace, *Greek Grammar Beyond the Basics*, 244, on this indefinite sense of anarthrous nouns.

[10] Cullmann, *Christology*, 35. France, *Matthew*, 300, suggests, in addition to the primary function of identification, a secondary allusion to the Deuteronomy passage.

[11] R. Horsley, 'Like One of the Prophets of Old: Two Types of Popular Prophets at the Time of Jesus' *CBQ* 47 (1985), 435-63.

[12] Wright, *Jesus and the Victory of God*, 163: 'the great bulk of the relevant evidence does not point to Jesus being seen in terms of Deuteronomy 18' and 'I suggest that Jesus was seen as, and saw himself as, *a* prophet, not a particular one necessarily...' He goes on to qualify these statements, 'This is not to say that Jesus did not regard his prophetic ministry as in some way unique, and able to be combined with other roles. It certainly does not rule out the possibility of him, and/or his followers, regarding his work as in some way climactic within Israel's long story. As we shall see, this is in fact highly likely to have been the case. It is simply to stress that we cannot confine the investigation to the use, explicit or implicit of Deuteronomy 18 and the figure of 'the prophet' mentioned there; and that the initial impression made on Jesus' hearers would not have been that Jesus was claiming to be a particular figure, of whom they had had advance expectations.' Dunn, *Jesus*, 82, believes that the case is not clearly decisive either way, but does not believe that the lack of certainty on this point affects the fundamental point that Jesus exercised a prophetic ministry.

[13] Hagner, *Matthew 14-28*, 596.

belief on the part of *some* who observed Jesus' ministry, and that Matthew would no doubt have been aware of the *resonance* with the Hebrew Scriptures when he wrote the words. Whatever is the case, Matthew clearly has an interest in Jesus the prophet.[14] Though Jesus only makes reference to himself as a prophet in oblique comments in Matthew's account, he takes on the role of a prophet in many ways and several of these may be seen particularly clearly in Matt. 21-25. Our interest in the following passages is two-fold. Firstly, we will note passages that clearly indicate the prophetic character of Jesus' words and actions. However, secondly, and more importantly, we will note passages that point to prophetic sayings and actions of judgement.

Jesus the Judge as Performer of Prophetic Acts: Old Testament Background

Particularly striking at the beginning of our section are the three prophetic acts[15] of chapter 21. The concept of a 'prophetic act' or 'prophetic drama' (to use Stacey's term) is very clearly illustrated in numerous OT texts. A brief survey of three prophetic books will suffice.

Hosea

The astonishing demands placed by Yahweh on the eighth century BC prophet Hosea epitomise the nature of the prophetic act (Hosea 1:2-9).[16] Rather than incorporating accounts of prophetic acts into a broader narrative of the prophet's activities, the narrative is completely devoted to the activities which Hosea is required to carry out and their significance. Hosea indicates in striking terms that prophetic acts may well not make any sense apart from the divine interpretation that they are given by God who instructs that they be done.[17]

---

[14] With particular reference to chapters 21-23 of Matthew's gospel, Marguerat, *Le Jugement*, 347, comments: 'Plus important encore est de relever que tout au long de ces trois chapitres, *la figure du Christ est résolument décrite sur le modèle de la tradition prophétique*' (author's italics).

[15] See particularly W. D. Stacey, *Prophetic Drama in the Old Testament* (London: Epworth Press, 1990), and now the recent work of M. Hooker, *The Signs of a Prophet* (London: SCM Press, 1997).

[16] Stacey, *Prophetic Drama*, 96-111. See also W. VanGemeren, *Interpreting the Prophetic Word* (Grand Rapids: Zondevan, 1990), 105-20.

[17] R. C. Ortlund, Jr., *Whoredom* (NSBT 2; Leicester: IVP, 1996), 47-75. Ortlund writes, 'God called Hosea not only to speak to the nation but also to serve as a living symbol of the larger spiritual reality of Yahweh's love for promiscuous Israel' (47). Cf. D. Stuart, *Hosea-Jonah* (WBC 31; Waco: Word, 1987), 24: 'Divine command to perform a symbolic act is followed by divine explanation of the act's symbolic importance. The act itself is then done in obedience to the command and in service of the symbolism.'

Jeremiah

The first symbolic act we encounter in Jeremiah's ministry is recorded in
Jeremiah 13:1-11.[18] Jeremiah is given detailed instructions by Yahweh ('the
Lord said to me', v.1) to purchase a 'linen waistband',[19] to put it round his
waist, and to refrain from washing it. The Lord then gave instructions to bury
the waistband in a crevice in a rock by the Euphrates. After 'many days' (v.6)
Jeremiah is told to uncover the cloth,[20] and when he finds that it is ruined (v.7),
'the word of the Lord' came to him (v.8), saying

> 9 Thus says the LORD: Just so I will ruin the pride of Judah and the great pride of
> Jerusalem. 10 This evil people, who refuse to hear my words, who stubbornly
> follow their own will and have gone after other gods to serve them and worship
> them, shall be like this loincloth, which is good for nothing. 11 For as the
> loincloth clings to one's loins, so I made the whole house of Israel and the whole
> house of Judah cling to me, says the LORD, in order that they might be for me a
> people, a name, a praise, and a glory. But they would not listen.

The following verses indicate by means of vivid images the judgement that
the Lord will bring upon his rebellious people. Harrison comments that this
'acted parable'

> made clear that idolatry, with its attendant moral corruptions, would be the ruin of
> the people.

And that

> The damaged waistcloth indicated that proud Judah would be humbled and
> punished for her idolatry.[21]

Thus the 'acted parable' is associated with the declaration of judgement. The
human agent (the prophet) is required to undertake an action which is then
given meaning by the divine interpretation which is supplied.

When we turn to Jeremiah 16:1-13, we find a startling composite 'acted parable' where Jeremiah is instructed firstly *not* to take a wife nor have children as
a symbol of the devastation that will fall upon the families of the land (16:1-
4).[22] Secondly, Jeremiah is not to follow the normal conventions of mourning

---

[18] Stacey, *Prophetic Drama*, 131-38.

[19] This is probably an undergarment, though the meaning 'belt' is possible. Stacey,
Prophetic Drama, 131, n. 4.

[20] Stacey, (*Prophetic Drama*, 131), correctly notes that the text explicitly records three
direct commands from Yahweh with respect to the garment: 1. Buy and wear; 2.
Remove and bury; 3. Recover.

[21] R. K. Harrison, *Jeremiah and Lamentations* (TOTC; Leicester: IVP, 1973), 99.

[22] This is an interesting reversal of the command given to Hosea. J. A. Thompson, *The
Book of Jeremiah* (NICOT; Grand Rapids: Eerdmans, 1980), 403, draws attention to

(5-8). The reason for these peculiar responses to death are explained in the following words, in which Yahweh addresses the people directly:

> 9 For thus says the LORD of hosts, the God of Israel: I am going to banish from this place, in your days and before your eyes, the voice of mirth and the voice of gladness, the voice of the bridegroom and the voice of the bride.

Once more, the prophetic act, though apparently bizarre and even vindictive in and of itself, becomes by divine interpretation a signpost of imminent judgement on the people.

A further example is found in 19:1-13.[23] The account of a very brief and simple action (v.1, 10) is given great significance by means of the interspersed prophetic oracles (3-9, 11-13).[24] The power of the combination of action and word as a declaration of judgement is exemplified in verses 10 and 11:

> 10 Then you shall break the jug in the sight of those who go with you, 11 and shall say to them: Thus says the LORD of hosts: So will I break this people and this city, as one breaks a potter's vessel, so that it can never be mended.

Verse 4 is of particular significance for understanding, by analogy, the full extent of Jesus' prophetic ministry. The people of Judah are condemned for their rejection of their God, Yahweh. They have 'profaned this place by making offerings in it to other gods whom neither they nor their ancestors nor the kings of Judah have known'. But they are also condemned because they 'have filled this place with the blood of the innocent, and gone on building the high places of Baal to burn their children in the fire as burnt offerings to Baal, which I did not command or decree, nor did it enter my mind.' Though there is clearly a reference to religious practice here, it appears clear that the judgement that is to fall on the people comes equally because of a blatant lack of compassion for the vulnerable.

One final example of this genre from Jeremiah is recounted in 27:1-22. In this case the yoke that Jeremiah is instructed to wear (v.2) is referred to in the prophetic interpretation of the action (vv.8, 11, 12). This prophetic act is interpreted as a call to submit to the Lord's judgement (against the advice of the false prophets who say that there is nothing to fear, vv.16-17) in case worse

---

several similar accounts of 'the proclamation of the word through family events' but notes that 'the call to celibacy is unique in the OT.' Given the understanding that lack of family was regarded as a curse, it is clear that the word that is proclaimed by this state of affairs is a word of judgement.

[23] Stacey, *Prophetic Drama*, 146-48. Stacey includes a discussion, (143-46), of 18:1-12 as a prophetic drama, although he notes that few commentators include this passage in their discussions of the phenomenon. See also Thompson, *Jeremiah*, 443-56.

[24] Thompson, *Jeremiah*, 445: 'The symbolic act was tantamount to a word from Yahweh'.

judgement should befall the people. Yet there is also a note of hope in the final words (v.22).[25]

Ezekiel

A brief survey of the prophecy of Ezekiel reveals a number of similar prophetic acts.[26] Particularly important are the events of 4:1-5:4.[27] In this section of the prophecy, Ezekiel is commanded by God to carry out intricate instructions which lead to a vivid visual symbol of Jerusalem under siege. The divine interpretation of the actions is given in Ezekiel 5:5-17. The Sovereign Lord will punish Jerusalem for her unfaithfulness. The passage is summed up in verses 5-8:

> Thus says the Lord GOD: This is Jerusalem; I have set her in the center of the nations, with countries all around her. 6 But she has rebelled against my ordinances and my statutes, becoming more wicked than the nations and the countries all around her, rejecting my ordinances and not following my statutes. 7 Therefore thus says the Lord GOD: Because you are more turbulent than the nations that are all around you, and have not followed my statutes or kept my ordinances, but have acted according to the ordinances of the nations that are all around you; 8 therefore thus says the Lord GOD: *I, I myself, am coming against you; I will execute judgments among you in the sight of the nations.*

Similar to the requirements laid upon Jeremiah is Yahweh's demand that Ezekiel should not mourn openly for his wife (24:15-27). The puzzled response of the people in verse 19 ('Will you not tell us what these things mean for us, that you are acting this way?') leads to a prophetic oracle of judgement which presents the purpose of Yahweh to bring great disaster on the people. The sanctuary will be profaned (v.21), and yet the people will not mourn outwardly (22-23); the mourning will be the inward sigh of Ezekiel (v.23, *cf.* v.17).

Jesus the Judge as Performer of Prophetic Acts in Matthew's Gospel

These OT events provide an appropriate backdrop for interpreting the actions of Jesus, so that the lack of judgement vocabulary in Matthew 21 does not detract from the significance of the actions of Jesus. However, Jesus' actions do not conform exactly to the pattern of these OT events. A distinctive characteristic of these and other OT 'sign-acts' is that they are initiated by the command of

---

[25] The note of hope does not suggest that judgement will be turned away, but rather that *through* the judgement Yahweh would sustain a faithful remnant which he will restore.

[26] See VanGemeren, *Interpreting the Prophetic Word*, 325.

[27] Stacey, *Prophetic Drama*, 180-92; J. Blenkinsopp *Ezekiel* (IBC; Louisville, Westminster/John Knox Press, 1990), 33-40; D. I. Block, *The Book of Ezekiel 1-24* (NICOT; Grand Rapids: Eerdmans, 1997), 164-217.

Yahweh.[28] The fact that no such words are recorded prior to the actions of Jesus must be taken into account when drawing conclusions from the text of Matthew about the nature of Jesus' prophetic activity. It appears that Jesus acts on his own initiative and with his own authority as he takes on these roles.

We will examine three prophetic acts described in Matthew's narrative. The entry into Jerusalem (21:1-11), Jesus' actions in the temple, particularly the clearing of the traders (21:12-17) and the withering of the fig tree (21:18-22).[29]

The Entry into Jerusalem (21:1-11)[30]

In the first of the actions that Matthew records, Jesus enters Jerusalem, the 'city of David'.[31] There can be little doubt that Jesus deliberately arranges his entrance into Jerusalem[32] as a fulfilment of Zechariah 9:9. When Matthew makes this explicit in 21:4-5,[33] we need not suppose that this is only the evangelist's perspective on the event.[34] There is every indication that Jesus intended his entry to be a prophetic act, in the tradition of the OT prophets surveyed above.[35]

---

[28] Cf. Jer. 13:1; 16:5; 19:1; 27:1-2; Ezek. 4:1, 2, 3, 4, 6, 9, *etc.*.

[29] Luz, *Matthäus 18-25*, 176, comments, 'In neuerer Zeit hat sich mit Recht die Tendenz verstärkt, Mt 21,1-17 als eine einzige Perikope zu betrachten.' However, the exclusion of the cursing of the fig tree from this unit fails to recognise sufficiently the common character of the three actions, and leads to lack of appreciation of the significance of the apparently arbitrary cursing of the fig tree. Furthermore, Mark's intercalation of the withering of the fig tree and the disruption in the temple (Mark 11:12-26) provides a secondary indication that these two events interpret each other.

[30] Cf. Mark 11:1-17.

[31] The account of the conquest of the Canaanite city known as Jebus is found in 2 Samuel 5. Quite clearly this account is written from the perspective of a time when the city is already known as 'the city of David' (7), and verse 9 indicates the way in which this name originated with David himself. Also of great significance is the reference to the cause of David's greatness: 'the LORD God of hosts was with him.' Thus the presence of God is associated with the city of David.

[32] Garland, *Reading Matthew*, 209, points out that the unit 21:1-11 is framed by two references to Jerusalem (1, 10), but, given the geographical necessity of reference to the city, these references do not seem greatly significant in literary or theological terms.

[33] Matthew is the only Synoptic Evangelist to include the citation of Zechariah 9:9. While this should certainly not be understood to indicate that the other Evangelists were unaware of the background to Jesus' action, it does highlight the particular dependence of Matthew on the prophetic literature of the OT, and on Zechariah in particular.

[34] The first four words of exhortation come from Is. 62:11, though they are reminiscent of similar language in Zech. 2:10 and at the very beginning of 9:9. On the significance of this, see comments below.

[35] So Davies and Allison, *Matthew*, 3:118; Keener, *Matthew*, 490. Wright, *Jesus and the Victory of God*, 490: 'This was not so much a matter of *teaching* as of *symbolic action*.

This view is far preferable to that which claims Matthew fabricated the account upon reflection on Zechariah 9:9, a position which, at the very least, fails to take seriously the multiple attestation of the event.[36] E. P. Sanders is much more historically sensitive in his verdict that,

> the entry was probably deliberately managed by Jesus to symbolize the coming kingdom and his own role in it. I account for the fact that Jesus was not executed until after the demonstration against the temple by proposing that it was an intentionally symbolic action, performed because Jesus regarded it to be true (he would be king, but a humble one) and for the sake of the disciples, but that it did not attract large public attention.[37]

While Jesus supplies no prophetic explanation of the action (such as accompany OT prophetic acts, as we have seen from the previously cited examples from the prophetic literature), the explanation is provided by the crowds that gather at the side of the road and shout out as Jesus proceeds along. Thus, in 21:9, Matthew presents Jesus as being 'the Son of David'[38] and 'the one who comes in the name of the Lord'. Both of these descriptions are of great theological significance.[39] They are both terms which reflect the hope of (at least some of) the Jewish people that 'David's son' would establish his rule,[40] and

---

> Jesus, as we have seen often enough, was as capable as any of his contemporaries of deliberately performing actions which had rich symbolic value. Within his own time and culture, his riding on a donkey over the Mount of Olives, across Kidron, and up to the Temple mount spoke more powerfully than words could have done of a royal claim.'

[36] So R. Bultmann, *The History of the Synoptic Tradition* (Oxford: Blackwell, 1968), 262. See the firm response by M. Hengel in 'Jesus, the Messiah of Israel' in *Studies in Early Christology* (Edinburgh: T&T Clark, 1995), 55: 'When Bultmann describes the second part of the narrative as "legendary or at least strongly influenced by legend" and grounds this judgement with the reasoning that "there can be no doubt about the [messianic] character of the animal", we may agree with the latter statement while doubting the former.' See also his several arguments against Bultmann's view.

[37] Sanders, *Jesus and Judaism*, 308.

[38] See also 15:22; 20:30; 21:15. Cf. *NIDNTT*, 3:648-53.

[39] See J. A. Sanders, 'A New Testament Hermeneutic Fabric: Psalm 118 in the Entrance Narrative,' in C. A. Evans and W. F. Stinespring (eds), *Early Jewish and Christian Exegesis: Studies in Memory of William Hugh Brownlee* (Atlanta: Scholars Press, 1987).

[40] 2 Sam. 7:12-16 is a fundamental text for proper understanding of this phrase. Sanders (*Judaism: Practice and Belief*, 295-97) claims that 'the expectation of a Messiah was not the rule' in second temple Judaism, but it does appear in PsSol 17. Theissen and Merz, *The Historical Jesus*, 537, concur to an extent, but are more circumspect than Sanders when they comment, 'The inner variety within Judaism shows that not all its hopes pointed in the direction of the Messiah. However, messianic hopes were alive among the people – probably more alive than appears from the sources.' See their helpful discussion on pages 531-67.

thus bring the Roman occupancy to an end.[41] Thus, on the lips of the crowd, these words may have had a significant political thrust.[42] They certainly imply royalty and thus authority.

It is significant that the words found on the lips of the crowds in Matthew 21:9 are exactly reproduced in 23:39 on the lips of Jesus.[43] They are a citation of Psalm 118:26.[44] While this fact may be regarded as one more example of a theme which runs through chapters 21-25 and thus indicates the literary coherence of the unit, it also suggests that, in the latter passage, Jesus sees a further enactment of the royal Psalm yet to come.

While we may well be suspicious of the expectations of the crowd, their words accurately capture the messianic significance of the event. This initial prophetic act is not an act of judgement in any obvious sense. The strongest motif is that of Jesus' humble kingship.[45] Yet attention to the original context of the words from Zechariah 9:9 quoted by Matthew reveals that 'Daughter Zion' can rejoice because 'the king' (humble as indeed he is) will overcome all who stand against her. While R. Smith claims that Jesus took up this passage for his entry into Jerusalem because 'the peaceful and universal reign of God was his goal,'[46] it is nonetheless clear from what follows in Matthew that such peace could not come without judgement on those who opposed Jesus as the embodiment of that reign. In fact, Matthew's citation of this text reinforces the implication of judgement as can be seen by a comparison between the MT/LXX and the text of Matthew. The text in its OT context reads (in the NRSV):

> Rejoice greatly, O daughter Zion! Shout aloud, O daughter Jerusalem! Lo, your king comes to you; triumphant and victorious is he, humble and riding on a donkey, on a colt, the foal of a donkey.

The first phenomenon that is noteworthy is that Matthew deletes Zechariah's exhortation to rejoice, replacing it with a command to declare (Εἴπατε τῇ θυγᾶ

---

[41] Keener, *Matthew*, 492.

[42] D. S. Russell, *The Method and Message of Jewish Apocalyptic* (London: SCM Press, 1964), 316-19.

[43] The former verse is preserved in the triple tradition, while the latter is Q material. Keener, *Matthew*, 494, correctly draws out the connection between 'the one who comes' in this verse and 'the one who comes' in 23:39.

[44] Psalm 118 is largely a psalm of individual thanksgiving. It may have been used on occasions when the Davidic king led the worship. See W. VanGemeren, 'Psalms' in F. Gaebelein (ed.), *The Expositor's Bible Commentary* (EBC 5; Grand Rapids: Zondervan, 1990), 729-36; L. C. Allen, *Psalms 101-150* (WBC 21; Waco: Word, 1983), 118-25.

[45] Strong as the emphasis on Jesus' humility is, it can only be secondary to the declaration of Jesus' status as king, which is the main focus of the Zechariah text.

[46] R. Smith, *Micah-Malachi* (WBC 32; Waco: Word, 1984), 257.

τρὶ Σιών),[47] suggesting that he regards this occasion, not as a celebration, but as a solemn visitation.

Furthermore, Zechariah's phrase (as per the NRSV) 'triumphant and victorious is he' is not found in Matthew, although both the MT and the LXX include two adjectival terms prior to the description 'humble'. The word rendered 'victorious' is נוֹשָׁע in the MT.[48] Petersen also translated the niphal participle 'victorious', but adds

> LXX translates with an active verb, i.e., "saving," which seems to be the required sense.[49]

Comparison of the LXX with Matthew yields the following results:

> LXX: χαῖρε σφόδρα θύγατερ Σιων κήρυσσε θύγατερ Ιερουσαλημ ἰδοὺ ὁ βασιλεύς σου ἔρχεταί σοι δίκαιος καὶ σώζων αὐτός πραῢς καὶ ἐπιβεβηκὼς ἐπὶ ὑποζύγιον καὶ πῶλον νέον

> Matt: Εἴπατε τῇ θυγατρὶ Σιών· Ἰδοὺ ὁ βασιλεύς σου ἔρχεταί σοι πραῢς καὶ ἐπιβεβηκὼς ἐπὶ ὄνον καὶ ἐπὶ πῶλον υἱὸν ὑποζυγίου.

Apart from obvious redactional activity such as the alteration of direct instruction to indirect instruction, and the famous 'doubling' of the beast,[50] Matthew appears to cite the LXX text *verbatim*, with the exception of the deletion of the phrase δίκαιος καὶ σώζων αὐτός. This suggests that Matthew has cited directly from LXX textual tradition, but has deliberately omitted a reference to salvific activity.[51]

There can be no mistaking the royal note that is sounded by both the action and the citation of Zechariah's prophecy.[52] This confirms our judgement that Matthew deliberately constructs an inclusion around chapters 21-25 by means of the royal motif, for the language of 'the king' is not used of Jesus in Mat-

---

[47] This phrase appears to be drawn from Isaiah 62:11.

[48] See *NIDOTTE*, 2:556-62.

[49] D. L. Petersen, *Zechariah 9-14 & Malachi*, 55. P. L. Redditt, *Haggai, Zechariah, Malachi* (NCBC; Grand Rapids: Eerdmans, 1995), 114, suggests the translation 'saved' for the niphal participle on contextual grounds.

[50] On this matter, see Keener, *Matthew*, 491-92. Also Garland, *Reading Matthew*, 210-11. In the face of some explanations of Matthew's text which appear to charge him with great naivity (for example, Beare, *Matthew*, 413), Keener (491) helpfully cautions that 'it is quite unlikely that Matthew would be *unfamiliar* with Hebrew parallelism.'

[51] See Garland, *Reading Matthew*, 210.

[52] Gundry, *Matthew*, 407, points to the work of Derrett who suggests that the claim Jesus makes on the animal is in fact an implicit claim to kingship. See Num 16:15 and 1 Sam 8:17.

thew elsewhere.[53] 'The king' does figure prominently in two Matthean parables, but the likelihood is that in such parabolic contexts, the king is normally understood to refer to God.[54] Of course, the concept of 'Messiah' also has a royal connotation, but again, the messianic theme in Matthew reaches a new level of intensity in chapters 21-25.

Although commentators agree that the king in Zechariah 9:9 is a human,[55] D. L. Petersen points out that comparison with similar prophetic passages indicates that the king is standing as the representative of Yahweh:

> Zephaniah 3:14-15 and Zech. 2:13 [10] address Daughter Zion in the imperative mood in much the same way that she is addressed in 9:9: Zephaniah: sing aloud, shout, rejoice, exult; Zechariah: sing, rejoice. And the reason is fundamentally the same in both cases. Zephaniah: 'the king of Israel, the Lord is in your midst'; Zechariah: 'I come and I dwell in the midst of you.' Yahweh's immediate presence provides the ultimate ground for the imperative rhetoric in these two prophetic texts, and Zephaniah especially makes it clear that the king is Yahweh, not a Davidide. By connotation through allusion, the author indicated that the arrival of this king should be celebrated in much the same way that Yahweh's presence as king deserves accolade. Moreover, the logic of the poems of Zechariah 9 suggests that the presence of the king depends on the prior presence of the deity in Jerusalem (Zech. 9:8).[56]

There is good reason, then, for suggesting that the quotation of Zechariah 9:9 amounts to Matthew's statement that Yahweh is (in some sense) entering his city. If this is the case, then this declaration will have a significant bearing on the interpretation of Jesus' words and actions in the following narrative.

The Clearing of the Temple (21:12-17)

The second prophetic act in Matthew 21 is the action commonly known as the 'cleansing' of the temple,[57] but so as not to prejudge the issue we have used the

---

[53] Keener, *Matthew*, 489, entitles the section of his commentary dealing with the entry to Jerusalem, 'Jerusalem's King Enters Her Gates'.

[54] So Marguerat, *Le Jugement*, 492. Marguerat notes that the unusual attribution of this title to 'the Son of Man' has led several commentators to the conclusion that the term is a redactional insertion, but argues that this view is unnecesary since Matthew maintains the proper subordination of the Son of Man to God by the use of the distinctive phrase 'my father' (34). The use of this phrase also removes all reasonable doubt that Jesus intends the Son of Man/king to be understood as a reference to himself.

[55] So, implicitly, Redditt, *Haggai, Zechariah, Malachi*, 114.

[56] Petersen, *Zechariah 9-14 & Malachi*, 57-58.

[57] So R. E. Brown, *The Death of the Messiah* (ABRL; New York: Doubleday, 1994), 1:455. See further Brown's useful discussion of this incident in pages 455-60. See also Wright, *Jesus and the Victory of God*, 413-28.

term 'clearing', though that should not be understood in an exhaustive sense. It is virtually certain that Jesus' action did not put an end to the business in the temple.[58] The temple was a massive building and Jesus' action would only have affected a small section of the commercial area.[59] This view is corroborated by the fact the Roman guards, stationed in the adjoining Antonia Fortress, did not immediately arrest Jesus in the temple.[60] If, then, Jesus did not put a stop to the trade in the temple, how are we to understand what he did? E. P. Sanders has claimed that the understanding of the activity of Jesus as a 'cleansing' of the temple has no substantial foundation. Instead, what Jesus did must be understood as a prediction or threat of the temple's destruction.[61] C. A. Evans has challenged this view, pointing to a significant body of OT, intertestamental and synoptic evidence which demonstrates that there was a critical attitude against the activities of much of the priesthood and that there was a contemporary expectation that the temple would be cleansed.[62] In this matter, it seems to us that D. C. Allison takes a wise line as he writes,

> Although current scholarship, following Sanders' statement of the problem, has tended to suppose that we should choose between two competing theories – either Jesus enacted a prophecy of destruction or he was unhappy with some aspect of the temple business – these two theories are scarcely at odds. Protest against abuses and symbolic expression of judgment could readily have gone together.[63]

Jesus' words in 21:13 are vital to understanding his actions. Quoting words from the prophets (Is. 56:7, and an allusion to Jer 7:11), he clearly challenges an ethical offence. He uses the strong term λῃστής which is used by Josephus[64] to refer to insurrectionists, militant bandits, so that Blomberg comments,

---

[58] So Davies and Allison, *Matthew*, 3:137, who refer to the comments of Origen to this effect in his commentary on John.

[59] Keener, *Matthew*, 498, comments, 'His act itself was undoubtedly more symbolic than efficacious. Jesus acted against only a small area in the crowded outer court which was 300 meters by 450 meters.' While Keener's assertion cannot be confirmed by the NT texts, it is a reasonable assumption. For descriptions of the temple, see *DJG*, 811-13.

[60] Witherington, *The Christology of Jesus*, 110.

[61] Sanders, *Jesus and Judaism*, 61-76. See also W. W. Watty, 'Jesus and the Temple – Cleansing or Cursing?' *ExpT* 93 (1981-82), 235-39.

[62] C. A. Evans, 'Jesus Action in the Temple: Cleansing or Portent of Destruction?' *CBQ* 51 (1989), 237-70.

[63] Allison, *Jesus of Nazareth*, 98.

[64] *Antiquities* 14:421. Cf. *NIDNTT* 3:377-79, *TDNT* IV:257-62.

Jesus may be accusing the leaders of having converted the temple into a "nationalistic stronghold".[65]

The reference to Jeremiah is illuminating when the wider context of the words alluded to is taken into account. The passage from 7:3 reads,

> 3 Thus says the LORD of hosts, the God of Israel: Amend your ways and your doings, and let me dwell with you in this place. 4 Do not trust in these deceptive words: "This is the temple of the LORD, the temple of the LORD, the temple of the LORD." 5 For if you truly amend your ways and your doings, if you truly act justly one with another, 6 if you do not oppress the alien, the orphan, and the widow, or shed innocent blood in this place, and if you do not go after other gods to your own hurt, 7 then I will dwell with you in this place, in the land that I gave of old to your ancestors forever and ever. 8 Here you are, trusting in deceptive words to no avail. 9 Will you steal, murder, commit adultery, swear falsely, make offerings to Baal, and go after other gods that you have not known, 10 and then come and stand before me in this house, which is called by my name, and say, "We are safe!" - only to go on doing all these abominations? 11 Has this house, which is called by my name, become a den of robbers in your sight? You know, I too am watching, says the LORD.

The allusion to Jeremiah 7 thus picks up the issues of compassion (vv. 5 and 6a, 9a) and religious faithfulness (6b, 9b) as equally deserving of condemnation. The issue of oppression cannot be separated from idolatry, and Jesus' use of this portion of the OT scriptures may be understood to recall the wider context of Jeremiah's prophecy and thus to condemn the injustice found in the Jerusalem temple. In fact, the context of Jeremiah suggests that undue confidence in the temple as a sign of the presence of Yahweh in the midst of his people will be followed by judgement which will give the lie to the claim 'we are safe'.

A further prophetic text which may be significant for understanding Jesus' action is Zechariah 14:21, which declares that 'a day is coming for Yahweh' (14:1, יוֹם־בָּא לַיהוה הִנֵּה) and that 'in that day' (14:4, 6, 8, 9, 13, 20, 21, בַּיּוֹם הַהוּא):

> there shall no longer be traders in the house of the LORD of hosts.

The Hebrew term כְּנַעֲנִי, which several translations (e.g., NASB, KJV) render as 'Canaanite', can equally well be translated 'trader' as the NRSV does.[66]

But there is more to this attack on the temple, and this is seen clearly in the

---

[65] Blomberg, *Matthew*, 315. So also Hagner, *Matthew 14-28*, 601. C. K. Barrett, 'The House of Prayer and the Den of Thieves' in E. E. Ellis and E. Grässer (eds), *Jesus und Paulus* (Göttingen: Vandenhoeck & Ruprecht, 1975), 13-20.

[66] See Job 40:30 [LXX 41:6 translates φοινίκων]; Isa 23:8; Zeph 1:11. *NIDOTTE* 2:669. See the comments in Wright, *Jesus and the Victory of God*, 491, n. 44 and, earlier, Meyer, *The Aims of Jesus*, 198.

account of the healing of the blind and the lame in verses 14-17, which immediately follows the account of the clearing of the temple. The common theme
that runs through this two-fold account is not simply the temple as location, but
the temple as the object of judgement.

In verses 12-13, the temple, or more precisely, those who operate the temple
system, is judged for fraudulent dealing (to some extent, at least). In verses 14-
17 the temple is judged for excluding those who are oppressed and for lacking
compassion. In other words (Borg's words), Jesus condemns the temple system
for operating the 'Politics of Holiness', and indeed for doing so hypocritically.
This has been recognised by D. E. Garland, whose comments on the temple
incident are particularly insightful,

> The blind and the lame, who were barred access to the sanctuary of God's
> presence (see Lev 21:18-19; 2 Sam 5:8 [LXX]; 11QTemple 45:13; *Mishna
> Hagiga* 1:1), come to Jesus and are healed. On the one hand, this healing is a
> fulfillment of Micah's prophesy that the lame and rejected will be gathered and
> restored (4:6-7). On the other hand, it is another token of the inadequacy of the
> temple. The temple and its purity system failed to make these people whole and
> only promoted social injustice by stigmatizing them and excluding them
> according to purity classifications. Jesus embraces all who are weak and burdened
> and renews them.[67]

Garland's comments are instructive for appreciating the nature of judgement in
Matthew's presentation of Jesus' proclamation. His words apply equally to the
passage alluded to by Jesus himself in Jeremiah 7. N. T. Wright makes the
very important observation that the two dramatic events of the entry into Jerusalem and the clearing of the temple correspond to two portions of an extremely
powerful prophecy in Zechariah. Wright comments,

> Zechariah 9 focuses on the king riding into Jerusalem on a donkey, as the agent of
> the return from exile and the renewal of the covenant; Zechariah 14, which
> celebrates the coming of YHWH and his kingdom, ends with the Temple being
> cleansed of traders. There should be no doubt that Jesus knew this whole passage,
> and that he saw it as centrally constitutive of his own vocation, at the level not just
> of ideas but of agendas.[68]

Wright's comments helpfully serve to further reinforce the position advo-
cated in this thesis that Jesus deliberately drew on the traditions of the OT (in
this case, the prophetic tradition) to give content and significance to his words
and actions of judgement. There is no good reason to restrict the creative use of

---

[67] Garland, *Reading Matthew*, 213.

[68] Wright, *Jesus and the Victory of God*, 599-600. Wright recognises in his footnote to
this paragraph that the same portion of Zechariah also influences Jesus' teaching in
Matthew 24:30, on which see more below. It is clear how significant the prophetic
literature was for Jesus' self-consciousness.

the prophetic writings to Matthew, as if Jesus were unable to recognise the resonances between his actions and the words of the prophet. Yet Jesus consistently went beyond the position of a prophet (i.e., one who bears witness to judgement, or who proclaims the judgement pronouncing words of another), taking on himself the role of the agent of judgement.

Clearly the latter portion of Zechariah's prophecy is of great significance for our appreciation of these first prophetic acts. It should then come as no surprise to find that this portion of the prophetic book is drawn upon in a number of other places in these five chapters. For example Zechariah 9:14 is alluded to in 24:27; Zechariah 12:10 in 24:30; Zechariah 14:4 is a possible background to 21:21; Zechariah 14:5 and 10 are echoed in 24:31 and 25:31; Zechariah 14:6 may lie behind 24:29; Zechariah 14:7 is significant with respect to 24:36. Other possible allusions to Zechariah include 4:6-9 (in 21:21) and Zechariah 4:7 (in 21:42). Although not cited by Matthew, John's reference in John 2:16 to Jesus citing Zechariah 14:21 is consistent with what we find in Matthew regarding the close association of this prophet with the temple incident(s).

The Withering of the Fig Tree (21:18-22)

The third prophetic act is the cursing of the fig tree (21:18-22).[69] That this incident strikes most modern readers as 'bizarre'[70] is undoubtedly due to the widespread lack of appreciation for the dramatic and startling characteristics of the *prophetic act*. One only has to read of the actions of Jeremiah or Ezekiel, as discussed above, to recognise that Jesus' reaction to the bare fig tree is much more than a fit of pique at being deprived of a snack. The widespread misreading of this passage as an act of rage or bitterness also reflects the tendency to ignore the relationship which Matthew sees between the various accounts he preserves for us.[71] For Matthew, this is not an isolated story which is included

---

[69] Davies and Allison, *Matthew*, 3:148: 'For the third time in three paragraphs Jesus the prophet performs a symbolic act.'

[70] So Garland, *Reading Matthew*, 213.

[71] While there might be some excuse for a reader of Matthew struggling to see the common theme in these accounts, there can be no excuse for those readers who have Mark available to them. Mark's intercalation of the turning of the tables in the temple and the withering of the fig tree leaves little doubt that both pericopae are, in his view, concerned with the same issue. On this pericope, see W. R. Telford, *The Barren Temple and the Withered Tree* (JSNTS 1; Sheffield: JSOT Press, 1980), and more recently Meier, *A Marginal Jew*, 2:884-96 (for a thorough treatment of the pericope, its possible sources and its historicity) and Brown, *Introduction*, 142-43 (for briefer comment). Telford (80) believes that Matthew's redaction of Mark's account has done away with the note of judgement so that the incident 'is treated as if it were a normal miracle story.' However, this judgement is premature as we shall indicate below. For now it is sufficient to point out, firstly, that Matthew retains the account of the overturning of the tables which points to a judgement theme in near proximity to the

simply to perplex his readers at Jesus' strange reaction. Instead, this 'prophetic act of power' is the third of a series of such prophetic acts, each of which contributes something vital to Matthew's portrait of Jesus the judge.[72]

N. T. Wright suggests that Jeremiah 8:11-13 is of particular importance in grasping the significance of Jesus' action.[73] The relevant verses read as follows:

> 11 They have treated the wound of my people carelessly, saying, "Peace, peace," when there is no peace. 12 They acted shamefully, they committed abomination; yet they were not at all ashamed, they did not know how to blush. Therefore they shall fall among those who fall; at the time when I punish them, they shall be overthrown, says the LORD. 13 *When I wanted to gather them, says the LORD, there are no grapes on the vine, nor figs on the fig tree; even the leaves are withered*, and what I gave them has passed away from them.

The significance of this passage, as Wright indicates, is that it comes in the context of the earlier citation of Jeremiah 7 found in Matthew 21:13. Jesus appears to be drawing on an entire prophetic narrative for the raw material of his entry to Jerusalem, and the implication of the action is that Israel is found barren when Yahweh comes to gather his fruit (in the person of Jesus).

In each of these prophetic acts we are clearly presented with Jesus as the one who brings judgement, but in the words of W. Trilling, Jesus

> does not merely lament like a prophet, he takes action. He does not call down judgement, he exercises it.[74]

What Trilling so concisely observes is what I believe Borg and many others have failed to observe, *viz.* although Jesus is *like* the prophets, he is not *just* like the prophets, but goes beyond what the prophets did, and indeed were, while still remaining in continuity with them. This insight makes a significant difference to what may be accepted as 'reasonable' behaviour for the prophetic Jesus. If Jesus is simply fulfilling the functions of the prophets who have come before him, then some of Jesus' words later in these chapters sound very unusual. However, if Jesus is declaring by these prophetic acts that he has authority not simply to declare the judgement of Yahweh but to exercise it, then this understanding of Jesus provides a proper context for interpreting Jesus' words concerning future judgement.

With the withering of the fig tree, the emphasis of Jesus' activities in Jerusa-

---

account of the withered tree and, secondly, that the withering of the fig tree would be a quite unique type of miracle in Matthew's account in that it is destructive and benefits no-one.

[72] T. W. Overholt, 'Seeing is Believing: The Social Setting of Prophetic Acts of Power' *JSOT* 23 (1982), 3-31.

[73] Wright, *Jesus and the Victory of God*, 421-22.

[74] W. Trilling, *The Gospel according to St. Matthew* (London: Burns and Oates, 1969), 2:140.

lem changes in Matthew's account. Not surprisingly, the Jewish authorities (specifically, 'the chief priests and the elders of the people', οἱ ἀρχιερεῖς καὶ οἱ πρεσβύτεροι τοῦ λαοῦ) challenge Jesus' authority to carry out these extraordinary activities. Jesus' responses are couched in the language forms of Jewish Wisdom literature, indicating that this man who stands in the line of the prophets also stands in the line of the sages.[75] These passages are dealt with elsewhere.[76] In this chapter, we will now turn our attention to chapter 23 of Matthew's gospel, where Jesus confronts the Jewish leaders in typical prophetic fashion.

Jesus the Judge as Prophetic Preacher against the Pharisees (23:1-36)

Chapter 23 of Matthew renews the emphasis on Jesus the prophet. This chapter contains some of the most vehement criticisms of the religious leaders (οἱ γραμματεῖς καὶ οἱ Φαρισαῖοι) in Palestine in the whole gospel tradition, and is unique to Matthew.[77] The passage is therefore of great importance to our thesis that Jesus' message of judgement was directed at his political/religious contemporaries as much as it was claimed for his future reign.[78] It is particularly interesting to note the frequency with which Jesus makes reference to the prophets (23:29, 30, 31, 34, 37). A strong case may be made that Jesus speaks of the leaders' opposition to the prophets as a veiled way of rebuking their opposition of his own prophetic ministry, and thus these references reinforce the argument that Jesus thought of himself in terms of a prophet and exercised a 'prophetic' ministry, even if such descriptions do not exhaust the nature of Jesus' ministry.

It has been claimed in recent times that the portrait of the Pharisees and other religious groups drawn by Matthew and the other Synoptists is a harsh caricature and in no way reflects the religion of grace that was Palestinian Judaism.[79] As the work of M. Borg is of such significance for the direction of this

---

[75] Of course, there are significant areas of continuity between the expressions of Wisdom literature and prophetic oracles as we shall see.

[76] See the discussion in chapter 6 below.

[77] Brown, *Introduction*, descibes this passage as 'an extraordinary Matthean construction' (197). Important studies of this portion of Matthew include D. E. Garland, *The Intention of Matthew 23* (NovTSup 52; Leiden: Brill, 1979); K. G. C. Newport, *The Sources and Sitz im Leben of Matthew 23* (JSNTS 117; Sheffield: Sheffield Academic Press, 1995).

[78] In spite of the significance of this passage for his argument, there is no sustained treatment of Matthew 23 in Borg, *Conflict*.

[79] See particularly E. P. Sanders, *Paul and Palestinian Judaism* (London: SCM Press, 1977), and *idem, Jesus and Judaism*. On the Pharisees, see the helpful discussions in *ABD*, 5:289-303; Wright, *New Testament and the People of God*, 181-203; Luz, *Matthäus 18-25*, 353-66. A recent and brief discussion can be found in W. R. Herzog,

thesis, it is important to note that challenges have been made against Borg's understanding of the social structure of Palestine, particularly with respect to his views on 'the quest for holiness'[80] or the 'Politics of Holiness'. D. A. Neale has severely criticised Borg's reconstruction of the attitude towards 'sinners' shown by those who followed the 'Politics of Holiness'.[81] Neale argues that the code of holiness followed by the Pharisees was supererogatory, that those who did not follow this self-imposed code were *not* regarded as sinful, and that, for these reasons, Borg's view that 'outcasts' (the lowest type of sinners) were treated like 'untouchables' in the Hindu caste system is wholly wrong.[82]

In response to Neale we may well say that Borg has perhaps overstated his case, particularly in his more popular volume. Witherington agrees with Sanders that the groups of *haberim* (which were probably not co-extensive with, but were rather sub-sets within, the Pharisees[83]) were 'small voluntary associations which accepted special rules for special reasons'.[84] But it may be that Neale has not treated the Pharisees' treatment of the 'sinners' with enough seriousness, perhaps because he regards the 'sinners' as a religious category which does not correspond to any observable social group.[85] Certainly Neale identifies a number of Rabbinical passages which, he claims, show that there was not the ostracism of the non-observant which Borg claims (though Pharisees were encouraged to avoid table fellowship with such people), but if the gospel accounts are to be allowed a fair hearing then we are faced with severe criticism of the Pharisees by Jesus on the grounds of their intricate observance of regulations to the disadvantage of others (particularly, but not exclusively, in Matthew 23), along with a constant refrain of complaint from the Pharisees that Jesus associated himself (even to the point of table fellowship) with 'sinners' (cf. Mark 2:16; Luke 19:7). Clearly something of the sort of 'Politics of Holiness' was in operation at some level.

The 'woes' of Matthew 23 certainly signify extreme displeasure with the Pharisees on the part of Jesus, and yet in verses 2-3a there may be a note of appreciation.[86] Whatever is the case regarding the interpretation of these verses, it is clear from the gospel narratives as a whole that Jesus did not regard the whole of Pharisaism as totally corrupt. He approved of the Pharisees' concern for the *Torah* but he saw that they were not all consistent in the way they responded to what they read. He also does not appear to acknowledge the notion

---

II, *Jesus, Justice and the Reign of God* (Louisville: Westminster/John Knox Press, 2000), 147-55.

[80] Borg, *Conflict*, 66-87.

[81] Borg, *New Vision*, 86-93.

[82] Neale, *None But The Sinners* 70-71, n. 6.

[83] Witherington, *Christology of Jesus*, 57-58.

[84] Witherington, *Christology of Jesus*, 58 citing Sanders, *Jesus and Judaism* 183.

[85] Neale, *None But The Sinners* 97. See the criticisms of Neale's work in J. B. Green's book review in *Themelios* 18.2 (1993), 28-29.

[86] See below for discussion of this issue.

of the dual *Torah*, written and oral, since he has particularly firm words of condemnation reserved for those who impose the oral traditions on others. These
comments indicate that Jesus' words in this chapter should not be understood as
a blanket condemnation of all Pharisees, but rather of those who fit the categories he goes on to describe.[87]

Although Hagner may be right to argue for a distinctive character for chapter
23 (rather than it being treated as a part of the following Olivet discourse), it is
no less the case that the solemn words of chapter 23 form the framework of
judgement in which the predictions and parables of chapters 24 and 25 make
sense. Thus, on the question of whether chapter 23 belongs with the discourse
of chapters 24 and 25, Garland notes the comment of Syreeni: 'Matthew could
have it both ways.'[88] This warns us against taking a dogmatic position, but it
does allow for an argument for unity being presented which may be evaluated
on the basis of the resultant reading of Matthew. Even if there are distinctive
characteristics to each of these sections, it is still possible to see an overall coherence. It can also be argued that there are strong grounds for seeing continuity between chapter 23 and chapters 21 and 22 which precede it. Having read of
Jesus' dramatic activities around the temple in chapter 21, and his not-so-veiled
criticisms of the religious authorities in chapter 22, it is no surprise to find him
speak in such strong terms in chapter 23. Garland writes in confirmation of this
position:

> This discourse is not simply polemic that impugns rivals who compete to make
> converts to their way of thinking and doing (23:15). The language is that of a
> prophet who chastises a stubborn people (see Jer 23:1; Ezek 34:1-6, 7, 9, 10; Isa
> 10:5-19). Jesus has identified himself as a prophet (13:57) and has been extolled
> as one by the crowds when he enters the city (21:11; see 21:46). He has acted like
> a prophet in the temple and linked his authority to that of John the Baptist,
> recognized as a prophet by everyone except the temple hierarchy (14:5-9; 21:23-
> 26). Now, Jesus pronounces doom-laden woes like a prophet (Isa 5:8-23; Hab 2:6-
> 20; Zech 11:17) and expresses the prophet's characteristic outrage at injustice
> (23:23) and greed (23:25; Mic 6:8; Zech 7:9-10). The ironic command to fill up
> the measure of your fathers' sins (23:32; Isa 8:9-10; Jer 7:21; Amos 4:4; Nah
> 3:14-15) and the concluding lament over the judgment that is to come on the city
> with its allusion to an apocalyptic visitation conforms to prophetic style. The
> accumulation of the sins of "this generation" (23:34) will result in the inevitable
> devastation of the temple (24:2).[89]

---

[87] Theissen and Merz, *The Historical Jesus*, 230, point out that there is an ambivalence in
the relationship between the Pharisees and Jesus, so that as well as fierce invective we
find Pharisees warning Jesus concerning Herod Antipas (Lk. 13:31) and Pharisees
inviting Jesus to meals (Lk. 7:36-50; 11:37; 14.1-24).

[88] Garland, *Reading Matthew*, 234, citing Syreeni, *The Making of the Sermon on the
Mount*, 94-96. Cf. also Blomberg's structure, *Matthew*, 338.

[89] Garland, *Reading Matthew*, 228.

Garland helpfully outlines the consistency in Matthew's presentation of Jesus in such a way that it is clear that chapter 23 acts as a balancing point in our narrative, expressing judgement on the Jewish authorities in unambiguous terms following the more allusive acts and parables of judgement in chapters 21-22 and setting the scene for the more predictive words of judgement in chapters 24-25.

The seven woes found in this chapter are distinctive in that they begin with an identical introductory formula (prefaced with Οὐαί - found in 23:13, 15, 16, 23, 25, 27, 29). While some might regard this similarity as a sign of Matthean redaction, it is entirely consistent with the teaching method of a person steeped in the prophetic literature of the OT. Hagner defines the 'woe saying' as 'a painful statement of displeasure involving an implied judgment'.[90] The Greek term Οὐαί is employed sixty-seven times in the LXX.[91] Behind the Greek word lie several Hebrew exclamations.[92] Hagner's observation is particularly important for the purposes of this thesis, *viz.* that Matthew is portraying Jesus as the agent of God's judgement. In pronouncing these woes, Jesus was not merely attacking verbally those who did not agree with him but he was formally pronouncing judgement on the Jewish leaders in a way that implies that he had the authority to do such a thing.[93]

The Structure of Matthew 23

The fundamental structure of Matthew 23 is quite plain. An introduction (23:1-12), in which Jesus is critical of the scribes and Pharisees is addressed to a broad group of his followers, including his disciples (τοῖς ὄχλοις καὶ τοῖς μαθηταῖς αὐτοῦ). This is followed by seven 'woes' directed at the Jewish leaders themselves (23:13-33). Finally, there is a poignant lament over Jerusalem

---

[90] Hagner, *Matthew 14-28*, 668.

[91] See for example Num. 21:29; 1 Sam. 4:7, 8, 21; 1 Ki. 12:24; Hos. 7:13; 9:12; Amos 5:16, 18; 6:1; Mic. 7:4; Nah. 3:17; Hab. 2:6, 12, 19; Zeph. 2:5; 3:18; Isa. 1:4, 24; 3:9, 11; 5:8, 11, 18, 20, 21, 22; 10:1, 5; 17:12; 18:1; 24:16; 28:1; 29:1, 15; 30:1; 31:1; 33:1; Jer. 4:13; 6:4; 10:19; 13:27; 22:18; 26:19; 27:27; 28:2; 31:1; Lam. 5:16; Ezek. 2:10; 7:26; 13:3, 18. It is clear that the exclamation is found predominantly in prophetic works, particularly Isaiah and Jeremiah. The form is also found occasionally in the Wisdom tradition (Prov. 23:29; Eccl. 4:10; 10:16; Sir. 2:12-14; 41:8).

[92] Particularly אוֹי, (defined by BDB as 'an impassioned expression of grief and despair: usually with dative. With the 2nd. or 3rd. ps. often implying a denunciation. With a voc. (or implicit accus.). Used as a subst.' [pg 17]). See Num. 21:29; 24:23; 31:8; Josh. 13:21; 1 Sam. 4:7, 8; Prov. 23:29; Is. 3:9, 11; 6:5; 24:16; Jer. 4:13, 31; 6:4; 10:19; 13:27; 15:10; 45:3; 48:46; Lam. 5:16; Ezek. 16:23; 24:6, 9; Hos. 7:13; 9:12) and the more general הוֹי and the related form הֹה meaning 'Alas!'

[93] Wright, *New Testament and the People of God*, 387, sees in the woes on the Pharisees a contrast with the blessings of chapter 5, and together a parallel with the list of covenant blessings and curses in Deut. 27-30.

(23:34-9), which is addressed to the city as a whole.[94]

Introduction to the Prophetic Woes of Matthew 23

In the first words of his address to the crowds and his disciples (verse 1), Jesus appears to employ deep irony as he apparently places them on a place of honour (verse 2)[95] and calls those who hear him to do whatever the scribes and Pharisees tell them to do (verse 3). It could be that Jesus is speaking plainly and encouraging obedience to the teaching of these leaders so far as it is in harmony with the Scriptures,[96] but it would be entirely in keeping with what we know of Jesus as a teacher skilled in using *meshalim*[97] if these words were to be read in almost exactly the opposite sense to their literal meaning.[98]

The final words of 23:3 almost demand the ironic reading of the earlier words. In drawing the contrast between what is said and what is done, Jesus identifies the Jewish leaders as 'hypocrites'. Davies and Allison comment astutely,

> To label one's opponents hypocrites or charlatans was standard fare for ancient polemics, Jewish and Graeco-Roman. It goes without saying that the charge was always credible, for hypocrisy belongs to the human condition, and so can always be found in the enemy camp.[99]

While they have correctly analysed the nature of fallen humanity, Davies and Allison tend towards indicating that the words of Jesus are simply a matter of convention, a touch of bravado. However, in the context of the whole of chapters 21-25, it is clear that Jesus is not simply following a path of conventional name-calling. Rather he is bringing about something very solemn indeed, and the words of chapter 23 must be read in the light of both what precedes and what follows. The 'woe' on the temple has already been dramatically enacted (21:1-22). The Jewish authorities (specifically, the chief priests and the elders of the people) have been exposed as hypocrites (21:23-27). This leads to the

---

[94] See Davies and Allison, *Matthew*, 257-58, particularly n. 2 which outlines many of the various competing proposals. Hagner, *Matthew 14-28*, 654, sub-divides the last section into two portions: a prophecy (34-36) and a lament (37-39), while Garland, *Reading Matthew*, 229, includes verses 34-36 with the central section addressed to the scribes and Pharisees. All are united in recognising the pivotal significance of the woe oracles.

[95] The reference to the 'seat of Moses' is an allusion to the claim of the Pharisees to be the guardians and interpreters of the Mosaic *torah*. Cf. *mAboth* 1:1.

[96] So Gundry, *Matthew*, 454-55.

[97] See chapter 5.

[98] So Carson, *Matthew*, 473-74; France, *Matthew*, 324; Davies and Allison, *Matthew*, 3:270.

[99] Davies and Allison, *Matthew*, 1:271.

conclusion that the 'woe' in Jesus' words is ominous indeed.

There are some striking similarities between the polemical descriptions of the Jewish leaders in Matthew 23, and the comments on piety in chapter 6, which indirectly address the religious practices of the 'hypocrites' (a term which may include both recognised 'leaders' in the Jewish community and those Jewish people who sought public recognition for their piety).[100] Thus, as we come to the woes against the Jewish leaders themselves, the hearers (and Matthew's readers) already have an appreciation of what practices and omissions lie at the heart of Jesus' critical remarks.

As we consider these woes, albeit briefly, it will become clear that Jesus is bringing prophetic judgement on his contemporaries, not simply on account of the lack in their relationship with their God (though that is without doubt a significant problem, which is made all the clearer by comparison of chapter 23 with chapter 6), but also on account of the way in which their actions have resulted in exclusion and oppression of others. In Borg's terms, they are being judged for exercising the 'Politics of Holiness' rather than the 'Politics of Compassion'.[101]

THE PROPHETIC WOES

First Woe (23:13-14)

The conventional prophetic woe formula is addressed to the scribes and Pharisees as hypocrites. The validity of that designation has already been established in the previous section of the chapter (23:1-12). The main thrust of this condemnation is not that the scribes and Pharisees have failed to enter the kingdom of heaven. That is certainly the case, but it remains their own responsibility as they have consistently rejected Jesus' proclamation of that dynamic reign.[102] What is particularly deserving of judgement, however, is that they have excluded others who wish to be part of God's reign from being so.[103] This is stated in the initial woe and reinforced again in the elaboration of it. Hagner is right to point out that the emphasis of the noun 'hypocrite' is on the deception

---

[100] The term is used in 6:2, 5 and 16. Also in 23:13, 15, 23, 25, 27, 29. It is also found in 21-25 in 22:18 and 24:51.

[101] Borg, *New Vision*, 157-59.

[102] *Cf.* 21:28-32.

[103] The view that this is a reference to hindrance of the proclamation of the gospel by Christian missionaries (so Davies and Allison, *Matthew*, 3:286) can only be supported by reading a meaning into Jesus' words which would have been incomprehensible to the addressees of these words in the setting of the narrative. While we might grant the continuing validity of the principle of Jesus' words ('do nothing to jeopardise the salvation of others') it seems methodologically dubious to give primary significance to any meaning that would not make sense in the context of the narrative.

of others, not self-deception.[104] Thus the title of Garland's chapter is entirely appropriate: 'False Teachers Lead Others to Ruin'.[105] There is no doubt that Jesus' powerful words are partly motivated by a concern for those who are excluded from the benefits of God's rule by the exclusivistic actions of the Jewish leaders.

Second Woe (23:15)
This brief rebuke challenges the Jewish leaders for producing converts, each one of whom is twice as much a 'son of hell' as are the leaders presently addressed.[106] This shocking language may be explained partly by the conventions of the day, but however we read it, there can be little doubt that Jesus is condemning the Jewish leaders as belonging to *Gehenna*. C. Milikowsky has discussed this term in a recent article.[107] He notes that Matthew uses the term seven times in his gospel, two of which occurrences are found in chapter 23, and claims that Matthew uses this term to refer to the final destination of the wicked after the general resurrection and the great Day of Judgement.[108] The reader cannot fail to notice the startling words with which Jesus addresses the Jewish leaders, but he or she might be misled by the conventions of the modern day to think that Jesus is simply throwing invective at those he opposed. However, this interpretation of Jesus' words does not do justice to their solemnity. It is important to recognise that Jesus does not simply use abusive language of these Jewish people, but rather pronounces their destiny in the context of a solemn vow. Thus Jesus demonstrates his authority as judge in the present age. This judgement will be confirmed in the last great act of judgement in which 'the sons of Gehenna' will be separated from the 'sons of God'.[109]

It could also be argued that Jesus is so critical of the Jewish authorities because of what they do to their proselytes. The implication of Jesus' words is that the final character of the proselyte is the responsibility in large measure of

---

[104] Hagner, *Matthew 14-28*, 668. *Cf.* the definition of ὑποκριτής offered by Louw-Nida (s.v.): ὑποκριτής οῦ *m*: (derivative of ὑποκρίνομαι 'to pretend,' 88.227) one who pretends to be other than he really is - 'hypocrite, pretender, one who acts hypocritically.' ὅταν δὲ νηστεύητε μὴ γίνεσθε ὡς οἱ ὑποκριταὶ σκυθρωποί 'when you fast, do not put on a sad face like the hypocrites' Mt 6.16. See also R. H. Gundry, 'Appendix: A Dialogue with Dan O. Via, Jr., on Hypocrisy in Matthew' in Gundry, *Matthew*, 641-47.

[105] Garland, *Reading Matthew*, 227.

[106] It is not the purpose of these words to delineate the extent of Jewish missionary activity in and around the first century AD. The words rather indicate that such conversion as does take place leaves the convert in a worse state than the first. See Davies and Allison, *Matthew*, 287-88.

[107] C. Milikowsky, 'Which Gehenna? Retribution and Eschatology in the Synoptic Gospels and in Early Jewish Texts' *NTS* 34 (1988), 238-49.

[108] Milikowski, 'Which Gehenna?', 244.

[109] Compare the use of 'son of...' language in 1QM.

those who make him a proselyte.

Third Woe (23:16-22)
This third woe focuses on the matter of holiness. Those who are condemned are described as 'blind guides'. That is, they are those who have been entrusted with the task of leading the people of God, but who have in fact led them astray. In particular, Jesus criticises the manner in which some objects within the temple are used as grounds for non-compliance with oath-taking. B. Chilton comments,

> Throughout [Matthew], the essential stance of Mt. 23.16-22, which portrays the Temple as the source of sanctification, rather than as an object of sacrificial activity, is clearly maintained. Jesus is consistently portrayed in the Synoptic Gospels as construing purity in terms of what the worshiper willingly does in respect of God's presence in the Temple, rather than as characteristic of or inherent within objects.[110]

It is this latter point that is surely particularly significant in this pericope. The pronouncement in verse 20 regarding the altar is heightened by the pronouncement in verse 21 which points out that it is the dwelling place of God, which in turn is overshadowed by the vision of the heavens as the place of God's throne.

Fourth Woe (23:23-24)
Jesus' fourth woe in this series finds a parallel in Luke 11:42, and may therefore be designated Q material. It is in this fourth woe that the 'Politics of Holiness' receives its most telling condemnation. Holiness is understood in terms of carrying out the obligations imposed by the *Torah* (as the activity of tithing crops undoubtedly was. See Lev 27:30).[111] However, Jesus proclaims fierce condemnation on the Jewish leaders, not because of their failure to fulfil elements of the *Torah* (that is explicitly stated),[112] but because they had their priorities entirely out of keeping with Jesus' priorities, which he declares to be 'the weightier matters of the law' (ἀφήκατε τὰ βαρύτερα τοῦ νόμου, τὴν κρίσιν καὶ τὸ ἔλεος καὶ τὴν πίστιν). This raises an important question: who is the arbiter of what are the 'weightier matters of the law'? Certainly there are OT precedents set. Particularly relevant are Micah 6:8 and Zechariah 7:9-10. Jesus appears to claim the right to declare what portions of the law are of greatest

---

[110] '[ὡς] φραγέλλιον ἐκ σχοινίων (John 2:15)' in W. Horbury (ed.), *Templum Amicitiae* (JSNTS 48; Sheffield: JSOT Press, 1991), 343.

[111] Hagner points out that the OT laws had proper crops in view, and that *m.Seb.* 9:1 actually exempts certain garden herbs from tithing (*Matthew 14-28*, 670).

[112] Hagner correctly notes that, even in the light of the literature Jesus is willing to accept their scrupulous behaviour, *provided* that they do not neglect other important aspects of the Torah, (*Matthew 14-28*, 670).

consequence in the eyes of the God of Israel.

Fifth Woe (23:25-26)

Jesus' words hit hard at matters of purity. Though the primary significance of his words is probably metaphorical,[113] Keener points out that the Mishnah does contain discussions 'which distinguish between inner and outer parts of vessels with respect to cleanness.'[114] These words suggest that the concern for purity which Borg describes in terms of the 'Politics of Holiness' was indeed a significant driving force in the life of the Pharisees.

Sixth Woe (23:27-28)

Davies and Allison are correct to point out the strong verbal continuities between this woe and the previous one, thus indicating that the subject matter is the same.[115] This prophetic denunciation bears a similarity to Luke 11:44. Both passages refer to the same custom, but appear to use it in somewhat different ways.[116] The reference is to the practice of identifying burial places with white substances so as to avoid contamination and thus uncleanness through unintentional contact with a grave.[117] In the context of the 'Politics of Holiness', this is a startling condemnation which ascribes the most pervasive impurity, unholiness, imaginable to those who considered themselves to be most holy. Borg believes Matthew to misrepresent the purpose of the act of whitewashing the graves:

> The purpose is to warn people away from the graves, not to make the tombs or graves beautiful.[118]

Borg regards Matthew's statement as an indication of his failure to appreciate the significance of the Jewish practice. However, this judgement appears unlikely in view of the fact that Matthew's gospel is clearly written from within the Jewish community, and Matthew may well have been familiar with pre-AD 70 Pharisaic traditions, even if he wrote post-AD 70. It seems as if Jesus is

---

[113] Keener, *Matthew*, 552; Davies and Allison, *Matthew*, 3:296.

[114] Keener, *Matthew*, 55. Keener cites *m.Kelim* 25:1-9; *Para* 12:8; *Tohar* 8:7.

[115] Davies and Allison, *Matthew*, 3:299-300.

[116] So Borg, *Conflict*, 128.

[117] *m.Shek.* 1:1; *bKat.* 1a, 5a. *Cf.* Num. 19:16. See Str-B 1:936-37 on the practice of whitewashing graves before passover. *Cf.* also Ezek. 13:10-12 (though not in connection with the use of whitewash on *graves*): '10 Because, in truth, because they have misled my people, saying, "Peace," when there is no peace; and because, when the people build a wall, these prophets smear whitewash on it. 11 Say to those who smear whitewash on it that it shall fall. There will be a deluge of rain, great hailstones will fall, and a stormy wind will break out. 12 When the wall falls, will it not be said to you, "Where is the whitewash you smeared on it?"'

[118] *Conflict*, 128.

making reference to an incidental effect of the whitewash used to betray the location of tombs, but an effect that would be perfectly comprehensible.[119]

Seventh Woe (23:29-32)
The final woe is a striking demonstration of Jesus' authority as judge. Condemning the teachers of the law and the Pharisees for their violent history, he urges them to realise their heritage of brutality! Yet, adopting the ironical stance of an ancient Israelite prophet, Jesus now calls on them to go deeper into sin and thus bring upon themselves the ensuing judgement: 'Fill up, then, the measure of your ancestors.'[120] Blomberg correctly points out the strong connection between these words and the parables of the wicked tenants and the wedding banquet (21:33-22:14).

Prophetic Conclusion (23:33-36)
The stream of woes reaches its culmination in this final denunciation. The question Jesus places before the Jews (πῶς φύγητε ἀπὸ τῆς κρίσεως τῆς γεέννης;) implies that there is no way of escape. The reference to Gehenna picks up the previous reference in 23:15.

Firstly, we notice that Jesus concludes his prophetic condemnation of the Jewish authorities with a reference to the prophetic figures that he will send after him. This remark has several interesting implications. The first is that Jesus, once again, classes himself as a prophet. The second is that Jesus appears to give tacit acknowledgement that his own prophetic ministry will shortly be brought to an end. The reference to the blood shed in past times seems to suggest that blood will be spilt in the days to come. This is confirmed in Jesus' lament over Jerusalem where he speaks of the killing of prophets and the stoning of those sent. The third implication is that Jesus ascribes to himself the authority to send prophets, a task which, of course, was normally the prerogative of Yahweh.[121] It is the brutal treatment of these sent ones (prophetically foretold) which is the final straw for Jesus.[122] This may well be seen in terms of assault on the one sent being equivalent to assault on the one who sends.

Secondly, Jesus' words in verse 36 are important for understanding both chapter 23 and the chapters that follow. Jesus says,

ἀμὴν λέγω ὑμῖν, ἥξει ταῦτα πάντα ἐπὶ τὴν γενεὰν ταύτην

which clearly bears considerable similarity to 24:34 which reads,

---

[119] So Keener, *Matthew*, 553, especially n. 58.
[120] 23:32. *Cf.* 1 Kgs. 18:27; Is. 6:9; 8:9-10; 29:9; Jer. 7:21; 23:28; 44:25-26; Ezek. 3:27; Amos 4:4-5. See in the NT, Rev. 22:11.
[121] See, e.g., Mal. 4:5 'Lo, I will send you the prophet Elijah before the great and terrible day of the LORD comes.' So Keener, *Matthew*, 555.
[122] Garland, *Reading Matthew*, 232; France, *Matthew*, 330.

ἀμὴν λέγω ὑμῖν ὅτι οὐ μὴ παρέλθῃ ἡ γενεὰ αὕτη ἕως ἂν πάντα ταῦτα γένηται

There are clear parallels between the wording of these two verses, and they can therefore be used, I submit, to interpret each other.

The first comment to make is in respect of 23:36 and its function as the climax of the prophetic woes against the Jewish leaders. The impact of Jesus' words is that what has gone before is not mere rhetoric which has no substance. Jesus has pronounced his judgement on the Jewish authorities, particularly for the way in which they have oppressed and destroyed others in the name of holiness, and now Jesus makes it quite plain that they will not be left unaccountable for such actions. Since Jesus is speaking to particular people, it would seem to be plain that the phrase τὴν γενεὰν ταύτην has reference to those to whom Jesus spoke and therefore can only be interpreted as a natural life span.

The implication of this for 24:34 must be that only a natural lifespan is a suitable interpretation of the same phrase in that context. But a further implication is that just as the words of 23:36 are clearly a reference to judgement on the Jewish leaders and their religious system, with not the slightest hint of a *Parousia* or other supernatural event, so 24:34 should be understood to refer to a similar situation.[123]

We regard 23:37-39 as a Wisdom saying and deal with that pericope elsewhere.[124]

Jesus the Judge as Prophetic Predictor (24:1-25:46)

In interpreting these chapters of Matthew's gospel, it is important to try to see the structure which Matthew has given to his account. Clearly this is ruled out as impossible if the discourse is either a Jewish apocalypse, and thus not a product of Matthew's redactional activity, or a disorganised collection of isolated sayings, in which case the search for order that never existed would be a vain exercise. The first of these theories has been admirably dealt with by Beasley-Murray,[125] who argues convincingly that the 'little apocalypse' theory is untenable, while the second is surely hard to accept given the clear and orderly structure which Matthew gives to his overall work.[126]

An issue that has come to particular prominence in recent years, which has a significant bearing on the interpretation of Matthew 24-25, is the interpretation of 'apocalyptic language'. In particular, commentators tend to focus on the texts which relate to the 'coming Son of Man', and those which contain lan-

---

[123] France, *Matthew*, 331.

[124] See the discussion in chapter 6.

[125] See on the 'Little Apocalypse' theory, Beasley-Murray, *Jesus and the Last Days*.

[126] If the suggestion that Matthew models his work on the five books of the Pentateuch contains any valid insight, then surely we must allow for more editorial care than many do in respect of the eschatological discourse.

guage of 'cosmic catastrophe'. It is important that we take some time at this
point to discuss this matter because our interpretative methodology will undoubtedly have a significant impact on our exegesis.

The Interpretation of Apocalyptic Language

In attempting to interpret Matthew's gospel, there can be no avoiding the essential hermeneutical issue of the interpretation of 'apocalyptic' language. To illustrate this, we may briefly note the positions of two contemporary scholars. On
one hand, Marcus Borg refers to the 'end-of-the-world Jesus' who was ob-
sessed with the cataclysmic conclusion of this present world order. He rejects
this conception of Jesus, tracing it to the work of Weiss and Schweitzer who
claimed that Jewish apocalyptic literature was crucial in the formation of Jesus'
future expectations. In complete contrast to Borg's position is that of R. H.
Hiers who argues that Jesus did expect an imminent end of the world. Hiers
criticises many scholars for neglecting the Jewish apocalyptic material in favour of the OT. The dramatic variation between the images of Jesus which are
offered by these two scholars is all the more startling when it is recognised that
both are in agreement regarding the need for careful treatment of apocalyptic
language and imagery as essential to a proper understanding of Jesus' views,
and it is a striking indication that we must give careful consideration to the issue of apocalyptic literature. We would, however, be quick to add that the two
extreme positions noted do not necessarily exhaust the possibilities.

The Definition of 'Apocalyptic'

Here, as everywhere in scholarship, precise definition is vital. Unfortunately,
we are faced with a discussion in which participants frequently employ two of
the most 'slippery' theological terms currently in use - 'apocalyptic' and 'eschatology'. These terms have sometimes been used as if they were interchange-
able, and frequently as if the very use of the word ushered the reader or hearer
into a state of total comprehension. Sadly, this is very far from being the case.
It is clearly of great importance to ascertain what the various authors mean by
the term 'apocalyptic', and then whether their various understandings of the
term are legitimate. Also of key importance is how we are to interpret the language which may be termed 'apocalyptic'.

The term 'apocalyptic' is derived from the Greek word ἀποκάλυψις, which is
found 18 times in the NT,[127] but in Revelation 1:1 the noun is uniquely employed as an apparent designation for the document that follows.[128] This usage

---

[127] *NIDNTT*, 3:310-16
[128] See especially the introductory section on 'Genre' in G. K. Beale, *The Book of
Revelation* (NIGTC; Grand Rapids: Eerdmans, 1999), 37-43. Also Aune, *Revelation
1-5* (WBC 52A; Dallas: Word, 1997), lxxvii. J. J. Collins, *The Apocalyptic*

led to the use of the term to describe other documents with characteristics judged by scholars to be similar to those found in the canonical document.[129] Thus the fundamental significance of the term is as a description of a literary genre, and it is this issue that has been the subject of the most intensive scholarly activity.

Intensive discussion of the genre of 'apocalyptic literature' issued in a definition of the genre which was published in the journal *Semeia*, and which has been (almost) definitive ever since. Though often reproduced, it is convenient to have it before us at this point. An apocalypse is

> A genre of revelatory literature with a narrative framework, in which a revelation is mediated by an otherworldly being to a human recipient, disclosing a transcendent reality which is both temporal, insofar as it envisages eschatological salvation, and spacial insofar as it involves another supernatural world.[130]

While the value of this statement has been widely recognised, it should be noted that it does not resolve all issues relating to the genre of a particular document. Even in the case of the canonical document which gives the genre its name, Beale can accurately comment,

> Commentators now generally acknowledge that John has utilized the three genres of apocalyptic, prophecy and epistle in composing the book.[131]

In fact the evidence for these three genres is so transparent that there can be little room for doubt that the document includes material of various genres.[132] This suggests that the expectation of identifying a distinct genre or a distinct style of language is rather unrealistic. What is more to be expected is some level of synthesis of a variety of influences. Quite clearly, the gospel of Matthew as a whole does not demonstrate the characteristics enumerated in the *Semeia* definition, and so cannot be described as an apocalypse. It is a matter of debate whether the eschatological discourse (found in somewhat different forms in each of the synoptic gospels) is best described as an apocalypse within a document of a different genre, but I favour the view that there are no exam-

---

Imagination (Grand Rapids: Eerdmans, 2nd edn 1998), 3, comments with reference to the occurrence in Revelation 1:1 that 'even there it is not clear whether the word denotes a special class of literature or is used more generally for revelation.'

[129] Kreitzer 'Apocalyptic, Apocalypticism', *DLNT*, 56.

[130] J. J. Collins (ed.), *Apocalypse: The Morphology of a Genre* (Semeia 14; Missoula MT: Scholars Press, 1979), cited in Collins, *Apocalyptic Imagination*, 5.

[131] Beale, *Revelation*, 37.

[132] Apocalyptic: the term ἀποκάλυψις is used in 1:1. Prophecy: the phrase τοὺς λόγους τῆς προφητείας are used in 1:3. Epistle: the epistolary prescript is found in 1:4 with an extended blessing, and the letters of chapters 2 and 3 appear to have been intended to circulate round the various churches.

ples of the apocalypse genre in Matthew's work.[133]

However, Collins points out that other definitions of 'apocalyptic' have been advanced besides that of literary genre. Of particular significance is the analysis of 'apocalyptic' as a world-view adopted by particular communities. Collins summarises Koch's[134] proposal of eight distinctive characteristics with may be used to identify an 'apocalyptic' community: (1) urgent expectation of the end of earthly conditions in the immediate future; (2) the end as a cosmic catastrophe; (3) periodization and determinism; (4) activity of angels and demons; (5) new salvation, paradisal in character; (6) manifestation of the kingdom of God; (7) a mediator with royal functions; (8) the catchword 'glory'.[135] D. C. Sim also identifies a distinctive apocalyptic world-view using similar categories,[136] and finds this world-view represented in the gospel of Matthew.[137] However, both Collins and Sim issue cautions to the effect that a given 'apocalyptic' movement may not exhibit each of these characteristics, while other characteristics, such as 'mysticism', may be found.[138] In addition to this *caveat*, it is important not to find evidence of these characteristics too readily. For example, the matter of an imminent end in the form of a cosmic catastrophe is the focus of intense debate relating to whether the language of cosmic catastrophe, which is undeniably found in numerous Jewish documents including those found in both the OT and the NT, is intended to be read literally or metaphorically. In the case of Matthew's gospel, to claim that the presence of imminent end-expectation points to an apocalyptic world-view is to pre-judge a contentious issue.

A third use of the term 'apocalyptic' is introduced as Collins takes up the issue of 'apocalyptic language'. He criticises several previous scholars including R. H. Charles, H. H. Rowley and D. S. Russell for demanding a consistency of the apocalyptic writings which, says Collins, simply is not to be found. In particular, Collins believes that these scholars failed to read apocalyptic language on its own terms. He says that Charles, Rowley and Russell,

---

[133] See especially Beasley-Murray, *Jesus and the Last Days*. One of the clearest methods of establishing this view is to carry out even cursory comparison with the canonical book of Revelation which demonstrates the radically different character of these two works.

[134] K. Koch, *The Rediscovery of Apocalyptic* (London: SCM Press), 28-33.

[135] Collins, *Apocalyptic Imagination*, 12.

[136] Sim, *Apocalyptic Eschatology*, 34-53. Sim's categories are (1) dualism; (2) determinism; (3) eschatological woes; (4) arrival of a saviour figure; (5) the judgement; (6) the fate of the wicked; (7) the fate of the righteous; (8) the imminence of the end.

[137] Sim, *Apocalyptic Eschatology*, 75-177.

[138] Collins, *Apocalyptic Imagination*, 12-14. Compare Sim, *Apocalyptic Eschatology*, 34: 'An apocalyptic-eschatological perspective, therefore, consists of a substantial cluster of these elements and need not necessarily contain them all.'

all sought the sources of apocalyptic language primarily in Old Testament prophecy. While prophecy may indeed be the single most important source on which the apocalyptists drew, the tendency to assimilate apocalyptic literature to the more familiar world of the prophets risks losing sight of its stranger mythological and cosmological components.[139]

This is clearly an issue which Collins believes lies at the heart of much misunderstanding of apocalyptic language. He writes again, this time more generally,

> Biblical scholarship in general has suffered from a preoccupation with the referential aspects of language and with the factual information that can be extracted from a text. Such an attitude is especially detrimental to the study of poetic and mythological material, which is expressive language, articulating feelings and attitudes, rather than describing reality in an objective way. The apocalyptic literature provides a rather clear example of language that is expressive rather than referential, symbolic rather than factual.[140]

Collins' comments above seem to me to alert the reader of 'apocalyptic' literature to the distinctive characteristics of the dramatic language he or she will encounter and aid sensitivity to the distinctives of the genre. At this juncture, Collins refers the reader to the work of G. B. Caird for discussion of this use of language, and so it is appropriate that we turn to a discussion of his contribution now.

The Interpretation of 'Apocalyptic' Language: Representative Positions

The matter of definition of 'apocalyptic' language has recently been addressed by Caird in his *New Testament Theology*.[141] In this work Caird raises the vital question of eschatology and notes that though the classical definition of the term is, 'The department of theological science concerned with the four last things, death, judgement, heaven and hell',[142] this definition has been almost completely ousted in the twentieth century by a second sense, introduced by Weiss and Schweitzer, that of the biblical teaching 'about the destiny of the world and the working out of God's purposes in and through his holy people'. Caird identifies the first sense with the term 'individual eschatology' and the second with the term 'historical eschatology'. He believes that the use of one word to describe two very different forms of future hope has led to great confusion. He writes,

---

[139] Collins, *Apocalyptic Imagination*, 15.

[140] Collins, *Apocalyptic Imagination*, 17.

[141] G. B. Caird, *New Testament Theology*, (Completed and edited by L. D. Hurst; Oxford: Clarendon Press, 1994). This section of the book draws on the previously published, and more famous, book, *The Language and Imagery of the Bible* (London: Duckworth, 1980).

[142] Oxford English Dictionary (1891 and 1933).

its use has almost inevitably led to the quite baseless assumption that the finality which attaches to death, judgement, heaven and hell must be characteristic also of national eschatology, and therefore to an intolerable kind of literalism in the interpretation of the imagery used by prophet and apocalypticist to describe the Day of the Lord.

The situation is particularly complicated in the New Testament due to a developed belief in the afterlife being common to Jews and Christians.

It is therefore not always easy to tell whether we are dealing with national or individual eschatology, and, as the Church moved more and more away from its original Palestinian setting into the Gentile world, there must have been a tendency to reinterpret the national in terms of the individual.[143]

This, however, is a later development. Caird claims that, 'The historic is almost the only kind of eschatology we find in the Old Testament - hardly surprising when it is remembered that almost all the books of the Old Testament were already written before the Jews achieved a belief in an afterlife.'[144] Caird notes the tendency, when using the term 'eschatology', to think in terms of an *eschaton*, a final day defined as 'that beyond which nothing can conceivably happen.' While he agrees that such a day awaits both the individual and the world, he adds, 'But at least 90 per cent of what we have come to call 'eschatology' in the Bible has nothing to do with an *eschaton* in this strict sense; it is rather the use of eschatological language to describe something quite different.'[145] This view, however, is not accepted by scholarship in general and it is necessary to look at an example of interpretation which stands against Caird's view before we look at how Caird works out his own approach.

Representative of the typical twentieth century interpretation of 'apocalyptic' is the work of R. H. Hiers, whom we have already mentioned, and so we will now look at this aspect of his work a little more closely.

R. H. HIERS

R. H. Hiers is convinced that we will only understand Jesus' view of judgement through understanding the apocalyptic literature of second temple Judaism, and certainly his discussion of the intertestamental documents is wide-ranging and thorough. He recognises, however, that although there is much value in a detailed investigation of these works, we must beware of neglecting the importance of the OT. In Hiers' view, the roots of Jesus' expectation of judgement are traced back to the OT expectation of the *Yom Yahweh*,[146] but even more so

---

[143] Caird, *Theology*, 243-44.
[144] Caird, *Theology* 243.
[145] Caird, *Theology* 246-47.
[146] Cf. Hos. 2:16-20; Is. 2:2-4; 11:1-10; 19:19-25; Jer. 31:31-34; Hag. 2:6-9, 21-23; Zech. 2:10-12; 3:6-10; 14:1-21, [Hiers *Jesus and the Future*, 129n. 101].

to the expectations expressed in the literature of second temple Judaism. Hiers indicates that a shift occurs in this literature to an even more future oriented expectation of the final judgement which would bring history to an end. Hiers does not want to draw too sharp a distinction between OT prophecy and intertestamental apocalyptic literature, claiming that they are, in many respects, 'contiguous'.[147] In this body of literature, Hiers identifies several important themes such as the 'Day of Judgement',[148] and the 'Judge' (who is usually understood to be God himself, often referred to by some circumlocution such as 'the Lord of the Spirits' or 'the Most High').[149] In addition to this belief, Hiers notes,

> In Enoch, two different terms are used for a figure other than God, who was expected to appear or come as Judge: "Mine Elect One," and "Son of man".[150]

The judge is also identified as 'a new priest' in the *Testament of Levi* (18:2-14). In *2 Baruch* 72:2-73:7, 'a passage reminiscent in its latter verses of various Isaianic themes', the Messiah is explicitly said to be judge over the nations, sparing those which have been merciful to Israel and giving the others over to destruction.

Hiers states that the general expectation was that the judgement would be universal, referring to *1 Enoch* 1:7-9; 25:4; and *Testament of Benjamin* 10:8f. as examples. The latter text indicates an expectation that the dead would also rise to judgement. While Hiers acknowledges a nationalistic flavour to some texts he also identifies an expectation that some Gentiles would share in 'the new era of peace'.[151]

As to the basis for judgement in the apocalyptic literature, Hiers claims that it is on the basis of 'the attitudes and actions of each person'.[152] He quotes the following significant passage from *2 Enoch* 44:4f:

---

[147] Hiers *Jesus and the Future*, 41. However, at this point Hiers seems to regard the intertestamental literature as giving more support to his thesis since he laments that 'there is a tendency for both modern Jewish and Christian interpreters to ignore or bypass the intertestamental writings in order to leap directly from canonical Hebrew scriptures into "normative" Judaism or post-apostolic Christianity.'

[148] Cf. *Apoc Moses* 26:4; *T. Levi* 3:3; *2 Enoch* 51:1-3; 2 Esd. 7:38, 104, 113; 12:34; Wis. 3:18. Cf. *1 Enoch* 22:4, 11; 65:6f; 103:8.

[149] Cf. *Vita Adae et Evae* 29:10; *1 Enoch* 1:1-4, 9; 45:6; 53:2; 90:20-27; 91:7, 15; 100:4; *T. Levi* 4:1; *T. Asher* 7:3; *Sib. Or.* 3:659ff, 741ff; 4:41, 176f, 183f; *As. Moses* 10:7; *2 Bar.* 83:2f; 2 Esdras 7:33; 9:2; *Pss. Sol.* 15:12, 14; 17:51.

[150] Hiers *Jesus and the Future*, 42.

[151] Hiers *Jesus and the Future*, 43. See *2 Bar* 72:1-5; *Sib Or* III:652-54, 741-60, 772-82. Cf. Is. 2, 19, 49; Jon., in the prophetic tradition.

[152] Hiers *Jesus and the Future*, 44. He cites *1 Enoch* 58:2f; 98:9f; and also 38:1-4; 103:3-8; *2 Bar* 54:21; *Wisd Sol* 3:1-19; *2 Enoch* 61:1-3.

> Blessed is the man who does not direct his heart with malice against any man, and
> helps the injured and condemned, and raises the broken-down, and shall do
> charity to the needy, because on the day of the great judgment every weight, every
> measure and every make-weight (will be) as in the market, that is to say they are
> hung on scales and stand in the market, (and every one) shall learn his own
> measure, and according to his measure shall take his reward.

After the judgement the righteous were expected to inherit the earth. This might
entail a recreation, as the old passed away to be replaced with the new. The
wicked would be punished eternally.

All this was to happen in the future, at the end of the 'present age'. Hiers
notes the use of vivid imagery in 4 Ezra 5:4f. He goes on to write,

> it is characteristic of apocalyptic writing to look for the time of final Judgment
> and deliverance in the near future. Thus from the standpoint of those living at the
> time in and for which an apocalypse was written, most of the signs pertaining to
> the course of history have already occurred; what remain are the final cosmic
> signs and the events which they herald (e.g., II Esdras 9:1-9).[153]

From these words it is clear that Hiers understands the apocalypticists and their
readers to have interpreted the 'cosmic' language in a literal sense. He also understands them to have had an expectation of these events happening imminently.

> That the end events are expected in the near future is stated expressly in several
> places, especially in *II Baruch*; e.g., "For truly my redemption has drawn nigh,
> and is not far distant as aforetime"; "For the Judge shall come and will not
> tarry."[154] This is also affirmed in II Esdras: "The age is hastening swiftly to its
> end"; "Therefore my judgment is now drawing near."[155]

Finally, Hiers deals with the reason for writing about the coming judgement.
He suggests that some of the literature was intended to make sense of periods
of hardship, and he acknowledges that some of it is speculative, but he claims
that the main intention is to call the readers to repentance and righteousness.[156]

So one scholar claims that we have to take the apocalyptic language of the
intertestamental documents at its face value. Is that our only option?

I believe that the answer is no. So the question that lies before us is, how are
we to interpret this kind of language, if not as Hiers does? This question leads
us to note G. B. Caird's stress on metaphor. Particularly important in regard to
this is his book, *The Language and Imagery of the Bible*. His position is clearly
set out in chapter 14 of this work and we will briefly examine it now.

---

[153] Hiers *Jesus and the Future*, 47.

[154] *2 Bar* 23:7; 48:39.

[155] 2 Esdras 4:26; 8:61. See also 4:27-52. Hiers *Jesus and the Future*, 47.

[156] Hiers *Jesus and the Future*, 47-48.

G. B. CAIRD

After a helpful survey of the various uses of the term 'eschatology' from Weiss and Schweitzer, through Dodd and Bultmann, to Clements, Caird goes on to outline his own understanding of eschatological language. He states his position in three theses:

1. The biblical writers believed literally that the world had had a beginning in the past and would have an end in the future.
2. They regularly used end-of-the-world language metaphorically to refer to that which they well knew was not the end of the world.
3. As with all other uses of metaphor, we have to allow for the likelihood of some literalistic misinterpretation on the part of the hearer, and for the possibility of some blurring of the edges between vehicle and tenor on the part of the speaker.[157]

This seems to me to be a useful starting point in appreciating the language of some of the OT prophets from which Caird draws examples in order to illustrate his position. The first proposition is beyond doubt as is seen from texts such as Ps 72:7 and Ps 102:25-26. It is important that we do not lose sight of this fact for it may have significance for our interpretation of biblical texts. If the writers believed so strongly in the end of the world, we should not be too surprised if that conviction was expressed in their writings, and indeed we should be very surprised if it were not. That is not to say, however, that language which we immediately associate with descriptions of the end of the world was intended to have that meaning in its original context.

The second proposition raises more questions but Caird effectively establishes the point with discussion of the phrases 'the latter end of the days'[158] and 'the day of the Lord'.[159] Caird notes the definition of the former phrase as 'a prophetic phrase denoting the final period of the history so far as the speaker's perspective reaches.'[160] He understands this to be similar to the English phrase 'sooner or later', thus leaving it somewhat ambiguous and so, he claims, he is justified in bringing his third proposition into play. With regard to the phrase 'the Day of the Lord', Caird points to Amos' use of the phrase in the eighth century BC when it already had 'a long history behind it.'[161] It is significant for our present study that several of the occurrences of this phrase refer to the disaster which would fall on a particular city or nation, whether it be Babylon or

---

[157] Caird, *The Language and Imagery of the Bible*, 256.

[158] Gen. 49:1; Num. 24:14; Deut. 4:30; 31:29; Hos. 3:5; Is. 2:2; Jer. 23:20; 30:24; 48:47; 49:39; Ezek. 38:16; Dan. 2:28; 10:14.

[159] Amos 5:18, 20; Is. 2:12; 13:6, 9; Zeph. 1:7, 14; Jer. 46:10; Ezek. 13:5; 30:3; Obad. 15; Zech. 14:1; Mal. 4:5; Joel 1:15; 2:1, 11, 31; 3:14.

[160] BDB, 31, *s.v. 'akarît*.

[161] Caird, *The Language and Imagery of the Bible*, 258.

Edom or Judah. Caird makes it clear, however, that the perspective of the prophets was not limited to the events of their own day alone. The prophets are said to have 'looked to the future with bifocal vision', seeing both the historical events of their own day and the final 'Day of the Lord', and producing a 'synthetic picture'. Caird writes,

> With their near sight they foresaw imminent historical events which would be brought about by familiar human causes; for example, disaster was near for Babylon because Yahweh was stirring up the Medes against them (Isa. 13:17). With their long sight they saw the day of the Lord; and it was in the nature of the prophetic experience that they were able to adjust their focus so as to impose the one image on the other and produce a synthetic picture.[162]

At the same time, the prophets were able to distinguish between the two visions. Thus they might say that 'the Day of the Lord' had come (Joel 2:2) in that judgement was being poured out on the people calling them to repentance. Caird speaks then of a 'panorama' view which sees the judgement of God's people in the context of a universal judgement (Joel 3:14). But, Caird claims, this is not a final judgement as the doorway to an afterlife, since there is the prospect of the fortunes of the people being reversed so that,

> there shall be people living in Judah forever,
>   in Jerusalem generation after generation. (Joel 3:21)

Thus there can be talk of 'the Day of the Lord' without implying that this was *the definitive* 'Day of the Lord'.[163] However, the short and the long term views are intimately related. In the light of his discussion it would seem to be more helpful to say that the biblical writers *sometimes* used 'end of the world' language to refer to this-worldly events, but never in a way that was detached from the ultimate event of God's judgement. It is perhaps significant that the body of Caird's discussion focuses on the message of certain OT prophets. We may pose the question, Are there occasions in the New Testament, and specifically in Matthew's gospel, which take a view which is more specifically future oriented? Or are we to pay closer attention to the fact that Jesus was steeped in the OT Scriptures and was perhaps using the conventions of the prophets in his own teaching?

Caird's third thesis (which he introduced during the discussion of the phrase 'the latter end of the days') is, perhaps, more controversial yet. It implies that we should expect to find misrepresentations of the metaphorical message and

---

[162] Caird, *The Language and Imagery of the Bible*, 258.

[163] Caird, *The Language and Imagery of the Bible*, 259-60. In speaking of a definitive Day of the Lord it is necessary to heed Beasley-Murray's point, *Jesus and the Kingdom of God* (Exeter: Paternoster, 1986), 11, that 'It is commonly acknowledged that the Day of the Lord in the Old Testament is not a date but an event.'

that we should not be distracted by them. Does this mean that when we find portions of the Scriptures which seem to have a future referent, we are to disregard them as evidence that the author of that document simply has a mistaken understanding of the language? Does this serve to rule out of court any interpretation which clashes with Caird's? Are we in danger of suggesting that we in the twentieth century understand the Jewish metaphorical language better than first century Jews? We certainly have to be careful here, and we must be guided by the literary context of a particular occurrence of a phrase at all times, but Caird's point does remind us that it is possible for language bearing one significance to be misconstrued by another writer who gives it a very different significance.

One of the areas where Caird believes there has been gross misunderstanding in the past is that of Jewish apocalyptic literature. He notes that Weiss and Schweitzer believed this literature to be decisive in the interpretation of Jesus' message, and that it evidenced a vastly different world-view from the OT prophetic books.[164] Caird argues, on the other hand, that apocalyptic literature shares much with the OT prophetic works and that differences are accounted for largely on the grounds of two key factors. First, the conquests of Alexander the Great which broke down so many national boundaries led to the necessity of Jewish writers seeing their situation in the context of a much wider world than the OT prophets had done. Secondly, the apocalyptic works were all written in a period of intense nationalism, which is expressed with little disguise in the symbolism of their pages.[165]

We must be wary, however, of accepting 'apocalyptic' literature in the Bible as no more than a literary mirror of the political events of the writer's day. While it is without doubt the case that the author, for instance, of 4 Ezra has mirrored the catastrophic events of the destruction of Jerusalem in his work,[166] this may not always be the case in every document that contains apocalyptic language. Caird identifies the book of Daniel as a prime example of the incorporation of present events into apocalyptic literature.[167] But this depends on his understanding of Daniel as a pseudepigraphical second century work, containing *vaticinia ex eventu*, rather than a sixth century work containing real prophecy. If the latter view is taken, there is no compelling reason to limit the scope of the prophecies to the immediate period.[168] Regardless of authorship, however, it has been shown on numerous occasions that the book of Daniel does not demonstrate the most typical characteristics of later apocalyptic literature and is

---

[164] This is basically the position Hiers adopts, although he would probably see a little more continuity between the two bodies of literature.

[165] Caird, *The Language and Imagery of the Bible*, 261.

[166] This Jewish document is usually dated about AD 100. See M. Reddish, *Apocalyptic Literature* (Peabody: Hendrickson, 1995), 58; Evans, *NWNTI*, 11.

[167] Caird, *The Language and Imagery of the Bible*, 261-65.

[168] See J. G. Baldwin, *Daniel* (TOTC; Leicester: IVP, 1978).

therefore not the best example for Caird's point.[169] Here we need to recall the distinction between the genre of a document and the genre of language. Daniel contains apocalyptic language, though the book is not typical of the later apocalypses. It is perfectly feasible to understand the language of Daniel 7 as apocalyptic symbolism while still accepting that Daniel contains true prophecy.

The particular strength of Caird's understanding is that it makes the eschatological language of the Bible comprehensible to those who first heard it and who best understood its genre. It also means that eschatological language is not regarded as simply the longing of the pious. Rather it challenges the culture to which it speaks. He writes,

> If Weiss and Schweitzer were correct in thinking that apocalyptic provides the indispensable background for the understanding of the teaching of Jesus, then the one inescapable inference is the one which they and their successors persistently refused to draw: that the gospel of Jesus was directed to Israel as a nation with a summons to abandon the road of aggressive nationalism and return to a true understanding of her historic role as the people of God.[170]

It is this interpretative approach, developed by Caird, which is adopted by Marcus Borg, even if, as I believe, he does not work it out with sufficient consistency. Caird has also been followed by another of his doctoral students who is developing his approach with a new vigour.

N. T. WRIGHT

In the course of an extensive study of first century Judaism, Wright discusses the way in which apocalyptic literature functions as an expression of the hope of Israel. Using examples from *Apoc. Abr.* 12:3-10 and *2 Bar.* 36:1-37:1, Wright points to characteristics of apocalyptic literature as including the revelation of secrets of the universe (seen in the former text) and more specific references to the history of Israel, couched in symbolic language (as found in the latter). The effect of using such language, according to Wright, is 'to awaken the echoes of earlier biblical prophecy for hearers whose minds were attuned to such things, and to cast his message of patient hope into a form which lent it divine authority.'[171] The rich language of apocalyptic discourse invests the reality referred to with greater meaning and therefore meaning will be lost if the richness of the language is flattened out in interpretation. Wright contends that apocalyptic language was one of several forms of language available to the ancient Jews by which to describe the act of God to deliver his people, and that it signifies the conviction that however 'this worldly' the event might be, it is an event of cosmic significance.

The significance of this understanding, in Wright's view, is that a literalistic

---

[169] See Ladd, *The Presence of the Future*, 84-86, 97-98, 100-101.
[170] Caird, *The Language and Imagery of the Bible*, 265.
[171] Wright, *New Testament and the People of God*, 282.

interpretation of the imagery of apocalyptic language does it violence. It must be seen to be a complex of rich metaphors which points to the extraordinary significance of historical events.

This being the case, the thesis of Schweitzer that Jesus expected the imminent end of the world is due to a complete misunderstanding of the function of apocalyptic language. While Wright agrees that the Jews may have perceived certain events such as earthquakes as portents of the anticipated events, he states,

> the events, including the ones that were expected to come as the climax of YHWH's restoration of Israel, remained within (what we think of as) the this-worldly ambit.[172]

Thus 'the problem of the delay of the *Parousia*', with which notion Wright associates Schweitzer, Bultmann and Käsemann, is, in fact, no problem at all because it arises by reading apocalyptic language in a literalistic way which would never have occurred to a first century Jew.

Wright's understanding of apocalyptic texts is attractive in that it pays due attention to the symbolic nature of the language employed, and also avoids the gulf between the first century Jews and our own day, as is established by the view of Schweitzer and his followers, which he describes in the following way:

> We know that they were crucially wrong about something they put at the centre of their worldview, and must therefore either abandon any attempt to take them seriously or must construct a hermeneutic which will somehow enable us to salvage something from the wreckage.[173]

This is a major step forward in evaluating the first century religious expectation. We must avoid the temptation to ascribe to the early Christians views which require that they constantly have to extricate themselves from awkward positions. We should rather seek an understanding which does justice both to the texts in question, and to the early Christian interpretation of those texts.

It is somewhat difficult to relate Wright's discussion to the language of Jesus since the main focus of his discussion is on *Jewish* apocalyptic, rather than Christian. However, we may raise one issue; that of the 'Son of Man' in Daniel 7:13. Wright argues that justice is done to the literary genre of the chapter if the various creatures in the early part of the chapter represent the nations which war against Israel. Therefore, he says, the Son of Man must be understood as a representation of Israel, and his coming with the clouds and his being led into the presence of the Ancient of Days indicate vindication for Israel; a vindication, Wright claims, which Israel would have understood and expected to come

---

[172] Wright, *New Testament and the People of God*, 285.
[173] Wright, *New Testament and the People of God*, 285.

in historical terms.[174]

When Wright then moves on to discuss Mark 13, he agrees that it has a recognisable apocalyptic form but he argues that to distinguish between an apocalyptic chapter 13 and a non-apocalyptic remainder is to create a false dichotomy. While an apocalypse, according to his definition, would tell the story of Israel through an intermediary such as an angel and in the typical symbolic language of apocalyptic literature, in Mark's gospel the evangelist has 'told *the story of Jesus telling the story of Israel* by such means.'[175] This raises the question of how Jesus understands the term 'Son of Man' which he clearly uses as a self-designation. Does he understand himself to be taking on the role of Israel (an understanding in continuity with Wright's proposed interpretation of Daniel 7:13), or has Wright overlooked a more personal reference in Daniel 7:13 which Jesus takes up in his use of the phrase? Another alternative is that Jesus has adopted a phrase from Dan 7 which was interpreted in a corporate way by the original hearers, but has *reinterpreted* the phrase to suit his purposes. Some of these questions will be dealt with in later exegesis.

D. C. ALLISON

D. C. Allison, like Hiers, argues firmly for a Schweitzer-like interpretation of Jesus' eschatological expectation. However, unlike Hiers, he has written in the wake of Caird and Wright, and so provides a trenchant critique of their similar positions. In his most recent monograph, and more intensively in a recent contribution to a book-length response to Wright's *Jesus and the Victory of God*, Allison draws on a number of arguments to counter the metaphorical hermeneutic of Caird and Wright. Firstly he draws on a comparative approach to claim that expectation of a future golden age, to come in the imminent future, is common to world religions.[176] This may be the case, although I believe that Allison draws on his history-of-religions methodology too freely throughout his book, but that does not determine whether *all* language which seems to suggest future turbulent events need *necessarily* refer to cosmic dissolution. Some might indeed, but this cannot be assumed from the start.

Secondly, Allison draws attention to a number of Jewish texts which appear to have a very concrete referent in view when they use the language of dramatic future occurrences. For example, he cites the War Scroll (1QM) and claims that it is

> Ostensibly a prophecy of a real eschatological battle complete with fighting angels.[177]

---

[174] Wright, *New Testament and the People of God*, 291-97.

[175] Wright, *New Testament and the People of God*, 394. Author's italics.

[176] Allison, *Jesus of Nazareth*, 153-57.

[177] Allison, *Jesus of Nazareth*, 157.

However, the fact that Allison is able to locate examples of Jewish writings from the first century which appear to take cataclysmic language literally does not demonstrate that Jesus and the writers of the gospels took the same hermeneutical approach, though it does give us reason for being cautious in our conclusions regarding Wright's position. While adopting the hermeneutical approach of Caird, Borg, and, in its most nuanced form, Wright, would certainly make several vexed issues of NT interpretation, such as the problem of the delay of the *Parousia*, vanish at a stroke, we cannot accept their view simply because it would make our life simpler. It must reflect the understanding of the Jewish people who read the ancient documents, as far as we can discern that understanding from the ancient texts available to us.

'Apocalyptic' Language in the Old Testament

The first place for us to begin is the OT, and this for several reasons. Firstly, Matthew quotes frequently from the canonical[178] books, but never quotes from the various other Jewish works which were commonly known in his day. Although he does appear to draw upon Ben Sira 51:23-27 at 11:28-30, there are no clear allusions to non-canonical literature in Matthew 21-25. We do well to analyse thoroughly the understanding of symbolism found in the OT texts, and even give them a certain priority in our interpretation of the NT allusions. Secondly, the apocalyptic language found in the so-called intertestamental works is derived in large measure from the prophetic works of the OT. Thus knowledge of the primary sources is necessary for a true understanding of the documents that drew from them. It should also be noted that if the apocalyptic works have indeed drawn on the prophetic tradition, that does not imply that they have preserved the same hermeneutical approach. Thus we may well find that language used in a certain way in Isaiah is used in a dramatically different way in Enoch or 4 Ezra (recall Caird's caution, in the third of his theses above, to the effect that apocalyptic imagery may be liable to misinterpretation. If that is true of modern interpreters, it was surely also a possibility for ancient interpreters). If this is found to be the case, we will have to ask which understanding was most likely to be in the mind of Matthew (and Jesus). We cannot examine all of the instances of apocalyptic language in the OT and pseudepigrapha, so we will restrict ourselves to several examples of the use of language which resembles that used in Matthew 21-25, particularly Matthew 24. They fall into two categories: those that appear to speak of cosmic catastrophe, and those that speak of the coming Son of Man, or of the clouds.

---

[178] I recognise that this is a contentious term when we are looking at things from the perspective of first-century Jews. However, I am adopting the position, argued thoroughly by R. T. Beckwith, *The Old Testament Canon of the New Testament Church* (London: SPCK, 1985), that the 39 (according to the LXX reckoning) books which form the modern OT were regarded as canonical by the first century AD.

COSMIC CATASTROPHE

We begin our survey of texts in Isaiah, which is alluded to (if not quoted) several times in the eschatological discourse of Matthew 24:

> Isaiah 13:9-10.
> See, the day of the LORD comes,
>   cruel with wrath and fierce anger,
> to make the earth a desolation,
>   and to destroy its sinners from it.
> For the stars of the heavens and their constellations
>   will not give their light;
> the sun will be dark at its rising,
>   and the moon will not shed its light.

When the wider context of this passage is considered, it becomes clear that the oracle is directed against Babylon (v. 1) as an historical entity, however much Babylon might also be utilised as a type of rebellion against Yahweh. Through the use of vivid language concerning the great lights of the sky being darkened, we are presented with the awesome effects of God's judgement. D. C. Allison points out that darkness is associated with mourning in several Jewish texts.[179]

It is important to note that this cosmological language comes early in this particular oracle, not at its end. It should not be thought of as the 'final judgement', but a picture of great judgement. Some of the language which follows suggests existence beyond the point of verses 9-11 (e.g., v. 20). Van Gemeren writes,

> Isaiah was a master of the Hebrew language. His style reflects a rich vocabulary and imagery with many words and expressions unique to him.[180]

It is this use of language that we must beware of turning into something much more prosaic. Commenting on this particular passage, Van Gemeren continues,

> The terror of that day *may be compared to* that brought about by earthquake (13:9, 13), war (v. 4), and cosmic upheaval (vv. 10, 13).[181]

It is this aspect of comparison which is so important to notice. These are God-directed events in the realm of history and politics, which are compared to various other events, including the destruction of creation. Watts sums up the section 13:1-14:32 in the phrase, 'Yahweh has broken the scepter of rulers'.[182]

---

[179] Allison, *The End of the Ages*, 28

[180] VanGemeren, *Interpreting the Prophetic Word*, 252.

[181] Van Gemeren, *Interpreting the Prophetic Word*, 265. Emphasis added.

[182] J. D. W. Watts, *Isaiah 1-33* (WBC 24; Waco: Word, 1985), 185.

Similar language is found later in the same work:

> Isaiah 34:4
> All the host of heaven shall rot away,
>   and the skies roll up like a scroll.
> All their host shall wither
>   like a leaf withering on a vine
>   or fruit withering on a fig tree.

This language, when read out of context, certainly appears to be another prediction of cosmic destruction. However, it is always dangerous and misleading to interpret texts apart from their context, and these words too are best explained by reference to the clearer portions of the chapter. The nations are called as witnesses as God challenges Edom. The cumulative effect of the images in the chapter is a warning: overwhelming judgement is coming. But to take the language too literally means that the thorns will overrun Edom's fortresses (v. 13) *after* the stars have been dissolved and the sky rolled up (v. 4). Jeremiah later refers to the historical catastrophe of the desolation of Bosrah, essentially Edom's capital,[183] in Jeremiah 49:13.

If we compare Jeremiah 4:23-28 we find a similar vocabulary employed to describe the approaching destruction of Judah and the temple:

> I looked on the earth, and lo, it was waste and void; and to the heavens, and they had no light. I looked on the mountains, and lo, they were quaking, and all the hills moved to and fro. I looked, and lo, there was no one at all, and all the birds of the air had fled. I looked, and lo, the fruitful land was a desert, and all its cities were laid in ruins before the LORD, before his fierce anger. For thus says the LORD: The whole land shall be a desolation; yet I will not make a full end. Because of this the earth shall mourn, and the heavens above grow black; for I have spoken, I have purposed; I have not relented nor will I turn back.

N.T. Wright comments that Jeremiah,

> invest[s] that space-time reality with a theological interpretation: this is like the unmaking of creation itself.[184]

More fully, G. B. Caird writes,

> Jeremiah's vision is of the whole creation returning to its primaeval chaos; in the first line he uses the phrase *tohu wabohu*, which is used elsewhere only of the empty turbulence out of which God created heaven and earth (Gen. 1:2; cf. Isa.

---

[183] See G. Keown, P. J. Scalise, T. G. Smothers, *Jeremiah 26-52* (WBC 27; Dallas: Word, 1995), 330.

[184] Wright, *New Testament and the People of God*, 299 n. 42.

34:11). But the referent of the vision, what it is intended to predict, is the coming devastation of Israel.[185]

Another passage which contains similar language is Ezek 32:7-8:

> When I blot you out, I will cover the heavens,
>   and make their stars dark;
> I will cover the sun with a cloud,
>   and the moon shall not give its light.

> All the shining lights of the heavens
>   I will darken above you,
>   and put darkness on your land,
>   says the Lord GOD.

Once more, the beginning of the oracle gives the key to correct interpretation of the passage. Verse 2 indicates that Ezekiel is to speak against the Pharaoh of Egypt, who is portrayed in the metaphorical language of the monster. The oracle then picks up the metaphor in verse 3 with the image of a monstrous fishing match! When we come to the cosmological language of verses 7 and 8, we should be ready for a metaphorical significance.[186] The parallelism between verses 8 and 9 reinforces the view that destruction of a nation, and resultant mourning are in view.

In his important article, T. R. Hatina points to Joel 2:10, 31; 3:15 and Amos 8:9 as parallel instances of cosmological language and demonstrates that each has a temporal referent rather than picturing the end of the world.[187]

Though we have focused our attention on texts from the OT, D. C. Allison has pointed out that the 'rending or dissolution of the heavenly firmament occurs in the Old Testament and later came to be a fixed item of the eschatological scenario.'[188] Russell cites a similar passage from the Assumption of Moses 10:5:

---

[185] Caird, *The Language and Imagery of the Bible*, 114.
[186] M Greenberg, *Ezekiel 21-37* (AB 22A; New York: Doubleday, 1997), 655, speaks of 'these densely symbolic passages'.
[187] T. R. Hatina, 'The Focus of Mark 13:24-27: The Parousia, or the Destruction of the Temple?' *BBR* 6 (1996), 43-66, at 55-6.
[188] Allison, *The End of the Ages*, 33. Allison cites the following examples from the OT and pseudepigrapha: Job 14:12 LXX; Ps. 102:26; Is. 34:4 (see the discussion above); 63:19 (64:1); Hag. 2:6, 21; *Sib. Or.* III, 82; *Sib. Or.* VIII, 233, 413.

> The horns of the sun will be broken
>> and he will be turned into darkness;
> and the moon will not give her light,
>> and be turned wholly into blood.
> And the circle of the stars will be disturbed.

This text is also perfectly compatible with the literary reading of these catastrophic events as symbols of disaster,[189] but when Russell goes on to cite descriptions of cosmic confusion such as the roles of sun and moon being reversed (4 Ezra 5:4) we find that we are into a different kind of meaning altogether.[190] What is common to the texts cited above is the deprivation of light, and Allison has pointed out that darkness is associated with mourning,[191] clearly an appropriate response to great national catastrophe. The text from 4 Ezra is quite different in that there is still light, and the text seeks to highlight a strange and foreboding event. Yet we need not regard this as a completely legitimate development of the sense of the OT texts, but instead as quite a new departure.[192]

COMING SON OF MAN WITH CLOUDS

The most famous, and the most relevant, of the texts that we must comment on is found in the book of Daniel. It is greatly debated which genre Daniel belongs to; is it prophecy or apocalyptic. We will not attempt to discuss this large-scale question here, although we may be more cautious in our interpretation if we remember that the debate continues. Debate also extends to the date of Daniel; most scholars placing it in the second century BC,[193] in the same age as many of the extant Jewish apocalypses, but a substantial minority maintaining the position of a sixth century BC date, which would place it along with several other OT prophetic works.[194] I assign Daniel a sixth century date, although the exegetical argument should stand regardless of which position on date is adopted.[195] The key text for our purposes reads as follows:

---

[189] Hatina ('Focus', 57) comments, 'The prediction should probably be read in the context of Roman intervention in Palestine during the first-century CE, an event which the author most likely experienced,' referring the reader to J. Tromp, *The Assumption of Moses: A Critical Edition with Commentary* (Leiden: Brill, 1993).

[190] Russell, *Method and Message of Jewish Apocalyptic*, 276.

[191] Allison, *The End of the Ages*, 28.

[192] See the discussion in Hatina, 'Focus', 57.

[193] So Collins, *Apocalyptic Imagination*, 87-88.

[194] So Baldwin, *Daniel*, 35-46.

[195] Goldingay, *Daniel* (WBC 30; Waco: Word, 1989), xxxix-xi, who favours a second century date, calls the reader to read the document on its own terms. Glasson highlights one important issue related to the dating of Daniel and *1 Enoch*. If Daniel should be dated in the Maccabean period (c. 165 BC) then it is possible to regard Daniel as later than, and even dependent on, portions of *1 Enoch*. See Glasson, *The*

Dan 7:13-14.

As I watched in the night visions,
    I saw one like a son of man
        coming with the clouds of heaven.
    And he came to the Ancient One
        and was presented before him.
    To him was given dominion
        and glory and kingship,
        that all peoples, nations and languages
            should serve him.
    His dominion is an everlasting dominion
        that shall not pass away,
    and his kingship is one
        that shall never be destroyed.

When attempting to interpret this familiar passage, it is crucially important to pay close attention to its context. Its wider context is that it forms part of Dan 7. The beginning of chapter 7 presents a dream-vision[196] of four great beasts (v. 3), all of which are either composite creatures with parts from various known beasts, or, in the case of the fourth beast, completely unrecognisable and hideous. The explicit description of the genre of literature in the chapter (7:1) should immediately suggest to us that we are dealing with symbolism, and not with literal anatomical description, a suggestion which gains strength when the immediate context speaks of a night vision (v. 13). Furthermore, as Goldingay correctly points out, there is repeated use of the particle כ (like).[197] When we are told later in the chapter that these beasts are four kings (v. 17), this is confirmed, and we are also allowed to see that we are thinking of political entities as we consider the beasts. N. T. Wright surely asks a sensible and incisive question when he comments,

> Reading the chapter as far as verse 12, there is no problem. The monsters 'represent' (in the literary sense) nations that war against Israel. Why then have critics read the 'son of man' figure, whom the beasts attack but who is finally vindicated, as a reference either to an individual human, or possibly divine, being, or to an angel?[198]

In fact, the whole of this chapter is a *literary* work intended to convey a meaning beyond the details on the page. Wright continues to explain,

---

Second Advent, 2-6. In notes to the third edition of his book, Glasson appears to express a little caution about his earlier view of dependence, but not of his dating.

[196] Collins, *Apocalyptic Imagination*, 79. Also Goldingay, *Daniel*, 146, 157.

[197] Goldingay, *Daniel*, 146.

[198] Wright, *New Testament and the People of God*, 291.

What we have in this chapter, I suggest, is a *literary* representation, whereby a figure in the story - a human figure, surrounded by monsters - functions as a symbol for Israel, just as the monsters function as literary representations of pagan nations. This symbol is obviously pregnant with the meaning of Genesis 2, evoking the idea of the people of God as the true humanity and the pagan nations as the animals. This strongly implies, with all the force of the imagery, that Israel, though beleaguered and battered, is about to be vindicated.[199]

T. F. Glasson concurs with this approach to the text. He writes of Daniel's 'son of man',

This figure, like the beasts earlier in the chapter, is a symbolic one representing the community of 'the saints of the Most High', as explicitly interpreted in verse 27.[200]

The scene provides us with a contrast between the beastly nature of the pagan nations and the true humanity of God's people. The 'Son of Man' comes to the Most High to receive vindication and exaltation, a picture of God's commitment to his people even in a time of distress. The clouds represent the might and the glory of God, as we can see by looking at just two further examples:

Is 19:1
See, the LORD is riding on a swift cloud
    and comes to Egypt;
the idols of Egypt will tremble at his presence,
    and the heart of the Egyptians will melt within them.

Ps 97:2-3
Clouds and thick darkness are all around him;
    righteousness and justice are the foundation of his throne.

As Caird has rightly and humorously said,

The coming of the Son of Man on the clouds of heaven was never conceived as a primitive form of space travel, but as a symbol for a mighty reversal of fortunes within history and at a national level.[201]

If this interpretation of Dan 7 is correct, then it has profound implications for our interpretation of this passage when we encounter it in the gospels, and in Matthew in particular. We should be warned against importing the expectation of a literal event into the citation of a passage which originally had a literary function.

---

[199] Wright, *New Testament and the People of God*, 291-92.

[200] Glasson, *Jesus and the End of the World*, 21.

[201] G. B. Caird, *Jesus and the Jewish Nation* (London: Athlone Press, 1965), 20.

As we examine the OT evidence for eschatological expectations we must beware of assuming that Jesus or Paul could only hold views which conform completely to those of the OT writers. We must recognise that, as Witherington reminds us,

> It was not a part of early Jewish expectations about a Messiah that he would *return* to earth after his death. The idea of a *second* coming does not appear in the literature prior to the time of Jesus and Paul.[202]

However, this does not mean that the views of Jewish writers prior to Jesus and Paul are *determinative* for those of Jesus and Paul. Witherington goes on,

> We might well expect to find something unique about the teaching of Paul and perhaps even Jesus that stands out from its Jewish matrix.[203]

It is this distinctiveness which is perhaps being disallowed in contemporary studies of Jesus' eschatology, whether it is Schweitzer and Hiers who cast Jesus as an apocalyptic preacher moulded by that literature, or Borg and Crossan who try to remove every trace of apocalyptic influence. However, having made allowance for distinctiveness in the views of Jesus and Paul, we must equally beware of detaching them from their roots in first century Palestine and particularly in the Hebrew scriptures.

Early Christian Interpretation

The most important text from the early Christian church related to the interpretation of apocalyptic texts is Acts 2:16-21. As Peter begins his sermon to the astounded crowd, following the coming of the Spirit, he is anxious to establish the scriptural foundation for what has happened and so he quotes from Joel 3:1-5 [LXX 2:28-32].[204] There are several important points to note about the way in which he treats this text.

Firstly, Peter says to the crowd '*this* is what was spoken' (v. 16). In other words he makes a direct identification between Joel's prophecy and the events of Pentecost.[205]

Secondly, he quotes more of the passage from Joel than is necessary to es-

---

[202] B. Witherington III, *Jesus, Paul and the End of the World* (Exeter: Paternoster, 1992), 147.

[203] Witherington, *Jesus, Paul and the End of the World*, 147.

[204] Parts of this portion of Joel are also found quoted in Matt. 24:29; Mark 13:24-25; Lk. 21:25; Acts 2:39; 22:16; Rom. 10:13; Tit. 3:6; Rev. 6:12.

[205] J. A. Fitzmyer, *The Acts of the Apostles* (AB31; New York: Doubleday, 1998), 252. Fitzmyer believes that Peter understands the events of Pentecost to be the *Yom Yahweh* in a way that Joel could not envisage. See the excursus on this citation of Joel in T. J. Finley, *Joel, Amos, Obadiah* (Chicago: Moody, 1990), 76-81.

tablish the scriptural warrant for the strange phenomena brought about by the Spirit, which suggests that he sees relevance to the events in the cosmological language also.[206] It is possible that the quotation is extended simply so as to include the statement 'whoever will call on the name of the Lord will be saved.'[207] The implication of this view is that the issue of whether the cataclysmic language refers directly to the events experienced on that day of Pentecost is beside Peter's point.[208] However, the fact that Peter's speech comes immediately after dramatic manifestations of the Spirit's activity suggests that the explicit reference to the cosmological signs is intentional, but not literal.[209] It is worth noting that Stuart identifies both 'chiastic structure' and 'synonymous parallelism' in the Hebrew text of Joel 3:3-4, which suggests that we may be dealing with poetic language.[210]

Thirdly, there is no other reference to the end of the world in any of the remainder of Peter's sermon, but there are numerous references to the events surrounding Jesus' death at the hands of wicked men (v. 23), his vindication by resurrection (vv. 24, 31-33), and the threat of judgement (v. 40).

Thus, the method of interpreting apocalyptic imagery that we wish to advance in this thesis appears to be in accord with early Christian interpretation of apocalyptic imagery in an OT text.

Matthew and Apocalyptic

The final question we wish to deal with in this section is the extent to which Matthew is influenced by apocalyptic. Since T. Colani proposed the 'Little Apocalypse' theory of the composition of the apocalyptic discourse, scholars have sought remnants of apocalyptic documents in Matthew, or at least significant influence from such documents.[211] It is clear, however, that Matthew has made chapters 24 and 25 his own, and they now stand as a literary unit. It is also clear, as we have said already, that Matthew drew frequently from the OT

---

[206] J. Stott, *The Message of Acts* (Leicester: IVP, 1990), 74-75, presents the metaphorical interpretation as one possible reading of this portion of Peter's speech, the other being as a reference to real upheavals in nature already begun at the cross.

[207] Fitzmyer, *Acts*, 253, comments, 'In the context of Peter's speech, this concluding clause of Joel's prophetic utterance becomes climactic.'

[208] I am grateful to a member of the University of Aberdeen New Testament Postgraduate Seminar for suggesting this view to me.

[209] It is clear from other NT texts (e.g. Romans 10:13) that NT authors could cite the words of Joel 3:5 without feeling obliged to set them in their broader context. Thus, when the context is included in a citation, it is important to give that fact due weight.

[210] Stuart, *Hosea-Jonah*, 261. See also VanGemeren, *Interpreting the Prophetic Word*, 124-27.

[211] Kümmel, *Promise and Fulfilment*, 88-9, accepts that Mark 13 (and parallels) is indeed 'an extensive apocalyptic text'. See the detailed discussion in Beasley-Murray, *Jesus and the Last Days*.

but never (explicitly) from a contemporary apocalypse. Rather than look for pieces of apocalypses, I believe that we should recognise in Matthew the presence of 'apocalyptic' language, which is drawn primarily from the 'apocalyptic' or symbolic language of the *OT prophetic literature*. This approach does most justice to Matthew's presentation of Jesus as a prophet.

G. B. Caird illustrates his method of interpreting apocalyptic language from various passages in Matthew's gospel. Caird's initial comment seems, at first glance, to indicate some concern for his thesis in the case of Matthew. He admits that, 'Of the four Gospels, Matthew's is, at first blush, the most resistant to such an explanation.'[212] He goes on to draw attention to Matthew's use of the technical term παρουσία ('coming') and the phrase συντέλεια αἰῶνος ('the end of the age', cf. 13:39, 40, 49; 24:3; 28:20). On the other hand, Caird notes Matthew's willingness to allow apparently contradictory statements stand in tension (e.g., Christians are to let their light shine (5:16) but are to do their acts of piety in private (6:2-6, 16-18); 'they are to pass no judgement on anyone (7:1), but must avoid throwing their pearls to those they judge to be pigs (7:6).') and claims that in keeping with this he is 'far from being a thoroughgoing literalist in his eschatology.'[213] Caird recognises Matthew's emphasis on judgement and even on the Last Judgement but claims that this is

> to be seen not as the product of a dominating interest in the end of the world, but of an awareness...in which the Last Judgement is constantly impacting upon the present in both offer and demand.[214]

It is our contention that the interpretative method developed by Caird and Wright is the way forward

(i) in doing greatest justice to the original prophetic context of the apocalyptic language.
(ii) in making sense of many of the most difficult passages in Matthew.
(iii) in enabling us to see the theme of judgement come through in Matthew's gospel.

Having laid the foundation in this discussion of hermeneutics, we must now put these insights into practice as we seek to interpret Matthew 24-25.

---

[212] Caird, *Theology*, 261.
[213] Caird, *Theology*, 262.
[214] Caird, *Theology*, 263.

The Structure of Matthew 24-25

If Matthew 24-25 has a recognisable structure it will not only allow us to interpret the text in an orderly way but should also give us an insight into the thinking that led Matthew to present his material as he did. Blomberg[215] suggests the
following structure for chapters 24 and 25:

**1. Signs and Times of the Temple's Destruction and of Christ's
Return (24:1-35)**
(a) Introduction (24:1-3)
(b) Signs that do not yet herald the end (24:4-14)
(c) Destruction of the temple (24:15-20)
(d) The Great Tribulation (24:21-28)
(e) Christ's second coming (24:29-31)
(f) Concluding implications (24:32-35)

2. Commands to Perpetual Vigilance (24:36-25:46)
(a) Introduction and thesis: No-one but God the Father knows the time of
     Christ's return (24:36-42)
(b) The Parable of the Householder and Thief (24:43-44)
(c) The Parable of the Faithful and Unfaithful Servants (24:45-51)
(d) The Parable of the Ten Bridesmaids (25:1-13)
(e) The Parable of the Talents (25:14-30)
(f) The Sheep and the Goats (25:31-46)

Blomberg admirably recognises that the language of 24:4-20 refers primarily
(not discounting possible secondary references) to the first-century situation.
He also recognises that verse 35 forms a clear pause in the discourse, while
verse 36 indicates a new beginning, thus picking up two of the clearest literary
signals in the text. He struggles, however, with the language of v. 21 and feels
compelled to generalise this verse into a reference to the 'great tribulation' of
the 'church age'. This immediately introduces a long-term view into the section
which naturally leads Blomberg to regard vv. 29-31 as a description of the Second Coming. However, this generalisation is unnecessary and in fact stands in
contradiction to the clear division which Blomberg has recognised in verses 35
and 36. The horrors of the siege of Jerusalem could quite legitimately be described in the dramatic language of v. 21,[216] and then vv. 23-26 return to the

---

[215] Blomberg, *Matthew*, 338

[216] So, correctly, Carson, *Matthew*, 501. See the description in Josephus, *Jewish War*
v.424-438 and 512-518. For example, Josephus writes in 5.442, 'I shall therefore
speak my mind here at once briefly: - That neither did any other city ever suffer such
miseries, nor did any age ever breed a generation more fruitful in wickedness than this
was, from the beginning of the world.'

discussion of false messiahs begun earlier in v. 5.[217]

France[218] on the other hand offers the following structure:

(i)   Jesus foretells the destruction of the temple (24:1-2)
(ii) Warnings against premature expectation (24:3-14)
(iii) The coming crisis in Judea (24:15-28)
(iv) Climax of the crisis within 'this generation' (24:29-35)
(v) The unexpected *Parousia* of the Son of Man (24:36-25:13)
(vi) The Parable of the Talents (25:14-30)
(vii) The Last Judgement (25:31-46)

This approach to the discourse follows a view held by Tasker,[219] and Kik,[220] and others which understands the discourse to fall into two clear sections: 24:1-35 and 24:36ff. There are two significant advantages in this approach:

(a) It allows the discourse to be understood as a coherent and ordered response to the two-part question of verse 3.[221] It avoids the complications of continually switching back and forth between references to the judgement on Jerusalem and references to the *Parousia*. This is not to say that we ignore the theological connection between the two events but it allows us to recognise connection without confusion.

(b) The understanding of the phrase τὸν υἱὸν τοῦ ἀνθρώπου ἐρχόμενον in terms of apocalyptic imagery allows us to make sense not only of this passage but of the other similar difficult texts (10:23; 16:28; 26:64) without either impugning the integrity of Jesus by claiming that he was mistaken or straining the language of the texts beyond what they can bear. It has the added advantage of retaining the natural sense of Dan 7:13 which would have been appreciated by the original readers. If we are to truly understand Jesus in the context of his own time and culture then we have to beware of imposing an interpretation on his words which, while appearing 'obvious' to us, would not have been the natural meaning for his original audience.

The section of the discourse found in 24:36-25:46 is distinguished from what precedes it in two respects. Firstly, it is separated from the earlier portion of Matthew 24 by the transitional verse 36. Secondly, it is largely composed of

[217] Carson, *Matthew*, 502-503, fails to make this connection and therefore blurs the distinction between the events of the first century and those of the continuing experience of the church in his interpretation of 24:22-28.
[218] France, *Matthew*, 66-67.
[219] R. V. G. Tasker, *The Gospel according to St. Matthew* (TNTC; London: Tyndale Press, 1961).
[220] J. M. Kik, *An Eschatology of Victory* (Phillipsburg: Presbyterian and Reformed Publishing Co, 1971).
[221] So also Garland, *Reading Matthew*, 235.

material of quite different form to that found in 24:1-35, namely *meshalim* of one kind or another. For this reason, while emphasising the balance and coherence of the whole section found in Matthew 24-25, we will delay discussion of 24:36-25:46 until chapter 6. At this point, we will proceed to the detailed exegesis of the first part of the passage (24:1-35).[222]

Setting and the Disciples' Question

The statement that Jesus left the temple forms a conclusion to the temple scenes begun at the beginning of chapter 21 and running right through chapters 22 and 23, thus also forming a link between chapters 21-23 and the eschatological discourse of chapters 24-25. Besides being a statement of historical fact, the action is symbolic of Jesus' abandoning the temple.[223] The account recalls Ezekiel's vision of the departure of the glory of God from the temple (Ezek. 10:18-19), particularly when the link is made with the Mount of Olives in verse 3 (cf. Ezek. 11:22-23).[224] Davies and Allison comment that they do not agree with those who claim that here Jesus abandons Israel, because the mission to Israel continues through his followers and because 'the repentance of Israel is an eschatological hope.'[225]

Though Jesus is leaving the temple, the temple is still the subject of Matthew's discourse. Matthew does not record the reason why the disciples drew Jesus attention to the temple structure, but this brief comment may well reflect the sense of bewilderment felt by Jewish men who have just heard their master pronounce judgement on the heart of their religious life.[226]

The question Οὐ βλέπετε ταῦτα πάντα; is formed in such a way (using the negative particle οὐ) as to imply that a positive response is expected.[227] The phrase ταῦτα πάντα recurs four more times in the first section of the discourse (3, 8, 33, 34) but in this case the reference is not to the various events which Jesus will go on to describe (if the disciples had 'seen' them, then Jesus would not have gone on to detail them so fully) but most naturally to the magnificent structures of the temple which have just been mentioned by the disciples. Jesus goes on to use the formula of solemnity ἀμὴν λέγω ὑμῖν, the first of three instances in chapter 24 (see also verses 34 and 47) and of a total of six instances in 24-5 (see also 25:12, 40, 45), in order to predict complete devastation on the temple buildings. The certainty and completeness of the destruction are empha-

---

[222] The structure follows closely that offered by Garland, *Reading Matthew*, 236-39.

[223] *Cf.* 23:38-9. So Davies and Allison, *Matthew*, 3:334.

[224] Garland, *Reading Matthew*, 234; Davies and Allison, *Matthew*, 3:334.

[225] Davies and Allison, *Matthew*, 3:334 n. 38.

[226] France, *Matthew*, 336.

[227] Wallace, *Greek Grammar Beyond the Basics*, 449-50; Porter, *Idioms of the Greek New Testament*, 278.

sised by the use of the two negative particles (οὐ μή).[228] While Davies and Allison are correct in affirming that the majority view of these words is that they are 'usually thought of as a fulfilled prophecy for the reader, who knows the events of AD 70,' the precise date of final composition of the gospel is of little consequence to the narrative which quite clearly presents the events as taking place at some undefined point in the future.[229]

By this dramatic act Jesus again indicates his role as a prophet in two ways. Firstly, his spoken words are to be regarded as themselves a prophetic act for the sake of those who hear them. Thus Jesus reinforces the message of the prophetic actions of chapter 21 with a prophetic utterance.[230] Secondly, these words move Jesus beyond the prophetic ministry of proclaiming judgement on his contemporary society into the associated ministry of proclaiming the future

---

[228] Porter, *Idioms of the Greek New Testament*, 283. Wallace, *Greek Grammar Beyond the Basics*, 468-69.

[229] It should not be necessary to treat Jesus' words regarding the fall of the temple as *vaticinia ex eventu* simply on the basis of choosing a post-AD 70 date for the composition of the gospel. If the author of Matthew was indeed able and willing to distinguish the 'past of Jesus' from his own day, then we could expect that he would record Jesus' pre-AD 70 words accurately even if he was writing post-AD 70. It is well known that the words of Jesus do not conform as closely to the precise events of the sacking of Jerusalem as we might expect of *vaticinia ex eventu*, for example in that he does not indicate destruction by fire, and that some of the massive stones of the temple's retaining wall did remain on top of each other, and can still be seen today. For full discussion see Keener, *Matthew*, 561-62. Thus I can agree in part with T. R. Hatina, 'Focus', 44, who, in reference to the parallel discourse in Mark 13 states that, 'Whether the final form of the discourse was written prior to 70 or as an *ex eventu* prophecy just after 70 has little bearing on determining the function of the quotations in Mark's narrative world. The important point from a literary perspective is that the prophecy is attributed to Jesus who, as a character in the story, antedates the destruction of the temple.' I would add that it is not only from a literary point of view that this issue should be viewed. If we are to believe that Matthew intended to portray Jesus with historical credibility then it is acceptable to believe that Matthew would record Jesus' point faithfully whether the temple had been destroyed or not. Thus Casey's criticism of France to the effect that 'the foundation of France's expectation is a dogmatic belief in the authenticity and accuracy of Jesus' predictions so strong that he expects the Marcan prophecy to read like some pedant's account of the event written after it' (173), apart from revealing clearly Casey's own presuppositions, is not telling. It does not matter when the account was written; what matters is whether it accurately reflects what Jesus prophesied. Keener cites 1QpHab 9.6-7 (which is quite clearly to be dated pre-AD 70) as a contemporary 'prediction' of the raiding of the temple which cannot, by that very fact, be turned into a post-AD 70 document: 'but in the Last Days their riches and plunder alike will be handed over to the army of the Kittim, for they are "the rest of the peoples".'

[230] See Byrskog, *Story as History*, 104, on the relationship between words and actions in Jesus' ministry.

acts of God.

This element of Matthew's portrait of Jesus the prophetic judge must be taken seriously, and must not be casually dismissed as unhistorical. It is entirely in keeping with the model of prophetic ministry presented in the Hebrew Scriptures that Jesus should be a prophet in the two-fold sense of 'forth-telling' a message of judgement to his contemporaries and 'fore-telling' events yet to take place. Indeed, there is a clear sense of progression which links chapter 24 with the three previous chapters. Where they have indicated Jesus' proclamation of judgement on the temple, chapter 24 indicates that this judgement will be devastating and complete. Garland comments,

> Jesus' answer goes beyond repudiation of the temple to a prophecy of its total destruction.[231]

That these words were startling to Jesus' disciples is indicated clearly in verse 3 where Matthew allows his readers to 'overhear' the amazed questioning of the disciples. Jesus is once more found on the Mount of Olives (cf. 21:1) where he takes up the posture of the Rabbi. This place was 'already resonant with apocalyptic overtones', being associated with the judgement of the Messiah on his enemies (Zechariah 14:4, καὶ στήσονται οἱ πόδες αὐτοῦ ἐν τῇ ἡμέρᾳ ἐκείνῃ ἐπὶ τὸ ὄρος τῶν ἐλαιῶν τὸ κατέναντι Ιερουσαλημ ἐξ ἀνατολῶν καὶ σχισθήσεται τὸ ὄρος τῶν ἐλαιῶν τὸ ἥμισυ αὐτοῦ πρὸς ἀνατολὰς καὶ τὸ ἥμισυ αὐτοῦ πρὸς θάλασσαν χάος μέγα σφόδρα καὶ κλινεῖ τὸ ἥμισυ τοῦ ὄρους πρὸς βορρᾶν καὶ τὸ ἥμισυ αὐτοῦ πρὸς νότον).[232] Matthew agrees with Mark's form of the question concerning 'these things' (ταῦτα) but introduces the words 'of your coming' (τῆς σῆς παρουσίας) to the section concerned with 'the end of the age' (συντελείας τοῦ αἰῶνος). The 'end of the age' indicates the apocalyptic scheme of dividing time into two parts which are separated by the decisive act of God (cf. Matt 12:32).[233] While some have interpreted the term to refer to the end of the 'Jewish age', the more natural reading is a reference to the final and climactic act of God (cf. Matthew's use of the phrase in 13:39, 40, 49; 28:20).[234] The *Parousia* and the end of the age are closely linked here by the use of a single definite article.[235] While some have suggested that this is a reinterpretation by Matthew which departs from the simple question recorded in Mark, it is better to understand Matthew's form either as indicating the full implications of the disciples' question, or perhaps more likely, the fact that the disciples were unable at that point to comprehend that there was a distinction

---

[231] Garland, *Reading Matthew*, 235.
[232] Blomberg, *Matthew*, 353.
[233] See Allison, *The End of the Ages Has Come*.
[234] See France, *Matthew*, 337.
[235] So Blomberg, *Matthew*, 353 n. 37.

between the destruction of the temple and the end of the age.[236] It is perhaps because of this confusion of the two events in the minds of the disciples that Jesus concentrates his attention first of all on the danger of being deceived, but a fair reading of the disciples' question will reveal that it is quite possible to understand the question as being composed of two distinct issues, however much the disciples may have confused the two. Understanding the question in this way allows us to recognise a very ordered response on the part of Jesus which is conveyed by Matthew in a similarly ordered way.

As this saying includes the first occurrence of the important term παρουσία in Matthew, it is necessary at this point to consider briefly its significance.[237] Although Matthew's account of the eschatological discourse is in many ways parallel to those of Mark and Luke, the use of this term is unparalleled.[238] It is quite clear from both the parallel accounts of the 'eschatological discourse' in the other synoptic gospels and from the traces of Jesus' Aramaic teaching in the gospels, that the use of this precise Greek term almost certainly does not originate with Jesus and that Matthew's use of the term is redactional. Yet Matthew's understanding of this term is so distinctive that the question arises, What does he understand it to signify? And why does he use it at certain points in the discourse and not at others? There is some NT evidence to indicate that παρουσία was beginning to take on the character of a technical term in early Christian discourse about Jesus' future return. Important passages include 1 Cor. 15:23; 1 Thess. 2:19; 3:13; 4:14; 5:23; James 5:7,[239] 9; 2 Peter 1:16; 3:4, 12; 1 John 2:28.[240] The Matthean context of these occurrences of παρουσία indicates that Matthew uses them to refer to a climactic appearance of Jesus at the close of the age (see 24:3). Thus, while we can admit that the term probably does not belong to the vocabulary of Jesus himself, it may nonetheless help us to recognise a nuance in Jesus' eschatological teaching as presented by Matthew which distinguishes the final appearance of Jesus from more imminent expressions of his activity as judge. If we can see consistency in the usage of

---

[236] So J. Calvin, *Matthew, Mark and Luke, Vol III* (Translated by A. W. Morrison; Grand Rapids: Eerdmans, 1972 [1555]), 75. Also Garland, 235.

[237] The fullest study of the term, with particular reference to its use by Paul in the NT, is J. Plevnik, *Paul and the Parousia* (Peabody: Hendrickson, 1997). The first two chapters of this book are particularly useful for their survey of canonical and non-canonical Jewish literature. The term is found only in Matthew 24:3, 27, 37, 39. It is also found in Jud 10:18; 2 Macc 8:12; 15:21; 3 Macc 1:27; 3:17 where it has the meaning 'coming', 'arrival' or presence'. See Plevnik, *Parousia*, 4. See also *NIDNTT*, 2:898-901.

[238] In these parallel accounts, the verb ἔρχομαι is employed.

[239] Although the precise referent of the term is debated, Davids can conclude 'The Christian hope, then, is the coming of Christ when all the wrongs suffered will be set right.' See P. H. Davids, *Commentary on James* (NIGTC; Grand Rapids: Eerdmans, 1982), 182-83.

[240] Plevnik, *Parousia*, 4.

this term, that will add further weight to this argument.

Answer 1. Jesus' Reply re the Destruction of the Temple (24:4-35)

PRELUDE TO THE CATASTROPHE (24:4-14)

Jesus begins his discourse with an imperative (Βλέπετε[241]) which sounds a note of urgency that recurs throughout the discourse. Ladd is correct to note that here Jesus is closer to the prophets than to the apocalypticists (or at least some of them) in that knowledge of the future is not regarded as an end in itself but rather a spur to faithful discipleship.[242]

Verse 4 also marks the discourse off from apocalyptic concerns in that the emphasis here and in the following verses to verse 14 is on the events which should *not* be regarded as signalling the end.[243] D. Sim misses this point entirely when he writes,

> In 24:4-31 Matthew details not merely the arrival of the Son of Man, but the events which precede and herald this event. This section of the gospel is equivalent to the eschatological woes and signs of the end which are normally a part of Jewish apocalyptic-eschatological schemes and which provide information on the timing of the end.[244]

And further,

> In 24:4-14, which is a heavily edited version of Mark 13:3-8, 13, the Matthean Jesus sets out a timetable of the end.[245]

This could only be written by an author who is not prepared to allow Matthew's words in 24:4-14 and 24:36 to carry equal weight.

It is significant that throughout the section comprising verses 4-35 the second person is used extensively. While it could be argued that this is Matthew's editorial work serving to apply the passage specifically to the readers within his community, the more natural reading, on the assumption that Matthew is a faithful recorder of traditional material, is that it is the disciples who will witness and experience the events described.[246] This stands in contrast with the more detached language in the section vv. 36-40. The form of the language, therefore, helps to sustain the view that the events described in verses 4-35 are

---

[241] On Mark's use of this verb, see especially T. J. Geddert, *Watchwords: Mark 13 in Markan Eschatology* (JSNTS 26; Sheffield: JSOT Press, 1989).

[242] Ladd *The Presence of the Future*, 327-28.

[243] Garland, *Reading Matthew*, 236.

[244] Sim, *Apocalyptic Eschatology*, 99.

[245] Sim, *Apocalyptic Eschatology*, 99-100.

[246] So Garland, *Reading Matthew*, 235.

events of the first century which were indeed witnessed by the disciples or their contemporaries.

Jesus' concern is that the disciples be 'deceived'. We must briefly consider how such deception might come about.

FALSE CHRISTS

Matthew portrays Jesus as predicting false Christs who come in his name (v.5). This does not require that they claim identity with him, or that they explicitly claim to be the Messiah, but that they claim to be what (Jesus implicitly claims) he alone is. [247] The fact that the prediction refers to roughly contemporaneous events does not minimise the real note of prediction. Matthew has Jesus exercise the role of a true prophet bringing both insight into the future and ethical exhortation to his disciples. The deceivers will be significant in number (πολ λοί). This word recurs frequently in vv. 4-14 indicating the scale of deception and the need for the disciples to be on their guard (*cf.* 10, 11 [*bis*], 12). A number of commentators point to bar Kochba in the early second century,[248] but the fact that he fits the picture does not rule out the possibility of such claims being made significantly earlier.

POLITICAL UPHEAVAL

Jesus indicates that the conflicts which arise from time to time (particularly so in the turbulent political conditions of first century Palestine[249]), and which could perhaps be interpreted as signs of 'the end' by anxious onlookers, are *not* to be interpreted as such but are to be seen as the inevitable outworking of the desires of sinful humanity, within the overarching control of God (δεῖ is indicative of God's activity). The list of disasters, both political and natural, continues in verse 7.

NATURAL UPHEAVAL

The image of labour-pains was commonly used in apocalyptic literature to signify extreme suffering and more specifically the 'Messianic woes'.[250] While there is recognition of the distressing nature of these experiences, they are only the 'beginning' (ἀρχή) of the labour-pains and must not be construed as indica-

---

[247] Davies and Allison, *Matthew*, 3:338-39, comment, 'The first and second centuries saw quite a few famous false prophets who made eschatological claims. That any of them (before Bar Kochba) said, in so many words, "I am Messiah", is undemonstrated by the sources. But several of them did identify themselves as the eschatological prophet like Moses, a figure Matthew equated with Messiah.'

[248] E.g., Blomberg, *Matthew*, 353.

[249] Borg's revised thesis, *Conflict, Holiness and Politics in the Teachings of Jesus*, gives a valuable insight into this aspect of first century life. See particularly pp. 43-87.

[250] See *1 Enoch* 62:4; *4 Ezra* 4:42; *Tg. Ps.* 18:14. For a recent discussion of this imagery see C. Gempf, 'Birth Pains in the New Testament' *TynB* 45 (1994), 119-135. See also Allison, *The End of the Ages has Come*.

tions of an imminent end.

'Then' (τότε) is to be understood in the sense of 'at that time'; it does not imply chronological sequence.[251] The progression in the discourse is not temporal (i.e., a list of consecutive events) but by category, as the focus of the discourse shifts from the grand scale in referring to trials that will affect the Jewish nation to the smaller scale in taking up trials through which the disciples must pass. This is most clearly seen in the shift from the third person to the second.

The reference to ψευδοπροφῆται sounds a note of stark contrast between Jesus (the true prophet) and those who will come. It is interesting to note the use of this term in connection with Jesus' predictive discourse on the future faced by the disciples. The mark of a false prophet, clearly established by Deut 18:18-22 is that his words do not come true. Jesus freely speaks as a prophet who has an insight into the counsel of God which he shares with his disciples. Note the repeated use of the future tense (παραδώσουσιν ὑμᾶς εἰς θλῖψιν καὶ ἀποκ τενοῦσιν ὑμᾶς, καὶ ἔσεσθε μισούμενοι ὑπὸ πάντων τῶν ἐθνῶν διὰ τὸ ὄνομά μου), and Matthew apparently has no fear that Jesus himself will be shown to be a false prophet.

Our reading of this first section of Jesus' teaching as primarily concerned with the events of the early first century might be challenged on the basis of verse 13, where Jesus speaks of 'the end'. Do these words indicate that Jesus anticipated 'the end', in the sense of the final judgement, to come in the lifetime of some who were enduring these hardships? Or is it that he called his disciples to remain faithful 'until their last breath'? France claims that the phrase 'to the end' here,

> does not necessarily point to the apocalyptic consummation (as though those who have lived earlier cannot be saved!), but is a standard phrase for 'right through' (it lacks the article, which would be needed, as in vv. 6 and 14, to refer to '*the* End'). The whole verse is repeated from 10:22, where it clearly related to the contemporary situation of the mission to Israel, not to 'the close of the age'.[252]

Verse 14 picks up the same word to claim that 'the end' (τὸ τέλος) will be preceded by the preaching of the 'gospel of the kingdom' in the 'whole world'. Here, in contrast to verse 13, the articular noun τὸ τέλος is used, and appears to refer to the final consummation, but there is no specific timing implied by the verse. What is clear is that Jesus expects his disciples to be actively involved in a programme of preaching the gospel, not waiting for an end to the world in passive resignation.

Garland compares Jesus' description of coming events with the perception of Tacitus of his own day:

---

[251] So, Hagner, *Matthew 14-28*, 694.
[252] France, *Matthew*, 339.

The history on which I am entering is that of a period rich in disasters, terrible with battles, torn by civil struggles, horrible even in peace. Four emperors fell by the sword; there were three civil wars, more foreign wars, and often both at the same time ... Italy was distressed by disasters unknown before or returning after the lapse of the ages ... Beside the manifold misfortunes that befell mankind there were prodigies in the sky and on the earth, warnings given by thunderbolts, and prophecies of the future, both joyful and gloomy, uncertain and clear.[253]

Tacitus seems to have drawn on idioms similar to those found the gospels. His account indicates that Jesus was by no means using language inappropriate for what was to come in the following decades.

WARNINGS TO FLEE BEFORE ERUPTION OF HOSTILITIES (24:15-22)

The connective particle οὖν at the beginning of verse 15 indicates that the events described in verses 4-14 are to precede the events of 15-22. Matthew introduces his readers to 'the abomination of desolation' (τὸ βδέλυγμα τῆς ἐρημώσεως)[254] which is explicitly identified as a reference to Daniel (specifically to Dan 9:27; 11:31 [where the phrase in the LXX is anarthrous] and 12:11. The equivalent Hebrew phrase is שִׁקּוּץ מְשֹׁמֵם/ שִׁקּוּצִים מְשֹׁמֵם). Once again, Jesus is presented as deliberately aligning himself with the prophets of a previous time. The significance of the phrase is not transparent, quite probably intentionally so.

The call to pray is not simply a convention meaning 'hope for the best'. It is an imperative to the disciples to recognise the sovereign rule of God even in the darkest hour. Does it suggest that because the devastation which will occur is the judgement of God which vindicates Jesus as the true prophet, the disciples can be assured that the one who is in control of the devastation is also willing to hear their prayers? G. Stanton notes that though Matthew follows Mark closely throughout most of this section of the discourse, he adds two phrases at this point: ἡ φυγὴ ὑμῶν and μηδὲ σαββάτῳ. He helpfully surveys the various opinions on this verse. He then goes on to discuss the first of the additional phrases. The subjects of ἡ φυγὴ ὑμῶν are most naturally identified as 'those in Judaea' (v. 16, where the cognate verb is used). Stanton argues, on the basis of his understanding of Matthew's redaction, that the words indicate that the believers of Matthew's day will be persecuted so that they will have to flee.[255] Thus, on this reading, Matthew has quite significantly altered the thrust of Mark's account.[256] Stanton then goes on to argue that the prayer to avoid the Sabbath is not due to legalism on Matthew's part but rather to the desire to avoid hostility from the Jewish authorities. While there is much to be said for Stanton's exegesis, it is not helpful that he largely removes the verse from its setting in the teaching of

[253] *Histories*, 1.2, 3.
[254] *Cf.* Mark 13:14
[255] Stanton, *A Gospel for a New People*, 199.
[256] Stanton, *A Gospel for a New People*, 200.

Jesus and instead finds its relevance in a post-AD 70 Matthean community.[257] While any late-first-century readers of Matthew's gospel could doubtless find relevance for their own situation in Jesus' words, that does not limit their relevance to the pre-AD 70 disciples who might face arduous conditions, limited possibilities for travel and perhaps direct opposition from Jewish authorities if flight on a Sabbath became necessary due to the devastation brought upon Jerusalem in the coming crisis.[258] Blomberg helpfully writes,

> Undoubtedly, much that surrounded the destruction of the temple and the Jewish war of A.D. 70 will be repeated, probably on a larger scale, just prior to Christ's return. But given the thoroughly Jewish nature of all of the details of vv. 15-20, their close correspondence to the actual events of the mid-first century, and the more explicit wording of Luke 21:20-24, there is no reason to take any of Matthew's text here as looking beyond the events that culminated in the destruction of the temple in A.D. 70.[259]

The comments of Sim regarding the significance of verse 20 are also misguided, and require to be corrected by Blomberg's position:

> The addition of the sabbath reference makes no sense at all if the flight is an event of the past and the day of flight is already established; clearly here Matthew is thinking of an event which has yet to take place. This means that all the material in the immediate context of this verse, Matthew 24:15-28, seems to pertain to the future and not to the past.[260]

Aside from the problem of making verse 20 the key to such a large portion of the discourse, Sim's view suffers from the fallacy that because Matthew is (assumed to be) writing after the events of the fall of Jerusalem, he cannot accurately record Jesus speaking of these events with a perspective from which they are yet to take place. That Matthew's readers might know the date of 'the flight' has precisely no bearing on the accuracy of Matthew's recollection and transmission of Jesus' words, nor on the significance that these words would have had for Jesus' audience in the setting of the narrative.

A passing comment in an article by A. Saldarini indicates something of the absurdity brought about by reading 24:20 as a reference to the end of the world. In the context of a discussion of the place of Sabbath observance within the early Christian communities, he writes:

---

[257] See now the important volume edited by R. Bauckham, *The Gospels for All Christians* (Edinburgh: T&T Clark, 1998).

[258] See Blomberg, *Matthew*, 358.

[259] Blomberg, *Matthew*, 359.

[260] Sim, *Apocalyptic Eschatology*, 157.

Matthew's group observes the Sabbath seriously enough to forbid Sabbath flight from the dangers and horrors of the end of the world (24:20).[261]

According to Saldarini's reading, we must reckon with (a) words ascribed to Jesus actually originating in a much later Matthean community; (b) a group who will attempt to flee from the destruction of the cosmos (an activity doomed from the start?), and who have 'the words of Jesus' to encourage them in their enterprise; and (c) a group who are instructed by Jesus to pray that 'the end of the world' will not take place on a sabbath because if it does, they will not be allowed to flee! Such an approach to interpretation completely prevents Matthew from being heard as a narrator of the ministry and teaching of Jesus, and locates the key to interpretation in the reconstructed Matthean community of the late first century. This thesis is an attempt to redress this imbalance.

Thus, up to verse 22, Matthew has recorded Jesus' teaching on distress that will come upon the disciples themselves within a relatively short period of time because of their location in Judea. When the climax of the distress comes upon Jerusalem, the disciples are instruced to flee to the mountains for safety. All of Jesus' teaching can quite naturally be interpreted as predictions of the events of the Jewish war.

DESTRUCTION OF JERUSALEM DESCRIBED IN STEREOTYPED IMAGES OF THE 'COMING SON OF MAN' AND COSMIC CATACLYSM (24:23-31)

In attempting to interpret what is by any standards a rather difficult passage, care must be taken to avoid taking any single pericope or phrase out of its context. The context, of course, is not simply the immediate sentence or paragraph but the whole of Jesus' discourse as recorded by Matthew. Any interpretation must do justice to the progression of thought in the Matthean discourse as a whole.

It is in this section that the term 'Son of Man' (in the context of the longer phrase ἡ παρουσία τοῦ υἱοῦ τοῦ ἀνθρώπου) makes its first appearance in Matthew 21-25, and so we must take some time to consider the meaning of this phrase in its Matthean context. It is important to note, for example, that the reference to the Son of Man comes towards the end of a series of verses that otherwise speak of the appearance of counterfeit Christs, an issue that has already been introduced in 24:5.

Previously we argued that Jewish writers (in the OT, in the intertestamental literature and in early Christian literature) often used language, which might appear to modern western readers to have its primary referent in the end of the physical universe, in a figurative sense in order to refer to the activity of God in history. This has been described by some authors as 'apocalyptic' language, but given that it frequently appears in documents which do not exhibit the typical

---

[261] A. Saldarini, 'Comparing the Traditions: New Testament and Rabbinic Literature' *BBR* 7 (1997), 195-204, here at 199-200.

features of 'apocalyptic literature', it is probably best to describe such language as 'figurative' or 'visionary'. In the present section we wish to test this view on some of the most controversial passages in the gospel of Matthew - the 'coming Son of Man' sayings.

These sayings are important to our argument for several reasons.

1. So far as the historical Jesus is concerned, they are regarded by Borg as being inauthentic, and therefore receive no serious exegetical treatment in his writings. Yet these sayings are exceptionally important for a discussion of judgement in Matthew since, according to the majority of interpreters, they refer to the complex of events associated with the return of Jesus, including eschatological judgement.

2. The coming Son of Man sayings employ language which has been described as 'apocalyptic' (better, 'figurative and visionary') in a way that makes them excellent examples with which to test the validity of our earlier conclusions about the proper interpretation of such language.

3. These sayings provide a valuable sample of texts to test in order to provide indications of Matthew's reliability as a source of information on the historical Jesus. There are a number of these texts, found in various sections of the gospel, and they have been highly contested as to their authenticity, not only by Borg, but by many scholars before and since he wrote. They are, then, some of the hardest possible texts to justify as authentic teaching of Jesus. We do not intend to argue for their authenticity directly, but we believe that evidence that Matthew has set them in appropriate contexts will indicate that Matthew's competence as a communicator of factual information is confirmed, and this will have implications for the authenticity of these sayings.

It is my intention now to indicate how the 'coming Son of Man' sayings can be interpreted naturally in the context of Matthew's narrative without resorting to an 'end of the world' interpretation. In this way, I hope to show the invalidity of the view of M. Borg that these sayings cannot be accepted as authentic words of Jesus because they present an 'end of the world Jesus.'

We must be clear that it is only this group of 'Son of Man' sayings in particular which are in view. As is well known, the gospels portray Jesus using the phrase[262] 'Son of Man' in various ways. Scholars have categorised the various sayings as follows:

Group A: sayings about the earthly activity of the Son of Man.

Group B: sayings about the suffering, death and resurrection of the Son of Man.

Group C: sayings about the future coming and glory of the Son of Man.[263]

---

[262] We refrain here from use of the term 'title' since the validity of this term is disputed.

[263] The basic analysis may be traced, at least, to R. Bultmann, *Theology of the New Testament* (London: SCM Press, 1952), 1:30. Compare C. Caragounis, *The Son of*

The first thing to be said about the language of the 'coming Son of Man' sayings is that there is an obvious Jewish background for the NT usage of the phrase in the prophecy of Daniel.[264] The fact that the language is entirely Jewish should lead to an inclination to accept its authenticity (as it would be an entirely reasonable thing for Jesus to draw on language from his scriptures) and to concentrate on its interpretation. However, few scholars have been so accepting of the phrase, as we shall see. While we would hold that it is a defensible position that Jesus had the figure of Daniel 7:13 in mind when using the phrase in any context, we want to focus particularly on the occasions in Matthew when there appears to be a very conscious allusion to the 'apocalyptic' language of Daniel 7.

A primary reason which Borg offers for abandoning the 'end-of-the-world Jesus' is that the exegetical base of this position has been eroded. He develops this position most fully in his article, 'An Orthodoxy Reconsidered: The "End-of-the-World Jesus"'.[265] He cites the common scholarly agreement that the 'coming Son of Man' sayings are inauthentic.[266] In particular, he mentions the six such sayings which are threats: Luke 12:8-9;[267] Mark 8:38;[268] Luke 12:39-40;[269] Luke 17:23-4, 37;[270] Luke 17:26-7; Luke 17:28-30. In these he finds no unambiguous element of imminence, though he does find such a note of imminence in Mark 13:26-7 and in Matt 10:23.[271]

The struggle is thus abandoned; the hard work is avoided. We regard this aspect of Borg's work as being particularly weak, and unfortunate. It is, unfortunately, not unique, however. D. R. A. Hare similarly writes

> If *bar enasha* was used by Jesus as a modest self-designation, it is unlikely that any of the apocalyptic Son of man sayings are authentic. They conform so closely

---

Man (WUNT I 38; Tübingen: JCB Mohr, 1986), 145-47; I. H. Marshall, 'The Synoptic "Son of Man" Sayings in the Light of Linguistic Research' in T. E. Schmidt and M. Silva (eds), *To Tell the Mystery* (JSNTS 100; Sheffield: JSOT Press, 1994), 72-94, here 74.

[264] See Caragounis, *Son of Man*, 35-81, 168-243; Casey, *Son of Man: The Interpretation and Influence of Daniel 7* (London: SPCK, 1979).

[265] See also Borg's article, 'A Temperate Case for a Non-Eschatological Jesus' *Foundations and Facets Forum* 2.3 (1986), 81-101.

[266] He points particularly to the work of G. Vermes and N. Perrin.

[267] The parallel passage in Matthew 10:32 omits the phrase 'Son of Man'.

[268] // Matthew 16:27. Also Mark 8:38.

[269] // Matthew 24:43-44.

[270] // Matthew 24:23, 27

[271] However, his response to these latter texts, 'An Orthodoxy Reconsidered', 214, is, 'But it is precisely the "coming Son of man" sayings which modern scholarship increasingly views as not coming from Jesus'.

to the expectation of Jesus' Parousia that soon prevailed in the post-Easter church that all can be readily explained on this basis.[272]

Claiming, as he does, to stand within a stream of scholarship which rejects the unhealthy scepticism of the past regarding what we can know of Jesus, it is frustrating to see Borg (and others) resort so quickly to the cry of 'inauthentic' when he comes to these sayings.[273] The frustration is exacerbated when we see the slender foundation on which he rests this judgement. The first plank is the 'psychological difficulty' which demands that we ask the question:

> what kind of consciousness is attributed to Jesus if he is thought to speak of several stages of his own activity *after death*?[274]

This question indicates that Borg is making the *a priori* assumption that Jesus *could not* have understood himself to have a future role in the purposes of God, unless that view is to be attributed to the state of his 'mental health'.[275] This raises the question of how Jesus understood himself and his mission. The recent careful work of B. Witherington[276] has established, on the basis of the most securely authentic texts, that Jesus understood himself to have a unique role in the purposes of God which he expressed through his relationships with John the Baptist, his disciples and the religious leaders of his day, through his actions and through his words. If Jesus could speak in startling terms derived from the OT about his present activity, [277] there is surely no reason why he could not have derived, from the same source, startling views about his future activity. The fact that Borg has more recently rested his dismissal of these sayings on the tradition analysis of J. D. Crossan has done little to bolster his foundation, or to convince other scholars.[278]

The second plank on which Borg builds his case is the argument that there was no expectation of an apocalyptic 'Son of Man' in contemporary Jewish

---

[272] D. R. A. Hare, *The Son of Man Tradition*, 277. Hare cites Schweitzer, 'Der Menschensohn', 192; Glasson, 'Theophany and Parousia', 265ff.; and Wrede, *Messianic Secret*, 220 in support of his position.

[273] Allison, who himself is not unwilling to declare synoptic material secondary, challenges this perception of current scholarly opinion: 'in order to be fair it should be added that there is hardly here a consensus' (*Jesus of Nazareth*, 115-16, n. 81). Allison cites J. Becker, D. R. Catchpole, J. J. Collins, A. Y Collins, V. Hampel, U. Luz, M. Reiser and E. P. Sanders as witnesses against Borg's blanket claim.

[274] Borg, *Conflict*, 231. The italics are Borg's. Borg traces this view particularly to John Knox, *The Death of Christ* (London, 1959), 54-60.

[275] Borg, *Conflict*, 232. The latter comment is also drawn from Knox, 58.

[276] Witherington, *The Christology of Jesus*. Compare Witherington's follow-up essay 'The Christology of Jesus' in M. A. Powell and D. R. Bauer (eds), *Who Do You Say That I Am?* (Louisville: Westminster/John Knox Press, 1999).

[277] So Hare, *The Son of Man Tradition*, 278.

[278] See the discussion of these sayings in Allison, *Jesus of Nazareth*, 116-20.

literature. The only source which might be adduced in support of such a figure, the Similitudes of Enoch (*1 Enoch* 37-71) is ruled out on the basis that there is no evidence of its existence at the time of Jesus.[279] This point of view is, of course, hotly debated in contemporary scholarship.[280] Following a brief discussion of the evidence, M. Reddish concludes, contrary to Borg, that, although the available data are not conclusive,

> they do strongly suggest that the 'Similitudes' were probably produced during the first half of the first century CE.[281]

Thus, though his conclusion *may* be correct, Borg's confidence in the scholarly consensus on this matter should be treated with great caution.

As the third plank in his argument, Borg also refers to the work of G. Vermes which, he claims has established that

> *bar nasha* was such a common expression (meaning "man", "someone", or used as a circumlocution in certain well-defined circumstances) that it would have been virtually impossible for somebody to invest it with titular significance.[282]

Once again, it is true that Borg has some significant figures within biblical scholarship on his side in this matter. Notable supporters (at least in part) of Black, Vermes and (by extension) Borg include B. Lindars[283] and M. Casey.[284] R. J. Bauckham holds that the phrase means 'someone'.[285] However, there have been strong challenges to this viewpoint.[286] For example, C. F. D. Moule, in a brief note, reaffirms the view that the arthrous form of the phrase '*the* Son of Man' indicates an anaphoric use of the article to indicate that Jesus spoke of

---

[279] *Cf.* J. T. Milik, *The Books of Enoch: Aramaic Fragments from Qumran Cave 4* (Oxford: Clarendon Press, 1976), 89-98.

[280] Collins, *The Apocalyptic Imagination*, 177-78.

[281] Reddish, *Apocalyptic Literature*, 164-65. So also Collins, *The Apocalyptic Imagination*, 178: 'The Similitudes, then, should be dated to the early or mid first century CE, prior to the Jewish revolt of 66-70 CE, to which it makes no reference.'

[282] Borg, *Conflict* 222-5. Borg cites two works of Vermes for support: 'The Use of *bar nash/bar nasha* in Jewish Aramaic' in M. Black, *An Aramaic Approach to the Gospels and Acts* (Oxford: Clarendon, 3rd edn 1967), 310-28, and *Jesus the Jew* (London: SCM Press, 1973), 160-91.

[283] *Jesus – Son of Man* (Grand Rapids: Eerdmans, 1981). 'Response to Richard Bauckham: The Idiomatic Use of *Bar Enasha*' *JSNT* 23 (1985), 35-41.

[284] *Son of Man: The Interpretation and Influence of Daniel 7* (London: SPCK, 1979).

[285] 'The Son of Man: "A Man in my Position" or "Someone"' *JSNT* 23 (1985), 35-41.

[286] See particularly Caragounis, *The Son of Man*, 21-33 on Vermes, Lindars and Casey. Also Marshall, 'The Synoptic "Son of Man" Sayings in the Light of Linguistic Research' 72-94, especially 79-94.

'*the* Son of man [whom you know from that vision]' and that he used Daniel's human figure as not primarily a title so much as a symbol for the vocation to victory through obedience and martyrdom to which he was called and to which he summoned his followers (so that they would together constitute 'the people of the saints of the Most High').[287]

Quite clearly there are many who would take issue with Moule's view. The debate continues and there is no sign of it subsiding, particularly with respect to the possible Aramaic background of the phrase.[288] Yet, the above discussion raises serious questions about the confidence with which Borg dismisses the 'coming Son of Man' sayings. Typical of his approach, Borg sums up his discussion by quoting the conclusion of Leivestad approvingly:

> Der apokalyptische Menschensohn ist eine theologische Erfindung der letzten hundert Jahre.[289]

However, I believe that Borg's attempt to dismiss the 'coming Son of Man' sayings does not stand up to scrutiny, and in the course of this section I will attempt to demonstrate that Matthew understood these words to be perfectly coherent and indeed necessary in his overall portrait of Jesus. While this argument cannot demonstrate the authenticity of these texts as accurate representations of the words of Jesus, it can indicate that these words may be interpreted in such a way that they conform to what we might expect Jesus to say, as a Jew steeped in the Hebrew scriptures.

While claiming that the 'coming Son of Man' sayings are 'unlikely' to be authentic, Hare nonetheless recognises the consistency with which Matthew uses this language:

> It is indisputable that Matthew not only uses the term more frequently than any other Gospel writer but uses it more often in an apocalyptic context.[290]

---

[287] Moule, ' "The Son of Man": Some of the Facts' in *Forgiveness and Reconciliation*, 207.

[288] See particularly the numerous publications of P. M. Casey. The printed version of a discussion of the work of N. T. Wright involving Casey and C. Marsh, together with a response by Wright highlights fundamental disagreement concerning the proper methodology for, and indeed the benefits of, studying first century Aramaic in order to understand Jesus' words. See C. Marsh 'Theological History? N. T. Wright's *Jesus and the Victory of God*', P. M. Casey, 'Where Wright is Wrong: A Critical Review of N. T. Wright's *Jesus and the Victory of God*' and N. T. Wright, 'Theology, History and Jesus: A Response to Maurice Casey and Clive Marsh' *JSNT* 69 (1998), 77-94, 95-103, 105-112.

[289] Borg, *Conflict* 371, n. 79, quoting R. Leivestad, 'Der apokalyptische Menschensohn: ein theologisches Phantom' *ASTI* 6 (1967), 101. Hare draws on both Vermes and Leivestad in his volume, *The Son of Man Tradition*. See pages ix-x.

The accuracy of Hare's observation suggests that Matthew uses this phrase deliberately and with some measure of care. Our intention here is to examine the 'coming Son of Man' sayings in their Matthean context, based on the understanding that Matthew's redactional skill was such that any saying in his gospel is used in a way that is consistent with his own interpretation.[291] Hare supports such an approach, claiming,

> It must be insisted that Matthew's understanding of the term can be obtained, if at all, only through careful observation of how he places Son of man sayings in context. An unprejudiced investigation must depend heavily on composition and redaction criticism.[292]

Thus, we will not favour any interpretation which requires an understanding of a particular saying which is in radical discontinuity with the Matthean context in which that saying is found. What we are suggesting is that an author has a right that his work should be read as a coherent expression of his thought, and that some degree of effort should be expended in the process of trying to trace that coherent position. It may be that after much effort it is found to be impossible to trace any coherence in a part or the whole of a piece of literature, but that should be a conclusion that is come to when all other possibilities have been exhausted.[293] It is our conviction that Matthew's text is coherent as it stands and represents the intended narrative of the author. To dismember the author's narrative and to separate texts from their present context serves only to limit our opportunities for accurate interpretation, not to broaden them.

To examine a text in its context is particularly vital in the case of these 'coming Son of Man' sayings in that the verb ἔρχομαι is not used technically, even in conjunction with the phrase ὁ υἱὸς τοῦ ἀνθρώπου.[294] Thus, although the verb may have an apparently obvious meaning, we must recognise that it has a broad semantic field and its precise meaning can therefore only be established

---

[290] Hare, *The Son of Man Tradition*, 114.

[291] Thus Caird, *The Language and Imagery of the Bible*, 268, in discussing the words 'from now on' found in Matt. 26:64, comments, 'It little matters whether these words are his own editorial insertion or came to him from a traditional source. He was quite capable of deleting anything that did not express his own conviction.'

[292] Hare, *The Son of Man Tradition*, 115.

[293] It would appear that Hare jumps too quickly to accuse Matthew of inconsistency in his placing of sayings of Jesus so that 'the Matthean Jesus speaks prematurely of his future heavenly role (10:23, 32f.), before the disciples confess their faith in him as the Son of God (14:33; 16:16).' Hare is then forced to maintain that 'Matthew is not a theologian for whom consistency is the foremost virtue' and that 'Matthew's mind is not so disordered that we should expect "the Son of Man" to be used without consistency' (*The Son of Man Tradition*, 116). This equivocation makes it difficult for Hare to maintain his commitment to respecting the Matthean context.

[294] BAG, 310-11. In Matthew we find ἔρχομαι used with ὁ υἱὸς τοῦ ἀνθρώπου in 11:19 and 18:11, both in reference to the present earthly situation.

by the literary context. This approach, of course, does not resolve the question of whether Matthew is *justified* in placing such words on Jesus' lips, (*i.e.* whether any given saying is authentic) or, if he is, whether Matthew understands the words in the same way as Jesus did. While a great deal of time is spent in some works discussing the authenticity of individual sayings, I will focus on Matthew's use of the text, seeking to find a coherent interpretation of the text as it stands. It is not my intention to demonstrate the authenticity of each saying, but if sayings of Jesus as found in Matthew's narrative may be interpreted in a way that makes sense in their narrative setting *and* in the context of the conceptual and literary world of *Jesus'* day (in so far as we are able to construct that) then this will be a *prima facie* indicator that Matthew has accurately preserved and interpreted Jesus' words.[295]

Neither can our approach to the texts resolve the issue of whether the saying may have had a different original context than the one that Matthew assigns to it. However, it seems to me not unreasonable to assume that a saying should be interpreted by its present context in the gospel unless there is clear evidence that the Evangelist has placed a saying where it does not belong. That is to say that if we remove particular sayings from their present canonical contexts, then we will almost inevitably limit our ability to effectively interpret them.[296]

It is noteworthy that the first occurrence of a 'coming Son of Man' saying is found towards the end of the thirteenth chapter of Matthew's gospel. It is quite clearly the case that this particular expression is not essential to the presentation of Jesus as the eschatological judge, since there are several occasions earlier in the gospel where Matthew presents Jesus as the eschatological judge without using that term. For instance, Hare notes the absence of the phrase from the climactic conclusion of the Sermon on the Mount (7:22ff.), and correctly states that

Matthew's avoidance of the term at this important juncture should ... at least cause us to ponder whether he regards "the Son of man" as an apocalyptic title

---

[295] See the discussion of authenticity in Caragounis, *Son of Man*, 145-67.

[296] This is frequently done by commentators when they discuss Matthew 16:28. Seeking to offer a cautious corrective to this approach, Caragounis, *Son of Man*, 166-67, having affirmed his basic confidence in the genuine character of the 'Son of Man' tradition, writes, 'This is not to deny, however, that the exact wording of the contexts in which the SM term is embedded is often the wording of the evangelists. After all we need to recall the fact of translation. But this does not necessarily mean that the evangelists created the contexts and the sayings in which they merely inserted Jesus' phrase *bar-nasha*. Such sayings as contain this title were no doubt too specific, too poignant, "too catchy" to be forgotten in the tradition and therefore had a better chance than other things Jesus had said to survive intact.'

whose *primary* linguistic function is to identify Jesus as the eschatological judge.[297]

However, it is important to pay attention to these sayings because they have been identified by so many as a vulnerable part of the Jesus tradition. Since the primary focus of this thesis is on Matthew 21-25, we will devote our most sustained attention to the 'coming Son of Man' texts which are found within these chapters. Other such texts occurring beyond these chapters will be noted more briefly as confirmatory material in an Appendix. After each text reference, we have included a reference to the particular Greek term used in the pericope to designate the 'coming'.[298]

24:27 (παρουσία)

ὥσπερ γὰρ ἡ ἀστραπὴ ἐξέρχεται ἀπὸ ἀνατολῶν καὶ φαίνεται ἕως δυσμῶν, οὕτως ἔσται ἡ παρουσία τοῦ υἱοῦ τοῦ ἀνθρώπου·

Matthew introduces his eschatological discourse with the question about the destruction of the temple which is common to all the synoptic writers (24:3. *Cf.* Mk. 13:4; Lk. 21:7). However, he alters the latter part of the question concerning the sign, from a reference to 'these things' to 'your coming (τῆς σῆς παρουσίας) and the end of the age'.[299] This indicates that, in Matthew's view, the disciples had some form of expectation that Jesus would 'come' *even prior to* Jesus' death and resurrection. Caird believes that Matthew has recast the original question of Mark to accommodate his situation writing after the fall of Jerusalem.[300] It is certain, however, that in Matthew's mind there was an intimate connection but also a distinction between the two events. The two elements of the disciples' question are not epexegetical; the destruction of the temple is not (at least in a complete sense) the coming of Jesus at the end of the age.[301] However, it may indeed be the case, as Kik suggests, that the disciples anticipated an imminent end of the world which they would have linked with the destruction of the temple.[302] In this case the question which Matthew re-

---

[297] Hare, *The Son of Man Tradition*, 128.

[298] See Caragounis, *Son of Man*, 204-12, on the arguments for and against the authenticity of these sayings. Caragounis comes to positive conclusions regarding authenticity.

[299] Hare, *The Son of Man Tradition*, 168, regards this change as being 'the key to Matthew's understanding of the entire discourse'.

[300] Caird, *Language and Imagery*, 267-68.

[301] So Hare, *The Son of Man Tradition*, 168. However, Hare completely misses the point of this distinction when he goes on to write, 'In the succeeding discourse the destruction of Jerusalem is forgotten; attention is focused rather on Jesus' Parousia, the events or signs leading up to it, and the necessity of preparing oneself spiritually and ethically.'

[302] Kik, *Eschatology of Victory*, 83.

cords in verse 3 is an accurate account of the thought of the disciples while at the same time being at variance with Jesus' own future expectations.

When we come to verse 27, then, we are prepared for some reference to Jesus' 'coming'. Verses 23-26 makes it clear that people are always looking for the Messiah and will claim to have found him in secret. Jesus rejects such claims, after the fashion of verse 5, responding with a vivid simile. The language of lightning, while it no doubt implies suddenness, speaks primarily of the fact that all will know when the *Parousia* of the Son of Man takes place.[303] Verse 27 marks the first use of the term ἡ παρουσία in Jesus' discourse which alerts us to the fact that a comment is being made here which relates to the second part of the disciples' question (*cf.* v. 3). Witherington is correct to note that Jesus almost certainly never referred to his future return using the term *Parousia* since (1) he would have taught in Aramaic and (2) the term is used only by Matthew and is quite clearly redactional.[304] This does not, however, mean that its use is insignificant. Matthew appears to have intended a distinction between the παρουσία and other events which might be described in terms of 'coming' and so his use of this distinctive term is helpful in guiding our exegesis. Here the reference is to ἡ παρουσία τοῦ υἱοῦ τοῦ ἀνθρώπου, which indicates that Matthew (at least) regards the 'coming of the Son of Man' as synonymous with 'your [i.e. Jesus'] coming' in verse 3. Since this reference comes in the course of what we argue to be the first distinct part of Jesus' response to the disciples, it might be counter-argued that there is therefore evidence that Jesus is not presented as teaching on two distinct subjects but rather blends discussion concerning the destruction of the temple with discussion of *Parousia*. This argument would miss the point of this reference, however. Verses 27-28 can only be properly understood with reference to the prophecy of 'false christs' and 'false prophets' in verses 23-26. It is these counterfeits who are to appear in the days of 'this generation' (v. 34), not the *Parousia*. However, the way in which Jesus alerts his disciples to the spurious character of these pretenders' is by pointing to the circumstances that would attend the true appearance of the Christ, that is, the *Parousia*. The purpose of the reference in verses 27-28 is to contrast the false claims of verses 23-26 (previously mentioned in 24:4-5[305]) which would abound pre-AD 70,[306] with the unmistakable nature of the true *Parousia* of the Son of Man. It is important to note that this is the only occurrence of ἡ παρουσία prior to verse 37, and here it forms an aside to the

---

[303] So Keener, *Matthew*, 582. Compare Hare, *The Son of Man Tradition*, 169.

[304] Witherington, *Jesus, Paul and the End of the World*, 171.

[305] 24:4-5 combine with 24:23-28 to form a literary inclusion, indicating that the primary concern of Matthew in this section of the narrative is to present Jesus' explicit warnings to his disciples against presuming that historical events occuring in the first century are indicators of 'the end' or of his *parousia*.

[306] Josephus mentions numerous figures who might be included in this category. See Carson, *Matthew*, 498, for further references.

main theme under discussion (the imminent disaster to befall Judea, and Jerusalem in particular) which serves to draw a clearer distinction between these events and the final return of Jesus. Thus verses 27-28 should be understood as a proleptic reference to the subject taken up properly in verse 37.

To conclude this discussion of 24:27, Matthew clarifies Jesus' words by using the language of the *Parousia* to refer to the literal final appearance of Jesus. This will be an event that will be dramatically different from the 'comings' which are proclaimed to the disciples in their own generation, and an event distinct from any other 'coming' of Jesus.

The note of *immediate subsequence* (Εὐθέως δὲ Μετά)[307] in verse 29, related to what appears to be a clear reference to the trying circumstances ('tribulation') foretold for Judea (15-26, but not including the parenthetical remarks of 27-28), strongly suggests that the following refer to the actual fall of Jerusalem which has still not been described in the discourse up to this point.[308] It is very difficult to make sense of this adverb by any other interpretation unless we are to assume both that Jesus was entirely mistaken and that Matthew was completely unconcerned about that fact, particularly since Matthew would not usually retain the stress on immediacy from his sources.[309] In other words, Matthew creates, in a way that is not typical of his own use of language, a link between the distressing events of his own day (described up to verse 26) and the cataclysmic events of verse 29. The words of verse 29 should be read as markers of an event of similar, and even far greater, significance to the national calamities which befell Babylon (Isaiah 13) and Edom and the nations (Isaiah 34).[310] If Matthew is writing in the latter part of the first century and there is no apparent sign of the return of Jesus, would he not be more likely to play down that temporal connection? Only, we might respond, if he believed that the language did indeed refer to the return of Jesus. Caird notes that,

---

[307] Note the definition of Louw-Nida, (s.v. εὐθέως): a point of time *immediately subsequent to a previous point of time* (the actual interval of time differs appreciably, depending upon the nature of the events and the manner in which the sequence is interpreted by the writer) - 'immediately, right away, then.' εὐθύς: καὶ εὐθὺς ἐκ τῆς συναγωγῆς ἐξελθόντες 'and immediately they left the synagogue' or 'then they left ...' Mk 1.29; καὶ εὐθὺς τοῖς σάββασιν εἰσελθὼν εἰς τὴν συναγωγὴν ἐδίδασκεν 'and immediately on the Sabbath he went into the synagogue and taught' Mk 1.21. εὐθύς probably implies what was done on the immediately following Sabbath. Accordingly, one may translate this expression in Mk 1.21 as 'and on the next Sabbath he went into the synagogue and taught. εὐθέως: εὐθέως δὲ μετὰ τὴν θλῖψιν τῶν ἡμερῶν ἐκείνων ὁ ἥλιος σκοτισθήσεται 'immediately after the trouble of those days, the sun will grow dark' Mt 24.29.

[308] France, *Matthew*, 343-44.

[309] Blomberg, *Matthew*, 361-62, on the assumption for the sake of argument that Matthew depends on Mark.

[310] France, *Matthew*, 343.

if Matthew, not to mention the other New Testament writers, had taken his eschatology with a strict literalism, one would have expected the fall of Jerusalem in AD 70, unaccompanied by a Parousia, to be an emergency of the first order for Christian theology. But there is no sign that in fact it was so.[311]

Caird's comments are particularly pertinent when the assumption is made (as it is in his quotation) that Matthew's gospel is to be dated post-AD 70. If that were the case, and Matthew is writing a religious document for the instruction and encouragement of believers in his community, it is surely inconceivable that he understood Jesus' words to mean that the end of the world would occur at the same time as the destruction of Jerusalem. If that were the case then the post-AD 70 church would have had a religious disaster on their hands.

This point is particularly significant as a response to M. Casey's criticism of France's approach to the chapter. In commenting on France's treatment of the language of Mark 13:24-25 in the light of OT parallels, he writes,

There is nothing 'consistent' about restricting the application of Jesus' words to their OT sphere of reference, because the OT sphere of reference has been misleadingly stated and because in the intertestamental period it was common to describe new events in OT language. Any attempt to use OT language to describe the parousia of Jesus was bound to result in some shift of use of OT phrases because there is not really any OT description of the parousia of Jesus, but this does not constitute a good reason for supposing that the parousia of Jesus could not be described in OT terms, which is the necessary effect of arguing that the OT phrases must be used according to France's idea of consistency. France further ignores the use of this imagery in contemporary apocalyptic writings, an omission of relevant evidence that would be remarkable if it were not so distressingly common. What would he make of 1 Enoch 80; IV Ezra 5.4ff?[312]

Casey has not, however, dealt with the point made by Ladd and others (including France himself[313]) that there are many ways in which this discourse does not relate to the form and themes of contemporary Jewish apocalyptic writings, and that, if indeed Jesus is drawing primarily on the prophetic tradition of the OT Scriptures for his use of apocalyptic imagery, undue reliance on such contemporary works might well prove to be a distraction rather than a help. This point is forcefully presented by A. Schlatter in the first volume of his New Testament Theology when he writes,

We do not have a single concrete parallel to individual statements in the apocalypses. Not one of Jesus' statements, for example, is reminiscent of 1 Enoch...That signs are expected before the final revelation of God and that these would consist of great misery was no particular characteristic of apocalypses. This

---

[311] Caird, *New Testament Theology*, 263.
[312] Casey, *Son of Man*, 174.
[313] See France, *Matthew*, 334-36.

understanding was widespread in the Jewish community on the basis of the prophetic description of the Day of the Lord.[314]

It should be carefully noted that Jesus shows no evidence of being under any compulsion to use his words in the way expected by his contemporaries.[315]

24:30 (Μκ. 13:26/Lκ. 21:27; ἐρχόμενον)

καὶ τότε φανήσεται τὸ σημεῖον τοῦ υἱοῦ τοῦ ἀνθρώπου ἐν οὐρανῷ, καὶ τότε κόψονται πᾶσαι αἱ φυλαὶ τῆς γῆς καὶ ὄψονται τὸν υἱὸν τοῦ ἀνθρώπου ἐρχόμενον ἐπὶ τῶν νεφελῶν τοῦ οὐρανοῦ μετὰ δυνάμεως καὶ δόξης πολλῆς·

We will deal first with the reference to the coming Son of Man in 30b. That this is an allusion to the events surrounding the mysterious figure (אֱנָשׁ בַּר) of Dan 7:13 is beyond doubt.[316] The critical question is, To what event does it refer? The most widely held interpretation is that this is a reference to the 'second coming' of Jesus, the *Parousia* (as that term is commonly understood).

The interpretation of the reference to the 'coming Son of Man' in verse 30 clearly is tightly bound to the interpretation of verse 29. Many interpret 30b as a reference to the *Parousia*, but this view faces the difficulty that, if our interpretation of verse 29 is correct, it is tied to 'that time' which appears to be directly connected to the fall of Jerusalem ('immediately', v. 29).[317] France argues that this is apocalyptic language which must be interpreted figuratively, pointing out that Dan 7:13 is an account of an approach to the throne of the Ancient of Days, not a *Parousia* to earth. In connection with this, Caird comments,

> When the figure like a Son of Man comes on the clouds of heaven to the Ancient of Days, this is an enthronement scene. It has, of course, been correctly said that this is not a coming from heaven to earth, but of earth to heaven - there is no *Parousia* here. But such a statement takes the imagery too literally, failing to recognise that *the entire scene is symbolic.*[318]

It would certainly seem to do most justice to the context of these words in Daniel 7 to recognise that they are symbolic in nature. However, even symbolic

---

[314] A. Schlatter, *The History of the Christ* (trans. A. Köstenberger; Grand Rapids: Baker, 1997), 233.

[315] Witness, particularly, his use of the phrase ἡ βασιλεία τοῦ θεοῦ.

[316] Hare, *The Son of Man Tradition*, 170, notes the similarity between Matthew's text and the LXX reading of Daniel 7:13.

[317] So J. W. Wenham, *Christ and the Bible* (Downers Grove:IVP, 1973), 68. Of course, most interpreters who hold that verse 30 refers to the *parousia* would also hold that verse 29 is a reference to final literal cosmic catastrophe and so the two verses do speak of the same time.

[318] Caird, *New Testament Theology*, 377.

language is intended to convey information or impressions and Caird may be underestimating the significance of the detail of the vision. Is it not in coming into the presence of the Ancient of Days and receiving a place of honour from him that we recognise that the 'one like a Son of Man' is receiving authority and vindication? This echo of Daniel 7 appears to indicate that some event will take place which will be an open vindication of Jesus before 'the tribes of the earth' although the precise nature of the event is disguised by the figurative character of the allusion. That power and glory attend the coming of the Son of Man does not imply that the event must be seen as 'glorious' in and of itself. If we argue that the language is a figurative reference to the devastation of Jerusalem, it might be objected that the fall of Jerusalem was a disaster for the Jewish people which could hardly be described as 'glorious'. So it was but it may still be understood to be the sign that Jesus had been vindicated before those (the Jewish authorities of Jerusalem) who rejected him.

The sign of the Son of Man is mentioned nowhere else in the NT and so is difficult to interpret. The mention of τὸ σημεῖον, however, should immediately remind the reader of the disciples' question in verse 3. As to the precise significance of the phrase, there is debate at the grammatical level as to whether the genitive is objective ('the sign which points to the Son of Man') or appositional ('the sign which is the Son of Man'). As to the image itself, while some commentators cite with some favour the interpretation of Glasson[319] that it is a reference to the ensign or banner of the king,[320] the cautionary note of France to the effect that this is apocalyptic symbolism for which we may be unable to find a specific referent is worth heeding and most contemporary comentators are reluctant to make any decisive judgement between the various views.[321] That we are unable to find a clear referent for this statement does not invalidate the general principle of interpreting this section of text as figurative language rather than as descriptive of the end of the world.

The words τότε κόψονται πᾶσαι αἱ φυλαὶ τῆς γῆς are a 'loose quotation' of Zechariah 12:12 (which reads, in the LXX, καὶ κόψεται ἡ γῆ κατὰ φυλὰς φυλάς· φυλὴ οἴκου Δαυιδ καθ' ἑαυτὴν καὶ αἱ γυναῖκες αὐτῶν καθ' ἑαυτάς· φυλὴ οἴκου Ναθαν καθ' ἑαυτὴν καὶ αἱ γυναῖκες αὐτῶν καθ' ἑαυτάς). While they are often translated 'then all the tribes of the earth will mourn' (so NRSV), France points out that the reference in Zechariah 12:10-12 is to the tribes of the nation of Israel and that is how the Greek reading of the LXX should be understood. Thus there is no reference to a world-wide event here; it is the mourning

---

[319] T. F. Glasson, 'The Ensign of the Son of Man (Matt. XXIV.30),' *JTS* 15 (1964), 299-300.

[320] See Carson, *Matthew*, 505.

[321] France, *Matthew*, 344-45. So too Hagner, *Matthew 14-28*, 713-14. Garland, *Reading Matthew*, 238-9, appears to be content to leave the question open also. In addition, see A. J. B. Higgins, 'The Sign of the Son of Man (Matt. XXIV.30),' *NTS* 9 (1962-63), 380-82.

of the nation of Israel over the destruction of Jerusalem.[322] This would be an entirely natural reading if verse 29 is understood to be a declaration of the destruction of the temple, the symbol of God's presence with the Jewish people.[323]

The reference to τοὺς ἀγγέλους αὐτοῦ in verse 31 may be translated 'his messengers' and understood in terms of the preaching of the disciples. This is, of course, a perfectly acceptable translation as far as the Greek is concerned,[324] but it is not a translation that has received wide approval, largely because this verse in Matthew is taken to be a reference to the events of the final days of the existence of this world.[325] Certainly, the verse does allude to important themes from the OT and the intertestamental literature (Ex. 19:16; Is. 18:3; 27:13; *Pss. Sol.* 11:1). Hagner points out the allusion to Zechariah 2:10 (LXX): ἐκ τῶν τεσσάρων ἀνέμων τοῦ οὐρανοῦ συνάξω ὑμᾶς λέγει κύριος, but his assumption that this verse is necessarily a reference to the end is unwarranted. If the theme of this first portion of chapter 24 is indeed the destruction of the key building in the religious life of Judaism then this would clearly have dramatic repercussions for the mission of the first Christians.[326]

We conclude, then, that an appropriate awareness of the figurative or symbolic nature of clear allusions to Daniel 7:13 and other similarly symbolic passages of the OT leads to an interpretation of 24:1-31 that is consistent and would be understood by those, like Jesus and his disciples, who were steeped in the OT scriptures.

---

[322] France, *Matthew*, 345, with cross-reference to France, *Jesus and the Old Testament*, 237, 257. So also Garland, *Reading Matthew*, 238.

[323] There are a number of occasions in the NT where the language of Dan. 7:13 is echoed, apart from the synoptic parallels. Particularly Acts 7:56; Rev. 1:7, 13; 14:14-16. The familiar passage in 1 Thes. 4:13-18, although it includes references to meeting the Lord in the clouds, does not include reference to the Son of Man and so is discounted as a direct allusion to Dan. 7:13. The only text which appears to cause significant problems for this interpretation is Rev. 1:7. Here the reference seems to be quite clearly to the *Parousia*. This does not, however, cause the downfall of the figurative approach for two reasons. First, as Wenham tentatively suggests, the apocalypse could be dated prior to the fall of Jerusalem in which case the reference might be a variation on the theme of Mt. 24:30, without any necessary reference to the *Parousia* (J. W. Wenham, *Christ and the Bible*, 70). Second, since the language refers to an event which demonstrates the authority and kingship of Jesus, it is quite appropriate for the *Parousia*, though its suitability does not imply that it would always be used in that context.

[324] See, for example, Louw-Nida's lexicon, s.v. ἄγγελος, which offers the two possible meanings of (a) messenger (33.195) or (b) angel (12.28)

[325] See Hagner, *Matthew 14-28*, 714.

[326] So Garland, *Reading Matthew*, 239.

THE ASSURANCE OF THE CERTAINTY OF THE PROPHECY (24:32-35)

If Jesus is indeed being presented (and had previously presented himself) as a prophet, then in the light of the OT background (particularly Deut. 18:18-22) it was essential that he was recognised to be a true prophet rather than a false one. This is Wright's reading of the text,

> As a prophet, Jesus staked his reputation on his prediction of the Temple's fall within a generation; if and when it fell, he would thereby be vindicated. As the kingdom bearer, he had constantly been acting...in a way which invited the conclusion that he thought he had the right to do and be what the Temple was and did, thereby implicitly making the Temple redundant. The story he had been telling, and by which he ordered his life, demanded a particular ending. If, then, the Temple remained forever, and his movement fizzled out (as Gamaliel thought it might), he would be shown to be a blasphemer. But if the Temple was to be destroyed and the sacrifices stopped; if the pagan hordes were to tear it down stone by stone; and if his followers did escape from the conflagration unharmed, in a re-enactment of Israel's escape from their exile in doomed Babylon - why, then he would be vindicated, not only as a prophet, but as Israel's representative, as (in some sense) the 'son of man'.[327]

The formula of solemnity in verse 34 (ἀμὴν λέγω ὑμῖν), combined with the emphatic negative (οὐ μή, 'certainly not'), draws attention to these words as being of particular significance, which is entirely appropriate if they are the concluding remarks of this dramatic prophetic discourse on the temple and Jerusalem; it is also highly ironic if one takes the view that it was on this very point that Jesus was so wrong.

This problem seems to be exacerbated by the fact that Jesus puts such a precise time constraint on the accomplishment of all that he has predicted. His words appear plain: ἀμὴν λέγω ὑμῖν ὅτι οὐ μὴ παρέλθῃ ἡ γενεὰ αὕτη ἕως ἄ∏ν πάντα ταῦτα γένηταί. And yet, from our modern perspective as also from the perspective of Matthew and his contemporaries, there is no sign of a *Parousia*, either in the sense of the return of Jesus or in the sense of the end of the world. There seems to be only a limited number of alternative solutions to this problem.[328]

a) The least defensible is that we should translate ἡ γενεὰ αὕτη in such a way that it can refer to however long a period proves to be required before the *Parousia* happens.

b) A second, and commonly held, position is that Jesus had a firm expectation of an imminent *Parousia* which proved to be completely unfulfilled.

c) Yet another possibility is that Jesus never said these words at all. While this might appear to absolve Jesus of responsibility, it does not really

---

[327] Wright, *Jesus and the Victory of God* 362
[328] *NIDNTT*, 2:35-39. See also the helpful discussion of the various suggested interpretations in Davies and Allison, *Matthew*, 3:367.

remove the problem since whether or not Jesus used these words, Matthew certainly did and we must attempt to understand what he meant by them.

On the grounds of the usage of ἡ γενεὰ [αὕτη] in 11:16; 12:39, 41, 42, 45; 16:4 and 17:17, we conclude that Matthew intends a reference to the contemporaries of Jesus.[329] It seems inescapable, therefore, that Jesus is talking about an event which is about to overtake his contemporaries. Wright develops the point in the following way,

> Already present in Jesus' ministry, and climactically inaugurated in his death and resurrection, the divine kingdom will be manifest within a generation, when Jesus and his followers are vindicated in and through the destruction of Jerusalem. The generation that rejects Jesus must be the last before the great cataclysm. There can be no other, because if there were they would need another warning prophet; once the father has sent the son to the vineyard, he can send nobody else. To reject the son is to reject the last chance. The prophecy of 'this generation' is thus closely tied to Jesus' view of his own role within the eschatological process.[330]

The interpretation argued for here is given additional support in that the phrase πάντα ταῦτα of verse 34 echoes the πότε ταῦτα ἔσται of the disciples' question in verse 3. The words indicate that Jesus has indeed given the disciples an answer to their question.

The fundamental point of the words in verse 35 is to contrast the complete authority and unfailing nature of Jesus' words with the changeable nature of all else. There is no intention to indicate a time after which Jesus' words may pass away. However, the choice of the phrase 'heaven and earth' indicates an awareness that the present world order will be brought to an end. This echoes 5:18 and makes both for a very appropriate conclusion to predictions of the fall of the temporal Jerusalem, and for a very natural stepping-stone onto the subject of the final return of Christ.

It is also the case that Jesus' emphatic statement here presents us with one who considered his prophetic words to be entirely dependable; this is no false prophet, but the true prophet who, whether recognised as such or not, comes in fulfilment of Moses' prediction.

Answer 2. Jesus' Reply re the End of the Age and Jesus' Parousia (24:36-25:46)

The section of text from 24:36 to the end of chapter 25 also portrays Jesus as a prophetic predictor of future events, but now the focus changes to events which are certain to happen, but unknown with respect to their timing. It should be carefully noted that to say that the timing of the events in 24:36-25:46 is un-

---

[329] So Davies and Allison, *Matthew*, 3:367-68.
[330] Wright, *Jesus and the Victory of God* 365.

known is not the same as to say that they were assigned to a time beyond the 'generation' of 24:35 or beyond the lifetime of the disciples, since such statements imply an element of knowledge. Jesus declares quite categorically that he does not know when these events will take place and therefore that none of disciples can know either. Thus, 'ignorance' should not be set against 'imminence' as if it were a direct alternative.

A full discussion of Jesus' reply to the second part of the disciples' question can be found in chapter 6. For the moment, however, we may note that Matthew offers us a finely balanced, two-part response to the disciples' question reflecting what we might expect of Jesus the teacher.

Excursus: Matthew's 'Coming Son of Man' Sayings Outside Chapters 21-25

Although our primary focus in this thesis has been on the 'coming Son of Man' sayings which occur within the bounds of Matthew 21-25, there are several 'coming Son of Man' sayings which are found in other parts of Matthew's gospel. It is necessary to give some attention to these because several of them highlight the importance of recognising the figurative nature of the language used and the importance of the motif of vindication. Study of these texts in their Matthean context may, therefore, help us to confirm the analysis which has been presented in chapter 4 of this thesis.

We should emphasise that we interpret these texts as they appear in Matthew's narrative, for regardless of any hypothetical original setting (and of course such judgements often rest on rather frail source-critical assumptions concerning which evangelist used which sources), we must seek to find an interpretation that indicates how Matthew understood the words he was writing, and our intention is to demonstrate that Matthew is consistent in his use of 'coming Son of Man' texts. I do not consider the charge of incoherence on the part of Matthew to be a legitimate interpretative option unless all other avenues have been exhausted and it is clear that the coherence of Matthew's account can only be maintained by arguing for improbable interpretations of individual sayings.

There are three texts to consider: Matthew 10:23; 16:27-28; 26:64.

10:23.

ὅταν δὲ διώκωσιν ὑμᾶς ἐν τῇ πόλει ταύτῃ, φεύγετε εἰς τὴν ἑτέραν· ἀμὴν γὰρ λέγω ὑμῖν, οὐ μὴ τελέσητε τὰς πόλεις τοῦ Ἰσραὴλ ἕως αⱷν ἔλθῃ ὁ υἱὸς τοῦ ἀνθρώπου.

This saying, which is unique to Matthew, lay at the foundation of A. Schweitzer's understanding of Jesus as an eschatological prophet of the imminent end. Ben Witherington makes it quite clear what was at stake for

Schweitzer in the interpretation of this short pericope:

> We can hardly underestimate [*sic*][331] the importance of Matthew 10:23 to
> Schweitzer's estimation of the character of Jesus' proclamation. Largely on the
> basis of this text alone Schweitzer argued that Jesus expected the parousia of the
> Son of Man (someone other than himself) before his disciples had completed their
> preaching tour of Galilee.[332]

In looking at this verse with the question of Matthew's understanding of it in
mind we must avoid separating it from the context in which it is found, both the
immediate passage and the gospel of Matthew as a whole. Source-critical perspectives often militate against such a reading. It is recognised that material in
the 'missionary discourse' of chapter 10 of Matthew's gospel finds parallels in
the other synoptic gospels. Meier, for example, points out that portions of
10:17-25 are paralleled by material in Mark's eschatological discourse (Mark
13:5-37).[333]

This issue of the relationship of a pericope to its context is often sadly side-
stepped in discussions that focus particularly on the question of authenticity.
Meier writes openly,

> Needless to say, such a detailed scenario about the disciples' being involved in
> legal procedures before Jewish courts and before the tribunals of pagan governors
> and kings, to say nothing of suffering the death penalty for acknowledging one's
> allegiance to Jesus, reflects the time of the early church, not the time of the
> historical Jesus.[334]

It should be noted, however, that in Matthew 23:34 Jesus also refers to persecution of Christians by the Jewish authorities,[335] and while these events might
well be understood to lie some distance in the future, they are not far away. The
authenticity of this verse has also been challenged on the basis that it simply
reflects the eager expectation of the church for the return of Jesus.[336] However,
several factors tell against the view that this verse is a creation of the Christian
church. Firstly, on the assumption of those who argue for inauthenticity that the

---

[331] Witherington undoubtedly means to say 'overestimate'.

[332] Witherington, *Jesus, Paul and the End of the World*, 39. On the history of
interpretation of this verse, see particularly, M. Künzi, *Das Naherwartungslogion
Matthäus 10, 23. Geschichte seiner Auslegung* (BGBE 9; Tübingen: Mohr, 1970).

[333] Meier, *A Marginal Jew*, 2:339.

[334] Meier, *A Marginal Jew*, 2:339.

[335] See Gundry, *Matthew*, 194.

[336] E. Schweizer, 'The Significance of Eschatology in the Teaching of Jesus', in
Eschatology and the New Testament (Peabody: Hendrickson, 1988), 1-13 (here, 3),
cited in Witherington, *Jesus, Paul and the End of the World*, 262, n. 3. See also Borg,
'A Temperate Case' 87, n. 16, for the names of scholars who have denied the
authenticity of this verse, including Bultmann, Perrin, Bammel and Tödt.

text is a reference to the imminent return of Jesus, we might ask why Matthew
would create a prophecy of the end/Jesus' *Parousia* which remained unfulfilled
in his own day.[337] Secondly, the fact that there is an explicit limitation of the
mission to the Jews would suggest that it was not the invention of a mixed
church community.[338] Jeremias points, thirdly, to Semitisms in the text (on the
understanding that they reflect the original Aramaic of Jesus), and, fourthly, to
the fact that there is no 'rival' (a parallel version of the text which does not include the 'Son of Man' phrase).[339]

Whatever scholars may make of the authenticity of the present location of
this verse in Matthew's narrative, it is inescapable that the conjunction γάρ
relates the 'coming Son of Man' saying (23b) to the previous part of the verse
(23a) thus providing the explanation for the instruction to flee from one town to
the next. While the connection between verse 23 and its immediate context is
not so clearly marked, the common theme of persecution suggests that the present setting for verse 23 is quite plausible. Thus it is unhelpful to attempt to
understand this text as an independent saying if we are seeking Matthew's understanding of its significance, since Matthew clearly believed it to fit appropriately into its present setting, and France is correct to say that 'Any proper
exegesis must take it in its context: the Christian missionary's response to Jewish persecution must be to move on, for there will always be further scope for
the mission to Israel until "the Son of Man comes".'[340] On the understanding
that Matthew has placed the saying in at least an appropriate context, in which
Jesus is instructing his disciples on the opposition which they will face during
their mission, we must ask *how* Matthew understood this saying to be relevant
to this teaching.[341]

---

[337] If, on the other hand, the early Christians did not read these words in such a way, but
read them metaphorically, as argued for in this book, then this embarrassment
vanishes to a large extent. However, in that case the challenge to the saying's
authenticity on the basis of it being a projection onto Jesus of the church's expectation
of the parousia would also vanish. Allison (*Jesus of Nazareth*, 9) objects to this use of
the criterion of embarrassment on the ground ('a difficulty so fundamental that one
wonders how anyone could ever have missed it') that the saying was established in the
tradition as authentic long before embarrassment arose. However, this claim does not
adequately address the evident selectivity of the evangelists as they use the tradition
available to them. Why would Matthew include this saying at a time when it would
cause embarrassment when he clearly felt no obligation to include everything he
knew.

[338] See Witherington, *Jesus, Paul and the End of the World*, 40.

[339] Jeremias, *New Testament Theology*, 135-6, n. 4. McKnight, *A New Vision for Israel*,
134. Davies and Allison, *Matthew*, 2:189.

[340] France, *Matthew*, 184.

[341] Hare, apparently accepting the saying as an isolated logion, nonetheless states that our
task is to determine how Matthew understands it in view of the context in which he
has placed it (*The Son of Man Tradition*, 141). While this does not resolve the issue of

We are faced with a choice between one of two fundamental interpretations, although there are variations within these two main options.[342] The first interpretation is that the words indicate the physical appearance of the Son of Man. This view was espoused in its most memorable form by A. Schweitzer[343] who claimed that Jesus expected the coming of the Son of Man to be the climactic appearance of the glorious figure (Schweitzer thought that Jesus expected a figure distinct from himself) within the brief period of the disciples' mission. A more widely accepted variation of this view is that Jesus was referring to his own return sometime in the future. This view requires us to make some sense of the time scale involved. What does it mean that the Son of Man will come before the disciples have completed the towns of Israel? We can respond either by understanding these words as a reference to the immediate mission of the Twelve, in which case we must also accept that Jesus was mistaken; or we can protect Jesus' integrity by understanding the time scale in a much more open ended fashion. Thus verse 23 has been understood as a reference to the entire Jewish mission throughout church history.

The other major interpretative option is that we must interpret the coming of the Son of Man more figuratively in accordance with the discussion of 'apocalyptic' language in chapter 4 above. That is to say, that we allow the literary background of Daniel 7 to have more significance for our interpretation of what 'the coming Son of Man' means than popular understandings of the language.

Several points suggest that Matthew understands Jesus to be looking somewhat beyond the very immediate work of the disciples. Firstly, the situation described in verses 17-22 is that of widespread and official hostility towards the followers of Jesus, a situation which did not obtain at the time of the initial ministry of the disciples. Secondly, the reference to the help of the Spirit in these verses points beyond the present experience of the disciples to (in canonical terms) a post-Pentecost time. The relationship between 10:23 and the verses which precede it is demonstrated partly by the close connection between the language of 10:23 and 10:19-20, as can be seen below:

10:19-20

ὅταν δὲ παραδῶσιν ὑμᾶς, μὴ μεριμνήσητε πῶς ἢ τί λαλήσητε· δοθήσεται γὰρ ὑμῖν ἐν ἐκείνῃ τῇ ὥρᾳ τί λαλήσητε· 20 οὐ γὰρ ὑμεῖς ἐστε οἱ λαλοῦντες ἀλλὰ τὸ πνεῦμα τοῦ πατρὸς ὑμῶν τὸ λαλοῦν ἐν ὑμῖν.

---

whether Matthew has placed the logion in a legitimate setting, it does at least take the Matthean context seriously.

[342] See Carson, *Matthew*, 250-3, for a valuable discussion of seven major interpretations.

[343] Schweitzer, *Quest of the Historical Jesus*, 257-8. See Keener, *Matthew*, 325, n. 36.

10:23

ὅταν δὲ διώκωσιν ὑμᾶς ἐν τῇ πόλει ταύτῃ, φεύγετε εἰς τὴν ἑτέραν· ἀμὴν γὰρ λέγω ὑμῖν, οὐ μὴ τελέσητε τὰς πόλεις τοῦ Ἰσραὴλ ἕως ἂν ἔλθῃ ὁ υἱὸς τοῦ ἀνθρώπου.

In both cases there is a similar pattern of (i) a description of the disciples' future experience (ὅταν δὲ ... ὑμᾶς); (ii) instructions couched in the form of an imperative; (iii) an explanation of the instructions given, introduced by γὰρ.

The saying in 10:23 is preceded by the formula ἀμὴν γὰρ λέγω ὑμῖν, indicating a solemn affirmation. Matthew frequently has Jesus using the phrase 'I say', indicating a particular interest in the weight which Jesus laid upon his words.[344] We may therefore assume that this is a saying of particular importance. This tells against any interpretation which regards these words as a simple promise that Jesus would meet up with his disciples again before they had finished their missionary activity.[345] Such an approach is also suspect because of the note of urgency which is quite clearly present, and it is perhaps this point which points the way forward.

The phrase φεύγετε εἰς τὴν ἑτέραν employs the same verb as the phrase τότε οἱ ἐν τῇ Ἰουδαίᾳ φευγέτωσαν εἰς τὰ ὄρη in 24:16. The latter phrase comes in the context of a passage dealing with the devastation that will soon come upon the city of Jerusalem, and it may therefore be that Jesus here gives a similar warning to that given in the eschatological discourse. This position is reinforced by the presence of the words τότε παραδώσουσιν ὑμᾶς εἰς θλῖψιν καὶ ἀποκτενοῦσιν ὑμᾶς, καὶ ἔσεσθε μισούμενοι ὑπὸ πάντων τῶν ἐθνῶν διὰ τὸ ὄνομά μου in 24:9, which reflect the words of 10:19-20, including the use of the verb παραδιδώμι.

If we treat the connection with chapter 24 seriously, then we may suggest that Jesus is giving a two-part warning to his disciples. Firstly, though they are to be engaged in proclaiming the message of the kingdom of God throughout the towns of Israel, they should expect rejection and persecution. Yet, they should also be aware that before they have completed the task of mission to the towns of Israel, the Son of Man (that is, Jesus himself) will be vindicated after the fashion of Daniel 7 as those who have rejected him (and particularly the authorities in Jerusalem, though this identification is not yet clear in Matthew's

---

[344] It is important to note that several of the texts under consideration in this chapter are prefaced by this solemn formula. In addition to 10:23, see 16:28; and see also 26:64 where there is a somewhat less forceful clause: λέγω ὑμῖν. Some more of these verses are within a few verses of the use of this formula and are clearly in the related context; see 24:39 and 44 with the formula in 24:47.

[345] Cf. Witherington, *Jesus, Paul and the End of the World*, 40-1. Witherington offers Mt. 11:19/Lk. 7:34 as an example of 'Son of Man' and ἐλθών used in conjunction to refer to an earthly activity of Jesus.

narrative) are visited in judgement.

It is certainly the case that this is not in all respects an easy reading of the text, yet I believe that it does justice to the literary background of the text and also to the use of similar language in other parts of Matthew's gospel. The validity of the interpretation of this text is in many ways bound up with the interpretation of similar texts, to which we must now turn.

16:27-8 (Mк. 8:38-9:1/Lк. 9:26-7)

μέλλει γὰρ ὁ υἱὸς τοῦ ἀνθρώπου ἔρχεσθαι ἐν τῇ δόξῃ τοῦ πατρὸς αὐτοῦ μετὰ τῶν ἀγγέλων αὐτοῦ, καὶ τότε ἀποδώσει ἑκάστῳ κατὰ τὴν πρᾶξιν αὐτοῦ. 28 ἀμὴν λέγω ὑμῖν ὅτι εἰσίν τινες τῶν ὧδε ἑστώτων οἵτινες οὐ μὴ γεύσωνται θανάτου ἕως ἂν ἴδωσιν τὸν υἱὸν τοῦ ἀνθρώπου ἐρχόμενον ἐν τῇ βασιλείᾳ αὐτοῦ.

In Matthew, both verses speak of the coming of the Son of Man, but it should be noted that in Mark and Luke there is a change in terminology within the pericope. In both cases there is an initial reference to the Son of Man, but the verse that speaks of some not tasting death refers to the coming of the βασιλεία. There appears, then, to be some distinction drawn between the two events.

Verse 27 speaks of a coming of the Son of Man 'in the glory of his Father with his angels' which certainly utilises 'apocalyptic' language similar to that which elsewhere we have interpreted figuratively. However, this highlights the problem that the term 'apocalyptic' does not really clarify the significance of such language. The real issue with such references is whether they are intended to be understood figuratively of some event other than the final event of judgement or whether they are intended to give accurate descriptions of observable events at the eschatological judgement. I believe that contextual considerations lead to the conclusion that verse 27 refers to a future expectation of the *Parousia*. At that time (τότε) there will be the Judgment. This is spoken of in very personal terms; the Son of Man will reward (ἀποδώσει) each (ἑκάστῳ) person according to what they have done. Therefore, a universal judgement is also in view. This verse appears to comport with the scene presented in Matt 25:31-46. Indeed, there are a number of conceptual and verbal parallels.

But what of verse 28? The first thing to note is that, despite the similarity of language, v.28 is isolated from v.27 by the formula ἀμὴν λέγω ὑμῖν. It is important to recognise that this solemnising formula is applied only to the words following.[346] In what follows, we have what appears to be a prediction of the *relatively* imminent *Parousia* of the Son of Man. E. Schweizer's comments (on the parallel saying in Mark 9:1) indicate his interpretation of these words as an imminent expectation of the *Parousia*:

---

[346] Compare the similar formula in Mt. 10:23.

some of the first generation will live to see Christ's coming.[347]

Yet Schweizer also appears to recognise the indication of some delay.[348] Kümmel also argues that the words indicate a short delay and then the *Parousia*.[349] The key to interpretation seems to me, again, to lie in taking the redaction of the evangelist seriously. This is particularly so in this case since the three synoptic witnesses agree in placing these words immediately before their accounts of the Transfiguration.[350] Moore points out that

> If the context is taken fully into account, it suggests that the early church, so far as its views are reflected in the Synoptic tradition, did *not* regard this saying as a community-formulation sustaining it in its crisis, but as a promise fulfilled in some sense in the Transfiguration.[351]

Moore's premise, it appears to me, is precisely the position that is rejected in most treatments of this verse, and therefore misunderstanding inevitably follows. In Matthew, there is a connective καί to reinforce this conclusion. G. R. Beasley-Murray finds this interpretation unconvincing for two reasons. First, he ascribes the placement of the saying solely to the evangelist. His second argument is that this interpretation requires a gross distortion of the force of the phrase, 'there are some standing here who shall certainly not taste death until...' He argues that to use such language of an event in the immediate future (six days later, 17:1) would be extremely unnatural.[352] In response to the first objection we may say that this does not seem to do justice to the interpretation of the evangelist and particularly to the unanimity of the synoptic authors that this saying belongs directly before the Transfiguration account. Could this arrangement not point to the correct interpretation preserved in the placement of the saying, rather than being purely arbitrary? As for the second objection, it is true that we may read Jesus' words as being strange but this may be because we lay stress on the wrong part of the statement. Witherington cites Cranfield as stating that the phrase 'shall not taste death' is an idiom which stresses the fact that some *will* see the event rather than saying that any *will not* see it.[353] If we interpret the phrase in terms of the Transfiguration then the 'some' makes complete sense; the distinction is not based on who is alive but on who is *present* at the event (Peter, James and John, 17:1). That Jesus says that they will not taste

---

[347] *Jesus* (London: SCM Press, 1971), 63.

[348] *Jesus*, 63-4.

[349] Kümmel, *Promise and Fulfilment*, 28. So also McKnight, *A New Vision for Israel*, 136.

[350] McKnight, *A New Vision for Israel*, 135.

[351] A. L. Moore, *The Parousia in the New Testament* (Leiden, 1966), 127.

[352] Beasley-Murray *Jesus and the Kingdom of God*, 188. So also, McKnight, *A New Vision for Israel*, 136.

[353] Witherington *Jesus, Paul and the End of the World*, 38.

death perhaps indicates that the disciples expected to see Jesus in power only after their own deaths. Jesus here raises an expectation of his kingdom being demonstrated before then. If this is the case then it is clear that the evangelist (and Jesus) can use the language of 'coming' to refer to an event other than the final *Parousia*. This interpretation avoids the significant difficulty that Beasley-Murray faces:

(a) Jesus refuses to speak in concrete terms about the time of his *Parousia*. The *Parousia* interpretation places 16:28 in direct conflict with 24:36, 44.

(b) The reality is that the *Parousia* did not occur in the lifetime of Jesus' disciples.

S. McKnight follows Beasley-Murray in rejecting the transfiguration as the true referent of this saying, but chooses to link it with the vindication of Jesus in the future devastation of Jerusalem.[354] I find this view generally acceptable, on the basis of McKnight's attention to the context (speaking of the parallel verse in Mark 9:1):

> Jesus therefore predicted a vindication of himself and his followers before the death of the disciples. This view fits admirably with the previous context (Mark 8:34-38) and gives adequate ground for Mark's insertion of the logion before his account of the transfiguration. In the previous context, Jesus promises the disciples that, though they would suffer like him, they would be vindicated by God. And just as Jesus was to suffer the ignominy of a humiliating death at the hands of the leaders in Jerusalem, so he would be vindicated. The disciples need to be assured of Jesus' vindication, and this is precisely how the transfiguration ought to be understood – a proleptic vindication. Hence Mark's redaction.[355]

This is a reasonable position to take, except that there is no reason to demand that the time reference in Jesus' words cannot be specifically related to the immediately following event, and so it is possible to regard the transfiguration as the primary referent of Jesus' words, and yet also a proleptic vindication. McKnight suggests, with Beasley-Murray that 'it hardly seems realistic' that Jesus would use such words of a forthcoming event, but since both appear to attribute the placement of the saying to Mark with the implication that Mark saw a connection, how can we be certain that what seemed 'realistic' to Mark was not realistic to Jesus also? Furthermore, while Matthew's narrative of the transfiguration resolves the question of which of the disciples might observe this vindication, a reference solely to the devastation of Jerusalem leaves that matter without resolution.

To summarise this discussion, I believe that Matthew presents Jesus' words in 16:28, not as an unfulfilled prophecy of the *Parousia*, but as a declaration that even within the lifetime of the disciples (indeed within a few days) some of

---

[354] McKnight, *A New Vision for Israel*, 136-7.
[355] McKnight, *A New Vision for Israel*, 136-7.

them would witness an event that would demonstrate that Jesus was indeed God's Son. Matthew then recounts the narrative of the transfiguration as the natural and primary fulfilment of that declaration, though there may be a secondary reference to further future vindication, particularly the judgement on Jerusalem.

26:64 (Mκ. 14:62/Lκ. 22:69)

λέγει αὐτῷ ὁ Ἰησοῦς, Σὺ εἶπας· πλὴν λέγω ὑμῖν, ἀπ' ἄρτι ὄψεσθε τὸν υἱὸν τοῦ ἀνθρώπου καθήμενον ἐκ δεξιῶν τῆς δυνάμεως καὶ ἐρχόμενον ἐπὶ τῶν νεφελῶν τοῦ οὐρανοῦ.

This saying stands out among the other 'coming Son of Man' sayings in that it is particularly clearly linked to the context in which it is found. That context is the interrogation before the High Priest and the Sanhedrin (v.59).[356] The religious leaders set themselves up as judges over Jesus with the express intention of condemning him (v.59). The precise cause of these words being uttered by Jesus was the demand of the High Priest, in the form of an adjuration (ἐξορκίζω σε κατὰ τοῦ θεοῦ τοῦ ζῶντος), that Jesus declare if he was ὁ Χριστὸς ὁ υἱὸς τοῦ θεου. Jesus' reply has been understood to be evasive when compared with the direct affirmative in Mk. 14:62 (ἐγώ εἰμι). Matthew's phrase (σὺ εἶπας. Also used in 26:25) has, however, been shown to be 'affirmative in content, and reluctant or circumlocutory in formulation.'[357] It is also quite clear that Caiaphas understood the reply as affirmative from his dramatic and accusatory response. However, it is necessary to note that Jesus does express a certain reserve concerning the High Priest's charge. The word πλήν carries the force of 'only', 'nevertheless', 'however', 'but'.[358] Jesus indicates that he accepts the terms which the High Priest has used, but that he does not understand them in the same sense as Caiaphas does. The following OT allusions serve to illuminate Jesus' self-understanding, and to leave no doubt that it was not in terms of some political messianic pretender. There is no doubt whatsoever that, in these words, Jesus alludes to Dan. 7:13, and this adds weight to the view that Jesus' conception of 'the Son of Man' derives from that passage. In this instance, however, he combines that allusion with one from Psalm 110:1 also. The combination implies that Jesus regarded himself as the one who would be given the place of honour and glory beside God and who would then be given his enemies for his footstool.

There are important differences in Matthew's wording and that of the LXX

---

[356] While many scholars have questioned the historicity of the trial account, there are good reasons for accepting it as an accurate recollection of either a sympathetic participant or a later convert.

[357] D. R. Catchpole, 'The Answer of Jesus to Caiaphas (Matt. xxvi.64)', *NTS* 17 (1970-71), 213-26, at 216.

[358] BAG, 675 (*s.v.*).

of Dan. 7:13 which may help us to understand the significance of these words for Jesus. The introduction of a visionary ('I saw', ἐθεώρουν) is replaced by a future expectation ('from now on', ἀπ᾿ ἄρτι; 'you will see', ὄψεσθε). Clearly Jesus does not envisage the High Priest and Sanhedrin[359] having Danielic visionary experiences. Rather, he anticipates something which they will be able to observe or experience[360] *in the future*. If we take Jesus' words as a reference to his visible return[361] then we are left with difficult questions. In what sense could the authorities see the return of Jesus 'from now on'? We might certainly accept that Jesus could predict that those present would be witnesses of his physical return either in the near future or along with all of resurrected humanity in the distant future, but it is hard to avoid the conclusion that he would speak of such a situation in more definitive terms. His return would surely be a single event.

Excursus Summary and Conclusion

Having examined these three important texts in the light of the approach to apocalyptic language proposed in chapter 4, what conclusions can be drawn?

Firstly, none of the texts need be interpreted as predictions of the final *Parousia* of Jesus as the eschatological judge. This is in keeping with what we might expect given our interpretation of Matthew 24:36, for there Jesus avoids any reference to the time of his *Parousia* whereas in each of the texts examined above there is reference to a limited period of time within which Jesus' words will be fulfilled.

Secondly, each of the texts may be interpreted in accordance with the use of language found in the OT scriptures (particularly Daniel 7, but also Psalm 110:1) as expectations on the part of Jesus of vindication by God, and therefore our interpretation suggests that these words would be appropriate on the lips of the Jewish Jesus in Palestine in the early part of the first century.

Two implicatons are particularly significant, one negative and the other positive.

First of all, negatively, our analysis of these texts has done away with any need for discussion of 'the problem of the delay of the *Parousia*'. These texts lie at the root of the idea that Jesus proclaimed his imminent return to earth to

---

[359] Note that the initial response to the charge of Caiaphas in the singular (σὺ εἶπας) is followed by the plural verb, ὄψεσθε, which has reference to the whole assembled gathering.

[360] BAG, 581-2, *s.v.* ὁράω. The verb does not *necessarily* imply physical observation but it certainly may bear that meaning. Moore (*Parousia*, 140) quotes Lagrange (*Marc*, 403): 'Le terme "vous verrez" ne signifie pas toujours "vous verrez de vos yeux" (Cf. Dt. 28:10; Ps. 48:11; Ps. 88:49).' See also Glasson, *Advent*, 65. Kümmel, on the other hand, claims that 'to transfer ὄψεσθε to a spiritual experience is as arbitrary as to contest that Dan 7:13 points to an eschatological cosmic event' (*Promise* 50, n. 102).

[361] As does Moore, *Parousia* 140.

bring about the end of the world and the final judgment. Clearly the non-occurrence of this event would have been of great consequence for the early Christian church, and several valuable essays have been devoted to explaining why the early church did not collapse.

D. E. Aune agrees with the view of Kümmel and Beasley-Murray that texts such as Matt 10:23 indicate that Jesus envisaged 'a continuation of the present age for a short period after his death', but that this period was 'bounded by the lifetime of those in his own generation'.[362] On this basis, he offers the following summary of what I regard as the most attractive alternative to the position argued for in this thesis:

> it may be said that the imminent expectation of earliest Christianity anticipated neither the immediate consummation of the Kingdom of God momentarily, nor the delay of that consummation beyond the generation contemporaneous with Jesus. However, the lack of specificity with regard to the exact date of the Parousia made it impossible for its non-occurrence to become a critical problem at any point in the subsequent history of early Christianity.[363]

In other words, Jesus gave the impression that he would return within the life-time of his followers but because he did not set a specific date for his return there could never be a point at which the delay of the *Parousia* brought their hope to an end. That is, Jesus made it impossible to prove that the *Parousia* would not occur.

This view has a certain appeal to it in that it allows the difficult sayings to stand at what appears to be their face-value, and yet allows the future hope of the early Christians to be maintained. However, it ascribes to Jesus a vagueness of teaching which seems particularly uncharacteristic of him; it leaves us with the problem that Jesus appears to give semi-precise indications of the time of his return in one part of the gospel (e.g., Matt. 10:23, where he accompanies his words with a solemn declaration) and then later in the same gospel he denies all knowledge of its timing (24:36). This leaves Matthew in the precarious position of writing thirty to fifty and more years after the ascension of Jesus, with no sign of his return, and yet placing *numerous* sayings in his gospel which, it is claimed, indicate that the *Parousia* must occur within a *very short time* in order that Jesus' words are vindicated.

If these texts are understood to include figurative language, however, there is no need to explain why the early church did not find the delay of the *Parousia* a problem; the early church certainly expected Jesus' return, and they expected it *eagerly* on the basis of the teaching of Jesus himself (particularly, for example, Matthew 24:36-25:46), but they never understood the *Parousia* to

---

[362] D. E. Aune, 'The Significance of the Delay of the Parousia for Early Christianity' in G. F. Hawthorne (ed.), *Current Issues in Biblical and Patristic Interpretation* (Grand Rapids: Eerdmans, 1975), 87-109, at 97.

[363] Aune, 'The Significance of the Delay of the Parousia', 98.

be *necessarily* imminent. The early Christians understood the language of these verses in what was its natural sense to a first century Jew as assurances that Jesus would be given authority by his Father, and be vindicated before his enemies after the pattern of Daniel 7. This vindication came partially, of course, in the resurrection (see Paul's views in Romans 1:3-4) and so the view of Barrett is partially correct.[364]

The second, positive conclusion which may be drawn from our study of these texts is that they all make reference to the giving of authority, or the vindication of Jesus. This has great significance for our understanding of Matthew's theology. O. Michel claims that the whole of Matthew should be understood in the light of 28:18 where Jesus says, 'All authority in heaven and on earth has been given to me.' As we have studied the important section comprised of chapters 21-25 we have seen that throughout this section there is a continual reinforcing, in a variety of ways, of the authority of Jesus to act as Judge, both in the context of his Palestinian environment and at the final judgement.

The fact that Jesus used the kind of pictorial language which we have looked at in this chapter suggests that he was deliberately drawing on a tradition stretching back to the prophets of Israel which brought the message of God's judgement on rebellious people in a way which dramatically indicated the way in which God would bring a decisive blow to the religious/political/social world of the day. This serves to confirm strongly the argument that in Matthew 21-25, Jesus is bringing judgement on his contemporaries and their society, as well as demonstrating his authority to judge not only Israel but also all the nations.

Chapter Summary and Conclusion

In this chapter, I have attempted to demonstrate that Jesus is portrayed by Matthew as one who takes upon himself roles associated with the prophets of the Hebrew scriptures, particularly in the enacting of symbolic actions, in the proclamation of woes against the Jewish authorities and in the prophetic prediction of the destruction of the temple. Despite the clear continuity between Jesus' actions and the OT prophets of Yahweh, there is yet a discontinuity in that while the OT prophets acted on the instruction of God and declared the approaching judgement of God, Jesus is presented as one who acts on an authority which, while not an independent authority, is nonetheless authority beyond that of the prophets. In fact, several elements of Matthew's presentation (particularly the entry of Jesus into Jerusalem) might be regarded to echo prophetic language regarding Yahweh so closely that it would be regarded as inappropriate for a mere prophet to carry them out. Jesus does not simply announce judgement, but he enacts it as the judge. He takes on the role of Yahweh himself.

---

[364] See the discussion of Barrett's position on the resurrection as vindication in chapter 2.

In the prophetic woes which Jesus declares against the Jewish leaders in chapter 23, Matthew portrays Jesus as one who is angered by the injustice of the activities of the leaders which lead to status for them and oppression for the people. Echoing the form of words of OT prophets, Jesus can nevertheless declare his own judgement on the Jewish authorities, exposing their inner attitudes and declaring their fate (compare 23:33).

Further, Matthew presents Jesus as the one who declares the future judgement that will fall upon the Jewish nation (chapter 24). He does so carefully distinguishing for his disciples what will mark the devastation of Jerusalem from the events of the final judgement, yet with a confidence and certainty of fulfilment regarding the events of that generation that marks out his authority to make this declaration, and demonstrates that he is unlike the false prophets about whom he warns his disciples. In this regard, we have seen that Jesus employs allusions to the OT literature, used in a manner in keeping with their original context, to point to events of judgement in the coming generation which will vindicate the message and ministry of Jesus.

It is clear throughout Matthew 21-25 that not only has Matthew recorded the actions and words of Jesus which echo the actions and words of the prophets, but he draws on the prophetic literature as a resource for interpreting the narrative of Jesus' ministry which he presents. This points us to the significance of the prophetic literature for interpreting Jesus' actions and words and provides a corrective to the emphasis of recent interpreters on the pseudepigraphical 'apocalyptic' literature of second temple Judaism as the primary background for interpretation of the teaching of Jesus. This gives due weight to the fact that Matthew frequently quotes from or alludes to canonical prophetic literature (particularly Zechariah and Isaiah) in chapters 21-25 while he never quotes from the pseudepigraphical literature, and even the few proposed allusions (to *1 Enoch*, for example) are highly debatable.[365]

Our analysis of the prophetic aspects of Matthew's portrayal of Jesus in chapters 21-25 confirms Borg's argument that Jesus declared judgement on the Jewish nation because of its misuse of religion to support the 'Politics of Holiness', although we believe that Borg does not appreciate the full significance of Jesus' claim to authority to judge. We can also see that Jesus exercised what might be described as 'the Politics of Compassion' in his ministry. However, we contend that our reading of Matthew shows that Borg's rejection of an 'eschatological' Jesus is based on an inappropriate reading of the 'coming Son of Man' texts, and in the next chapter we will see that there is a substantial body of material in Matthew 21-25 that should be read as proclamation of final judgement in which Jesus will play a decisive role.

In the following chapter we shall see that Jesus, according to Matthew, also declared the final judgement of all humanity. He does so in a manner that sets

---

[365] These comments are based on the discussion of chapters 21-25 and are not intended as an evaluation of the possible reference to Ben Sira in Matt 11:28-30.

him apart from the apocalypticists of his day in that he shows no interest in pointing to the precise time of this event. Using distinctive *meshalim*, Jesus emphasises the paraenetic import of the coming reality – his disciples must be ready. While this aspect of his proclamation draws on the Wisdom background to his teaching, it nevertheless reflects an important aspect of the prophetic tradition also.

CHAPTER 6

Jesus the Judge in Matthew: As Sage

Introduction

The Wisdom tradition was a vital strand in the development of Jesus' self-understanding, as it was for any Jew steeped in the Hebrew Scriptures.[1] It is the contention of much recent scholarship that it had great significance for the way in which he exercised his teaching and preaching ministry.[2] Crenshaw offers the following definition of Wisdom literature,

> ...formally wisdom consists of proverbial sentence or instruction, debate, intellectual reflection; thematically wisdom comprises self-evident intuitions about mastering life for human betterment, groping after life's secrets with regard to innocent suffering, grappling with finitude, and quest for truth concealed in the created order and manifested in Dame Wisdom. When a marriage between form and content exists, there is wisdom literature. Lacking such oneness, a given text participates in biblical wisdom to a greater or lesser extent.[3]

Clearly, Jesus was not the author of 'Wisdom literature' in the sense defined by Crenshaw,[4] but he nonetheless demonstrates his dependence on it in both the

---

[1] For discussion of the impact of Wisdom literature on a group of Jews roughly contemporary with Jesus, see D. J. Harrington, *Wisdom Texts from Qumran* (London: Routledge, 1996).

[2] For a valuable discussion of Jewish Wisdom literature, both canonical and non-canonical, with particular reference to its significance for understanding the New Testament understanding(s) of Jesus, see particularly, Witherington, *Jesus the Sage*. See also the work of R. E. Murphy, *The Forms of Old Testament Literature. Vol XIII Wisdom Literature* (FOTL; Grand Rapids: Eerdmans, 1981), and J. L. Crenshaw, *Old Testament Wisdom: An Introduction* (Atlanta: John Knox Press, 1981), the multi-author work, *The Sage in Israel and the Ancient Near East* ed. J. G. Gammie and L. G. Perdue (Winona Lake: Eisenbrauns, 1990) and more recently, J. Day, R. P. Gordon and H. G. M. Williamson (eds), *Wisdom in Ancient Israel* (Emerton FS; Cambridge: Cambridge University Press, 1995).

[3] Crenshaw, *Old Testament Wisdom – An Introduction*, 19.

[4] He is not, of course, the author of *any* form of literature. Therefore, we can only establish connections (if they exist) with the literature of the Old Testament on the

content and the form of his teaching, and thus we may say that his teaching 'participates in biblical wisdom'.[5] This is as evident in Matthew 21-25 as it is anywhere in the gospel tradition, as we shall see.

The purpose of this chapter is to investigate the significance of the theme of judgement in a range of Jewish literature, all of which might be described as 'Wisdom literature', and then to examine the ways in which chapters 21 to 25 of Matthew reflect the findings of that survey. In the course of the discussion, I intend to demonstrate that:

a)   Wisdom literature and/or teaching contain an emphasis on God as judge, including both acts of judgement in the present experience of human beings and at some future eschatological judgement.

b)   Wisdom literature and teaching provide an appropriate context for understanding aspects of Jesus' ministry, both conceptually and formally. In particular, they provide a background to significant elements of Jesus' ministry as presented in Matthew 21-25.

c)   When Jesus' sayings are read against their OT background, they demonstrate that a correct application of the model of 'teacher of Wisdom' to Jesus does not require that a distinct expectation of future judgement in his teaching must be abandoned (as Borg asserts).

Following a survey of the relevant material from selected ancient Jewish Wisdom texts, we will proceed to examine certain important passages from Matthew 21-25. If Jesus is to be described as a 'sage' (as he is in numerous contemporary works of biblical scholarship),[6] and if judgement is indeed a dominant theme in his teaching (as we have argued it is), we must ask whether ancient documents that stand within the Wisdom tradition reflect this same emphasis. It is also important to investigate whether there are background materials in the Wisdom tradition which have a direct influence on Jesus' ministry. M. Hengel, for one, considers these two aspects of who Jesus was to be intimately related, particularly in Matthew:

> In the portals of certain Gothic cathedrals we meet Christ the teacher. Perhaps the finest example of this is the 'Beau Dieu' in Chartres. Above this, by contrast, Christ as judge appears in the tympanum of the doorway arch, this representation being even more frequent. The two belong together: the gift of the divine Wisdom binds the teacher with the judge; they are its exponents, indeed its embodiments. In other words, in Jesus as teacher, and in the Son of Man as judge, God's wisdom becomes manifest...The teaching and judging Christ of the Gothic cathedral is the

---

basis of allusions (whether linguistic or formal) in the oral teaching and in the activities of Jesus.

[5] So Harrington, *Wisdom Texts*, 88: 'That Jesus was to some extent a Wisdom teacher is clear from even a cursory look at the Gospels.'

[6] Borg is just one example among several. The theme is picked up most fully and consistently by Witherington, *Jesus the Sage*.

Christ of the First Gospel, which became in a special way the gospel of the Church.[7]

The term 'wisdom' (σοφία) does not appear in Matthew 21-25. There is only one occurrence of the cognate Greek adjective σοφός used substantively meaning 'sage' in chapters 21 to 25, namely 23:34 which reads:

> Therefore I send you prophets, sages, and scribes (προφήτας καὶ σοφοὺς καὶ γραμματεῖς), some of whom you will kill and crucify, and some you will flog in your synagogues and pursue from town to town

It is unlikely that this occurrence of σοφός is a reference to Jesus himself, since he is the one who makes the declaration (ἐγὼ ἀποστέλλω πρὸς ὑμᾶς), though it is possible that he adopts the first person declaration of God as the OT prophets frequently did.[8] Indeed, in the parallel passage in Luke 11:49-51 it is Wisdom who speaks these words.[9] The prophecy that the Jews will 'crucify' some of the messengers is certainly striking in the context, but Gundry is probably correct to see this as a parallel between the experience of the master and his disciples, rather than a veiled reference to Jesus.[10] The fact that more than one ('some') will be killed and crucified militates against a direct reference to Jesus, as does the reference to other experiences which are not most naturally predicated of Jesus ('some you will flog in your synagogues and pursue from town to town'). However, the presence of the term is still significant for our understanding of Jesus in terms of Wisdom, in that it alerts us to the importance of the sage in his understanding of the way God presents his will to humanity. In fact, the very fact of the striking variation between Matthew and Luke with regard to this pericope may suggest that, from the perspective of the early Christians, Jesus is to be understood *as* Wisdom incarnate.[11]

---

[7] Hengel, *Studies in Early Christology*, 73, 87.

[8] Compare the sending activity of Yahweh in the OT scriptures. Mal. 4:5: 'I will send you the prophet Elijah before the great and terrible day of the LORD comes.'

[9] D. E. Orton, *The Understanding Scribe* (JSNTS 25; Sheffield: JSOT Press, 1989), 153.

[10] Gundry, *Matthew* 470.

[11] So Hengel, *Studies in Early Christology*, 87: 'Matthew...consistently identif[ies] the divine Wisdom with Jesus himself.' See also M. J. Suggs, *Wisdom, Christology and Law in Matthew's Gospel* (Cambridge MA, Harvard University Press, 1970), 13-16. Orton, *The Understanding Scribe*, 154, raises a caution based on the fact that Matthew does not actually mention Wisdom, and therefore any identification of Jesus with Wisdom is based on a comparison with Luke's Gospel. So also R. Pregeant ('The Wisdom Passages in Matthew's Story,' in D. Bauer and M. A. Powell (eds), *Treasures Old and New* [Minneapolis: Fortress, 1996], 197-232, here 198) rightly raises cautions about the work of Suggs because Suggs assumes that readers will be able to compare the redactional activity of Matthew with his sources (here Luke). While we accept in this thesis that there is probably an identification of Jesus with the Wisdom of God, we must be cautious about our use of supposed redactional activity to construct a view of

Judgement in Jewish Wisdom Literature

The question of whether there is a doctrine of retribution in the OT was asked
by K. Koch in an important article first published in 1955.[12] In that article,
Koch developed the view that there is an 'act/consequence' doctrine of retribution in the OT, meaning that every deed brought about a consequence in keeping with that deed. This issue is of particular import in the case of the OT Wisdom writings, where such a doctrine appears to be more pronounced. More
recently, drawing on the work of L. Boström, R. E. Clements has claimed that
the answer to Koch's question must be 'yes' in the case of the Wisdom literature, on the basis of a strong conviction of a divine order. He does indicate,
however, that there is some ambiguity as to whether God directly intervenes to
bring about retribution, or whether it happens by natural consequence[13] and
thus largely follows in the footsteps of Koch in favouring the latter position.
We will attempt to clarify the issue raised by Koch's article in our investigation
of the Wisdom material.[14] In particular, we will seek to demonstrate that while
the Wisdom literature does not present a developed doctrine of the active
judgement of God, yet there are numerous texts which indicate that the authors
of the Wisdom literature held to the belief that God was concerned for justice
and that he would ensure that justice was upheld in the end.

Judgement in Proverbs

The title 'Proverbs' with which readers of the English translations of the Bible
are so familiar, translates the Hebrew term *meshalim*[15] which includes a broad
range of literary forms, from brief provocative expressions to lengthy stories.[16]
In the case of this particular document, the former variety predominates, so that

---

Matthew's thought. It is important that we are able to make sense of Matthew's
narrative on its own terms.

[12] 'Gibt es ein Vergeltungsdogma im Alten Testament?' *ZThK* 52 (1955), 1-42. An
English translation is found as 'Is There a Doctrine of Retribution in the Old
Testament?' in J. L. Crenshaw (ed.), *Theodicy in the Old Testament* (London: SCM
Press, 1983), 57-87.

[13] R. E. Clements, 'Wisdom and Old Testament Theology' in Day, Gordon and
Williamson (eds), *Wisdom in Ancient Israel*, 269-86, here 279.

[14] For the significance of this concept throughout the OT, see *NIDOTTE* 4:837-46.

[15] The Hebrew term occurs e.g., Num. 23:7, 18; 24:3, 15, 20, 21, 23; Deut. 28:37; 1 Sam.
10:12; 24:14; 2 Sam. 23:3; 1 Kgs. 5:12; 9:7; 2 Chr. 7:20; Job 13:12; 27:1; 29:1; Ps.
44:15 (LXX 43:15); 49:5 (LXX 48:5); 69:12 (LXX 68:12); 78:2 (LXX 77:2); Prov.
1:1, 6; 10:1; 25:1; 26:7, 9; Ecc. 12:9; Is. 14:4; Jer. 24:9; Ezek. 12:22, 23; 14:8; 17:2;
18:2, 3; 21:5; 24:3, Joel 2:17; Mich. 2:4; Hab. 2:6. In every case, bar three, the term is
translated in the LXX with παραβολή. In Job 27:1 and 29:1, Job's words are prefixed
with a standard formula for which the LXX uses τῷ προοιμίῳ. In Is. 14:4 the term
used is τὸν θρῆνον. See *NIDOTTE* 2:1134-36.

[16] See *NIDOTTE*, 2:1134-36; *TDNT*, 5:744-51.

John Collins accurately comments that,

> From a literary point of view, Proverbs is neither narrative nor law nor prophecy. Neither is it liturgical poetry such as we find in Psalms. The greater part of the book (chapters 10 to 30) is a collection of sentences that are sometimes strung together by catchwords or a common theme, but on the whole defy continuous reading.[17]

This characteristic of the collection makes it difficult to trace a developed view on any subject in Proverbs.[18] Certainly, we do not find here the kind of 'parables' that we find in Matthew's gospel (e.g., Matthew 25:14-30). However, I believe that it is possible to identify a consistent strand of judgement teaching in the collection, even if it is not developed in any pronounced way.

The 'descriptive' character of many of the proverbs is frequently noted. For example, after quoting a number of proverbs, Crenshaw comments,

> Such observations about 'the way things are' scarcely pronounce judgment upon one or the other phenomenon being described. We must guard against an assumption that Israel's maxims underwent a gradual development from wholly secular proverbs to fervently religious precepts. Presumably, even the most devout sage was capable of describing reality without always feeling obligated to affix a moral.[19]

Such statements are not the whole story, however. There are a number of passages that indicate a moral perspective. For instance, Proverbs 6:16-19 reads,

> 16 There are six things that the LORD *hates*, seven that are an abomination to him: 17 haughty eyes, a lying tongue, and hands that shed innocent blood, 18 a heart that devises wicked plans, feet that hurry to run to evil, 19 a lying witness who testifies falsely, and one who sows discord in a family.

While there is no explicit indication of the outcome expected for those who exhibit such characteristics, there is an implicit indication that the Lord's hatred (שָׂנֵא)[20] of such things is not a small matter, and that those who are the objects of this hatred will be held accountable.

From the very beginning of this collection of Jewish Wisdom, the reader is informed that what is written is provided,

> for gaining instruction in wise dealing, righteousness, justice, and equity (1:3)

---

[17] Collins, *Jewish Wisdom*, 2.
[18] Though Kidner, *Proverbs* (TOTC; Leicester: IVP, 1964) does provide a useful discussion of dominant themes.
[19] Crenshaw, *Old Testament Wisdom*, 77.
[20] *NIDOTTE* 3:1256-59.

This portion of the 'mission statement' of the book highlights the themes of righteousness and justice and equity, thus indicating concerns that lie at the heart of Israel's God, and suggesting themes that will be prominent throughout the rest of the book. Not only so, but the bringing together of these themes with the 'instruction in wise dealing' suggests a link between wisdom and justice that may be traced as we proceed.

In chapter 2 of the book, the reader is encouraged to take careful note of the words of the sage

> 1 My child, if you accept my words and treasure up my commandments within you, 2 making your ear attentive to wisdom and inclining your heart to understanding; 3 if you indeed cry out for insight, and raise your voice for understanding; 4 if you seek it like silver, and search for it as for hidden treasures - 5 then you will understand the fear of the LORD and find the knowledge of God. 6 For the LORD gives wisdom; from his mouth come knowledge and understanding; 7 he stores up sound wisdom for the upright; he is a shield to those who walk blamelessly, 8 guarding the paths of justice and preserving the way of his faithful ones.

In these words, the sage identifies several important issues for the purposes of this thesis. Firstly, wisdom is closely identified with the 'fear of the LORD'. This connection is introduced at the beginning of the book with the statement in 1:7,

> The fear of the LORD is the beginning of knowledge; fools despise wisdom and instruction.

This is described by Scott as a 'motto' which stands at the beginning, and in slightly different form, at the end (9:10), of the first series of admonitions in Proverbs.[21] He translates 'the fear of the LORD' as 'to hold the Lord in awe', and indicates that part of the meaning is 'to avoid wrongdoing'.[22] If this is the case, then there must be an implicit justification for this exhortation to the effect that the Lord will hold the wrongdoer accountable for his or her actions, whether immediately or in the distant future. If this is not implied, it is hard to see what need there is to fear the Lord for wrongdoing. Secondly, the claim that the Lord guards the 'paths of justice' would seem to indicate an active involvement in preserving justice in the land. This phrase does not necessitate that all actions within the land will, in fact, be just, but it indicates that the Lord will not overlook deviations from the paths of justice and will hold accountable those who do so deviate.

In a more positive light, the warm and tender words of 3:11-12 still maintain

---

[21] R. B. Y. Scott, *Proverbs, Ecclesiastes* (AB 18; New York: Doubleday, 1965), 36. Compare W. J. Dumbrell, *The Faith of Israel* (Leicester: Apollos, 1989), 225; Kidner, *Proverbs*, 59.

[22] Scott, *Proverbs, Ecclesiastes*, 37.

a perspective of the Lord's active correctional activity in the lives of his people. Although he recognises a clear theology of 'retribution' in Proverbs,[23] Collins claims that Proverbs exhibits no sign of God's active involvement in that process.

> God is the guarantor of this system but his role is like that of a midwife. No miraculous interference is needed.[24]

Whether one can accept Collins' judgement depends on what one understands by his phrase 'miraculous interference'. If he means that Proverbs gives no indication of an expectation that God will intervene in 'supernatural acts', perhaps to be compared with the fate of Ananias and Sapphira in Acts 5, then there can be little disagreement with his statement. If, however, he means that God is not presented as actively concerned with the upholding and administering of justice, both in the present experience of society and in future judgement, then we must take issue with that position. In addition to the implicit evidence to the contrary noted above, there are some further more explicit statements that appear to reflect a clear interventionist view of the judgement of God, such as Proverbs 10:3:

> The LORD does not let the righteous go hungry, but he thwarts the craving of the wicked.

On this latter line, McKane comments,

> The wicked are condemned to live forever with their unfulfilled, and so sterile, desires, which cannot be transformed into practical attainment.[25]

To dismiss this text as an example of 'doctrinaire pietism', as Collins does,[26] will not do. Although one might argue that nothing more than retribution is suggested here, the issue is not primarily what experience the wrongdoer endures, but rather who is responsible for that experience. Even if the statement in Proverbs 10:3 indicates no more than a life of unfulfilled desires, the significant point for our purposes is that *the Lord* is the one who 'thwarts the cravings of the wicked'. A similar text is found in 11:21:

---

[23] He identifies Proverbs 22:8 as an example: 'Whoever sows injustice will reap calamity, and the rod of anger will fail.' Collins, *Jewish Wisdom in the Hellenistic Age*, 4.
[24] Collins, *Jewish Wisdom in the Hellenistic Age*, 3-4.
[25] W. McKane, *Proverbs* (OTL; Philadelphia: Westminster, 1970), 426.
[26] Collins, *Jewish Wisdom in the Hellenistic Age*, 3. Collins claims that it is 'reasonable to suppose' that this statement 'represents a distinct redactional stage in the development of the collection.' This may be so, but such a view is only significant if it also holds that the later statements are incompatible with those made earlier.

Be assured, the wicked will not go unpunished, but those who are righteous will escape.

The niphal form of נקה suggests a 'divine passive'.[27] The emphatic character of this pronouncement[28] indicates that it is not a matter of uncertainty, and therefore it is not a matter outwith God's sovereign control.

Towards the conclusion of Proverbs, there is a reminder that the Lord requires justice to be carried out in the present world. In 31:9 we read,

Speak out, judge righteously, defend the rights of the poor and needy.

This verse, while not relating to the judgement of God himself, may be understood to indicate the *priorities* of God and thus to indicate something of the character of God's own justice.

It can be stated then, that Proverbs does assume a theology of judgement, though admittedly it is not developed. However P. House can write of Proverbs' view of justice that,

God vindicates the righteous by actively moving or reproving the wicked. God blesses the righteous with food but chastises the wicked (10:3). Yahweh promises that willful sinners will not go unpunished (11:21). It is God alone who is able to weigh human hearts (21:2), so only the Lord is capable of just punishment and reward.[29]

It is also true that there is no explicit reference to any future 'eschatological' judgement, although we might ask how Yahweh can uphold justice in the way that Proverbs does suggest without some form of eschatological judgement, since presumably not all the oppressed were vindicated within their own life span. However, there is no data that can be cited for developing an investigation into this question. Although Proverbs cannot be cited as providing a challenge to Borg's 'non-eschatological Jesus', our survey does raise questions about his treatment of the fundamental reason for Jesus' proclamation of judgement. Borg claims that Jesus' words of judgement were directed against the 'Politics of Holiness' being exercised in Palestine in the first century AD rather than personal sinfulness. However, Proverbs appears to indicate that the abandonment of justice is intensely displeasing to Yahweh and will bring judgement upon those who act in such a way.

---

[27] A. P. Ross, *Proverbs* (EBC 5; Grand Rapids: Zondervan, 1991), 964: 'God's just retribution is certain.'

[28] The idiomatic phrase is *yad liyad*, 'hand to hand'. See M. Anbar, 'Proverbs 11:21; 16:15: *yd lyd* «sur le champ»' *Biblica* 53 (1972), 537-38.

[29] P. R. House, *Old Testament Theology* (Downers Grove: IVP, 1998), 447.

Judgement in Job

Job shares sufficient characteristics with Proverbs that it may also be classed as Wisdom literature.[30] On the other hand, according to J. J. Collins, Job 'represents a reaction, however, against the more dogmatic doctrine of retribution found in one stratum of Proverbs.'[31] Thus, he identifies the words of Job's friends - 'Think now, who that was innocent ever perished? Or where were the upright cut off?' (Job 4:7)[32] - as representative of the strong doctrine of retribution that Job will not tolerate.

It is certainly true that the book of Job 'modifies a simplistic, fatalistic understanding of the doctrine of retribution that condemns all who suffer and praises all who prosper regardless of their moral integrity.'[33] What is not so obvious is that any of the sages of Israel ever held to such a simplistic principle of retribution.[34] It may in fact be the case that the critique of Job's friends found in this document would have been applauded by many of Israel's sages.

We can trace two types of texts in Job. One group of texts appears to speak of final eschatological judgement. (It is important to maintain that note of caution, as we do not wish to prejudge the issue.) The other group appears to speak of temporal judgement as God intervenes in the affairs of human life.

Belonging to the first class of texts are the following:

> There an upright person could reason with him, and I should be acquitted forever by my judge (23:7).

The context of these words of Job is a longing on the part of Job for a hypothetical audience with God. The preceding verses read:

---

[30] D. J. A. Clines, *Job 1-20* (WBC 17; Dallas: Word, 1989), lx; House, *Old Testament Theology*, 424. B. S. Childs, *Introduction to the Old Testament as Scripture* (London: SCM Press, 1979), 547, says that 'Job and Ecclesiastes are secondarily related' to 'biblical wisdom' for study of which Proverbs is the 'basic source'.

[31] Collins, *Jewish Wisdom in the Hellenistic Age*, 13. Collins' language indicates his view of Proverbs as an essentially schizophrenic work, containing multiple worldviews that stand in tension with one another. He illustrates his point (13): 'The contrast between Job and Proverbs can be seen clearly by contrasting the great Wisdom poem in Job 28 with its counterpart in Proverbs 8. While Wisdom in Proverbs can be encountered in the city gate, in Job it is hidden, and only God knows the way.'

[32] Collins, *Jewish Wisdom*, 13.

[33] J. E. Hartley, *Job* (NICOT; Grand Rapids: Eerdmans, 1980), vii.

[34] See the comments of R. Murphy, *Ecclesiastes* (WBC; Waco: Word, 1992), 142-3: 'Were the sages so obtuse that they failed to note the constant breakdown of such a theory in their daily experience?...If the wit and perception displayed by the teachers of Israel are widely acknowledged, the theory of mechanical correspondence between act and result has to be recognised as a gratuitous generalization that suffers from countless exceptions.'

Then Job answered: 2 "Today also my complaint is bitter; his hand is heavy despite my groaning. 3 Oh, that I knew where I might find him, that I might come even to his dwelling! 4 I would lay my case before him, and fill my mouth with arguments. 5 I would learn what he would answer me, and understand what he would say to me. 6 Would he contend with me in the greatness of his power? No; but he would give heed to me."

The everlasting nature of the acquittal in this text suggests that this is more than a temporal judgement made by a human judge. On the other hand, we have to beware of the fact that Job is speaking in rather dramatic style. Yet, it would seem that we have some indication of Job's conviction that God could provide him with a final court of appeal.

The sense of this kind of climactic judgement is confirmed by chapter 34. We must be careful in interpreting these words for they are the words of Elihu, and thus they must not be understood *necessarily* to reflect the perspective of the author of the book. However, they reflect an understanding of the character of God that is in keeping with what we find in Job's own words. In challenging Job's attitude, Elihu asks the question (17), 'Shall one who hates justice govern?' The question is quite clearly rhetorical since it concludes with the statement 'for they are all the work of his hands,' thus pointing to the creator who stands above all human judges. Elihu goes on to indicate the fate of those who do not act justly, and it is inescapable that he implies divine intervention in the affairs of humanity:

20 In a moment they die; at midnight the people are shaken and pass away, and the mighty are taken away by no human hand. 21 "For his eyes are upon the ways of mortals, and he sees all their steps. 22 There is no gloom or deep darkness where evildoers may hide themselves. 23 For he has not appointed a time for anyone to go before God in judgment.

The judging activity of God is further elaborated in verses 24 to 26 ('knowing their works, he overturns them in the night, and they are crushed,' 25), and then is explained on the grounds of turning away from God (27) with the result that injustice and oppression followed: 'so that they caused the cry of the poor to come to him, and he heard the cry of the afflicted' (28). The same two sins of godlessness and oppression are linked in verse 30 also: 'so that the godless should not reign, or those who ensnare the people'. This portrayal of God leaves no doubt that he is active in judgement of all kinds, whether national or individual.

The second class of texts, relating to this-worldly acts of judgement include the following passages:

be afraid of the sword, for wrath brings the punishment of the sword, so that you may know there is a judgment (Job 19:29).

It is important to note that the temporal judgement by the sword that is the main subject of the warning is actually a sign of a more fundamental judgement. The words stand at the end of one of the most startling passages in Job (19:23-29):

> O that my words were written down! O that they were inscribed in a book! 24 O that with an iron pen and with lead they were engraved on a rock forever! 25 For I know that my Redeemer lives, and that at the last he will stand upon the earth; 26 and after my skin has been thus destroyed, then in my flesh I shall see God, 27 whom I shall see on my side, and my eyes shall behold, and not another. My heart faints within me! 28 If you say, 'How we will persecute him!' and, 'The root of the matter is found in him'; 29 be afraid of the sword, for wrath brings the punishment of the sword, so that you may know there is a judgment.

The broader context indicates an apparent expectation on the part of Job of future vindication by his 'Redeemer'. While numerous commentators have argued that this Redeemer is God, Clines rejects this view on the basis that it is inconsistent with Job's perspective on God as reflected in the rest of the work. He believes that his position is established by two important propositions:

> (i) that there is a contrast between what Job *believes* will happen (his death before vindication, but vindication thereafter) and what he wishes would happen (a face to face encounter with God this side of death); and (ii) that what pleads for Job in the heavenly realm is nothing but his own protestation of innocence.[35]

While one can have sympathy with Clines' hermeneutical approach to the text, it would seem to be going too far to forbid Job from expressing convictions which appear to be in tension, since the context is one of great distress. F. I. Andersen reading the contested words of verse 25 in the context of the following verses states,

> Verses 25-27 are so tightly knit that there should be no doubt that the *Redeemer* is *God*. NEB is to be commended for securing this, and also for bringing out the forensic connotations: the 'vindicator' who 'will rise...to speak in court' as Job's 'witness' and 'defending counsel' is none other than 'God himself'.

This reading is to be preferred to Clines' for several reasons. Firstly, it does not require the pessimistic reading of Clines. Job is, without doubt, wrestling with his present circumstances, but there is no indication that he has abandoned his hope in God. Secondly, it does not require the rather peculiar notion of the personification of Job's plea of innocence. Thirdly, it comports with verses 28-29 which appear to warn those who plot against Job that there is an objective arbiter of justice who will not hold them unaccountable.

This view leads us to the conclusion that Job expresses a conviction that

---

[35] D. J. A. Clines, *Job 1-20*, 465.

vindication will come at some future *post mortem* judgement. The final words cited are particularly important in this regard as they speak of 'a judgement'. However, this is a difficult verse in various ways[36] and thus resists giving a clear statement. Once again, Clines hovers on the verge of appealing to Job's typical attitude in the rest of the book, yet he pulls back, stating,

> So he does not believe that God is fundamentally unjust and that evil will always win; but he has had too bad an experience of God to have more faith in God than he has in himself.[37]

While we have to be careful in our use of a disputed text, it would seem possible on the basis of our position on verses 25-27, to argue that a reference to future judgement would be quite in keeping with Job's thought.

We might briefly mention several other texts in Job which point towards a conviction that God will act as judge. A text that indicates the authority of God to judge even the highest in human society is Job 21:22:

> Will any teach God knowledge, seeing that he judges those that are on high?

The question that arises is, When does this judgement take place? The impression given is of ongoing judgement, but there may well be an indication of final judgement. Again, in Job 22:4, Eliphaz asks Job the sarcastic question,

> Is it for your piety that he reproves you, and enters into judgment with you?

Our interest is not in the accuracy of Eliphaz's perspective on Job, but of his perspective on God, for Eliphaz clearly ascribes to God an active role in judgement that has led to Job's present position. While Eliphaz is not understood to be a faithful speaker in Job, yet his words here indicate not a belief in 'retribution' in a mechanical sense, but an interventionist perspective on God's judgement. A little further on in Eliphaz's speech (22:13), he claims of Job,

> Therefore you say, 'What does God know? Can he judge through the deep darkness?

While Andersen is correct to state that Eliphaz perverts Job's true understanding of God,[38] this text is evidence of a belief that God *could* see through darkness in order to pronounce and execute judgement.

There are also some passages in Job which are difficult to classify exactly as to the view of judgement that they present. One such is 11:7-11:

---

[36] F. I. Andersen, *Job* (TNTC; Leicester: IVP, 1975), 195, claims that 'these verses are largely unintelligible.'

[37] Clines, *Job 1-20*, 468.

[38] Andersen, *Job*, 204.

7 "Can you find out the deep things of God? Can you find out the limit of the Almighty? 8 It is higher than heaven - what can you do? Deeper than Sheol - what can you know? 9 Its measure is longer than the earth, and broader than the sea. 10 If he passes through, and imprisons, and assembles for judgment, who can hinder him? 11 For he knows those who are worthless; when he sees iniquity, will he not consider it?

In this case, it is not clear to what verse 10 refers. Is this temporal judgement, or a final eschatological assembly for judgement? Whatever is the case, it is the Almighty who 'assembles for judgment'.

Judgement in Ecclesiastes

The words of Qohelet, 'the Teacher', are frequently enigmatic. Indeed, Crenshaw describes Ecclesiastes as 'the Bible's strangest book'.[39] In particular, Qohelet is said to rebel against the conservative teaching of Proverbs, with its neat doctrine of retribution, and even Job who appears to hold to a similar position in the face of all his suffering.[40] Ecclesiastes 3:17 reads,

> I said in my heart, God will judge the righteous and the wicked, for he has appointed a time for every matter, and for every work.

These words follow a meditation on the order which God has established in this world, but also an expression of awareness that all was not as it should be. Particularly, the structures that should have provided justice were not doing so (3:16):

> Moreover I saw under the sun that in the place of justice, wickedness was there, and in the place of righteousness, wickedness was there as well.

The writer does not despair at this state of affairs because he is confident that, just as God has established a time for all other things, so he has established a time for judgement when the injustices of which he is all too aware will be rectified. This has appeared to some commentators (e.g., Podechard, Galling, and Lauha[41]) as a change in the typical tone of Qohelet, and therefore an editorial addition. However, Murphy notes that while it is true that Qohelet does not believe that people receive justice in this world, yet he never denies that God is indeed judge. Indeed in 5:6 (Hebrew, 5:5) and 11:9 he upholds just such a position. The former text reads

---

[39] J. L. Crenshaw, *Ecclesiastes* (OTL; Philadelphia: Westminster, 1987), 23.
[40] Though note well the cautionary comments of Murphy as cited in footnote 34 above.
[41] As cited by Murphy, *Ecclesiastes*, 36.

> Do not let your mouth lead you into sin, and do not say before the messenger that
> it was a mistake; why should God be angry at your words, and destroy the work
> of your hands?

This seems to be a clear reference to judgement in the context of on-going human life, but it is far from being an example of cold retribution theology. It
displays a clear understanding that if there is to be judgement, then it will be
carried out by God himself. The latter text (11:9) reads,

> Rejoice, young man, while you are young, and let your heart cheer you in the days
> of your youth. Follow the inclination of your heart and the desire of your eyes, but
> know that for all these things God will bring you into judgment.

These words similarly attribute judgement quite clearly to God and not to some
principle of cause and effect. It is not so clear whether the judgement envisaged
in this case will take place during life or at its end. Whybray notes, however,
that the same commentators who question the authenticity of 3:17, also question this text (e.g., Galling and Lauha) on the same grounds. On the other hand,
he points out contrary voices in Gordis and Herzberg.[42]

Another passage which is significant in determining the doctrine of judgement in Ecclesiastes is chapter 3, verses 18ff., which read as follows:

> I said in my heart with regard to human beings that God is testing them to show
> that they are but animals. 19 For the fate of humans and the fate of animals is the
> same; as one dies, so dies the other. They all have the same breath, and humans
> have no advantage over the animals; for all is vanity.

An apparent confidence in God's activity in the world seems, in this case, to be
held in tension with a rather bleak perspective on life.

As the book comes to a conclusion, there is a further note of judgement
sounded in 12:14:

> For God will bring every deed into judgment, including every secret thing,
> whether good or evil.

This is an interesting text for it refers to both complete judgement and judgement of matters hidden from the eyes of human beings. This would suggest
something more than simply the retributive functions of the human authorities
even when understood to be acting as God's agents. The language echoes 11:9,
where

---

[42] See bibliographical details in R. N. Whybray, *Ecclesiastes*, (NCBC; Grand Rapids:
Eerdmans, 1989), 162.

God will call you to account if you do not enjoy life to the height of your capacity.[43]

Crenshaw understands these final words to be the work of an 'epilogist' who is at odds with the view of Qohelet:

> The epilogist insists that nothing will fall between the cracks. God will uncover the secret villanies and the secret deeds of charity. This comforting word for good people and frightening word for sinners is, again, totally alien to Qohelet's thinking.[44]

That 12:9-14 is an addition to the book is widely accepted, and the inclusion formed by 1:2 and 12:8 provides strong evidence for this view,[45] but Crenshaw is perhaps too bold in his dismissive statement. Murphy is more cautious, but still tends towards the view that the verse 'goes beyond the perspective of Qohelet.'[46] Whatever is the case with respect to the editorial involvement in 12:9-14, it is clear that the echo of 11:9 is deliberate, and there one can detect a definite (if somewhat more muted) reference to divine judgement.[47] Even if we must dissociate 12:14 from the document that precedes it, the author of these words stood in the same tradition as Qohelet and so we may still understand these words as evidence of a strong understanding of divine judgement in the Wisdom tradition.

Judgement in Ben Sirach

When we turn from the canonical Wisdom texts of the Hebrew scriptures to the later hellenistic Jewish Wisdom texts found in the LXX, we may observe a development of the theme of judgement. The book known as the Wisdom of Jesus ben Sirach (or Ecclesiasticus) was originally written in Hebrew (around 180 BC), and was later translated into Greek by ben Sirach's grandson around 132 BC.[48] It is recognised that a parallel to Matthew's interest in the scribe is found in the Wisdom of Jesus ben Sirach:

> 38:34 How different the one who devotes himself to the study of the law of the Most High! 39:1 He seeks out the wisdom of all the ancients, and is concerned with prophecies; 2 he preserves the sayings of the famous and penetrates the

---

[43] Crenshaw, *Ecclesiastes*, 184.

[44] Crenshaw, *Ecclesiastes*, 192.

[45] See Murphy, *Ecclesiastes*, 124, Crenshaw, *Ecclesiastes*, 189, Scott, *Proverbs, Ecclesiastes*, 255-6.

[46] Murphy, *Ecclesiastes*, 126.

[47] On this text Murphy (*Ecclesiastes*, 117) is more assured: 'as far as divine judgement is concerned, Qohelet never denies the *fact* (cf. 3:17).'

[48] Evans, *NWNTI*, 13.

subtleties of parables; 3 he seeks out the hidden meanings of proverbs and is at home with the obscurities of parables.

The context of this text is a discussion of those who have no time for the calling of the scribe.[49] The scribe, on the other hand, is described as 'one who devotes himself to the study of the law of the Most High.' In the description of his task, there is an emphasis on his desire and responsibility to delve into the mysterious words of parables.[50]

The theme of judgement in ben Sirach is relatively reserved – there is no clear reference to eschatological judgement – but he nonetheless presents Yahweh as the one who upholds justice. Thus in ben Sirach 35:15, we read,

> and do not rely on a dishonest sacrifice; for the Lord is the judge, and with him there is no partiality.

This theme is developed even more fully in 35:21-25, where the Lord's acts of judgement are spoken of in very bold images which perhaps hint at a reckoning beyond simply the day to day workings of temporal justice. J. J. Collins writes,

> With the exception of the disputed passage in chapter 36, which follows directly on this passage, this is the closest Sirach comes to the typical biblical picture of a God who intervenes in history on behalf of his people.[51]

The 'disputed passage' in question is a prayer for deliverance, and Collins comments that it 'burns with eschatological fervor.'[52] It pleads for Yahweh's judgement upon the nations. As to the nature of the judgement, there is some ambiguity. Verse 10 refers to 'the day', which may be a reference to the eschatological *Yom Yahweh*:

> Hasten the day, and remember the appointed time, and let people recount your mighty deeds.

The following verse then asks that 'survivors be consumed' which suggests some degree of historical continuity following 'the day'. Regardless of the precise interpretation of the passage, it is a clear call for judgement on the part of Yahweh. For this reason, its authenticity is disputed, and Collins concludes his discussion,

---

[49] See H. Stadelmann, *Ben Sira als Schriftgelehrter* (WUNT 6; Tübingen: JCB Mohr, 1980). D. E. Orton, *The Understanding Scribe.*

[50] Orton, *The Understanding Scribe*, 68.

[51] Collins, *Jewish Wisdom*, 91.

[52] Collins, *Jewish Wisdom*, 109.

> This prayer in chapter 36 is remote in spirit from the rest of the teaching of Sirach, and was most probably inserted into the book at the time of the Maccabean crisis.[53]

Once again, we are faced with a lack of explicit eschatological perspective in a Wisdom text. Collins comments,

> Sirach's lack of eschatological concern is typical of the biblical wisdom tradition. Eschatology is equally absent from Proverbs, Job, and Qoheleth.[54]

Although our discussion of Proverbs, Job and Qoheleth has suggested that Collins' conclusion is too hasty, it is also important to notice that Collins does not consider a lack of eschatological perspective to be inherent in the Wisdom tradition. He continues,

> We should not necessarily conclude that eschatology is incompatible with wisdom literature as such...Ben Sira's lack of eschatology is a result not of the genre he uses but of his social location.[55]

By this he appears to mean that the particular socio-political circumstances in which Sirach was written accounts for the lack of eschatological perspective rather than the genre of literature to which it belongs. Thus Ben Sira should not be regarded as a touchstone for what we may or may not find in the pages of Wisdom writings.

Judgement in the Wisdom of Solomon

The volume known as the Wisdom of Solomon (though it is accepted that it is a pseudepigraphical document dating from the first century BC[56]) includes a great deal of material which deals with the issue of judgement from a Wisdom perspective. This is particularly true in the first five chapters of the work. In chapter 1 there are a number of references to the judging activity of God. Following a call to righteousness in the first two verses, the author provides a reason for taking his words seriously:

> 3 For perverse thoughts separate people from God, and when his power is tested, it exposes the foolish

Furthermore, Wisdom, it is claimed (1:6),

> will not free blasphemers from the guilt of their words

---

[53] Collins, *Jewish Wisdom*, 111.
[54] Collins, *Jewish Wisdom*, 111.
[55] Collins, *Jewish Wisdom*, 111.
[56] Evans, *NWNTI*, 13.

The reason given for this statement is 'because God is witness of their inmost feelings, and a true observer of their hearts, and a hearer of their tongues.' Thus it would appear that it is God who will not free blasphemers from their guilt. Indeed there is a consistent testimony to the fact that justice comes upon the unrighteous because of the active intervention of the Lord. So we find the following statements (emphasis mine):

> 7 Because the spirit of the Lord has filled the world, and that which holds all things together knows what is said, 8 *therefore those who utter unrighteous things will not escape notice, and justice, when it punishes, will not pass them by.* 9 For inquiry will be made into the counsels of the ungodly, and *a report of their words will come to the Lord, to convict them of their lawless deeds*; 10 because a jealous ear hears all things, and the sound of grumbling does not go unheard.

At the same time, the author of Wisdom can write in a way that suggests a somewhat more distant activity on the part of God (emphasis mine):

> 11 Beware then of useless grumbling, and keep your tongue from slander; *because no secret word is without result, and a lying mouth destroys the soul.* 12 Do not invite death by the error of your life, or bring on destruction by the works of your hands; 13 because God did not make death, and he does not delight in the death of the living. 14 For he created all things so that they might exist; the generative forces of the world are wholesome, and there is no destructive poison in them, and the dominion of Hades is not on earth. 15 For righteousness is immortal. 16 But the ungodly by their words and deeds summoned death; considering him a friend, they pined away and made a covenant with him, because they are fit to belong to his company.

Chapter 2 is a reflection on the attitudes of the foolish regarding the righteous and does not further our discussion. However, chapter 3 begins with a rebuttal of the foolish perspective in which it is declared that the righteous are actually safe in the care of God. But the second half of the chapter turns to the ungodly who had so callously determined to oppress the godly (emphasis mine):

> 10 But the ungodly will be punished as their reasoning deserves, those who disregarded the righteous and rebelled against the Lord; 11 for those who despise wisdom and instruction are miserable. Their hope is vain, their labors are unprofitable, and their works are useless. 12 Their wives are foolish, and their children evil; 13 their offspring are accursed. For blessed is the barren woman who is undefiled, who has not entered into a sinful union; she will have fruit when God examines souls. 14 Blessed also is the eunuch whose hands have done no lawless deed, and who has not devised wicked things against the Lord; for special favor will be shown him for his faithfulness, and a place of great delight in the temple of the Lord. 15 For the fruit of good labors is renowned, and the root of understanding does not fail. 16 But children of adulterers will not come to maturity, and the offspring of an unlawful union will perish. 17 Even if they live long they will be held of no account, and finally their old age will be without

honor. 18 *If they die young, they will have no hope and no consolation on the day of judgment* (οὐχ ἕξουσιν ἐλπίδα οὐδὲ ἐν ἡμέρᾳ διαγνώσεως παραμύθιον). *19 For the end of an unrighteous generation is grievous.*

Thus Wisdom presents a kind of balanced retribution (or better, recompense); the ill-treated righteous are blessed with acceptance by God, while the oppressors find themselves condemned 'on the Day of Judgement' (ἐν ἡμέρᾳ δι αγνώσεως).[57]

Chapter 4 contrasts, in typical sapiential fashion, the situation of the godly and of the ungodly. From verse 3 the ungodly are described as those who may prosper in the short term, but who ultimately experience desolation. Verses 16-19 read,

16 The righteous who have died will condemn the ungodly who are living, and youth that is quickly perfected will condemn the prolonged old age of the unrighteous. 17 For they will see the end of the wise, and will not understand what the Lord purposed for them, and for what he kept them safe. 18 The unrighteous will see, and will have contempt for them, but the Lord will laugh them to scorn. After this they will become dishonored corpses, and an outrage among the dead forever; 19 because he will dash them speechless to the ground, and shake them from the foundations; they will be left utterly dry and barren, and they will suffer anguish, and the memory of them will perish.

Verses 18-19 leave little doubt that the author regarded the downfall of the wicked to be the direct result of the actions of the Lord.

Chapter 5 contains a passage which is striking in its similarity to material in Matthew's gospel.

1 Then the righteous will stand with great confidence in the presence of those who have oppressed them and those who make light of their labors. 2 When the unrighteous see them, they will be shaken with dreadful fear, and they will be amazed at the unexpected salvation of the righteous. 3 They will speak to one another in repentance, and in anguish of spirit they will groan, and say, 4 "These are persons whom we once held in derision and made a byword of reproach - fools that we were! We thought that their lives were madness and that their end was without honor. 5 Why have they been numbered among the children of God? And why is their lot among the saints? 6 So it was we who strayed from the way of truth, and the light of righteousness did not shine on us, and the sun did not rise upon us. 7 We took our fill of the paths of lawlessness and destruction, and we journeyed through trackless deserts, but the way of the Lord we have not known. 8 What has our arrogance profited us? And what good has our boasted wealth brought us?

Although somewhat removed from the sentiments of Matthew 25:31-46, the

---

[57] See T. W. Willett, *Eschatology in the Theodicies of 2 Baruch and 4 Ezra* (Sheffield: JSOT Press, 1989), 31-32.

above passage does present us with an interesting parallel of a dialogue that takes place on the Day of Judgement, and that relates to the reasons for acceptance or condemnation.

Another particularly striking passage is found in Wisdom 6, where those addressed are the 'kings' and the 'judges', that is, those who exercise authority. This authority, however, as verse 3 makes clear, was not their own, but delegated by God himself, and the failure of these leaders to live up to their responsibilities (verse 4) will bring judgement upon them in the most severe terms (verse 5):

> he will come upon you terribly and swiftly, because severe judgment falls on those in high places.

This proves an interesting parallel to Matthew 23 where the stinging woes of Jesus are addressed not to the Jewish people as a whole, but to the Jewish leaders who bore responsibility for guiding the people.

Thus, from this sample of texts, it can be seen that the direct judgement of God is a common theme in Wisdom of Solomon.[58]

Summary of Survey of Wisdom Literature

Thus there are frequent references in Jewish Wisdom literature to judgement, both temporal and, less frequently, eschatological. In addition, reference may be made to the *Psalms of Solomon* 17 where one finds a close connection drawn between judgement (apparently future) and wisdom,[59] and Testament of Levi 18:1ff. where the promise that the 'new priest' will 'execute a righteous judgement on the earth' stands beside the affirmation that the 'spirit of understanding' will rest upon him.[60] The investigation above would suggest that the Jewish Wisdom tradition provides a ready background for appreciating both the

---

[58] Other important texts which emphasise the judgement of God are: Wisdom 11:9 'For when they were tried, though they were being disciplined in mercy, they learned how the ungodly were tormented when judged in wrath'; 12:13 'For neither is there any god besides you, whose care is for all people, to whom you should prove that you have not judged unjustly'; 12:21 'with what strictness you have judged your children, to whose ancestors you gave oaths and covenants full of good promises!'; 12:22 'So while chastening us you scourge our enemies ten thousand times more, so that, when we judge, we may meditate upon your goodness, and when we are judged, we may expect mercy'; 12:10 'But judging them little by little you gave them an opportunity to repent, though you were not unaware that their origin was evil and their wickedness inborn, and that their way of thinking would never change'.

[59] See the discussion in Hengel, *Studies in Early Christology*, 96-98.

[60] See once more the discussion in Hengel, *Studies in Early Christology*, 98-99.

form and content of Jesus' proclamation of judgement.[61]

Jesus the Judge as Sage in Matthew 21-25

In his important monograph, Ben Witherington points to the work of two particular authors in presenting the evidence for Matthew drawing deeply on Jewish Wisdom material: M. J. Suggs[62] and C. Deutsch.[63] In both cases, he points out, the authors have been criticised for dwelling on just a few select passages. Witherington, on the other hand, seeks to take a more holistic approach.[64] The intention in this study is also to avoid looking only at those passages in our defined section which display verbal links with Wisdom literature, but to consider also those that clearly reflect the Wisdom tradition.

Meshalim

Throughout chapters 21-25 we see that Jesus' teaching is virtually all in the form of *meshalim*. This statement can only be made, and thus a true recognition of the influence of Wisdom tradition can only be had, if the flexibility of the term *mashal* is recognised. C. H. Peisker comments with respect to the noun *mashal* that, 'In its long history, which passed from (1) popular speech to (2) the language of wisdom and later (3) to prophetic speech, it acquired a very broad semantic field.'[65] This range of meanings is reflected in the use of παραβολή in the LXX. Peisker goes on to provide an analysis of the various forms of speech which may be understood as παραβολαί.[66] This analysis is complemented by C. Brown's list of all 'parables' in the gospels. I will proceed

---

[61] We have not investigated the wisdom texts from Qumran as there is no evidence of any dependence on these texts on the part of Matthew. However, Harrington (*Wisdom Texts*, 91) indicates the significance of these texts for modern debate when he writes, 'the Qumran wisdom texts can neither prove nor disprove the Jesus as Cynic hypothesis. But they do point to the existence of a more traditional style of Jewish wisdom activity in first-century Palestine. And they raise further questions. Why should we search for parallels and analogies far removed in time and place when we have some impressive evidence for Jewish wisdom movements in late Second Temple times? And why should we not better attribute the distinctive style and tone of the wisdom teachings in the Gospels to the religious genius of Jesus?'

[62] Suggs, *Wisdom, Christology and Law*. See also the discussion of Suggs by R. Pregeant, 'The Wisdom Passages in Matthew's Story' in Bauer and Powell, *Treasures New and Old*, 197-232.

[63] C. Deutsch, *Hidden Wisdom and Easy Yoke. Wisdom, Torah and Discipleship in Matthew 11.25-30* (Sheffield: JSOT Press, 1987). *Ibid.*, 'Wisdom in Matthew: Transformation of a Symbol' *NovT* 32.1 (1990), 13-47.

[64] Witherington, *Jesus the Sage*, 351.

[65] *NIDNTT*, 2:746-47.

[66] *NIDNTT*, 2:746-48.

to note these categories and how they relate to material within Matthew 21-25:
Figurative sayings
Metaphor
Simile
Parable
Parabolic story
Illustrative story
Allegory
I have adopted this term *mashal* in the light of our discussion of the pre-Christian Wisdom texts, and also following B. Gerhardsson who correctly notes with respect to the phrase ἐν παραβολαῖς (cf. Matt. 13:3) that,

> This does not mean 'in parables' - as we generally put it - but 'in meshalim'. When ancient Jewish teachers used the Hebrew word *msl* (mashal, meshalim in the plural) they had in mind a short, carefully formulated text, which could be of many different kinds: a maxim, a proverb, a riddle, a taunt, etc., as well as a brief narrative, an illustration, a parable, an allegory, or even a pregnant prophetic or apocalyptic saying, all distinguished by their skilful formulation from flat everyday speech.[67]

There is clearly a strong element of comparison in the categories proposed by Peisker and Brown,[68] and some scholars have claimed that only sayings which exhibit that comparative characteristic can properly be described as *meshalim*.[69] However, Gerhardsson's comments more accurately reflect the range of meanings of *mashal* and C. A. Evans demonstrates that *mashal* may be used of sayings in which there is no element of comparison.[70] In particular, he draws attention to 1 Samuel 10:12 and 1 Samuel 24:13, and it is worth noting these examples briefly.

---

[67] B. Gerhardsson, 'Illuminating the Kingdom: Narrative Meshalim in the Synoptic Gospels' in H. Wansbrough (ed.), *Jesus and the Oral Gospel Tradition*, 266. Cf. Witherington, *Jesus the Sage*, 19, and *idem*, *The Christology of Jesus*, 206-7. See also the discussion of G. M. Landes, 'Jonah: A Mashal?' in J. G. Gammie, W. A. Brueggemann, W. L. Humphreys and J. M. Ward (eds), *Israelite Wisdom: Theological and Literary Essays in Honor of Samuel Terrien* (Scholars Press, 1978), 137-58, on whether Jonah should be regarded as a *mashal*, which includes some helpful analysis of the genre.

[68] See also the categories offered, with examples, by R. H. Stein, 'The Genre of the Parables' in Longenecker (ed.), *The Challenge of Jesus' Parables*, 30-50, particularly 39-47.

[69] Stein ('The Genre of the Parables', 42) writes, 'Whereas a parable can be a proverb, this does not mean that every proverb can be classed as a parable. Only those proverbs in which a comparison of unlike things is found should be included in the genre "parable".'

[70] Evans, 'Parables in Early Judaism', 52-54.

1 Samuel 10:12:

A man of the place answered, "And who is their father?" Therefore it became a *proverb* (MT: לְמָשָׁל, LXX: εἰς παραβολήν) "Is Saul also among the prophets?"

1 Samuel 24:13

As the ancient *proverb* (MT: מְשַׁל, LXX: ἡ παραβολή) says, 'Out of the wicked comes forth wickedness'; but my hand shall not be against you.

In both of these examples it is quite clear that comparison is not an element of the saying. In the saying recorded in 1 Samuel 24:13 there is quite clear evidence of parallelism, but in the saying found in 1 Samuel 10:12 there is not even that structural indicator to suggest the appropriateness of the term *mashal*. It is therefore legitimate to recognise the breadth of the term *meshalim*, while nonetheless seeking to distinguish portions of Jesus' teaching that fall into this category from any portions of Jesus' teaching that should not be classed in this way.

With respect to both the quality and diversity of form of Jesus' *meshalim*, Martin Hengel states boldly,

> We are justified in seeing in Jesus the most impressive creator of מְשָׁלִים in ancient Judaism. Besides numerous parables and word pictures, there are 'makarisms', pregnantly formulated aphorisms, as well as artistic proverbial compositions...Jesus is as much the master of the laws of Semitic poetry as Sirach or other Wisdom poets. In him we find the *parallelismus membrorum*, rhythm, all types of word play and rhyme. Above all, he is the master of the sharply formulated logion with antithetic parallelism.[71]

With such an appropriately broad understanding of speech forms in the Wisdom tradition, we find various forms of *meshalim* in chapters 21 to 25. In confirmation of these findings, Witherington comments,

> ...even after the great revelations in Matthew 16 and 17, there is need for further teaching discourses in Matthew 18-25 which include a variety of parables as well as other sorts of teaching. The large bulk of the teaching material here too is sapiential in character which again drives home the point that Jesus is being likened to Solomon, not Moses.[72]

Gerhardsson identifies two broad classes of *meshalim*. 'Narrative *meshalim*' are understood to equate with 'parables' in the popular sense of the term, while 'Aphoristic *meshalim*' are diverse in character and include pithy sayings, rid-

---

[71] Hengel, *Studies in Early Christology*, 90.
[72] Witherington, *Jesus the Sage*, 364.

dles, etc. Among the passages described by Gerhardsson as 'narrative *meshalim*'[73] are the following passages:

The Two Sons (21:28-32), which is a brief story, might be included in this category, although it could barely be described as a narrative and might even be described as a riddle; The Tenants (21:33-41), on the other hand, has a much more developed narrative and is clearly to be categorised as Gerhardsson suggests; The Wedding Banquet (22:1-14) also contains a significant narrative; The Thief (24:43-44), has no developed narrative; three more developed narratives are The Servant (24:45-51); The Ten Virgins (25:1-13); and The Talents (25:14-30). Gerhardsson also includes the passage 25:31-46 under the title, 'The Last Judgment'[74] but I believe that this is not an accurate classification, noting that though there is imagery and identifiable structure in the passage, it does not truly conform to the pattern of a parable, particularly in that Jesus refers to the coming of the Son of Man which is never used elsewhere in the context of a narrative *mashal*.[75]

It is significant to note that in Gerhardsson's analysis of the 'narrative *meshalim*' found in Matthew (which, of course, is only one of several types of *mashal* employed by Jesus), one third are found in chapters 21-25, the remainder being found mainly in chapter 13. This indicates, firstly, that the narrative *meshalim* were recognised by Matthew to be of a distinct and common form and that they should therefore be gathered in particular collections; and secondly, that a substantial number are found in a section of Matthew which, we argue, presents the theme of judgement particularly strongly, suggesting that there may be a distinct connection between the form of the narrative *meshalim* and the theme of judgement. Witherington notes that 'narrative *meshalim*' were not characteristic of Wisdom literature, but rather are associated with the prophets, perhaps most famously Nathan in the account of 2 Samuel 12:1-4.[76] He suggests that they may therefore be regarded as a prophetic adaptation of a Wisdom form. It is worth noting this comment as we begin to study Matthew 21-25, looking at both its Wisdom and prophetic characteristics. We may well find that there is a relationship reflected there between the prophetic and the sapiential that will confirm Witherington's suggestion. For example, it may be the case that the Wisdom form (*mashal*) is used to convey prophetic themes, or to perform prophetic activities.

In Matthew 21-25 we might include in the category of 'aphoristic *meshalim*'

---

[73] Gerhardsson, 'If We Do Not Cut the Parables Out of their Frames' in *The Shema and the New Testament* (Lund: Novapress, 1996), 225-26.
[74] Gerhardsson, 'Illuminating the kingdom', 268. Garland (236) also classifies the passage as a parable.
[75] A substantial number of contemporary scholars would agree that Matt 25:31-46 is of a different character from the other material Gerhardsson helpfully classifies as narrative meshalim. See the comments of Blomberg, *Matthew*, 375.
[76] Witherington, *Jesus the Sage*, 158.

the riddles concerning John the Baptist's Authority (21:23-27); the issue of taxes for Caesar (22:15-22); and the question put to the Jewish authorities, 'Whose Son is the Christ?' (22:41-45). We might also include aphoristic sayings such as the children shouting (21:14-16); 'have faith' (21:21-22); 'the capstone' (21:42-44); 'God of the living' (22:29-32), (although both of the previous aphorisms have riddle-like qualities also); 'Love God and your neighbour' (22:34-40).

It may be objected that the breadth of the definition of *mashal* adopted in this work leads to almost all of Jesus' teaching being classified as *meshalim*. D. E. Aune, for instance, claims that

> The term 'mashal', however, is such a broad category that it is of little or no practical use in distinguishing between the various oral and literary forms of popular wisdom.[77]

It is true to say that 'The term "mashal" … is … a broad category', but I do not consider this reality to be a weakness of the classification, but rather a strength. In response to Aune's comments, we should say that the intention of this thesis is not to finely distinguish between the various sub-groups within the category of *mashal*. [78] Rather, we seek to demonstrate that Jesus used a variety of different types of saying, most of which were couched in the memorable forms encompassed by the term *mashal*. In fact, Aune's comment concerning the problem of 'such a broad category' adds support to our decision to adopt this broad category. There are several further reasons for maintaining the wide scope of the *meshalim*.

Firstly, this broad definition reflects the statement of Matthew (13:34-5) that '*All these things* Jesus spoke to the crowds in parables, *and he did not speak to them without a parable*. This was to fulfil what was spoken through the prophet: "I will open my mouth in parables; I will utter things hidden since the foundation of the world"' (emphasis mine). Quite clearly, the author of the gospel can make an inclusive statement of this sort and yet record sayings of quite diverse characteristics, far beyond a traditional definition of a 'parable'.

Secondly, although Peisker can begin his article in the *NIDNTT* with the words, 'It has been estimated that roughly one third of the recorded teaching of Jesus consists of parables and parabolic statements,'[79] more recent research leads R. Riesner to write:

> According to my estimate, about 80 per cent of the separate saying units are formulated in some kind of *parallelismus membrorum*. To this one has to add

---

[77] Aune, 'Oral Tradition and the Aphorisms of Jesus' in Wansbrough (ed.), *Jesus and the Oral Gospel Tradition*, 219-20.

[78] Drawing on research by Crenshaw and von Rad, Aune identifies at least nine such literary categories, 'Aphorisms', 220.

[79] *NIDNTT*, 2:743.

other poetical techniques such as alliteration, assonance, rhythm and rhyme. All these artificial forms were functional and not merely 'ornamental', as Rudolf Bultmann thought. The poetical structure of the words of Jesus made them, like the meshalim of the Old Testament prophets, easily memorizable and could preserve them intact.[80]

Thirdly, our emphasis on the *mashal* recognises the continuity between Jesus' teaching ministry and the important Wisdom and prophetic strands of Israel's history and literature, in which the term *mashal* is used frequently and in diverse ways.

Riesner's comments provide a useful starting point for classification of any given saying of Jesus as a '*mashal*'. While it has been suggested that only sayings which have some comparative element qualify for the designation '*mashal*', this would result in several peculiarities. It is more accurate and productive to say that a '*mashal*' should involve some element of literary quality, whether that means the form of parallel couplets, or the use of striking imagery, or the unusual use of language. This approach will distinguish the *meshalim* from teaching such as Matthew 4:17 (which may be a summary of teaching and therefore may not reflect Jesus' own form of speech) or the passion predictions of Matthew 17:22 and 20:18-19 (though even these statements exhibit a literary quality in their poetic progression).

Jesus the Teacher

This evidence suggests that Jesus should be regarded as a skilled Jewish teacher.[81] In fact, we find Jesus directly addressed as διδάσκαλε on three occa-

---

[80] R. Riesner, 'Jesus as Preacher and Teacher' in Wansbrough (ed.), *Jesus and the Oral Gospel Tradition*, 202. Compare Riesner's earlier monograph, *Jesus als Lehrer* (Tübingen: JCB Mohr, 1981), 392-94. Blomberg writes, 'the Gospels depict Jesus as ... a teacher of wisdom and phrase over 90% of his sayings in forms which would have been easy to remember, using figures and styles of speech much like those found in Hebrew poetry.' *The Historical Reliability of the Gospels*, 27, summarising the research of Riesner in *Jesus als Lehrer*.

[81] The noun διδάσκαλος and its cognates are used in the following verses of Matthew (with reference to Jesus, except where otherwise indicated): 4:23; 5:2, 19 (*bis*, used both of those who teach disobedience and those who teach obedience); 7:28, 29; 8:19; 9:11, 35; 10:24, 25; 11:1 (where 'to teach' and 'to preach' are distinguished); 12:38; 13:54; 15:9 (quotation from Isaiah applied to the Pharisees and scribes); 16:12 (a reference to the teaching of the Pharisees and Sadducees); 17:24; 19:16; 21:23; 22:16 (*bis*), 24, 33, 36; 23:8 (where the referent appears to be Jesus); 26:18, 55; 28:15 (used of the instructions given to the Roman guards), 20 (where the task of teaching is delegated to the disciples). In a discussion of the way in which the *narrator* uses these cognate terms, Byrskog (notes that eight out of nine instances are used in summary statements relating to Jesus' ministry with the result that the grammatical features

sions in the section under discussion (22:16, 24, 36), but always by opponents. This particular model for appreciating Jesus' ministry is given interesting support by the so-called *Testimonium Flavianum*, which, though almost certainly corrupted by Christian interpolation, is probably substantially genuine.[82] Josephus describes Jesus as σοφὸς ἀνὴρ παραδόξων ἔργων ποιητής and διδάσκαλος ἀνθρώπων (*Ant.* 18:63). Riesner picks up this reference in his article and points out the theme of Jesus as teacher.[83] He notes that Matthew tends to avoid διδάσκαλε on the lips of believers:

> On theological grounds the first evangelist preferred for Jesus the more distinguished κύριε as the address by followers, but Matthew preserved διδάσκαλε in the mouth of non-followers.[84]

This suggests that, for Matthew, Jesus was indeed a teacher, but also *more* than a teacher.[85] Thus, while Matthew is satisfied to have the appellation applied to Jesus, he points to a greater reality also.

Riesner briefly mentions a passage in John 18:20 in which Jesus appears to suggest that he plays the role of Wisdom (i.e. the Wisdom of God) speaking openly to people (cf. Prov 1:20-21). This is a theme which has been developed further by Witherington, who argues that Jesus was indeed not simply claiming to be a teacher of Wisdom, but to be Wisdom incarnate.[86] Perhaps this is why Jesus says to his disciples, ὑμεῖς δὲ μὴ κληθῆτε, Ῥαββί· εἷς γάρ ἐστιν ὑμῶν ὁ διδάσκαλος, πάντες δὲ ὑμεῖς ἀδελφοί ἐστε (23:8). Witherington writes,

> What this shows is that in the First Evangelist's view it is *inadequate* simply to call Jesus *a* rabbi or teacher. It is not, however, *inaccurate*. Indeed in the crucial passage in 23:8-10 Jesus makes plain that he alone is *the* teacher of the disciples, and that they should not assume the label of 'rabbi' or call any merely earthly teacher father, because they have a heavenly Father.[87]

So, Jesus was indeed a teacher, and the reports found in the other synoptic gospels suggest that he was an effective teacher who taught with authority (cf. Mark 1:22). This issue of authority is, of course, particularly important to Mat-

---

'*carry a foundational connotation as a positive description of extended parts of Jesus' active ministry*' [author's italics].)

[82] So Riesner, 'Jesus as Preacher and Teacher', 185. See Meier, *A Marginal Jew* 1:56-88 for a thorough discussion of Josephus in general and the *Testimonium* in particular. Also see Theissen and Merz, *The Historical Jesus*.

[83] The phrase echoes the title of Riesner's book, *Jesus als Lehrer*.

[84] Riesner, 'Jesus as Preacher and Teacher', 187. So also Witherington, *Jesus the Sage*, 344.

[85] Compare the way in which Matthew retains the description 'prophet' on the lips of the Jews, while not recording it as a typical appellation.

[86] See the discussion below, and further in Witherington, *Jesus the Sage*.

[87] Witherington, *Jesus the Sage*, 344.

thew and plays a key role in our understanding of the present section. Riesner suggests that the issue of authority is directly linked to Jesus' teaching which raised the question of just what kind of person could teach in such a manner. In other words, Yes he is a prophet, but is he more than a prophet? Yes he is a teacher, but is he more than a teacher?

B. Witherington provides a stimulating and insightful answer to this question in his important work, *Jesus the Sage*. Having previously pointed out the distinctive teaching method of Jesus, with its strong affinities with the Wisdom tradition found in the Hebrew Scriptures, he points out how a comparison with Solomon ('David's son') would be natural. Indeed Matthew records just such a comparison in 12:42 where he has Jesus say,

βασίλισσα νότου ἐγερθήσεται ἐν τῇ κρίσει μετὰ τῆς γενεᾶς ταύτης καὶ κατακρινεῖ αὐτήν, ὅτι ἦλθεν ἐκ τῶν περάτων τῆς γῆς ἀκοῦσαι τὴν σοφίαν Σολομῶνος, καὶ ἰδοὺ πλεῖον Σολομῶνος ὧδε.

As the text makes clear, Jesus understands himself to be in continuity with Solomon and yet, quite explicitly, greater than Solomon. Of course Matthew has already introduced the messianic concept of 'son of David' in his account of the triumphal entry into Jerusalem in 21:9. Now in the last verses of chapter 22 he raises that same theme but takes it to a new depth of significance. Witherington, in coming to 22:41-46 comments,

> It is, however, at the close of Matthew 22 that one finally learns that it is not enough to say merely that the messiah is the son of David.[88]

The pericope, of course, is framed in the typically riddle-like form of the Wisdom teacher, thus reinforcing the link with the composer of the book of Proverbs.[89] But the potent message of Jesus' *mashal* is (in verse 45),

εἰ οὖν Δαυὶδ καλεῖ αὐτὸν κύριον, πῶς υἱὸς αὐτοῦ ἐστιν;

Matthew emphasises the impact of this teacher of Wisdom by recounting the stunned silence of those who heard his words, but the inescapable point of Jesus' words is that the one hailed as 'the son of David' on his way into Jerusalem is also to be proclaimed as κύριος. So it is plain that Jesus regarded himself as taking the title of 'son of David' in a unique way. Witherington comments,

---

[88] Witherington, *Jesus the Sage*, 365.

[89] Of course, in drawing on the first verse of Psalm 110, Jesus also demonstrates his reliance on the poetic strand of OT literature.

If Jesus is by implication claiming to be David's Lord then he must be seen in more transcendental categories than either just sage, or teacher, or even Solomonic Son of David.[90]

We can affirm, then, that a significant proportion of Matthew 21-25 is couched in the forms of a teacher in the tradition of the sages of the OT Wisdom literature and its developments. Our next question is whether this teaching indicates that judgement is a dominant theme in the teaching of 'Jesus the Sage.'

Meshalim for the Jewish Authorities (21:23-22:46)

The first block of *meshalim* that we find in chapters 21-25 strictly extends from 21:23 to 22:46,[91] although we will also consider brief comments made by Jesus in the context of his prophetic actions in the temple (21:14-16) and against the fig tree (21:21-22). This block of material includes both narrative and aphoristic *meshalim*. We will examine these passages in the light of the Wisdom tradition and with a view to what they may tell us of Jesus' perspective on judgement as Matthew presents him to us. On certain occasions we will be able to indicate clear verbal connections between a pericope in Matthew and a portion of Jewish Wisdom literature. On other occasions, the connection will be conceptual or even allusive. It is important that we note all connections to gain an appreciation of the pervasive influence of this strand of thought.

Children Shouting in the Temple (21:14-16)

The brief aphoristic *mashal* of verse 16 (Ναί. οὐδέποτε ἀνέγνωτε ὅτι Ἐκ στόματος νηπίων καὶ θηλαζόντων κατηρτίσω αἶνον;) comes in the setting of a conflict story, which itself is situated within a series of three prophetic acts.[92] Though this section might be regarded as an intrusion into the dramatic series of actions, it in fact provides a commentary on the significance of the actions which surround it, thus serving Matthew's narrative purpose.[93] The conflict arises because Jesus heals in the temple, and because the children were crying out 'Hosanna to the Son of David.' This latter phrase is, according to B. Witherington, very significant in understanding Matthew's presentation of Jesus as a Sage,[94] and, in his view, even more than a Sage:

> Jesus is *the* teacher because he offers even greater Wisdom than Solomon, and indeed because he is Wisdom, as Matthew 11 makes clear, doing the deeds of

---

[90] Witherington, *Jesus the Sage*, 365.
[91] So Davies and Allison, *Matthew*, 3:249.
[92] See the discussion of these acts in chapter 5.
[93] The saying thus performs much the same function as the quotation from scripture performs in the account of the entry to Jerusalem.
[94] See Mt. 1:1, 20 (used of Joseph); 9:27; 12:23; 15:22; 20:30, 31.

Wisdom. In both word and even in deed (particularly the healing of the blind) he
is seen to be like but greater than Solomon, and so Solomon's title of being *the*
Son of David devolves upon Jesus.[95]

Thus right at the beginning of our chosen section, Jesus is identified twice as
the Son of David in the first few paragraphs (21:9, 15).[96] The only other reference to the Son of David within these chapters is found in 22:42-45, that is, at
the very end of this section of *meshalim*. This perhaps indicates an inclusion,
identifying the group of Wisdom-like sayings as a unit. While the phrase 'Son
of David' must inevitably have had strong regal and messianic tones,[97] it is at
least conceivable that it would have also resonated with the memory of the wise
king who was credited with the production of the collection of *meshalim*.

Jesus' response to the accusations of the Jewish authorities is to quote Psalm
8:2 (LXX, 8:3).[98] Although it clearly cannot be said that Jesus has created this
saying, he employs it as a *mashal*. That is, he takes a very familiar biblical text
(which itself is couched in poetic language and structure), and makes it provocative and enigmatic by the way in which he relates it to himself. Gundry is
probably correct to understand Jesus' citation of this appropriate verse as a
veiled reference to the whole of Psalm 8, which of course is a song of praise to
Yahweh.[99] This may therefore be a thinly-veiled claim to be more than just a
Jewish teacher and to stand in a unique relationship to Yahweh.

The impact of Jesus' citation of Psalm 8, then, is to bring implicit judgement
on the Jewish authorities for their unwillingness to recognise appropriate praise
directed towards Jesus, as the greater Son of David, the fulfilment of the promise of 2 Samuel 7.

'Have Faith' (21:21-22)

Likewise, this saying is closely related to the event of the withering of the fig
tree, which itself is part of the tightly connected complex of events found in
21:1-22. While it cannot properly be understood without reference to that incident, its startling content suggests that it is more than a matter-of-fact comment
on mountain removal and rather belongs in the category of a provocative
mashal.

---

[95] Witherington points out the way in which the use of this title closes chapter 20, and
opens chapter 21 (which he regards as the beginning of the passion narrative), *Jesus
the Sage*, 354-5. The phrase is used four times in chapters 21 to 25 (21:9, 15; 22:42,
45).
[96] See the discussion of 21:9 in chapter 5.
[97] 2 Sam. 7:11-16.
[98] The MT reads 'strength' instead of 'praise'. That Jesus draws on the commonly known
Greek reading rather than the Hebrew does not suggest inauthentic tradition. See
Keener, *Matthew*, 502-3.
[99] Gundry, *Matthew*, 414-5. So also Blomberg, *Matthew*, 316.

Jesus' use of the demonstrative pronoun ('this mountain'), combined with the close connection between the saying and the prophetic act directed against the temple,[100] has prompted commentators to ask whether Jesus is really giving a broad pronouncement on exercising faith,[101] or whether the statement relates much more closely to the mountain upon which the temple stood.[102] Comparison with the parallel account in Mark 11, where Mark creates an intercalation of the incident in the temple and the withering of the tree, points to the validity of Blomberg's conclusion:

> Given that the Old Testament described judgement on Israel in terms of the land producing no fig trees (e.g., Mic 7:1-6; Jer 8:13), and given that Mark sandwiches this episode around the temple purification (Mark 11:12-25), it is almost certainly correct to see in this passage a foreshadowing of the destruction of the sacrificial system in Israel.[103]

Keener is correct to suggest that the referent of the phrase 'this mountain' would have to be quite obvious for the benefit of readers who do not know the geography of Palestine. Thus, one would expect that the reference is to a mountain which takes some role in Matthew's narrative. Although the temple mount is not mentioned directly, the temple itself is very much in focus in the opening section of chapter 21. The possibility of a reference to Zechariah 4:6-9[104] or to the LXX text (πρὸς θάλασσαν) of Zechariah 14:4[105] would fit the pattern found in Matthew 21-25 of drawing on that particular prophetic work, and this language might well be echoed in Jesus' words even if the referent were not identical. Thus, in the light of these comments, I favour the interpretation of 'this

---

[100] See the discussion of this act in chapter 5.

[101] So Hagner, *Matthew 14-28*, 606.

[102] So Blomberg, *Matthew*, 318.

[103] Blomberg, *Matthew*, 318. Contra Carson, *Matthew*, 444, who sees the Mount of Olives 'as a sample of any mountain.' So also Keener, *Matthew*, 505. Carson's view does not do justice to the parallel account in Mark. Keener, recognises that the Temple Mount 'fits the literary context in Matthew and Mark' but suggests that such a reference would not be so natural, geographically speaking.

[104] 6 He said to me, "This is the word of the LORD to Zerubbabel: Not by might, nor by power, but by my spirit, says the LORD of hosts. 7 What are you, O great mountain? Before Zerubbabel you shall become a plain; and he shall bring out the top stone amid shouts of 'Grace, grace to it!'" 8 Moreover the word of the LORD came to me, saying, 9 "The hands of Zerubbabel have laid the foundation of this house; his hands shall also complete it. Then you will know that the LORD of hosts has sent me to you."

[105] So Davies and Allison, *Matthew*, 153, n. 40, but with the caution (n. 42) that the 'sea' in Zech 14:4 is the Mediterranean sea. The text reads: καὶ στήσονται οἱ πόδες αὐτοῦ ἐν τῇ ἡμέρᾳ ἐκείνῃ ἐπὶ τὸ ὄρος τῶν ἐλαιῶν τὸ κατέναντι Ιερουσαλημ ἐξ ἀνατολῶν καὶ σχισθήσεται τὸ ὄρος τῶν ἐλαιῶν τὸ ἥμισυ αὐτοῦ πρὸς ἀνατολὰς καὶ τὸ ἥμισυ αὐτοῦ πρὸς θάλασσαν χάος μέγα σφόδρα καὶ κλινεῖ τὸ ἥμισυ τοῦ ὄρους πρὸς βορρᾶν καὶ τὸ ἥμισυ αὐτοῦ πρὸς νότον.

mountain' as a reference to the temple mount,[106] though it is probably wise not to be dogmatic.

John the Baptist's Authority (21:23-27)

Matthew now continues his narrative with a new scene in the temple.[107] The temple is clearly the prime object of attention in this opening section of Matthew 21. There has already been a taste of confrontation between Jesus and the Jewish authorities in the temple in 21:15, but 21:23 marks the beginning of a carefully structured section, which presents sustained conflict between Jesus and the Jewish leaders, and which extends to the prophecy of the destruction of the temple in 24:2.[108]

Although this account might be classified as a 'confrontation story' or 'conflict narrative',[109] the narrative incorporates an 'aphoristic *mashal*' which demands attention at this point.[110] Although there is no comparative element to Jesus' words, they may be classed as a *mashal*, provided that their 'teasing' or 'riddle-like' nature is recognised. This saying is not included in Borg's analysis, but it may be considered a judgement saying in the sense that Jesus demonstrates his authority over the Jews and his ability to confound them. The story perfectly illustrates the conflict between Jesus and the Jewish authorities (οἱ ἀρχιερεῖς καὶ οἱ πρεσβύτεροι τοῦ λαοῦ)[111] which lies at the heart of Borg's presentation of Jesus' ministry.[112]

The opening words of the pericope (Καὶ ἐλθόντος αὐτοῦ εἰς τὸ ἱερόν) recall

---

[106] So, Telford, *The Barren Temple*, 110.

[107] Herzog, *Jesus, Justice and the Reign of God*, 233-38.

[108] So Sim, *Apocalyptic Eschatology*, 158. Though Sim clearly appreciates Matthew's careful work, I am cautious of his language of a 'carefully manufactured' episode. Garland (*Reading Matthew*, 215) regards the section as extending from 21:23 to 22:46 in two major parts. While this is a perfectly adequate approach to these verses in and of themselves, it does not give recognition to the continuity between these verses and chapter 23. Luz (*Matthäus 18-25*, 208) notes that 21:23 portrays Jesus entering the temple for the second time in Matthew's narrative and writes, 'Dort, im Zentrum Israels, wird er bis 24:1 bleiben und das Volk und seine Führer lehren, er, der messianische Lehrer Israels, der bisher immer wieder in den Synagogen das Volk gelehrt hat (vgl. 4:23; 9:35; 13:54).' See Keener's excursus on 'Conflict Narratives' in his *Matthew*, 351-53.

[109] Luz (*Matthäus 18-25*, 205) speaks of 'Das Streitgespräch über die Vollmacht Jesu'.

[110] Similarly, 22:15-22; 22:23-33; 22:34-40 and 22:41-46.

[111] This combination of Jewish figures appears again in 26:3, 47; 27:1, 3, 12, 20, where the chief priests and the elders play a significant part in the events of the passion narrative. However, this combination of leaders does not appear anywhere else in chapters 21-25. The expanded phrase οἱ πρεσβύτεροι τοῦ λαοῦ is Matthean. See Jeremias, *Jerusalem in the Time of Jesus* (London: SCM Press, 1969), 160-81 (chief priests) and 222-32 (elders).

[112] See Davies and Allison, *Matthew*, 3:156-57.

the words of 21:12, thus drawing the reader's attention back to the preceding narrative. Thus Davies and Allison are correct to regard ταῦτα in verse 23 ('Εν ποίᾳ ἐξουσίᾳ ταῦτα ποιεῖς;) as a reference to the whole complex of events from the beginning of chapter 21, and not simply any one aspect of Jesus' actions or teaching.[113] It is important for us to notice at this point the theme of the authority of Jesus, because it is part of the argument of this thesis that the question posed by the religious leaders in Matthew 21:23 is not impertinent, but is highly appropriate.[114] In the context of Matthew's narrative, it is only if Jesus can give a satisfactory answer to this question (though not necessarily to those particular leaders) that his actions in the temple can be justified. Matthew, therefore, in his development of chapters 21 to 25, provides us with a significant part of that necessary answer. Thus, while it may be correct to say that the Jewish leaders 'were crafty individuals,'[115] that is not to say that their two-part question ('Εν ποίᾳ ἐξουσίᾳ ταῦτα ποιεῖς; καὶ τίς σοι ἔδωκεν τὴν ἐξουσίαν ταύτην;) was an irrelevance. In fact, as custodians of the Jewish heritage, they would have been remiss if they had not been concerned for the question of authority when someone began to challenge that heritage. The problem with their question lay in the fact that the evidence had been laid before them already and they had not recognised, or more precisely had chosen to reject, the authority

---

[113] *Matthew*, 3:159. In a footnote (*Matthew*, 3:159, n. 9) they suggest that the withering of the fig tree is not to be included since this was probably only seen by the disciples. This is probably accurate at the level of historical circumstance. From the perspective of Matthew's readers, however, all the elements of Jesus' entry combine to demonstrate who Jesus is, and so Matthew's literary skill serves to make the answer to the leaders' question even more convincing than it could have been for most onlookers at the time. So Keener, *Matthew*, 506: 'The reader who has witnessed miracles such as the cursing of the fig tree understands that Jesus' authority is from God (21:21-22) ... The political leaders are not, however, privy to the information Matthew's audience shares.' Though Garland appears to omit reference to the fig tree in his list of convincing factors, he nonetheless shares the view that there is a cumulative impact on the reader of Matthew's literary work (*Reading Matthew*, 216) so that as Jesus asks his question, 'For the reader, the narrative has already furnished the answer.'

[114] This is not to say that commentators are in error when they attribute dubious motives to the chief priests and elders of the people. That is almost certainly the case in Matthew's presentation. However, that fact does not invalidate the legitimate question of whether someone *must possess authority* in order to legitimately do the things that Jesus has just done. See D. Bock, 'The Trial and Death of Jesus' in Newman ed.) *Jesus and the Restoration of Israel*, 113: 'it comes as no surprise that the first question Jesus is asked after the cleansing is where he gets the authority to do what he is doing...It is clear by his actions that he has intentionally bypassed the leadership's sanction.' So also Hengel, 'Jesus the Messiah of Israel' in *Studies in Early Christology*, 56, 'It is no wonder that the leaders – obligatorily – question him concerning his authority.'

[115] Davies and Allison, *Matthew*, 3:159.

possessed by Jesus.[116] It seems likely that the motive behind the question was to test Jesus, rather than to elicit information.[117]

The term ἐξουσία is particularly important in Matthew's gospel. It is found in the following verses which indicate important moments in the account of Jesus ministry: 7:29; 8:9; 9:6, 8; 10:1; 21:23, 24, 27, 28:18.[118] The significance of 28:18 for the gospel as a whole has been highlighted by O. Michel in an important essay, 'The Conclusion of Matthew's Gospel'.[119] That Michel draws particular attention to the similarities between the LXX version of Daniel 7:13-14 and Matthew 28:18-20 is suggestive for the relationship between the question of the Jews relating to authority and the 'coming Son of Man' sayings which are common in Matthew. Matthew's conclusion indicates that Jesus, the same Jesus whose ministry he records in his gospel, has all authority (ἐξουσία) from the Father to be the judge. It is particularly this fact of the authority of Jesus to judge, both in his earthly ministry and in his heavenly reign, that Matthew is determined to convey in chapters 21-25 of his gospel. We will explore this issue further in a later section.

Matthew has already placed his readers in a privileged position over the Jews, as Garland explains:

> For the reader the narrative has already furnished the answer. The Father has given all things to Jesus (11:27); and Jesus' presence is something greater than the temple (12:6).[120]

Jesus' response to the Jewish authorities' question is typically enigmatic, and takes the shape of a counter-question relating to the ministry of John (τὸ βάπτισμα τὸ Ἰωάννου πόθεν ἦν; ἐξ οὐρανοῦ ἢ ἐξ ἀνθρώπων;). Thus Jesus adopts the methods of the skilled teacher, effectively exercising the authority which is being questioned and placing those who claim authority for themselves in the position of the student. While his question appears to evade the Jewish leaders' question, in fact it addresses it in a pointed manner, since it highlights the intimate connection between the ministry of John and that of Jesus.[121] Matthew has already recounted Jesus' testimony about John (11:7-15), in the course of which he cites Mal 3:1 (verse 10) to indicate the preparatory role of John. Thus, the answer to Jesus' question has, once again, already been

---

[116] See Hagner, *Matthew 14-28*, 608.

[117] So Carson, *Matthew*, 447; Hagner, *Matthew 14-28*, 609: 'The questions are hardly asked for the sake of information. They represent an attempt to gain more ammunition against Jesus when the time was right.'

[118] *NIDNTT*, 2:606-11. See Byrskog, *Jesus the Only Teacher*, 279-84.

[119] Found in G. N. Stanton (ed.), *The Interpretation of Matthew* (Edinburgh: T&T Clark, 2nd edn 1995) 39-51.

[120] Garland, *Reading Matthew*, 216. On these texts see respectively Witherington, *The Christology of Jesus*, 221-28 and Witherington, *Jesus the Sage*, 361.

[121] Carson, *Matthew*, 447.

disclosed to Matthew's readers.

Matthew lets his readers listen in to the nervous considerations of the Jewish authorities, which are clearly presented as an exercise in calculated damage limitation (οἱ δὲ διελογίζοντο ἐν ἑαυτοῖς λέγοντες, Ἐὰν εἴπωμεν, Ἐξ οὐρα-νοῦ, ἐρεῖ ἡμῖν, Διὰ τί οὖν οὐκ ἐπιστεύσατε αὐτῷ; 26 ἐὰν δὲ εἴπωμεν, Ἐξ ἀνθρώπων, φοβούμεθα τὸν ὄχλον, πάντες γὰρ ὡς προφήτην ἔχουσιν τὸν Ἰωάννην), and show up the final answer (Οὐκ οἴδαμεν) to be not only cowardly but false. It is an attempt to maintain a vestige of their position of authority in spite of the fact that Jesus' question has penetrated through their sham.[122] It is clear to Matthew's readers, now, that the judgement which has come and is to come upon the Jewish leaders is entirely justified.[123] These religious leaders saw all too clearly the conclusion that they were obliged to reach, and simply refused to accept it. In the face of such clear face-saving, Jesus' refusal to sup-ply an answer to their original question serves to highlight the culpability of the Jewish leaders,[124] but it also leaves the true answer to their question quite obvi-ous. John's ministry was indeed from heaven, and was provided as the intro-duction to the ministry of Jesus which was also, and all the more so, from heaven.[125]

This pericope may be regarded as developing the theme of judgement in this section of Matthew in two ways. Firstly, it demonstrates Jesus' ability to con-found the Jewish authorities.[126] Matthew makes it clear that though Jesus is not one of the teachers of the temple establishment, yet he has more skill than they possess. Moreover, despite their own arrogation of authority to themselves, the Jewish authorities, in fact, have no power over him, and indeed, to the contrary, he has authority over them. Secondly, the Jewish authorities demonstrate them-selves to be corrupt and thus worthy of the condemnation which they implicity receive at Jesus' words and will receive, both in the destruction of Jerusalem and before the great judge at the eschatological judgement.

The Two Sons (21:28-32)

Verse 28 marks the beginning of a broadly recognised and acknowledged sec-

---

[122] See the comments to this effect in Herzog, *Jesus, Justice and the Reign of God*, 237.

[123] In particular, the apparently harsh designation of 'hypocrite' in 22:18 and 23:13, 15, 23, 25, 27, 29 is demonstrated to be literally true. 24:51 indicates the awesome end of such characters.

[124] Bock, 'The Trial and Death of Jesus', 115, highlights the implicit declaration of judgement in Jesus' words: 'Jesus' oblique reply by appealing to John is a reply that not only answers the question but reverses the implication of the alternatives the question was meant to raise. If Jesus is sanctioned from above, then the leadership is...!'

[125] See Herzog, *Jesus, Justice and the Reign of God*, 238.

[126] Luz (*Matthäus*, 209) comments, 'Die Frage Jesu stürzt die Hohenpriester und Ältesten in Verlegenheit.'

tion of 'parables' (better, *meshalim*) in Matthew.[127] The *mashal* in verses 29-32
is peculiar to Matthew.[128] Since it may be classed as a 'Matthean parable', Borg
regards it as evidence to reinforce his argument that Jesus was challenging the
"Politics of Holiness".[129] It is important to go beyond Borg, however, and to
regard this pericope as an intergral part of the narrative which Matthew shaped
into a literary whole with a coherent message. It is the first of three parables
which form a literary unit, and which thematically are united in their judgement
of the Jewish leaders.[130]

> 28 "What do you think? A man had two sons; he went to the first and said, 'Son,
> go and work in the vineyard today.' 29 He answered, 'I will not'; but later he
> changed his mind and went. 30 The father went to the second and said the same;
> and he answered, 'I go, sir'; but he did not go. 31 Which of the two did the will of
> his father?" They said, "The first." Jesus said to them, "Truly I tell you, the tax
> collectors and the prostitutes are going into the kingdom of God ahead of you. 32
> For John came to you in the way of righteousness and you did not believe him,
> but the tax collectors and the prostitutes believed him; and even after you saw it,
> you did not change your minds and believe him."

Borg rejects interpretations of this *mashal* which emphasise the contrast between what is said and what is done. Instead, he argues, Jesus should be understood as challenging the behaviour of the Pharisees because it was not what
God required. He writes,

> It seems best to discard the interpretations which depend upon a contrast between
> word and deed. When this is done, the nature of their [the Pharisees] "Yes"
> becomes clear; their "Yes" included both allegiance to *and* fulfillment of their
> understanding of the will of God; so the audience would have understood it, even
> if they might not have agreed that it constituted nonperformance of God's will.
> The parable claims that their "Yes" in both word and deed really amounted to
> nonperformance of the will of God – not because they failed to perform that to

---

[127] A. W. Martens, ' "Produce Fruit Worthy of Repentance": Parables of Judgment
against the Jewish Religious Leaders and the Nation (Mt. 21:28-22:14, par.; Lk. 13:6-
9)' in Longenecker (ed.), *The Challenge of Jesus' Parables*, 151-76.

[128] *NIDNTT*, 2:751.

[129] Borg, *Conflict*, 123-25, 220, 274.

[130] Keener, *Matthew*, 507. See W. Carter, *Matthew: Storyteller, Interpreter, Evangelist*,
(Peabody: Hendrickson, 1996), 169, 183. Martens, 'Parables of Judgment', 152-53,
identifies the careful literary structure of Matthew's account from the beginning of
chapter 21, linking three acts of judgement, followed by three parables of judgement,
followed by three 'controversy dialogues'. Whether we follow his analysis of how
'Matthew used Mark' or not, it is clear that Martens has correctly highlighted
considerable literary craftsmanship together with significant thematic continuity.

which they had committed themselves, but because that to which they had committed themselves was not the will of God.[131]

While Borg's comments point us in the right direction, they confuse the issue because they seek to emphasise the faithfulness of the Jewish leaders to the *Torah*, while the point of Jesus' *mashal* is that regardless of how faithful and obedient they *think* they are, they are in fact being *unfaithful* and *disobedient*.[132]

The reference to the ministry of John the Baptist in verse 32 performs two functions. Firstly, it relates this pericope to the preceding account of Jesus and the Jewish leaders and their discussion of John's ministry, thereby maintaining the flow of Matthew's narrative.[133] Thus it reinforces the significance of John as a witness-bearer. Secondly, it reinforces the condemnation of these religious leaders for not listening to John. It is, in effect, a second declaration of judgement on the Jewish leaders for the attitudes which Matthew has exposed for all to see in 21:25-26. In fact, Jesus so frames the question that the chief priests and elders pronounce their own condemnation in their answer in verse 31,[134] which is then confirmed by Jesus' words.

There is no clear parallel to the situation Jesus portrays here in any Jewish Wisdom literature, yet there is a clear reliance on the Wisdom genre in terms of formal characteristics. For example, Davies and Allison draw attention to the very striking parallelism in the structure of the saying.[135] Luke 15:11-32 records a *mashal* with a virtually identical opening sentence, yet with a different intention. There is, however, a parallel to the *message* of the *mashal* found in Sirach 3:3-11:

3 Those who honor their father atone for sins, 4 and those who respect their mother are like those who lay up treasure. 5 Those who honor their father will have joy in their own children, and when they pray they will be heard. 6 Those who respect their father will have long life, and those who honor their mother obey the Lord; 7 they will serve their parents as their masters. 8 *Honor your father by word and deed*, that his blessing may come upon you. 9 For a father's blessing strengthens the houses of the children, but a mother's curse uproots their foundations. 10 Do not glorify yourself by dishonoring your father, for your father's dishonor is no glory to you. 11 The glory of one's father is one's own glory, and it is a disgrace for children not to respect their mother (emphasis mine).

The most significant point for our purposes is that judgement is being pro-

[131] Borg, *Conflict*, 125.

[132] Hagner, *Matthew 14-28*, 613-14.

[133] Luz, *Matthäus*, 212: 'Nun gibt er die Antwort auf seine eigene Frage nach Johannes dem Täufer...'

[134] Davies and Allison, *Matthew*, 3:168.

[135] Davies and Allison, *Matthew*, 3:164. So also Hagner, *Matthew 14-28*, 612-13, and Keener, *Matthew*, 507, who draws attention to Rabbinic parallels such as Sifre Deut. 349.1.1.

nounced on the Jewish leaders by means of a Wisdom saying. It is true that the reference to judgement is rather indirect, yet there can be little doubt that Jesus' words, 'Truly I tell you, the tax collectors and the prostitutes are going into the kingdom of God ahead of you,' should be understood to mean that those people are going into the kingdom of God[136] *instead of* the religious authorities.[137] Jesus identifies two groups of people who were marginalised according to the 'Politics of Holiness', but who are drawn into the new experience of God's reign through the proclamation of Jesus.[138] While some scholars understand this statement to relate to the present situation in Jesus' day,[139] Jeremias argues that the underlying Aramaic verb is timeless and that, on the basis of Jesus' typical sayings on entering the kingdom of God, it should be translated as a future verb relating to the last judgement.[140] Davies and Allison regard the issue as impossible to decide conclusively,[141] but in either case the exclusivity implies an act of judgement on the Jewish leaders.

Borg identifies the warrant for the threat as 'You have not worked in the vineyard,'[142] but since Jesus is presented as giving an explicit warrant, it would seem better to take his words as the primary warrant.[143] The 'warrant' for the threat in verse 32 is in two parts of increasing seriousness and both are described in terms of 'belief'. In the first place, there is the stark and simple statement, 'you did not believe him' which stands as a condemnation that echoes the 'anticipated rebuke' of verse 25. This is followed by the even more tell-

---

[136] Matthew uses this phrase only occasionally, preferring 'kingdom of heaven'

[137] See Jeremias, *Parables*, 125. See also, Beasley-Murray, *Jesus and the Kingdom of God*, 179; Davies and Allison, *Matthew*, 3:169-70. See BDF § 245.a.3 on the use of comparison to indicate exclusion. Blomberg suggests that a certain ambiguity may remain to leave open the invitation to repent (*Matthew*, 322), but the context of other parables of judgement (such as the Wicked Tenants in 21:33-46) suggests a more decisive judgement.

[138] See K. E. Corley, *DJG, s.v.* 'Prostitute' for a discussion of the possible significance of this term.

[139] See e.g., Gundry, *Matthew*, 422: 'The present tense of the verb probably implies entrance into the current form of the kingdom (Cf. Luke 16:16).'

[140] Jeremias, *Parables*, 125 n. 46.

[141] Davies and Allison, *Matthew*, 3:169 n. 36.

[142] Borg, *Conflict*, 274.

[143] Borg (*Conflict*, 123) argues that this is a 'floating saying' that is not inherently part of the pericope, but which 'Matthew or a predecessor has attached to the parable.' However, Matthew's use of ἦλθεν γὰρ Ἰωάννης indicates that he regarded Jesus' statement in verse 32 as being the foundation for what came immediately before. Hagner (*Matthew 14-28*, 612) comments that 'The closest synoptic parallel, pertinent only to the application of the parable in vv 31-32, is found in Luke 7:29-30, which is not at all close to the actual wording of the Matthean pericope.'

ing offence that even in the face of the belief of others ('sinners' even!)[144], the Jewish leaders betrayed their hard hearts and would not change their minds 'and believe him'. Thus judgement comes upon them because of their refusal to accept the proclamation of the kingdom of God.

The Tenants (21:33-41)

This narrative *mashal*, found in the triple tradition,[145] follows a familiar pattern where an authority figure makes gracious provision[146] for others (tenants/ servants/ guests) who are then responsible for making appropriate use of that provision, and providing suitable returns to the benefactor.[147] Those who have been provided for fail to act appropriately, and treat their benefactor with both contempt and violence.[148] The inclusion of the son in the scenario (37) introduces an element of personal involvement that has been absent up to that point. The poignant words of the landowner ('They will respect my son.') provide a sense of tension in the narrative (surely every hearer anticipates that the hope of the landowner will be dashed) which reaches its climax at the point of the deliberate and premeditated murder of the son (38-39). Jesus' rhetorical question draws from his audience the inescapable verdict (41):

> He will put those wretches to a miserable death, and lease the vineyard to other tenants who will give him the produce at the harvest time.

Hagner draws attention to this verse as containing particularly distinctive themes: 'the motif of judgment against Israel and the concept of "transference" of the kingdom to a different people.'[149] Although vineyards are mentioned on a number of occasions in the Wisdom literature, there are no direct parallels to

---

[144] See Wright, *Jesus and the Victory of God*, 264-8, for a useful discussion of the category of 'sinner', in which he points out that 'sinner' would probably have been a sub-group of the 'people of the land'.

[145] Compare Mk. 12:1-12; Lk. 20:9-19. For a recent survey of research on this parable, see K. R. Snodgrass, 'Recent Research on the Parable of the Wicked Tenants: An Assessment' *BBR* 8 (1998), 187-216.

[146] The details of the fence, wine-press and watchtower, aside from adding colour to the image, serve no function other than to reinforce the provision of the landowner.

[147] Compare Matt 22:1-14 and 25:14-30. Matt 20:1-16 exhibits a similar form, although the point of that parable is the abundant generosity of the landowner, apart from any merit on the part of the workers.

[148] Though the evil character of the tenants combined with the consistently trusting attitude of the owner have led to questions over the authenticity of this *mashal*, on the grounds that the situation is ludicrous. C. A. Evans clearly demonstrates the use of such characterisation in Rabbinic parables and indicates the literary and pedagogical value of such features. See 'Parables in Early Judaism', 51-75 (here, 69-70).

[149] Hagner, *Matthew 14-28*, 617.

this account in that corpus. However, there is a close parallel to be found in the 'Song of the Vineyard' in Isaiah 5.[150] Thus, there may be a clear dependence on material from the prophetic tradition. On the other hand, this *mashal* is explicitly identified by the words Ἄλλην παραβολὴν ἀκούσατε.[151] Thus, Matthew (drawing on Jesus tradition?) classifies the portion of teaching as reflecting the type of literature that stands in the Wisdom tradition, though the distinction between these two strands of teaching should not be pressed too far, as the prophets were clearly capable of employing *meshalim*. We can clearly see an element of overlap between the function of prophetic proclamation and the form of Wisdom sayings which reinforces the importance of recognising the significance of both of these traditions in Jesus' ministry. It is not, however, unduly important for our purposes to be able to trace the words or broad content to other portions of Jewish Wisdom literature. We have already noted that *meshalim* are by their very nature diverse in form while yet displaying several important common features, such as story-telling, imagery, metaphor, riddle etc. In fact, the use of the vineyard as the setting for this parable establishes a clear narrative connection for Matthew,[152] with the result that the reader is drawn from one parable to the next and interprets the second parable in the light of the one before.

The purpose of the *mashal* is clearly to proclaim judgement, but not merely negatively.[153] While the kingdom is taken from the Jewish leaders, it will be given to those who have not previously enjoyed its benefits. The question which concludes Jesus' story leads to the impact of verse 41 in which the Jewish authorities, under the direction of Jesus' skilful story-telling, pronounce judgement on themselves (cf. 2 Samuel 12:5-6 where David pronounces judgement on the man of Nathan's story).

The Capstone (21:42-44)

Jesus follows up his powerful *mashal* of the tenant farmers with an elusive saying based on the text of Psalm 118:22. The rhetorical question with which the citation is introduced echoes the similar form of words in 21:16, and reinforces the portrait of Jesus as one who probes and challenges his hearers with perplexing words.

---

[150] So Charette, *Recompense*, 136, who notes the previous work of both Beare (*Matthew*, 426) with respect to the linguistic parallels between the LXX version of Isa 5:2 and Matt 21:33, and Jeremias (*Parables*, 74) with respect to the connection between Matt 21:40 and Isa 5:5 [LXX].

[151] A phrase Matthew commonly includes in his account. For the same or similar words, see 13:18, 24, 31, 33.

[152] So Charette, *Recompense*, 136 n. 1.

[153] Charette, *Recompense*, 135, writes: 'it is primarily in Matthew that it becomes a parable about judgement due to the absence of fruit.'

42 Jesus said to them, "Have you never read in the scriptures: 'The stone that the builders rejected has become the cornerstone; this was the Lord's doing, and it is amazing in our eyes'? 43 Therefore I tell you, the kingdom of God will be taken away from you and given to a people that produces the fruits of the kingdom. 44 The one who falls on this stone will be broken to pieces; and it will crush anyone on whom it falls."

In many ways this brief saying is highly significant. G. Stanton regards this section, and particularly verse 43, as being decisive in appreciating the status of the Christians to whom Matthew is writing. For Matthew, it is they who are the rejected stone.[154] While it is certain that the readers of Matthew's work would indeed have recognised themselves as the beneficiaries of the reversal of which Jesus speaks, Stanton's approach is once more too much governed by the circumstances of Matthew's audience.

Jesus draws his vocabulary from Psalm 118:22 (Psalm 117:22 in the LXX). The Psalms, of course, exhibit many similarities to the Wisdom tradition in the way language is used. In this particular case, the building image which is employed by the Psalmist is taken even further by Jesus. The significance of these words is that vindication awaits God's chosen one,[155] though the allusive nature of the saying veils its true reference to Jesus. This interpretation opens the reader up to the expectation of declarations of vindication in later parts of this section.

The words of verse 44 are the most explicit in terms of judgement, and yet at the same time they are couched in the riddle-like language so favoured by Jesus.[156] Luz notes that the image is not realistic ('Auf den obersten Eckstein eines Baus kann man ja nicht »fallen«') but evocative of a biblical theme.[157] For similar language in the Wisdom tradition, one might compare (with my emphasis in both cases) Proverbs 26:27:

> Whoever digs a pit will fall into it, and a *stone* will come back on the one who starts it rolling.

and later in Sirach 27:25:

> Whoever throws a *stone* straight up throws it on his own head, and a treacherous blow opens up many wounds.

The implication of this image is clear: disaster is coming.[158]

---

[154] Stanton, *Gospel for a New People*, 151-2.
[155] Hagner, *Matthew 14-28*, 622.
[156] Hagner, *Matthew 14-28*, 623: 'this obscure proverb-like logion'.
[157] Luz, *Matthäus 18-25*, 227.
[158] Luz, *Matthäus 18-25*, 227: 'Der Vers deutet also an, daß die jüdischen Führer (und indirekt auch das mit ihnen verstrickte Volk) ein schreckliches Geschick erleiden

The Wedding Banquet (22:1-14)

In formal terms, this parable bears strong resemblance to the parable of the wicked tenants, found in 21:33-44.[159] Charette identifies the important shared features as follows:

> The device of a father and son, the sending of servant envoys, the mistreatment and killing of these servants, the punishment of the murderers, and the transfer of privilege from an unworthy group to a new group.[160]

There can be little doubt that Jesus uses the 'rejected son' motif to point to the end of his own ministry at the hands of the Jewish authorities. This passage is similar to the parable in Luke 14:16-24, and so is assumed by many commentators to be Q material.[161] Jeremias, for instance, believes that Matthew has transformed an original story about a private individual into one about a king.[162] In fact, there are very few substantive parallels between the two accounts and so Reiser is correct to say that 'Whether it was found in Q is ... uncertain and rather improbable.'[163] Indeed, Blomberg highlights the fact that 'the structure of the alleged parallel is markedly different,' and contends that the Matthean and Lukan parables should be regarded as being independent stories used on different occasions, but utilising a similar theme.[164]

The theme of the wedding banquet is favoured by Matthew, appearing also in 25:10. On this occasion, however, the character of the one who makes the invitation (the king) raises the significance of this meal to a unique level. Thus the rejection of the invitation to the banquet on the part of those first invited is a much more serious act[165] than in the Lukan parable. Since those who have been given privilege have disregarded the honour (verses 5-6), their invitation is withdrawn (verse 8) and instead is extended to 'all', 'both bad and good' with the result that the king's intention to celebrate his son's wedding is fulfilled. The conclusion of the *mashal* echoes the conclusion of the story of the two sons in 21:31, thus reinforcing the theme of transfer.[166]

There is a strong similarity in the general outline of the story to Proverbs 9:1:

---

werden: Der Stein, Christus selbst, wird sie – nicht die Weltreiche – zerquetschen und zermalmen.' See also Hagner, *Matthew 14-28*, 623.

[159] So Charette, *The Theme of Recompense*, 148

[160] Charette, *Recompense*, 148.

[161] A. M. Hunter, *Interpreting the Parables*, (London: SCM Press, 1960), 55-56.

[162] Jeremias, *Parables*, 65.

[163] Reiser, *Jesus and Judgment*, 241.

[164] Blomberg, *Interpreting the Parables*, 237.

[165] Blomberg, *Interpreting the Parables*, 238, speaks of 'high treason'.

[166] The emphasis appears to be on the inclusion of the marginalised among the Jewish people (as in 21:31) rather than inclusion of the gentiles, although the latter interpretation is not inconsistent with the former.

Wisdom has built her house, she has hewn her seven pillars. 2 She has slaughtered her animals, she has mixed her wine, she has also set her table. 3 She has sent out her servant-girls, she calls from the highest places in the town, 4 "You that are simple, turn in here!" To those without sense she says, 5 "Come, eat of my bread and drink of the wine I have mixed. 6 Lay aside immaturity, and live, and walk in the way of insight."

However the tone of warm welcome is interrupted by verses 11-14 which appear to introduce a note of eschatological judgement.[167] In fact, this conclusion to the story bears comparison with 25:31-46 which is widely recognised to be about the final judgement.

Davies and Allison provide a valuable analysis of the vocabulary shared by the three (according to their division; note the somewhat different division above) *meshalim* of 21:28-32, 33-46 and 22:1-14. They comment,

These parallels do more than forge an artistic unity: they also create a thematic coherence by encouraging readers to expect similar meaning, which expectation is fully met.[168]

Reiser recognises that behind this *mashal* stands 'God's wrath' acting 'to intervene and bring punishment'.[169]

Taxes for Caesar (22:15-22)

Matthew follows Mark 12:13-17 closely.[170] Verse 15 introduces the theme of conflict, which continues from previous encounters between Jesus and the Jewish religious leaders, and which sets the tone of the passage.[171] The Pharisees' intention is to trap Jesus.

Is this pericope relevant to our understanding of Jesus as judge?[172] Marguerat[173] recognises the significance of the whole section 22:15-46, indicating that it forms 'une série de controverses (22,15-46), où le Christ Mt est confronté à l'animosité des divers groupes représentatifs de l'élite religieuse et politique d'Israël.' This sets the scene for 'la phase ultime de cet antagonisme: le réquisitoire du chapitre 23 contre les scribes et les pharisiens.' Thus, these confrontation pericopae serve to reinforce the theme of judgement in these

---

[167] So Davies and Allison, *Matthew*, 3:203-7. Garland, *Reading Matthew*, 220, draws attention to the blatant lack of realism as an indicator that the primary referent is always the eschatological judgement.

[168] Davies and Allison, *Matthew*, 3:189.

[169] Reiser, *Jesus and Judgment*, 245.

[170] See Davies and Allison, *Matthew*, 3:211 for details of minor differences.

[171] Hagner, *Matthew 14-28*, 634, suggests that it might be classed as a 'controversy' or more particularly a 'testing' pericope.

[172] It is not discussed by Borg or Reiser.

[173] *Le Jugement*, 346.

chapters, highlighting the deliberate antagonism to the ministry of Jesus found among the Jewish leaders, and throwing the woes of chapter 23 into sharper relief.[174]

In particular, the words of Jesus' opponents in 22:16 are quite clearly false flattery and demonstrate the hypocrisy of the religious authorities which will be condemned explicitly in chapter 23. However Matthew explains that Jesus knows 'their evil' (verse 18, thus demonstrating the insight into the hearts of human beings which qualifies him to be the righteous judge), and confounds the Pharisees and Herodians with a skillful question regarding the denarius which is handed to him. The aphorism which brings the encounter to its climax is deliberately opaque, thus demanding reflection on the part of the hearers. That Matthew still has the theme of judgement in view may be indicated by the fact that the verb used in 22:21 is the same as that used in 21:41.

λέγουσιν αὐτῷ, Κακοὺς κακῶς ἀπολέσει αὐτοὺς καὶ τὸν ἀμπελῶνα ἐκδώσεται ἄλλοις γεωργοῖς, οἵτινες ἀποδώσουσιν αὐτῷ τοὺς καρποὺς ἐν τοῖς καιροῖς αὐτῶν.

The judgement of the Jewish religious leaders on the wicked tenants in Jesus' story was that they should be destroyed on the grounds that they had not given to the landowner his due. Likewise, in 22:21 Jesus echoes that judgement as he implicitly condemns these leaders for not giving God his due. Finally, verse 22 is Matthew's declaration of Jesus' supremacy in the encounter. Jesus' opponents can say nothing in reply. It may be significant in Matthew's narrative that those who intended to trap Jesus 'went away' (ἀπῆλθαν) from Jesus. The same verb is used in Matthew 25:46 to refer to the separation of judgement, though on other occasions it has a more mundane significance.[175]

It is important to consider how this pericope promotes the intention of Matthew as he constructs his narrative rather than simply regarding this account as an isolated discussion of an abstract subject. It seems probable that Matthew emphasises Jesus' skill and authority as he condemns the failure of the Pharisees and their co-conspirators to give God his due.

'God of the Living' (22:23-33)

This pericope has, perhaps, less significance for the thesis than most in this section.[176] We will not, therefore, study this passage in depth. Yet it remains an integral part of Matthew's narrative and may be understood to continue the

---

[174] See also Luz, *Matthäus 18-25*, 251-52.

[175] The idea of separation (expressed in a variety of linguistic formulations) is certainly significant in Matthew in connection with the theme of judgement. See, for example, 21:17 (possibly); 22:13; 24:1 (probably); 24:40-41, 51; 25:10-12, 30, 41.

[176] It does not appear in Marguerat's scripture index.

theme of judgement to a limited extent and to reflect elements of the Wisdom tradition. We are once more confronted with teaching that certainly could not be described as 'prosaic', in two respects. Firstly, in verse 30 Jesus uses balanced phrases describing everyday life, which will be recalled in 24:38. Secondly, he takes a familiar, and apparently inconsequential, text of scripture (Exodus 3:6) and applies it in a provocative manner (verse 32). These words come at the conclusion of a contorted problem directed at Jesus by the Sadducees with the clear intention to trap Jesus. However, Jesus' words of judgement - 'you are wrong, because you know neither the scriptures nor the power of God' (verse 29) and 'have you not read what was said to you by God?' (verse 31) - clearly declare the Sadducees to be culpable. Gundry points out that Matthew heightens this note of accountability by means of the summary statement of verse 33,[177] which also serves to demonstrate Jesus' authority in the confrontation.[178]

'Love God and Your Neighbour' (22:34-40)

This brief pericope (cf. Mark 12:28-34 and Luke 10:25-28) is again without clear reference to judgement in word or action. Yet it is once more clear that the purpose of the question brought by the Pharisee is to 'test' Jesus (verse 35), and therefore we have another example of a 'test' narrative.[179] Yet Jesus' answer may be regarded as an implicit judgement in that Matthew presents the Pharisees as those who do not love their neighbours as themselves, perhaps with particular significance in the light of the *meshalim* which speak of those who have been marginalised by the interpretation of 'the Law and the Prophets' on the part of the Pharisees. Jesus thus demonstrates himself to be a true 'sage', that is, one who correctly interprets the *Torah*, but does so in a way that invalidates the interpretation of those who claim to be the interpreters of the Law.

'Whose Son is the Christ?' (22:41-46)

The confrontations of chapter 22 reach their climax[180] in this reversed confrontation, in which Jesus takes the initiative by presenting the Pharisees with a

---

[177] Gundry, *Matthew*, 447. Compare also 22:22 and 46. Gundry regards these statements as expressions of the authority of Jesus.

[178] Luz, *Matthäus 18-25*, 267: 'Für Matthäus heißt das: Die Lehre Jesu ist etwas ganz Besonderes, etwas ganz anderes als die der Schriftgelehrten.'

[179] In comparing the Markan and Matthean versions, Gerhardsson comments, 'the Markan narrative of a respectful and fruitful dialogue between a scribe and Jesus has become a fierce confrontation between the Pharisees and Jesus in Matthew, a confrontation that has the form of a thrust and counter-thrust – and then nothing more' ('The Hermeneutic Program in Matthew 22:37-40' in *The Shema*, 202-23.

[180] Hagner, *Matthew 14-28*, 649.

theological riddle.[181] Once again the reader is presented with a portrait of Jesus in the mould of a Wisdom teacher, as he gently invites them into familiar territory by means of a simple question (whose son is the Christ?) and then, using Psalm 110:1, lays a provocative question before them.[182] Then, typically, Jesus leaves the question unanswered when no answer is forthcoming (*cf.* 21:27). The numerous theological and exegetical issues relating to this text need not detain us at this point. What is significant for our purposes is the method by which Jesus confounds the Pharisees and highlights their hardness to Jesus who comes to them as the representative of Yahweh. However, it is also important to consider briefly the content of Jesus' question in so far as it is clearly intended to relate to his own ministry. In citing Psalm 110, Jesus brings before the Pharisees the prospect of his vindication by God ('sit at my right hand') in a way that will demonstrate the authority that has consistently been questioned in the confrontations recorded by Matthew up to this point. Highlighting the enthronement scene of Psalm 110, Wright comments,

> One of the most obvious points of such a scene is that the one thus enthroned is the judge who will pronounce the doom of YHWH's enemies; Jesus is again explaining the source of his authority, the reason for his sovereign prophetic act of judgment.[183]

With this confrontation, implicit claim to authority and demonstration of Jesus' superior skills as a teacher of wisdom (22:46), Matthew brings this substantial section of *meshalim* to a close.[184]

Meshalim for the Pharisees (23:34-39)

In the midst of the prophetic denunciations of chapter 23 there is a distinctive section in the language and form of a Wisdom saying. It reads,

> 34 Therefore I send you prophets, sages, and scribes, some of whom you will kill and crucify, and some you will flog in your synagogues and pursue from town to town, 35 so that upon you may come all the righteous blood shed on earth, from the blood of righteous Abel to the blood of Zechariah son of Barachiah, whom you murdered between the sanctuary and the altar. 36 Truly I tell you, all this will come upon this generation. 37 "Jerusalem, Jerusalem, the city that kills the proph-

---

[181] A full discussion can be found in Davies and Allison, *Matthew*, 3:249-57, who point out that 21:28-32 demonstrates a similar formal pattern. See also Wright, *Jesus and the Victory of God*, 507-09.

[182] See particularly, D. M. Hay, *Glory at the Right Hand: Psalm 110 in Early Christianity* (SBLMS 18; Nashville: Abingdon, 1973). M. Hengel, ' "Sit At My Right Hand!" The Enthronement of Christ at the Right Hand of God and Psalm 110:1' in *Studies in Early Christology*, 119-225.

[183] Wright, *Jesus and the Victory of God*, 509.

[184] Davies and Allison, *Matthew*, 249.

ets and stones those who are sent to it! How often have I desired to gather your children together as a hen gathers her brood under her wings, and you were not willing! 38 See, your house is left to you, desolate. 39 For I tell you, you will not see me again until you say, 'Blessed is the one who comes in the name of the Lord.'"

This latter part of this passage (verses 37-39) has a close parallel in Luke 13:34-35. Suggs writes that it 'is correctly identified as a Wisdom logion.'[185] He goes on to say that it 'follows right upon the heels of Wisdom's oracle of doom over those who persecute and kill the "prophets, wise men and scribes."'[186] There are thus two Wisdom sayings in this short section which we will look at in sequence.

'Oracle of Doom' (23:34-36)

Suggs provides a full source-critical discussion of verses 34-36 in which he justifies regarding them as an 'oracle of doom' on the basis of the setting.[187] He indicates that Isaiah 5:18-24 provides a model for comparison:

18 Woe, you who drag iniquity along with cords of falsehood, who drag sin along as with cart ropes, 19 who say, "Let him make haste, let him speed his work that we may see it; let the plan of the Holy One of Israel hasten to fulfillment, that we may know it!"

20 Woe, you who call evil good and good evil, who put darkness for light and light for darkness, who put bitter for sweet and sweet for bitter!

21 Woe, you who are wise in your own eyes, and shrewd in your own sight!

22 Woe, you who are heroes in drinking wine and valiant at mixing drink, 23 who acquit the guilty for a bribe, and deprive the innocent of their rights!

24 Therefore, as the tongue of fire devours the stubble, and as dry grass sinks down in the flame, so their root will become rotten, and their blossom go up like dust; for they have rejected the instruction of the LORD of hosts, and have despised the word of the Holy One of Israel.

---

[185] Suggs, *Wisdom, Christology and Law in Matthew's Gospel*, 63.
[186] Suggs, *Wisdom, Christology and Law in Matthew's Gospel*, 64.
[187] Suggs draws from the work of A. Bentzen, *Introduction to the Old Testament* (Copenhagen: G. E. C. Gads, 1948), 1:199.

Verse 24 comes at the conclusion of the repeated 'woes' with a 'therefore' indicating that it is the 'oracle of doom' declaring the outcome of judgement which the behaviour described in the woes is due.[188]

A Hen and her Chicks (23:37-39)

In this poignant passage, Jesus laments Jerusalem's rejection of himself as the last in a line of prophets who have been sent to,[189] and killed by, those who live in the city where God had chosen to dwell.[190] The reference to the prophets picks up the reference in 23:34, suggesting that the two sections (34-36 and 37-39) are closely related. The image Jesus uses here is found most strikingly, not in the Wisdom literature but in 5 Ezra (2 Esdras) 1:30:

> I gathered you as a hen gathers her chicks under her wings. But now, what shall I do to you? I will cast you out from my presence.

This parallel is so striking in part because of the difference in tone from the text in Matthew. Yet the lament in Matthew turns into a declaration, which is itself an act of judgement, and which closely parallels the final outcome as expressed in 5 Ezra 1:

> 31 When you offer oblations to me, I will turn my face from you; for I have rejected your festal days, and new moons, and circumcisions of the flesh. 32 I sent you my servants the prophets, but you have taken and killed them and torn their bodies in pieces; I will require their blood of you, says the Lord. 33 "Thus says the Lord Almighty: Your house is desolate; I will drive you out as the wind drives straw; 34 and your sons will have no children, because with you they have neglected my commandment and have done what is evil in my sight. 35 I will give your houses to a people that will come, who without having heard me will believe. Those to whom I have shown no signs will do what I have commanded. 36 They have seen no prophets, yet will recall their former state. 37 I call to witness the gratitude of the people that is to come, whose children rejoice with gladness; though they do not see me with bodily eyes, yet with the spirit they will believe the things I have said. 38 "And now, father, look with pride and see the people coming from the east; 39 to them I will give as leaders Abraham, Isaac, and Jacob, and Hosea and Amos and Micah and Joel and Obadiah and Jonah 40 and Nahum and Habakkuk, Zephaniah, Haggai, Zechariah and Malachi, who is also called the messenger of the Lord.

---

[188] See the fuller discussion in chapter 5.

[189] The passive participle may suggest that the sender is other than Jesus (so Davies and Allison, *Matthew*, 3:320), but this reference must be compared with 23:34 where the speaker uses the first person.

[190] The fate of those who have been sent to Jerusalem closely reflects the fate of those sent to the wicked tenants in 21:35. These texts clearly interpret each other in Matthew's narrative.

This passage displays several strong verbal similarities to Matthew 23, but since it is widely recognised that 5 Ezra is a second-century Christian addition to the original Jewish work 4 Ezra (3-14), it is likely that these reflect the influence of the canonical synoptic tradition.[191]

In Sirach 51:12 there is a less specific parallel:

> Give thanks to him who gathers the dispersed of Israel, for his mercy endures forever;

There are also numerous OT passages, particularly in the Psalms, which pick up this theme.[192]

Here Jesus speaks a lament over the city that has rejected him.[193] Yet he does not simply express sadness, but proclaims judgement.[194] Jesus declares that Jerusalem's 'house' is left 'desolate'. The language of 'house' immediately suggests an echo of the OT references to the temple. Particularly familiar is the play on 'house' in 2 Sam 7, though numerous other references could be cited.[195] The term for desolation is found frequently in the LXX. One striking example is found in Haggai 1:9, which speaks of the desolation of the temple.

> ἐπεβλέψατε εἰς πολλά καὶ ἐγένετο ὀλίγα καὶ εἰσηνέχθη εἰς τὸν οἶκον καὶ ἐξεφύσησα αὐτά διὰ τοῦτο τάδε λέγει κύριος παντοκράτωρ ἀνθ᾽ ὧν ὁ οἶκός μού ἐστιν ἔρημος ὑμεῖς δὲ διώκετε ἕκαστος εἰς τὸν οἶκον αὐτοῦ

A passage which takes up a similar theme, though using different vocabulary is Zechariah 7:8-14:

> The word of the LORD came to Zechariah, saying: 9 Thus says the LORD of hosts: Render true judgments, show kindness and mercy to one another; 10 do not oppress the widow, the orphan, the alien, or the poor; and do not devise evil in your hearts against one another. 11 But they refused to listen, and turned a stubborn shoulder, and stopped their ears in order not to hear. 12 They made their hearts adamant in order not to hear the law and the words that the LORD of hosts had sent by his spirit through the former prophets. Therefore great wrath came from the LORD of hosts. 13 Just as, when I called, they would not hear, so, when they called, I would not hear, says the LORD of hosts, 14 and I scattered them with a whirlwind among all the nations that they had not known. Thus the land they left was desolate, so that no one went to and fro, and a pleasant land was made desolate.

---

[191] See Evans, *NWNTI*, 10-11. See G. N. Stanton, '5 Ezra and Matthean Christianity in the Second Century' in *Gospel for a New People*, 256-77.

[192] See Davies and Allison, *Matthew*, 3:320. Among the passages they cite, see for example, Deut. 32:11, Ps. 17:8.

[193] Note the strong similarities in genre and content to Lamentations.

[194] Witherington, *Jesus the Sage*, 366.

[195] See, for example, the distinctive use of this language in Ezekiel.

This statement of Jesus, which confirms the significance of the prophetic acts of chapter 21 (compare Jesus' reference to the temple as 'my [God's] house' in 21:13), is most likely fulfilled in Matthew's narrative in two ways. Firstly, Jesus leaves the temple (24:1) and secondly, Jesus presents an account of the future devastation of the temple (24:4-35).

Meshalim for the Disciples (24:36-25:30)

Matthew portrays Jesus as a teacher of Wisdom clearly in the final section of the so-called 'eschatological discourse'. This is not to say that his ability as a teacher is not seen in the other portions of Matthew 21-25 (it certainly is, and we have already discussed some important texts earlier in this chapter), but it is particularly in 24:36-25:30 that we find once more the recourse to *meshalim* and vivid descriptive language. Davies and Allison accurately describe the structure of this section in terms of three 'sayings and similes' followed by three 'long parables'.[196] However, before we examine these *meshalim*, we must consider the way in which Matthew introduces this new section of his narrative.

Transitional Statement (24:36)

Blomberg describes verse 36 as 'a thesis statement for this entire section.'[197] The use of the disjunctive phrase περὶ δέ,[198] along with the technical term τῆς ἡμέρας ἐκείνης καὶ ὥρας signals the beginning of a new subject.[199] This is the first significant occurrence of the singular phrase with the demonstrative pronoun 'that day and hour'[200] (the plural αἱ ἡμέραι occurred in 24:19 and 24:22)[201] and so it is clear that reference is being made to 'the Day of the

---

[196] Davies and Allison, *Matthew*, 3:374.

[197] Blomberg, *Matthew*, 364, referring to the section extending to 25:46. See also Davies and Allison, *Matthew*, 3:374, who speak of verse 36 as 'the introduction.'

[198] Cf 22:31. With the genitive case, the phrase bears the sense of 'now concerning...'. Most occurrences of the phrase in Matthew are followed by the accusative case and have a temporal sense such as 'now around...' See Wallace, *Greek Grammar Beyond the Basics*, 379. For other NT occurrences of the phrase used as an introduction to a new subject matter, see particularly 1 Corinthians 7:1, 25; 8:1; 12:1; 16:1, 12; 1 Thessalonians 4:9; 5:1.

[199] See Garland *Matthew*, 235, who understands this as the beginning of Jesus' answer to the *second* half of the disciples' question in 24:3. So also France, *Matthew*, 347. We shall see, however, that Wright, *Jesus and the Victory of God*, does not see this as indicating a change of referent.

[200] The use of the singular ἡμέρα plus the demonstrative pronoun in 22:23 and 22:46 are so clearly references to the time of Jesus' ministry from the perspective of the narrator that they need not be included in this analysis.

[201] Cf 7:22: πολλοὶ ἐροῦσίν μοι ἐν ἐκείνῃ τῇ ἡμέρᾳ, Κύριε κύριε, οὐ τῷ σῷ ὀνόματι ἐπροφητεύσαμεν, καὶ τῷ σῷ ὀνόματι δαιμόνια ἐξεβάλομεν, καὶ τῷ σῷ ὀνόματι δυνάμεις πολλὰς ἐποιήσαμεν; In the light of usage in the OT (cf. Amos 8:9; 9:11; Is.

Lord'.[202] The singular form is consistently used in this second section of Jesus' answer (24:36, 42, 50; 25:13)[203]. It must be beyond the bounds of credibility to suggest that Jesus intends to indicate that while the generation in which the *Parousia* will occur is known ('this generation'), the precise time of arrival in hours and minutes cannot be given.[204] The whole thrust of verse 36 is that the timing of 'that day' is shrouded in complete mystery to all apart from the Father, even to 'the Son'.[205] Davies and Allison are correct in commenting that

> Its declaration of eschatological ignorance grounds the entire section: one must be prepared for what may come at any time.[206]

The staggering nature of this saying is seen in the fact that 'no-one' (οὐδείς) is reinforced with 'only' (μόνος). Also the force of the following comments on the OT is that the day is completely unpredictable. It surely places unbearable strain on Matthew's credibility as a redactor and/or on Jesus' credibility as a teacher to claim that Jesus is referring to the same event in vv. 33-4 and in v. 36.

The significance of this verse for appreciating Jesus' expectation with respect to future judgement can not be overestimated. Although B. Witherington

---

2:20; 10:20; Hos. 1:5; Zeph. 1:10, 14; Zech. 12:3-11; 13:1-4; 14:4, 6, 8, 9, 13, 20; Mal. 3:17-18) and other Jewish writings (cf. *1 Enoch* 45:3), there can be little doubt that this is a reference to the eschatological Day of Judgement (so Carson, *Matthew*, 193; Hagner, *Matthew 14-28*, 187; Davies and Allison, *Matthew*, less precisely, 1:714), though Davies and Allison point out the Rabbinic use of the phrase to refer to the messianic period (*Matthew*, 1:714, citing Str-B 1:468). Davies and Allison do not distinguish between the plural and the singular occurrences of the term, but this seems to me to be a distinction of some importance in the eschatological discourse.

[202] See Beasley-Murray, *Jesus and the Kingdom of God*, 11-16, 346-47.

[203] The final occurrence forms an inclusion with 24:36 which delimits the section.

[204] Caird justly criticises Beasley-Murray for this sort of view, *New Testament Theology* 255. Hatina, 'Focus' 51, n. 39, follows precisely the same path: 'it is quite probable that while Jesus, playing the role of prophetic critic, foreknew that a series of disastrous events would happen in a generation, he did not know the exact day or hour.' He continues, 'Ambiguity regarding precise timing is in continuity with prophetic figures in Jewish tradition.' Although he does not provide evidence to corroborate this latter statement, it is the violence done to the stark contrast between solemn certainty (v 34) and emphatic ignorance (v 36) that makes this interpretation unacceptable. McKnight, *A New Vision for Israel*, 132, follows the same pattern.

[205] It is Jesus' self-reference to 'the Son' which, of course, has led to significant doubt being cast upon the authenticity of this statement (despite the weight of the criterion of embarrassment). Though it is true that this language is not typical of Jesus in the Synoptic witnesses, it is not improbable that he said this or something very similar. For a helpful discussion, see Davies and Allison, *Matthew*, 3:378-9. See Carson, *Matthew*, 508, on the textual uncertainty surrounding the words 'nor the Son'.

[206] Davies and Allison, *Matthew*, 3:374.

is correct to say that 'Few scholars today are willing to dismiss the whole saying as inauthentic,'[207] yet the authenticity of the saying has been challenged in a variety of ways.[208] For the purposes of our argument, it is important simply to notice that Matthew places this saying at a crucial point in his narrative concerning Jesus' teaching about future events, and that he allows it to mark a notable difference in Jesus' knowledge regarding two types of future events – the devastation of Jerusalem and Jesus' own personal return in glory and judgement.

Five Meshalim *concerning the* Parousia

The five *meshalim* that follow reinforce this basic point: there will be no warning of the *Parousia* and so the only way to be ready for the event is to be *always* ready. Garland identifies 'several interlocking themes':[209]

> (a) The sudden arrival of something or someone that creates a crisis appears in all five parables (24:37, 39, 43, 44, 46; 25:6, 19). (b) A key figure is delayed in three of the parables (24:48; 25:5, 19). (c) The exhortation to watch (24:42, 43; 25:13) and be ready (24:44; 25:10) for the unknown time of arrival (24:37, 42-44, 50; 25:10) sets the tone for the first four parables. (d) The division of the characters into two separate categories (the wise, faithful and good versus the wicked, foolish and hesitant, 24:45, 48; 25:2, 21, 23, 26) appears in the last four parables. (e) The last three parables also contain a judgment scene in which the faithful and ready receive a joyous reward (24:46; 25:10-11, 21, 23), and the unfaithful and unready are banished and/or ruthlessly punished (24:39, 51; 25:10, 30).[210]

It would seem to be the case, therefore, that Matthew has recorded a group of *meshalim* which reinforce one another, whether this is because they were originally taught as a coherent unit or because Matthew has brought them together.

THE GENERATION OF NOAH (24:37-41)

The introductory words of the first *mashal* include the first reference to ἡ παρουσία since its first occurrence in 24:3 and its parenthetical use in 24:27:

ὥσπερ γὰρ αἱ ἡμέραι τοῦ Νῶε, οὕτως ἔσται ἡ παρουσία τοῦ υἱοῦ τοῦ ἀνθρώπου.

The term *mashal* is broad enough to cover all kinds of illustrative material, and it is clear that the narrative from Genesis (which Matthew presumably re-

---

[207] Witherington, *Christology of Jesus*, 229.
[208] See Witherington's helpful discussion of the matter in *Christology of Jesus*, 228-33.
[209] Garland, *Reading Matthew*, 239
[210] Garland, *Reading Matthew*, 239.

garded as historical) is used in an illustrative manner in this pericope. That the material is illustrative is clearly seen in the ὥσπερ...οὕτως construction.[211] This comparative structure is paralleled in verses 38-39 also, thus emphasising the carefully crafted character of the saying. The question then relates to the matter of comparison.

The reference to αἱ ἡμέραι echoes the reference to 'that day and hour' (τῆς ἡμέρας ἐκείνης καὶ ὥρας) in verse 36, though the referents are quite clearly different. This connection is then followed up by two references in verse 38. First there is a plural form referring to the 'days before the flood'. The second reference to the 'day' relates to the day when Noah entered the ark. Although this is not the moment of judgement in the Genesis narrative, yet it serves the purpose of Matthew to draw attention to momentous 'days'.

The true climax of the story comes in verse 39 with the description of the ignorance of the people of what was about to come upon them. The statement καὶ οὐκ ἔγνωσαν highlights the comparison with Jesus' words in verse 36, whereas the following words (ἕως ἦλθεν ὁ κατακλυσμὸς καὶ ἦρεν ἅπαντας) point to the devastating consequences of being unprepared.

The emphasis in this saying lies on the suddenness of the παρουσία, and so clearly there is a resumption of the theme of verse 27 where the term παρουσία was also employed. It should be noted that there is no mention of any of the attendant circumstances related to the 'coming Son of Man' found in Dan. 7 and in other texts in Matthew (clouds, glory, etc). This fact, coupled with the way in which Matthew once again compares the παρουσία to an historical event, indicates that this is not intended to be read as figurative language for Jesus' return in judgement on Jerusalem (as in 24:30) but is a more prosaic reference to the future and final glorious return of Jesus as the king and judge. It is vital to a consistent interpretation of Matthew's narrative that we bear in mind that future expectations may relate to one or other of these two events, and it is our contention that it is possible to distinguish between them without doing violence to Matthew's use of language.

If we then ask what the common theme is in this comparison then the answer is undoubtedly that judgement (πρὸ τοῦ κατακλυσμοῦ) is about to befall a people who continue to live according to the priorities of everyday life. More specifically we can say that the judgement will be entirely unexpected. The only way to come through this event safely (as did Noah in his day) is to be prepared for it whenever it happens.[212] Thus, there is an association of the *Parousia* and judgement.

The main theme of verses 40 and 41 is separation. There will be a division between one person and another person. We must surely follow Wright in dismissing any idea of a 'rapture' here, and can broadly concur with his statement,

---

[211] See Wallace, *Greek Grammar Beyond the Basics*, 675.
[212] France, *Matthew*, 348.

It should be noted that being 'taken' in this context means being taken in *judgment*. There is no hint, here, of a 'rapture', a sudden 'supernatural' event which would remove individuals from *terra firma*. Such an idea would look as odd, in these synoptic passages, as a Cadillac in a camel-train.[213]

Certainly the reference to the events in which Noah was involved indicates that the theme of judgement is pressing on Matthew's mind,[214] though it is not so clear that 'taken' bears connotations of judgement.[215] Whether we can accept the remainder of his paragraph, however, is up for discussion. Wright appears to understand these verses as a continuation of the theme of national catastrophe as he continues,

> It is a matter, rather, of secret police coming in the night, or of enemies sweeping through a village or city and seizing all they can. If the disciples were to escape, if they were to be 'left', it would be by the skin of their teeth.[216]

While Wright uses rhetorical language in this quotation, his words do indicate that he probably has events of the first century in mind. This view moves beyond those of others who would stand with Wright on the interpretation of 24:1-35 as an account of the fall of Jerusalem.[217] Wright's interpretation certainly has the benefit of continuity with the previous section, but in the light of Garland's analysis of the five *meshalim*,[218] I think that the distinct '*Parousia*' interpretation of the passage has the advantage for the following reasons.

Firstly, Garland noted that there was a recurrent theme of reward in several of the parables. This does not sit easily with Wright's interpretation for it is not clear who would provide the reward. Secondly, there is the fact that the 'parable' of the sheep and the goats is very likely to have a future referent, and there is no more obvious point in the passage than 24:36 for the transition from contemporary events to future events to take place.[219] Thirdly, there is the question of the interpretation of 'taken'. Wright interprets it in a sinister way, as the result of the 'secret police', but that is not the only possibility. France argues for a positive sense, as in 'take someone to be with you'.[220] Fourthly, there is

---

[213] Wright, *Jesus and the Victory of God*, 366.
[214] France, *Matthew*, 348.
[215] France, *Matthew*, 348, indicates that 'separation' is the dominant image in this text.
[216] Wright, *Jesus and the Victory of God*, 366.
[217] We might note D. E. Garland and R. T. France as prominent examples.
[218] See above.
[219] Wright gives no sustained attention to Matthew 25:31-46 so it is difficult to ascertain his views regarding its interpretation. However the brief references to this passage in *Jesus and the Victory of God* (533, 645) suggest that he would interpret this passage also as a reference to first-century events.
[220] France, *Matthew*, 348. The Louw-Nida lexicon offers the following possible meanings of παραλαμβάνω (s.v.):
(a) bring along with 15.168

the contrast between Jesus' exhortation to read the signs (24:32), and the clear thrust of the *meshalim* that of the events under discussion in these verses there will be *no sign*.[221] It is particularly important to recognise the force of this major change of theme between the two sections of chapter 24. Finally, there is the presence of the distinctive Greek term ἡ παρουσία which Matthew has clearly chosen to use in both the disciples' question (24:3) and in the section from verse 36 and following, even if it cannot be traced back to Jesus directly.[222]

Blomberg draws attention to the fact that verse 42 acts as a parenetic conclusion to the account of the days of Noah.[223]

γρηγορεῖτε οὖν, ὅτι οὐκ οἴδατε ποίᾳ ἡμέρᾳ ὁ κύριος ὑμῶν ἔρχεται.

Hagner correctly brings out the implication of the imperative γρηγορεῖτε, *i.e.* the necessity of being ready for the event watched for.[224] This readiness takes the form of the kind of ethical behaviour which will come into focus in the final pericope of chapter 25, and so Matthew links the whole section from 24:36 to 25:46 together. Blomberg suggests that Matthew draws a connection between 24:42 and 24:36 by the use of the word ὥρα. This is a noted variant reading,[225] but the reading ἡμέρᾳ should be accepted on the grounds that the use of ὥρα

(b) lead aside 15.180
(c) learn from someone 27.13
(d) welcome 34.53
(e) receive appointment 37.99
(f) be taught by 33.238
The verb is used 12 times in Matthew, and, although it certainly can bear the more forceful meaning Wright proposes (e.g., 27:27), the majority of instances of its use are in the much more positive sense which France suggests.

[221] Garland, *Reading Matthew*, 240: 'The first two parables address the second half of the disciples' question, "What is the sign of your coming and the end of the age?" (24:3). The answer is that there will be no sign.'

[222] See the comments of France, *Matthew*, 347, to the effect that ἡ παρουσία has been conspicuously absent from vv. 4-35 (except to state in v. 27 that the parousia is to be distinguished from the period then under discussion).

[223] Blomberg, *Matthew*, 366. This verse alone finds a parallel in Mark (13:35).

[224] Hagner, *Matthew 14-28*, 720. Cf. Louw-Nida, *s.v.* γρηγορέω which proposes the following three translations:
(a) stay awake 23.72
(b) be alert 27.56
(c) be alive 23.97
The entry for the second option reads as follows: 27.56 γρηγορέω: (a figurative extension of meaning of γρηγορέω 'to stay awake,' 23.72) to be in continuous readiness and alertness to learn - 'to be alert, to be watchful, to be vigilant'. γρηγορεῖτέ στήκετε ἐν τῇ πίστει 'be alert, stand fast in the faith' 1 Cor 16.13.

[225] In NA26, but not in UBS3. It is attested by K, L, G, 28, 565, 700, 1010, 1241, and the Majority Text.

appears to be an attempted harmonisation with verse 44.[226] Nevertheless, Blomberg's fundamental point may still stand as the use of ποίᾳ ἡμέρᾳ recalls the phrase τῆς ἡμέρας ἐκείνης in verse 36. We will notice in the following discussion that Matthew's use of ὥρα in other verses does indeed recall verse 36.

To sum up, this *mashal* is intended to impress on the reader three key points:

(a) Despite the continuance of day-to-day life, the climactic Day of the Lord is a reality which will come, and the reader should be assured of that fact. It is significant that Matthew uses the phrase ὁ κύριος ὑμῶν which hints at Christological significance left undeveloped by Borg.

(b) The timing of that event, in stark contrast to the timing of the devastation of Jerusalem, is a completely unknown factor.

(c) The time which the reader is afforded between the present moment and that unknown day is to be used profitably for living in a way that reflects Jesus' concern for compassion and *true* holiness.

THE HOUSEHOLDER AND THE THIEF (24:42-44)

Once more the most obvious point of this *mashal* is the unknown time of the entry of the thief.[227] We are not intended to draw theological conclusions from the ethical character of the thief, nor from the activity he intends to pursue when he arrives.[228] However, in the light of Matthew's emphasis on judgement, it is possible that the image of a thief was chosen as one of whom there should be a certain measure of apprehension. The point is made that *if* the householder had known that a thief was coming *then* he would have kept watch. Presumably the idea that a thief would advertise his arrival beforehand was as absurd in first century Palestine as it is in modern society, and so the exhortation is *not*, 'Find out when the event will take place', but, 'Ensure that you are ready at whatever point it might take place'.

Verse 44 performs the same function in relation to verse 43 as verse 42 does in relation to verses 37-41, *viz* to bring a telling and unambiguous exhortation to vigilance and right living, on the foundation of what has just been said (διὰ τοῦτο). The term for 'ready' (ἕτοιμοι - used again in 25:10) implies not simply awareness but preparedness in terms of action taken in the present. And what is the event that is to be awaited? The 'coming of the Son of Man' (ὁ υἱὸς τοῦ ἀνθρώπου ἔρχεται). Although in this thesis this phrase has been interpreted consistently in the light of the background of Daniel 7 in terms of the vindica-

---

[226] So Hagner, *Matthew 14-28*, 718.

[227] It is important to recognise that the image does *not* indicate imminence of arrival. If the householder knew that the thief was to arrive imminently, he could easily make and sustain arrangements for protection. The danger arises when no time of arrival is indicated, and watchfulness gives way to complacency.

[228] Davies and Allison, *Matthew*, 3:384, note that 'the likening of the eschatological end to an unexpected thief is unattested in ancient Jewish sources'.

tion of Jesus, yet here it appears to be a clear continuation of the theme of the return of Jesus to demonstrate his authority to judge not only Israel but the nations. While the term παρουσία is replaced here by the use of the verb ἔρχομαι, there is, once again, no reference to the attendant circumstances of the apocalyptic vision in Daniel 7. What is more, the use of the word ὥρα suggests a link with the phrase in verse 36, περὶ δὲ τῆς ἡμέρας ἐκείνης καὶ ὥρας. We hold the view, therefore, that this verse should be understood as a reference to the final and unmistakable (cf. 24:27) return of Jesus as the glorious judge rather than being interpreted figuratively as a reference to the vindication of Jesus through events other than the final judgement. This interpretation is entirely in keeping with the figurative use of the phrase, but simply takes the immediate context into account when determining the specific referent of 'Son of Man' terminology.

THE FAITHFUL AND UNFAITHFUL SERVANTS (24:45-51)

The next *mashal* continues the theme of delay and unexpected return (46, 48, 50). Sim argues that the reference to significant delay in return (Χρονίζει μου ὁ κύριος) in verse 48 cannot be understood to mean that Matthew did not expect the *Parousia* to appear imminently at the time he was writing.[229] However, this argument only has force if we assume that Matthew has included the aspect of delay in his narrative without any foundation in the teaching of Jesus. If Matthew believes Jesus to have predicted an imminent *Parousia*, and he has only inserted redactional material into his account to appease the members of his community who are concerned at the delay in the Lord's arrival, then it is certainly true that Matthew would have no reason to alter his expectation of an imminent end. If, however, the words of verse 48 reflect traditional material originating in the teaching of Jesus himself (and they certainly are consistent with 24:36, which would appear to be authentic material) then Matthew would be expected to incorporate the element of the unknown timing of the *Parousia* into his account with the express purpose of discouraging imminent expectation.

France helpfully points out the significance of the options open to the servant:

> He can exercise his stewardship well (vv. 45-47) or badly (vv. 48-51). The way in which these options are described helps to give more concrete meaning to 'being ready'; it is not to sit quietly waiting, but to provide for the *household* (vv. 45-46) - *i.e.* it is in service to others that we prepare for the parousia. In contrast, unpreparedness consists in selfish exploitation of others (v. 49).[230]

This latter point indicates Matthew's continuing emphasis on Jesus as the judge

---

[229] Sim, *Apocalyptic Eschatology*, 151.
[230] France, *Matthew*, 349

of the 'Politics of Holiness'. It is clear that Jesus' *mashal* is an assault on the Jewish leaders who have been entrusted with the riches of God's kingdom but have not acted responsibly. The fact that the servant is condemned, not only for his attitude to his master, but also for his unfair and hurtful treatment of his fellow servants (ἄρξηται τύπτειν τοὺς συνδούλους αὐτοῦ), reminds us that judgement, for Jesus and for Matthew, was not unrelated to human relationships.[231] However, what is particularly despicable about the wicked servant's actions is that he has been called to act as his master's representative.

The final part of the pericope introduces the most graphic description of judgement yet found in chapters 21-25.[232] Although the language of judgement is clearly related to the personal fate of the servant, that does not preclude the application of this language to the Jewish authorities. In other words, the Jewish leaders are condemned by the words of the *mashal* and are told that, while they will indeed experience the judgement prophesied on their city, after some delay they will also know the judgement of the returning king.

One of the purposes of the *mashal* is clearly to assure the readers that a delay before Jesus' return does not indicate that his return will not happen. The language describing the unexpected arrival of the returning master (ἥξει ὁ κύριος τοῦ δούλου ἐκείνου ἐν ἡμέρᾳ ᾗ οὐ προσδοκᾷ καὶ ἐν ὥρᾳ ᾗ οὐ γινώσκει) echoes the language of 24:36 and reaffirms that this event is in a completely different category to the events which will befall Jerusalem in the course of a delineated period. Yet the very fact that the master does return is equally significant for the assurance that this is not a vain hope. The combination of unknown timing but certain arrival is intended to have a positive ethical impact on Matthew's readers.

THE TEN BRIDESMAIDS (25:1-13)

This narrative *mashal* is closely linked to the previous one (Τότε),[233] and continues its theme of concrete action required for readiness for the Son of Man's return. The distinctive point it makes is that vague interest in the kingdom of heaven is not sufficient, and preparation (left undefined in this *mashal*) is the only way to be ready. The group of ten girls follows a numerical pattern familiar in Jewish literature,[234] and found in the Wisdom literature of the OT. Job 19:3 cites Job as complaining 'These ten times you have cast reproach upon me; are you not ashamed to wrong me?' while Ecclesiastes 7:19 indicates that 'Wisdom gives strength to the wise more than ten rulers that are in a city.' The

---

[231] Cf. Matthew 25:31-46.

[232] See O. Betz, 'The Dichotomised Servant and the End of Judas Iscariot' *RevQ* (1964), 43-58.

[233] Keener, *Matthew*, 595: 'This parable most naturally focuses on the same time of judgment as the preceding one'.

[234] See the numerous references in Davies and Allison, *Matthew*, 3:394.

connection with the Jewish Wisdom tradition is strengthened by the description of these girls as 'wise' and 'foolish' (πέντε δὲ ἐξ αὐτῶν ἦσαν μωραὶ καὶ πέντε φρόνιμοι). Davies and Allison correctly observe that parallels can be found in Proverbs 10:14; 14:33; 29:9, 11; Ben Sirach 20:7, 13, to name but a few examples.[235] An interesting example that picks up the same kind of imagery as is found here in Matthew is Ecclesiastes 2:14: 'the wise have eyes in their head, but fools walk in darkness.'[236]

It is interesting to note that both groups fell asleep (v. 5), due to the delay in the bridegroom's arrival. While this might be thought to be a fault on the part of all the girls, none are faulted for natural tiredness in the face of a long delay.[237] The fault lay in the lack of preparation while there was still time. While the delay relates primarily to the narrative framework of the *mashal*, it must raise the suggestion that Jesus was indicating the possibility of some kind of delay in his return. Sim takes his approach to the text from the perspective of Matthew writing late in the first century, and claims (of 24:48 and 25:5),

> While these texts certainly testify to Matthew's conviction that the parousia had been delayed, they tell us nothing about his future expectations.[238]

Sim is happy to affirm that Matthew presents Jesus telling a story which indicates a delay in the arrival of the key figure, yet he does not believe that this indicates anything about the expectations of Matthew as he writes late in the first century. Sim's comments only serve to highlight the assumptions about Matthew's historiography with which he comes to the text. Matthew does not purport to tell his readers anything about what he believes will happen in the future. Rather, he claims to present the teaching of Jesus. If Jesus did present the parable as Matthew presents it, then Matthew has every reason to expect that there will in fact be some delay in Jesus' return, even if that delay is only to the point of Matthew's writing. Sim argues that Matthew might still expect the *Parousia* within a very short time, and indeed Matthew may well have done so. However, we cannot claim from Matthew's text that Matthew expected the *Parousia* to be necessarily imminent, and if Matthew had appreciated the point of Jesus' parable we would expect him to lay the emphasis on being prepared rather than on specific timing.

As the *mashal* progresses, it is clear that realism is quickly sacrificed in the

---

[235] See Davies and Allison, *Matthew*, 3:396, n156. Other examples include, Proverbs 3:35; 10:1, 8, 23; 11:29; 12:15; 13:20, plus frequently in Ecclesiastes chapters 2, 7 and 10 and Ben Sirach chapters 20 and 21.

[236] Whybray, *Ecclesiastes*, 57, identifies this statement as a quotation. He states, 'In every respect – theme, language, poetical form, antithetical parallelism, brevity and striking imagery – it can be paralleled many times with sayings in the Book of Proverbs.'

[237] Keener, *Matthew*, 596-97. Keener emphasises the various ways in which such a delay might arise.

[238] Sim, *Apocalyptic Eschatology*, 151.

interest of making a powerful point. Thus the girls with oil do not share any (though for good reason),[239] and the door is shut in a way, as France notes, that 'hardly fits the atmosphere of a village wedding, but effectively makes the point that there is a 'too late' in God's timetable.'[240] These elements make it clear that this is a picture of judgement, and that point is made decisively in verses 11 and 12 by the appeal of the girls and the strongly worded rejection on the part of the bridegroom (Κύριε κύριε, ἄνοιξον ἡμῖν. ὁ δὲ ἀποκριθεὶς εἶπεν, Ἀμὴν λέγω ὑμῖν, οὐκ οἶδα ὑμᾶς).[241]

The applicatory verse 13 both reuses the exhortatory verb used in 24:42 (Γρηγορεῖτε οὖν), and recalls the stock phrase of 24:36 (ὅτι οὐκ οἴδατε τὴν ἡμέραν οὐδὲ τὴν ὥραν), thus indicating that once again this is a picture of final judgement.[242] McKnight is correct to recognise that

> Jesus surely intended in this parable to speak of himself and of his future acting as judge.[243]

Further, he recognises that 'Watchfulness is required if one wants to be ready for the final day.'[244] However, he appears to equate the 'final day' with the destruction of Jerusalem on the grounds that 'this parable is juxtaposed immediately alongside Jesus' predictions of the destruction of Jerusalem when God wreaks vengeance through Rome on unfaithful Israel.[245] This view misses the disjunctive nature of 24:36 entirely, along with the allusion to it in 25:13. In fact, the setting of the parable is the portion of the eschatological discourse which is primarily concerned with the *Parousia* – the future return of Jesus. While I believe that McKnight is correct to identify the earlier section of the discourse with the events of AD 70, in the latter section that matter has been superseded by a long-term perspective.

---

[239] Keener, *Matthew*, 598, points out that had the girls shared their oil with those who had none, then all the torches would have gone out too early and the whole event would have been spoiled.

[240] France, *Matthew*, 351

[241] France *Matthew*, 351-52 notes the striking parallel between 25:11-12 and 7:22-23. So also, Garland, *Reading Matthew*, 241. Reiser, *Jesus and Judgment*, 303, regards these verses as probably authentic material.

[242] Carson, 'Matthew', 514, is correct to criticise Jeremias (*Parables*, 52) for dismissing this verse on the grounds that it is inconsistent with the sleeping bridesmaids. Γρηγορεῖτε is not to be understood as 'stay awake', but 'be ready' (See Louw-Nida, *s.v.*). When it is considered that Matthew was writing decades after the death, resurrection and ascension of Jesus, it is hard to see what 'stay awake' would have meant to his readers in connection with Jesus' return!

[243] So McKnight, *A New Vision for Israel*, 144.

[244] McKnight, *A New Vision for Israel*, 144.

[245] McKnight, *A New Vision for Israel*, 144.

THE TALENTS (25:14-30)

This 'narrative *mashal*' is composed of three scenes, linked by phrases that act as temporal indicators ('immediately' [v. 15] and 'after a long time' [v. 19]).[246] It is 'Q' material.[247]

Borg[248] endorses the interpretation of this pericope supplied by C. H. Dodd and J. Jeremias.[249] He recognises that there is a clear allusion to the return of Jesus here, but regards this theme as secondary (following Dodd and Jeremias).

This final *mashal* in this section is very significant indeed, partly because it amplifies the point of the previous pericope.[250] Firstly, it points out that God has given responsibilities of stewardship to his servants. In Jesus' Jewish context that would clearly be understood as a reference to the Jewish leaders, though in Matthew's day it would be understood as referring to Jesus' followers.[251]

Secondly, the theme of delay is sustained as we are told in verse 19 that the servants' master returned 'after a long time' (μετὰ δὲ πολὺν χρόνον). Sim regards these words as probably redactional,[252] but argues that they do not indicate 'that Matthew had rejected the idea of an imminent *Parousia* and deferred it to the distant future.'[253] He writes,

> this interpretation has a hidden and fallacious assumption. It presumes that the fifty years or so which intervened between the resurrection and the composition of the gospel was not perceived as 'a long time'. But on what grounds do we know this? Surely it is likely that the five decades waiting for the parousia, the whole period of the church's existence, would have been accepted by the Christians of Matthew's time as a very long time indeed.[254]

It seems to me to be entirely true that fifty years could well have been 'a very long time indeed' for the early Christians. However, Sim's argument falls because of the assumption upon which he founds it. He assumes that Matthew holds to an expectation of an imminent *Parousia*, that he faces an unexpected delay, and that he maintains his imminent expectation despite that delay. He does not demonstrate Matthew's view but extrapolates it from the worldview which, according to Sim, he accepts:

---

[246] See the thorough analysis in Davies and Allison, *Matthew*, 3:401

[247] Cf Lk. 19:12-27. Reiser, *Jesus and Judgment*, 303, identifies this pericope as having at least a core of authentic tradition.

[248] Borg, *Conflict*, 131-32.

[249] Dodd, *Parables*, 114-21; Jeremias, *Parables*, 58-63.

[250] Note the use of γάρ in verse 14.

[251] Keener, *Matthew*, 600.

[252] Sim, *Apocalyptic Eschatology*, 151. So Gundry, *Matthew*, 504.

[253] Sim, *Apocalyptic Eschatology*, 152.

[254] Sim, *Apocalyptic Eschatology*, 152.

apocalyptic-eschatological schemes which accept the doctrine of the two ages almost without exception hold that the expected end events will occur in the imminent future. Since Matthew shows himself to be fully conversant with the other aspects of this perspective, we should expect that he too held fast to the imminence of the end.[255]

Even if we take the view that the delay envisaged is Matthew's (post-AD 70) perception of the delay between the fall of Jerusalem and the *Parousia* of Jesus, we are still faced with a problem in reconciling such an expectation with the rest of Matthew's narrative. Matthew has presented Jesus as teaching that disaster would fall upon Jerusalem within a clearly defined period of time. The *Parousia* of Jesus must either be immediately connected to that disaster or not. If it is, then Matthew writing (as is commonly held) around AD 80 must have faced a real problem which does not seem to be resolved by this *mashal*. If the temple has been destroyed for a decade and still there is no *Parousia*, how could Jesus' words concerning 'this generation' be fulfilled (some fifty years after Jesus spoke them) if there may still be 'a long time' to wait. If, on the other hand, Jesus distinguished the events to fall upon Jerusalem from his *Parousia* (as I believe Matthew indicates in his narrative), then there is no problem to be faced since Jesus explicitly denies the possibility of predicting the time of his *Parousia*.

Matthew's account is susceptible to a reading that takes seriously the *possibility* of delay, based on the ignorance of Jesus regarding that particular matter (cf. particularly 24:36). Sim is aware of this position, but claims that it 'reads far too much into this motif and is in fact based upon a false premise.'[256] The false premise is that imminent expectation of the end requires the setting of a specific time. Sim claims that,

> In reality there is almost no difference between reckoning with the possibility that the end might come at any time and actually expecting it in the imminent future. Consequently, this argument against Matthew's acceptance of the imminence of the end actually speaks in favour of it.[257]

Against Sim's contention, I would suggest that there is a significant point at issue. The first point relates to the foundation of one's expectation. Did Jesus teach that there would certainly be an imminent end, or did he teach that the end would come at some unknown time? The expectation of his followers, including Matthew and his community, must bear some relationship to Jesus' teaching. Sim appears to be rather unconcerned about this issue. The view that Jesus encouraged his followers to believe that the *Parousia* ('that day and hour') would certainly come imminently does not do justice to the contrast be-

[255] Sim, *Apocalyptic Eschatology*, 148.
[256] Sim, *Apocalyptic Eschatology*, 154.
[257] Sim, *Apocalyptic Eschatology*, 155.

tween Jesus' certainty concerning the events that will without doubt come upon 'this generation' (24:34) and his studied ignorance of the timing of the *Parousia* (24:36).[258]

Also against Sim's claim, there would seem to be a significant pastoral impact for early Christians who held to a strong expectation of an imminent *Parousia* rather than to its possiblity. Those who held to the former view would very soon have been demonstrated to have held a false expectation, whereas there is no such demonstration of misplaced belief for those who take the latter view.

It would appear to be indisputable that some of the early Christians expected the *Parousia* to come imminently and that they were deeply distressed when this did not occur (cf. 1 Thessalonians 4-5). However, Paul can be understood to challenge the expectation of the Thessalonians, and I submit that Matthew (along with the other Evangelists) may be read as making no commitment on the timing of the end, but rather calling for readiness at all times.

There can be no doubt, I suggest, in the face of this recurrent theme throughout these several parables, that Jesus (according to Matthew) made no claims of an imminent judgement day, and perhaps even gave strong hints that there would be some significant delay.

Thirdly, it illustrates what being prepared for the return of the master (ὁ κύριος) means. It is to faithfully carry out his commission, living as his representatives, moving his work forward. The 'settling of accounts' is clearly an image of a time of judgement.[259]

The response of the master to the servants is consistent. It is notable that reward plays a more significant role in this *mashal* than in those previously studied,[260] but yet the master is extremely displeased with the servant who had not used his talent, and expresses that displeasure in judgement. The final sentence gives the clue that something more significant than employment is at stake:

καὶ τὸν ἀχρεῖον δοῦλον ἐκβάλετε εἰς τὸ σκότος τὸ ἐξώτερον· ἐκεῖ ἔσται ὁ κλαῦ θμὸς καὶ ὁ βρυγμὸς τῶν ὀδόντων

These are 'Matthew's favourite metaphors for the final lot of the wicked.'[261] Keener is correct to argue that the very severity of the images of judgement points to the authenticity of the parable; it is implausible that the early Christian community would have attributed such words to Jesus were they not traditional.[262] Furthermore, the strong language provides a powerful warning not to treat the coming judgement with contempt. The point is that every person will

---

[258] See the discussion above.
[259] Keener, *Matthew*, 600.
[260] See the work of Charette, *The Theme of Recompense in Matthew's Gospel*.
[261] Hagner, *Matthew 14-28*, 736
[262] Keener, *Matthew*, 601.

be held accountable for their actions, whether they be the Jewish leaders (in Jesus' day) or the disciples of Jesus (in Jesus' day and beyond). Though the former may have found that judgement came particularly quickly in the crisis of AD 66-70, all will face judgement, whether favourable or critical, at the return of the master.

The Judgement of the Sheep and the Goats

This passage, unique to Matthew, is typically referred to as 'the Last Judgment',[263] but we will avoid this terminology at this point since such a title prejudges the question of whether this passage refers to an event at the end of time, or to an historical event couched in metaphorical language.[264] It is also often discussed as a 'parable',[265] and indeed Gerhardsson, in his careful study of the 'narrative meshalim', includes this pericope under that heading.[266] While the simile in verse 32 ('*as* a shepherd separates the sheep from the goats'), metaphorical features in verse 33 (the 'sheep' and the 'goats') and the stylised pattern of address[267] would justify the use of the term *mashal* to describe this passage, I would suggest that it is more helpful to avoid placing this passage in the same category as the preceding *meshalim*.[268] There are two main reasons for this. Firstly, the phrase 'Son of Man' is not used in the narrative of Jesus' parables, even where there is a clear indication that Jesus is making reference to himself.[269] Secondly, the narrative does not present a contemporary story in order to elucidate future events as parables typically do, but rather presents a direct (if image laden) insight into the judgement scene. Stanton claims that

---

[263] So Hagner, *Matthew 14-28*, 737.

[264] A thorough history of interpretation is found in S. W. Gray, *The Least of My Brothers: Matthew 25:31-46: A History of Interpretation*, SBLDS 114 (Atlanta: Scholars, 1989). For a discussion of the *Wirkungsgeschichte* of this passage, see U. Luz, 'The Final Judgment (Matt 25:31-46): An Exercise in "History of Influence" Exegesis' in Bauer and Powell, *Treasures New and Old*, 271-310.

[265] R. T. France, 'On Being Ready (Matthew 25:1-46)' in Longenecker (ed.), *The Challenge of Jesus' Parables*, 177-95] suggests that J. Jeremias has provided the impetus for many who take this view (190).

[266] Gerhardsson, 'Illuminating the Kingdom', 268. Also Garland, *Reading Matthew*, 242.

[267] See Hagner, *Matthew 14-28*, 740-41.

[268] McKnight, *A New Vision for Israel*, 148, describes the account as a 'parable', and believes it to refer to the events of AD 70.

[269] In fact, Jesus makes reference to 'the Son of Man' in the interpretation of the parable of the tares in 13:37.

The passage is neither an apocalypse, nor a parable, nor a poem, but an apocalyptic discourse.[270]

He comes to this conclusion by noting similarities in structure and theme in several 'apocalyptic' works such as *4 Ezra*, *1 Enoch*, *2 Baruch* and the *Apocalypse of Abraham*.[271] Although he is more cautious than Collins and others in tracing literary dependence between Matthew and apocalyptic literature (particularly *1 Enoch*), he can still write,

> The central theme of 25:31-46 is also found in several apocalyptic writings. Matthew's gospel, 4 Ezra, 2 Baruch, and at least two sections of I Enoch come from a broadly similar social setting. Their similar 'symbolic worlds' function as consolation to hard-pressed groups of God's people.[272]

This latter comment seems to me to be the foundation of Stanton's decision to treat this passage as an 'apocalyptic discourse'. He appears to work with an understanding of the Matthean community as an apocalyptic community, excluded from society, feeling marginalised, and in need of reassurance. Now there is something to be said for this reconstruction, but as with Sim's work, there is a great danger in portraying Matthew as simply an encourager for a somewhat sectarian group. I am concerned that Stanton appears to be driven to his conclusion by his construction of the Matthean community.

Stanton claims that 'the roots of this apocalyptic motif are deep' and then points to the '*locus classicus*' of Joel 3:1-3 (LXX 4.1-3), which reads:

> For then, in those days and at that time, when I restore the fortunes of Judah and Jerusalem, I will gather all the nations and bring them down to the valley of Jehoshaphat, and I will enter into judgment with them there, on account of my people and my heritage Israel, because they have scattered them among the nations. They have divided my land, and cast lots for my people, and traded boys for prostitutes, and sold girls for wine, and drunk it down.

Whatever the decision on the character of this passage, the genre of the passage is clearly of great significance for proper interpretation. In the light of the carefully crafted structure of the passage, and yet the dissimilarity between it and typical parables, I am inclined to regard it as a stylised account of the eschatological judgement.

There is no similar *mashal* in Jewish Wisdom literature. The closest parallel to the image of the separation of sheep and goats is found in Ezekiel 34:17, which reads,

---

[270] Stanton, 'Once More: Matthew 25:31-46' in *Gospel for a New People* , 207-31, here 209, n. 1.
[271] Stanton, 'Once More: Matthew 25:31-46' 221.
[272] Stanton, 'Once More: Matthew 25:31-46' 223.

As for you, my flock, thus says the Lord GOD: I shall judge between sheep and sheep, between rams and goats:

καὶ ὑμεῖς πρόβατα τάδε λέγει κύριος κύριος ἰδοὺ ἐγὼ διακρινῶ ἀνὰ μέσον προβάτου καὶ προβάτου κριῶν καὶ τράγων (LXX)

The account of Jacob's dealings with Laban in Genesis, chapter 30, may also serve to provide some conceptual background to this passage. However, there is an important passage in the prophetic tradition that picks up some of the themes of this portion of Matthew:

> A shoot shall come out from the stump of Jesse,
>> and a branch shall grow out of his roots.
> 2 The spirit of the LORD shall rest on him,
>> the spirit of wisdom and understanding,
>> the spirit of counsel and might,
>> the spirit of knowledge and the fear of the LORD.
> 3 His delight shall be in the fear of the LORD.
> He shall not judge by what his eyes see,
>> or decide by what his ears hear;
> 4 but with righteousness he shall judge the poor,
>> and decide with equity for the meek of the earth;
> he shall strike the earth with the rod of his mouth,
>> and with the breath of his lips he shall kill the wicked.
>
> (Isaiah 11:1)

In this passage there is an interesting and important link between the messianic figure's role as judge and 'the spirit of wisdom and understanding.' Also striking is the emphasis on the equitable judgement of the poor and meek of the earth. While there are a limited number of verbal links between this passage and Matthew 25:31-46, thematically there are close similarities which may indicate some form of dependence on the part of either Jesus or Matthew.[273]

It is notable that the Greek term ἡ παρουσία does not appear in this passage, but the theme is the 'coming' of the Son of Man. There can be little doubt that Daniel 7 continues to stand as the dominant backdrop to this scene, though France is correct to note that Matthew goes far beyond Daniel in that whereas in Daniel 7, the one 'like a Son of Man' comes to the throne of God, in Matthew 25:31, the Son of Man sits on the throne.[274] Hagner draws attention to the very close verbal and conceptual parallels between 25:31 and the earlier verse 16:27.[275] In the Appendix to Chapter 4, I argue that Matthew 16:27 should be

---

[273] Cf. also Is. 58:7 and Ezek. 18:7 for possible background material.
[274] France, *Matthew*, 356.
[275] Hagner, *Matthew 14-28*, 741.

understood as a reference to the final universal judgement, while the following verse 28 should be regarded as a reference to a contemporary event couched in figurative language. The correspondences which Hagner identifies suggests that 25:31 should also be regarded as non-figurative.

Verse 31 is frequently ascribed to the creativity of the Evangelist.[276] Indeed, the whole section from verse 31 to verse 46 is often understood to be inauthentic.[277] However, several characteristics point towards authenticity. First of all, there is the distinctive use of the phrase 'Son of Man' as a self-designation, which, if not unique to Jesus, is at least characteristic of Jesus. Secondly there is the careful structure and memorable 'parabolic' style of the pericope, typical of Jesus' teaching. Thirdly, the use of ἀμήν (25:40, 45) is typical of Jesus' style as presented in the gospel of Matthew.[278]

The passage has a very distinctive structure, which highlights its literary character:

A	Introduction (31-33)	
B		Declaration of Blessing (34)
C		Grounds for Declaration (35-36)
D		Questioning of Grounds (37-39)
E		Explanation of Grounds (40)
B'		Declaration of Banishment (41)
C'		Grounds for Declaration (42-43)
D'		Questioning of Grounds (44)
E'		Explanation of Grounds (45)
F	Conclusion (46)	

The scene is set with a brief introduction (A) which is phrased so as to suggest that this is the explanation of known material rather than the introduction of new material ("Οταν δὲ ἔλθῃ ὁ υἱὸς τοῦ ἀνθρώπου ἐν τῇ δόξῃ αὐτοῦ καὶ πάντες οἱ ἄγγελοι μετ' αὐτου τότε καθίσει ἐπὶ θρόνου δόξης αὐτοῦ).[279] There can be very little doubt that this is a pictorial account of an expected climactic event of judgement, in which Jesus understands himself to take the central role. The majesty of the scene is emphasised by means of three elements: glory, angels and the throne. The reference to the 'glorious throne' (τότε καθίσει ἐπὶ

---

[276] So, e.g., Schweizer, *Matthew*, 475.

[277] For example, Reiser, who tends to come to relatively conservative conclusions regarding authenticity of synoptic sayings tradition, does not mark this section of Matthew as having even a core of authentic material (*Jesus and Judgment*, 303).

[278] Keener, *Matthew*, 602.

[279] Previous references to the Son of Man within chapters 21-23 are all found in chapter 24: 27, 30, 37, 39, 44.

θρόνου δόξης αὐτοῦ)[280] of the Son of Man makes it clear that this is a royal event,[281] in which the Son of Man has a position of great authority. This is reinforced by the reference to πάντες οἱ ἄγγελοι μετ᾽ αὐτοῦ, the second important reference to ἄγγελοι in our section of Matthew. The previous occurrence of the noun is found in 24:31. The reference to angels (πάντες οἱ ἄγγελοι μετ᾽ αὐτοῦ) appears to be an allusion to Zech 14:5 (LXX - πάντες οἱ ἅγιοι μετ᾽ αὐτοῦ), though the ambiguous term 'holy ones' is made a clear reference to angels by a change of term.[282] While it is true that Zechariah 14:5 provides the most natural linguistic background, the context of the allusion in the OT prophecy does not tie in naturally with the context in Matthew.[283] It may be that there is some value in considering whether the reference to 'angels' is in fact drawn from the background of Daniel 7:9-22, for two reasons. Firstly, there can be no reasonable doubt that 25:31-46 resonates with echoes of Daniel 7.[284] Secondly, the phrase 'holy ones' is found five times in that brief passage.[285] D. Marguerat examines the references to the glory, the angels and the throne, concluding that these motifs reflect tradition drawn from *1 Enoch*.[286]

It is certainly true that striking similarities between Matthew's account and portions of *1 Enoch* may be noted, as may be seen in the following citations from *1 Enoch*:

---

[280] Compare Matthew 19:26: ὅταν καθίσῃ ὁ υἱὸς τοῦ ἀνθρώπου ἐπὶ θρόνου δόξης αὐτοῦ. Davies and Allison, *Matthew* 3:420, comment that they, along with most commentators, consider this clause to be redactional.

[281] This is the first indicator in this passage that there is a connection with the opening passage of chapter 21, though the contrast between humility (21) and glory (25) means that there are few common elements.

[282] Though many manuscripts read οἱ ἅγιοι, there is little doubt that this reflects harmonisation under the influence of the LXX of Zech 14:5. Compare the use of this text in Matthew 27:51-53.

[283] The most natural connections are the 'Day of Yahweh' motif and the location of the Mount of Olives.

[284] See France, 'On Being Ready', 190-91.

[285] 7:18, 21, 22, 25, 27.

[286] Marguerat, *Le Jugement*, 488-89. Similarly, Reddish claims 'Whereas most of the New Testament uses of the phrase "Son of man" can be explained from traditions arising out of the book of Daniel, several New Testament passages describe the Son of man in ways more similar to the Enochic Son of man than to the Danielic figure. Matthew 19:28 and 25:31 state that at the coming of the Son of man, he will sit on his "glorious throne" (compare to 1 Enoch 45:3; 55:4; 61:8; 62:5; 69:27, 29).' Reddish, *Apocalyptic Literature: A Reader*, 165, continues to bring out a point from John's gospel which has relevance for Matthew also: 'In John 5:22, 27 the Son (of man) is granted authority by God to execute judgment. This is a role performed by the figure in the "Similitudes" but not in Daniel'. Cf. Allison, *Jesus of Nazareth*, 134: 'With the exception of Matt 25:31-46, which may owe as much to the influence of 1 Enoch upon Matthew or his tradition as to Jesus, none of these logia contain vivid details.'

And the Lord of Spirits set the Chosen One on the throne of his glory, and he will judge all the works of the holy ones in heaven above, and in the balance he will weigh their deeds (61:8).

And the Lord of Spirits sat on the throne of his glory, and the spirit of righteousness was poured out on him, and the word of his mouth kills all the sinners and all the lawless and they are destroyed before him. And on that day all the kings and the mighty and the exalted, and those who possess the earth, will stand up; and they will see and recognise how he sits on the throne of his glory, and the righteous are judged in righteousness before him, and no idle word is spoken before him (62:2-3).

Marguerat notes that Matthew's account reflects that of *1 Enoch*, but with 'une nuance significative':

Le Fils de l'homme prend place non sur le trône de la gloire divine (Hénoch), mais sur le trône de *sa* gloire.[287]

Marguerat's comment highlights not a minor but a substantive difference between the two presentations. Yet there are numerous other differences between the passages from *1 Enoch* and the Matthean narrative also. In 61:8, judgement is carried out on 'the holy ones in heaven above' – surely a reference to angelic beings, while the account of judgement in 62:2-3 has quite a different tone to that in Matthew. Moreover, the dating of the Similitudes of Enoch is not certain, and any conclusions regarding Matthew's dependence on Enoch must be tentative.[288] In the end, the possibility of dependence on *1 Enoch* for certain elements of the imagery used in this passage is inconsequential for our interpretation.

The scene is further developed by the indication that the regal authority of the Son of Man is such that not only is he the judge of Israel but all the nations are gathered before him (καὶ συναχθήσονται ἔμπροσθεν αὐτοῦ πάντα τὰ ἔθνη).[289] The phrase πάντα τὰ ἔθνη is very common in the OT and other Hellenistic Jewish literature.[290] The phrase is also found in Matthew 24:9 and 24:14.

---

[287] Marguerat, *Le Jugement*, 489.

[288] See Evans, *NWNTI*, 23. See Keener, *Matthew*, 602, n. 225 for a similarly cautious position.

[289] Milikowsky, 'Which Gehenna?', in contrasting the theology of Matthew and Luke, claims that Matthew 'implies that reward and retribution are subsequent to the future coming of Christ and his judgment. After that judgment the sinner will be punished in the eschatological Gehenna, but he will receive no retribution until then' (243).

[290] In the LXX, see: Gen. 18:18; 22:18; 26:4; Ex. 23:27; 33:16; Deut. 7:6, 7, 14; 10:15; 11:23; 28:10, 64; 29:23; Josh. 4:24; 23:4; 24:18; 1 Sam. 8:20; 1 Chr. 14:17; 2 Chr. 33:9; Ezra 5:49; Neh. 6:16; Esth. 3:8, 4:11; Jdt. 3:8; Tob. 14:6; Tob (s). 13:13; 14:6; 1 Macc. 1:42; 2:18, 19; 4:11; 5:38, 43; 12:53; 13:6; 3 Macc. 7:4; Ps. 9:18; 46:2; 48:2;

The words of Isaiah 66:18 in the LXX may well provide the most natural background to this particular use in Matthew, though the difficulty of the Hebrew
text should make conclusions tentative:[291]

κἀγὼ τὰ ἔργα αὐτῶν καὶ τὸν λογισμὸν αὐτῶν ἐπίσταμαι ἔρχομαι συνᾶ
γαγεῖν πάντα τὰ ἔθνη καὶ τὰς γλώσσας καὶ ἥξουσιν καὶ ὄψονται τὴν
δόξαν μου

There can be no doubt that it indicates a universal judgement.[292] That the Son
of Man can now separate (ἀφορίσει αὐτοὺς ἀπ᾽ ἀλλήλων) the sheep from the
goats indicates his authority. This scene, then, is the dramatic answer to the
question of the Jewish leaders in 21:23. This is the demonstration of the authority that Jesus possesses. Yet, as Hengel indicates, the act of separation also portrays Jesus as

> the wise judge of the world who knows what the acquitted and condemned
> themselves do not recall.[293]

The first judgement is a declaration of blessing on those who are 'blessed of
my Father'. The co-ordination of 'the Son of Man', 'the king' and 'my Father'
can leave no reasonable doubt that Jesus is making reference to himself (using
the most distinctive phrases associated with him) in the most exalted terms (the
king).[294] When we come to consider the basis for judgement, it is striking to see
how far from the mark is Borg's assessment of Matthew's concept of judgement as non-political. In fact Borg recognises this passage (as a Matthean 'parable') as providing support for his view, but he can only do so by positing incoherence in Matthew's presentation.[295] It is my view that this does not do justice to Matthew's narrative. This passage is entirely political in the sense that it
relates to the activity of human beings towards other human beings. In Borg's
own words it identifies those who practised the 'Politics of Holiness' and those
who practised the 'Politics of Compassion'. As the King identifies the reasons

---

58:6, 9; 71:11, 17; 85:9; 112:4; 116:1; 117:10; Odes 7:37; Sir. 36:1; *Pss. Sol.* 9:9;
17:14, 34; Amos 9:12; Joel 4:2, 11, 12; Obad. 1:15, 16; Hab. 2:5; Hag. 2:7; Zech.
7:14; 12:3, 9; 14:2, 18; Mal. 2:9; 3:12; Is. 2:2; 14:12, 26; 25:7; 34:2; 40:15, 17; 43:9;
66:18; Jer. 3:17; 9:25; 25:9; 32:13, 15; 43:2; Lam. 1:10; Ezek. 25:8; 31:16; 38:16;
39:21, 23; Dan. 3:2, 7, 37; 7:14; Dan (t). 3:37.

[291] So Marguerat, *Le Jugement*, 490, n. 26. The difficult syntax has proved a challenge to
interpreters. J. A. Motyer, *The Prophecy of Isaiah* (Leicester: IVP, 1993), 540-41,
indicates the attractiveness of the LXX reading, but also highlights the problems it
raises for interpretation of the words in their context.

[292] So McKnight, *A New Vision for Israel*, 148-49.

[293] Hengel, *Studies in Early Christology*, 87.

[294] The reference to 'the king' echoes the reference in Mt 21:5 to Zechariah's prophecy.

[295] Borg, *Conflict*, 223.

for judgement, positive and negative, it becomes clear that the key issue is whether those concerned responded to human need. Indeed, the list of circumstances given encompasses the three most vital human needs - food, shelter and companionship.[296]

Is this passage, then, simply a call to humanitarian action? In a sense, the word 'simply' is not appropriate since true humanitarian action is to give human beings made in the image of God some dignity. However, the passage goes even further than this.

The king identifies the reason for blessing (C) or curse (C') as twofold. Firstly, he indicates whether there has been compassion (D) or no compassion (D') shown towards 'the least of these, my brothers' (τούτων τῶν ἀδελφῶν μου τῶν ἐλαχίστων). Although contemporary use of this passage frequently treats it as a reflection of classical Liberal theology of the fatherhood of God and the brotherhood of man,[297] the usage of this language in Matthew suggests a different interpretation. 'Brothers' in Matthew is a term used of Jesus' disciples (12:50; 28:10) and 'the least' is similarly predicated of those who are Jesus' followers (5:19; 11:11; 18:3-6, 10-14). Thus the phrase 'the least of these my brothers' should be understood in context as a reference to members of the Christian community, perhaps particularly those who were travelling around proclaiming the message of the kingdom (Matthew 10 suggests that the disciples might well face the situations described in this passage). Secondly, however, the more fundamental issue that the king highlights is that actions performed towards 'the least of these, my brothers' are understood by the king to be actions towards himself (25:35-36, 40, 42-43, 45). Thus the fundamental reason for blessing (E) or curse (E') is personal response to the king. This relates very closely to Jesus' words in 7:21-23.[298] France challenges this view on the grounds that neither the sheep nor the goats were aware that they were responding to the Son of Man/the king/Jesus.[299] However, while it is undoubtedly the case that neither group recognised that their actions would be treated as directed towards the king himself, such ignorance does not require that each group acted without an awareness of their response to the message and followers of Jesus. That is, there is no reason to believe that those who acted favourably towards 'the least of these my brothers' were unaware of the fact that these people were followers of Jesus which is what constitutes them 'my brothers'.

---

[296] Blomberg, *Matthew*, 377. Blomberg correctly notes that Marguerat (508-9) goes too far in claiming that the passage identifies food, shelter and freedom as the three necessities, as the passage gives no commitments of release for those in prison.

[297] Luz, 'The Final Judgement', 274-80, describes this view as an outworking of the 'universal interpretive model'.

[298] In fact, the vocative in verse 44 (Κύριε) recalls the repeated vocative in 7:21. Hagner, *Matthew 14-28*, 746, correctly points out that the address does not imply discipleship but simply confrontation with the glorious judge of the earth.

[299] France, 'On Being Ready', 193.

Likewise those who acted uncharitably may well have done so for the very reason that those who required their help were followers of Jesus.

Having discussed the significance of 'brothers', 'little ones', and 'least', and having demonstrated their application to believers in Jesus, Garland, following France[300], correctly notes,

> The picture of the judgment in this parable [*sic*] therefore does not reflect a "humanitarian ethic" of good works (salvation based on kindness to all in need) with no specifically Christian content (France, *Matthew*, 355). The nations are judged according to the way they treated Jesus' humble brethren who represented Christ to them.[301]

This passage demonstrates the reality of all that Jesus has done and said from the beginning of chapter 21 onwards. What right has Jesus to judge the temple? What right has he to judge the religious leaders? How can he predict the destruction of the heart of the Jewish religious system? It is because he is not simply the humble king on a donkey, but he is the great king on the throne (καθίσει ἐπὶ θρόνου δόξης αὐτοῦ) who will judge all people with all authority. Garland's conclusion to his chapter on the eschatological discourse, and this pericope in particular, is especially relevant to an interpretation which sees Jesus as the judge of the 'Politics of Holiness' and the promoter of the 'Politics of Compassion':

> This parable has often been used to emphasise the Christian's obligation to the down and out in society. Our interpretation calls this ethical reading of the parable into question. It does not negate the imperative to attend to the needs of the hungry, naked, and imprisoned that resounds throughout the Scripture (Isa 58:6-7; Ezek 18:7; Tob 4:16; Sir 7:35; 4 Ezra 2:20) but argues that the intention of this parable lies elsewhere. The ethical interpretation of this parable looks at things primarily from a position of superiority, from the perspective of those who have the material resources and ought to help the poor and needy (see 19:21). Matthew looked at the world from the perspective of the down and out, as a member of a group that was oppressed and dishonoured because of its commitment to Christ. The collective honour of Christians will not be made fully known until the judgment. Then, those who scorned and despised Christians will discover that

---

[300] As he expresses himself in his commentary – he appears to have since changed his mind. See France, 'On Being Ready'.

[301] Garland, *Reading Matthew*, 243. As Garland points out, the relationship of this pericope to 10:40-42 cannot be missed: 'Whoever welcomes you welcomes me, and whoever welcomes me welcomes the one who sent me. Whoever welcomes a prophet in the name of a prophet will receive a prophet's reward; and whoever welcomes a righteous person in the name of a righteous person will receive the reward of the righteous; and whoever gives even a cup of cold water to one of these little ones in the name of a disciple - truly I tell you, none of these will lose their reward.'

they scorned and despised the son of man who has all authority in heaven and earth.[302]

Chapter Summary and Conclusion

Having surveyed the material from both Jewish literature and Matthew 21-25, I submit that the following matters are clear:

(i)   the motif of divine judgement, including a future judgement, is an integral aspect of Wisdom teaching, even though it is not always conspicuous.

(ii) Matthew presents Jesus as a 'sage', a teacher of Wisdom, drawing on the form, techniques, and sometimes the themes of Wisdom literature. Within the Wisdom genre of sayings ascribed to Jesus by Matthew in chapters 21-25 of his gospel, proclamation of judgement on his contemporaries and at a future day of reckoning at which he himself would stand as judge (thus fulfilling the role previously understood to be the prerogative of God alone) figure prominently. In fact, the theme of judgement figures much more prominently in the *meshalim* of Jesus than it does in the Jewish Wisdom literature, possibly indicating the merging of the Wisdom and Prophetic traditions in the teaching of Jesus.

(iii) Matthew presents Jesus as one who proclaimed judgement on those who did not do the will of his Father. This condemned way of life included both a rejection of himself as God's chosen one (that is, a theological element) and oppression of others (that is, a social element). In the latter case, Matthew's portrayal of Jesus' teaching stands firmly in continuity with the tradition of the Wisdom literature of the OT and its later developments. In the former case, Matthew claims that Jesus introduced a new and striking criterion by which people are judged by God.

---

[302] Garland, *Reading Matthew*, 244-45.

CHAPTER 7

Conclusion

Introductory Remarks

In this brief chapter I intend to draw together the results of the exegetical work done in the previous chapters so that we may see the presentation of Jesus as Judge in Matthew 21-25 as it is unfolded in these chapters.

Jesus the Judge: Performer of Prophetic Acts of Judgement

Matthew presents Jesus as the one who enters Jerusalem in a royal *Parousia* (21:1-11). Matthew will present his readers with another royal arrival in 25:31-46 which forms an *inclusio* around the unit of the gospel. His citation of Zechariah 9:9 leaves the reader in no doubt that the king is entering his city, yet how it is true that Jesus, the human who comes in a clear reversal of the pomp and circumstance of the *Parousia* of a political ruler, can enter into the role of Yahweh is not yet clear. The second prophetic act recorded by Matthew (21:12-17. 'Clearing' of the temple) more transparently signifies judgement on the temple. That action is given further content by Jesus' appropriation of Isaiah 56:7 and Jeremiah 7:11. Jesus takes responsibility for the sanctity of the dwelling of Yahweh. However, his challenge to the present operation of the temple is not simply negative, but also has a positive aspect. Jesus heals those who are excluded from the life of the temple by their infirmities and thus presents the possibility of holiness which is not based upon exclusion. The third prophetic act (21:18-22. Withering of the fig tree) makes sense only when one sees the mutually interpretative relationship of the three prophetic actions and also when one is conscious of the deep resonances of the image of the fig tree in the OT prophetic literature. Jesus the prophet makes an unmistakable declaration of the impending (and irreversible) doom of the temple. In addition, Jesus makes a declaration that provides interpretation to the action, exhibiting his authority through the use of a distinctive formula. Thus Jesus enters Jerusalem with a complex of dramatic acts by which he claims to exercise authority to judge the very heart of the religion of the Jews, symbolically portraying the inevitable devastation of the temple. These prophetic actions are unmistakable demonstrations of unique authority, and this claim to authority in the actions he has performed is both recognised and questioned by the temple authorities.

Jesus the Judge: Proclaimer of *Meshalim* of Judgement against Jewish Leaders

Matthew presents Jesus to his readers as the one who teaches with amazing (22:22) and astonishing (22:33) teaching. By means of a series of narrative *meshalim* (21:28-32, *Mashal* of two sons; 21:33-46, *Mashal* of the wicked tenants; 22:1-14, *Mashal* of the marriage feast) Jesus demonstrates his unique authority and skill as a teacher in the tradition of the Jewish sages as he proclaims judgement on the 'Politics of Holiness', indicating, not only that those who have been privileged by God will have their privileges stripped from them on account of their rejection of God, but also those who have been marginalised will be brought in. Thus, the significance of the healings performed by Jesus in the temple (21:14) is confirmed by his teaching.

The *meshalim* of Jesus are not simply of the narrative variety. In a further series of three *meshalim*, this time of a more enigmatic nature and given in response to confrontations by various groups of the privileged among the Jewish people, Jesus condemns those who oppose him for their refusal to give God his due, for their refusal to recognise the voice of God in the scriptures and for their refusal to demonstrate love to God and love to fellow Israelites in like manner.

Finally, Jesus brings the confrontations to an end with a question of his own. Taking a familiar portion of scripture (Psalm 110:1) he turns it into a provocative question which once more (compare 21:23-27) confronts the Jewish leaders with Jesus' authority as he points them to the promise of divine vindication which is given to David's son, the Messiah.

Thus, Jesus brings judgement upon his Jewish opponents through both the content of what he says in *meshalim* and through the authority which he exercises as he demolishes their opposition.

Jesus the Judge: Proclaimer of Prophetic Woes against Jewish Leaders

In the prophetic woes against the Pharisees Matthew presents us with Jesus' deep anger regarding 'the Politics of Holiness'. Using the strongest terms, Jesus condemns a religious leadership that claims to provide for the people of God but in fact excludes them from what God intends for his people. Jesus' words are clearly not simply expressions of frustration vented in the hearing of those who oppose him. Rather they are declarations of the true experience of these unfaithful tenants. 'Woe' will indeed come upon them for Jesus the judge has declared it to be so.

Jesus the Judge: Prophetic Predictor of National Catastrophe

That Matthew portrays Jesus as fulfilling the role of a prophet can barely be disputed in the light of the prophetic acts of chapter 21. This prophetic role is extended in the predictions of the fall of Jerusalem which are recounted in chapter 24. These predictions are the counterparts of the prophetic acts of chapter 21, declaring in words the fate of the temple that was demonstrated in action previously. Though it is beyond the scope of this thesis to ask whether Matthew as he wrote already knew that Jesus had been shown to be correct, it is nonetheless clear that Jesus commits himself to firm and strongly emphasised declarations that devastation would hit the heart of Israel. In making such a prophetic declaration, it is no surprise that Jesus should use the language previously used by Isaiah and Daniel to speak now of the unspeakable event of the temple's destruction.

Jesus the Judge: Prophetic Proclaimer of Eschatological Judgement

Jesus' role as a prophet is not yet complete for Matthew. Combining the prophetic act of prediction with the Wisdom trait of effective images, Jesus presents several similes and stories which tell of a different phase in the judging activity of the Son of Man. Emphasising delay, uncertainty of timing and yet complete certainty of arrival, Jesus speaks of a master returning to reward or judge his servant, a bridegroom appearing to welcome or banish weary girls, a man returning to receive his due from his slaves. While the narratives have the elusive quality of the Sage's story, their combined effect is unmistakeable, particularly when they are set beside the less elusive account of the universal judgement in 25:31-46. Jesus is speaking of his own personal return as judge and those who follow him must abandon all concern to know what he declares to be unknowable and must simply devote themselves to being ready.

Jesus the Judge as Prophet and Sage

Our exegesis of Matthew 21-25 has attempted to demonstrate that, in this section of the gospel, Jesus is portrayed as a judge after the pattern of both the prophet and the sage, and that Matthew's presentation offers us an understanding of Jesus which is fundamentally Jewish, holding together divine judgement and social engagement, contemporary criticism and eschatological expectation. Thus Matthew presents to his reader a Jesus who exercises authority in his earthly ministry without hesitation or any sense of presumptiveness because he knows that he will exercise authority in his role as eschatological judge.

Is Matthew's Jesus 'Non-Eschatological'?

We have observed that the gospel material relating to Jesus' judging activities have been understood in two principal ways. Firstly, scholars have understood Jesus as an eschatological prophet after the fashion of Schweitzer and have regarded Jesus' actions and sayings to reflect an expectation of imminent cosmic catastrophe. According to this portrait, Jesus has little to say about matters of social justice because he single-mindedly proclaims the coming of the kingdom of God in the form of a cataclysmic event which is to take place in the near future. Alternatively, recent scholarship has rejected the 'eschatological' element of the Jesus tradition and has modelled Jesus after the sage, whether fundamentally Jewish (Borg) or Hellenistic (Crossan). In this latter scenario, if Jesus is a judge in any sense, it is as one who challenges the social structures of society, not as the proclaimer of the impending sovereign judgement of God.[1] The argument of this thesis is that the two models of prophet and sage are not mutually exclusive alternatives, but are complementary in providing appropriate ways of understanding the ministry of Jesus as judge. Further, I have sought to demonstrate that both models have suffered from being employed independently, and from the failure of scholars to draw on the most important Jewish roots for their basic principles.

With respect to the portions of Matthew 21-25 which have most frequently been regarded as predictions of the imminent end of the world, we have seen that Jesus' words must indeed be read and understood against the background of Jewish documents which contain analogous passages of symbolic or 'apocalyptic' language, as Schweitzer and Hiers correctly claim. This can only be properly done, however, when the 'apocalyptic' language employed by Jesus is interpreted in the way in which it was understood by Jesus' Jewish contemporaries, and this is the point at which Schweitzer, Hiers and many other interpreters fall into error.

Borg claims that the sayings of Jesus which appear to point to an imminent cataclysmic final judgment (particularly the 'coming Son of Man' sayings) must be regarded as inauthentic. Borg *does* accept that Jesus believed in a final Day of Judgment. What he does not accept is that Jesus preached that the end was imminent. We might ask if it is not rather misleading, then, for Borg to

---

[1] Cf. Powell, *The Jesus Debate*, 121: 'To put things a bit too simply, major historians of Jesus often seem to fall into two camps: those who accent the Hellenistic matrix for Jesus and downplay his eschatological teaching (the Jesus Seminar, Crossan, Downing, Mack), and those who accent the Jewish matrix for Jesus and emphasise his eschatological teaching (Meier, Sanders, Witherington, Wright).' It seems to me that this is not a simplistic classification, but has one notable exception in Marcus Borg. Powell goes on to note that Borg stands between these camps in that he emphasises the Jewishness of Jesus, yet declares him to be non-eschatological.

speak of a 'non-eschatological' Jesus.[2] However, Borg has a specific content in mind for the phrase 'the eschatological Jesus' which he wishes to challenge. He offers the following precise definition:

> an image or *Gestalt* of the historical Jesus which sees his mission within the framework of his expectation of the end of the world in his generation, understood in an objective and not a purely subjective sense.[3]

So the Jesus which Borg reacts against is one who is *driven* by his conviction that the end of the world will come within his generation, rather than one who does have an eschatological aspect in his teaching. This is clearly a reaction against the portrait of Jesus painted by Schweitzer, but it is not for that reason that we should question it. Rather, we should applaud Borg's rejection of Schweitzer's portrait of Jesus the preacher of the imminent end.

The most important interpretative canon to be observed when dealing with 'apocalyptic' language in the teaching of Jesus is that it must be understood in accordance with its meaning in its original historical and literary context.[4] As we have access to Jesus' words through Matthew's account, we must first interpret them in their Matthean context and then ask whether Matthew appears to have interpreted them in a way that makes sense in the setting of Jesus' ministry. Here it is important to recognise that the 'apocalyptic' language employed by Jesus according to Matthew is drawn (so far as clearly identifiable allusions are concerned) either from the prophetic literature of the Hebrew canon (particularly Isaiah and Zechariah) or from Daniel (regarded as one of the 'Writings' in the Hebrew canon), not from the extra-canonical 'apocalypses'. Having examined a selection of the most important of these texts from the Hebrew scriptures, we have seen that the allusions to Isaiah and Daniel make best sense in their present contexts in the gospel when they are interpreted with reference to their contexts in these two OT documents. That is to say, the citations from these OT documents should be regarded as figurative expressions used to describe events which may belong to the realm of historical experience.

This approach to 'apocalyptic' language stands in continuity with the stress of recent studies that Jesus must be understood in his first-century Jewish milieu. It is our contention, following Caird, France and Wright, that much of the confusion that has existed in the area of eschatology during this century, and even in recent years, is due to scholars failing to be rigorous enough in placing Jesus in such a first-century Jewish setting.

The test of this interpretative approach on the 'coming Son of Man' sayings in Matthew's gospel (both those present within chapters 21-25 and three sig-

---

[2] As we find, for example, in the title of his article, 'A Temperate Case for a Non-Eschatological Jesus' *Foundations and Facets Forum* 2.3 (1986), 81-102.
[3] Borg, 'Temperate Case', 81.
[4] Or 'context' and 'co-text' as P. Cotterell and M. Turner prefer. See their book *Linguistics and Biblical Interpretation* (London: SPCK, 1989), 16.

nificant texts outwith these chapters examined in the Appendix) revealed that it provided a coherent interpretation of these texts in their present Matthean contexts. Two results are particularly important to note: Firstly, it was established that the 'coming Son of Man' sayings may be convincingly interpreted so as to do away with the 'problem of the delay of the *Parousia*'. There is no need to try to justify Jesus' error in predicting his own imminent return which did not happen because the sayings, which have so often been interpreted in this way, do not refer to Jesus' return. The accuracy of this interpretative decision is seen by the fact that the majority of the early Christians were not devastated when the *Parousia* did not occur in the lifetime of their contemporaries because they did not understand the texts which refer to an imminent 'coming' as references to the *Parousia*. While some Christians clearly did become concerned at the delay of the *Parousia* (as is seen from 1 Thessalonians, for example), Paul's pastoral response challenges this concern on the grounds that it is based on a faulty expectation. Secondly, these texts may now be properly understood as predictions that Jesus would be openly given authority before his disciples (as is seen most clearly in the juxtaposition of the 'coming Son of Man' saying in Matthew 16:28 and the account of the transfiguration in Matthew 17:1-13), and openly vindicated before his accusers (as is seen most clearly in Matthew 26:64). In Matthew 21-25 this is particularly seen as authority to take the role of judge, and to execute judgment.

Our discussion of Jesus' teaching against the background of Jewish Wisdom literature has brought to light several issues. Firstly, it is now clear that there is no justification for the dichotomy that is created in some scholarship between the Wisdom tradition and some form of eschatological expectation. In particular, it has become clear that even if expectation of judgement is not pronounced in the Jewish Wisdom writings, it is certainly not absent.

We maintain that Borg misrepresents Matthew when he suggests that Matthew (at least in his special material) fails to portray Jesus as challenging the political and religious situation in Palestine, we have seen in chapters 21-25 of Matthew's gospel that Jesus is, indeed, concerned with the contemporary Jewish religion, and that he is portrayed as pronouncing judgment on Israel because of her wickedness, particularly by his prediction of the destruction of Jerusalem. This is entirely in keeping with what we should expect if indeed Jesus drew heavily on the Wisdom tradition, for much of the material surveyed from the OT Wisdom writings emphasised that judgement would come upon those who were unjust in their dealings with others. In this respect there is a substantial overlap between the prophetic and the Wisdom traditions in that the OT prophets also condemned injustice as deserving the judgement of God.

However, we have also seen that when chapters 21-25 are seen as a unit, they indicate that regarding Jesus as a temporal judge is not sufficient. The latter part of the unit, from 24:36 to 25:46, indicates by means of a series of *meshalim* that there will be a time, in the future but undefined (the lack of definite timescale sets these sayings apart from the previous predictions concerning the fall of Jerusalem), when Jesus will return as eschatological judge in order to judge all the nations. In the literary whole of Matthew 21-25 the final narrative in chapter 25 of the *Parousia* of the Son of Man provides the appropriate reflection of the *Parousia* that Matthew described in chapter 21. It is only in the light of this final judgment, in which it is evident that the Son of Man (Jesus) has all authority to judge, that Jesus' earthly judging activity in Jerusalem finds its true significance.

Borg is to be applauded for his concern to understand Jesus against the background of the political, social and religious situation of his time. In the light of Matthew 21-25 we cannot deny that Jesus exercised his ministry in such a context and also that he responded in his teaching to that context. The theme of 'conflict' which Borg has identified has much to commend it as a key for understanding Jesus' interaction with the various religious and political leaders of his day. We have seen that part of Matthew's presentation of Jesus as judge is to present Jesus in confrontation with the Jewish authorities, sometimes confounding them with the provocative *meshalim* of a teacher of Wisdom, sometimes condemning them with prophetic woes. However, our study of Matthew 21-25 indicates that it is inadequate and inaccurate to claim that Jesus was *exclusively* concerned with the immediate historical concerns of Israel. In fact, the political Jesus that Borg presents us with may be seen as being as much of a failure as the eschatological Jesus of Schweitzer since the warning he proclaimed to Israel, in the face of the disaster he perceived, was largely ignored, and, as we know, Jerusalem suffered devastation in AD 70.

Final Comments and Implications

In Chapter 1 of this book, we raised three issues that required clarification from Matthew's gospel: the *nature* of the judgement which Jesus preached; the *time* of the judgement; and *Jesus' own role* in judgement. As to the nature of Jesus' message of judgement, our studies in Matthew have revealed a portrait of Jesus as one who proclaims judgement for two main reasons. The first is that the religious leaders have not done God's will, even as they observe the regulations of the written (and oral) *Torah* scrupulously. The second is that they have rejected God in the figure of his son whom he has sent to them. Thus we cannot claim that Matthew holds that individuals receive reward or punishment on the basis of spiritual criteria alone. Matthew is also concerned for the social, religious and political situation in the first century and, in his gospel, Jesus is prepared (and authorised) to pronounce social, religious and political judgement on the people and structures which were out of step with God's will. Yet this aspect of judgement cannot be separated from the issue of how one responds to Jesus himself. The two issues are intertwined.

Regarding the timing of judgement, we have concluded that, according to Matthew, Jesus comes to Jerusalem as the one who enacts judgement on the temple. His own actions and words are declarations of the certainty of the devastation about to fall on the Jewish nation. Yet there is also a two-fold element of prediction of future judgement in Matthew's presentation of Jesus' teaching. Jesus predicts the outworking of his acts of judgement on the temple in the imminent future, using expressions of certainty that can leave no doubt regarding his confidence in his authority to make such predictions. Yet he also predicts a universal judgement with certainty regarding its occurrence but with no indication of its timing.

As to Jesus' role in judgement, Matthew clearly portrays Jesus as the one who will sit on the throne of judgement, the location of God himself. He did not only proclaim judgement but also exercised it, thus claiming a position unlike any prophet or sage before him.

Matthew 21-25 presents us with a coherent portrayal of Jesus as one who embodies the roles of both prophet and sage in his judging activity and yet also points to the conclusion (which becomes inescapable by the end of chapter 25) that this Jesus is no ordinary prophet or teacher of Wisdom – he is the judge of Israel and all the nations. If this is what Matthew believes to be the truth regarding Jesus, and if his portrait makes sense in the Jewish context in which Jesus carried out his ministry, and if there are good reasons for believing that Matthew has carefully transmitted traditions regarding Jesus, then it surely follows that we cannot be content to regard Matthew's narrative as simply a striking literary portrayal of Jesus but must consider its significance as a witness to the 'historical Jesus'.

Bibliography

Biblical Texts
Biblia Hebraica Stuttgartensia, Edited by K. Elliger and W. Rudolph, (Stuttgart: Deutsche Bibelgesellschaft, 1990).
Novum Testamentum Graece 27th Edition. Edited by B. Aland, *et al.*, (Stuttgart: Deutsche Bibelgesellschaft, 1994).
Septuaginta, Edited by A. Rahlfs (Stuttgart: Württembergische Bibelanstalt/ Deutsche Bibelgesellschaft, 1935).

Secondary Literature
Agbanou, V. K., *Le Discours Eschatologique de Matthieu 24-25: Tradition et Rédaction* (Paris: J. Gabalda, 1983).
Allen, L. C., *Psalms 101-150* (WBC 21; Waco: Word, 1983).
- 'Some Prophetic Antecedents of Apocalyptic Eschatology and their Hermeneutical Value,' *Ex Auditu* 6 (1990) 15-28.
Allison, D. C., *The End of the Ages has Come* (Edinburgh: T&T Clark, 1985).
- *Jesus of Nazareth: Millenarian Prophet* (Minneapolis: Fortress, 1998).
- 'Matt. 23:39 = Luke 13:35b as a Conditional Prophecy' *JSNT* 18 (1983) 75-84.
- *The New Moses* (Edinburgh: T&T Clark, 1993).
- 'A Plea for Thoroughgoing Eschatology' *JBL* 113/4 (1994) 651-68.
Andersen, F. I., *Job* (TOTC; Leicester: IVP, 1975)
Aune, D. E., 'Oral Tradition and the Aphorisms of Jesus' in H. Wansbrough (ed.) *Jesus and the Oral Gospel Tradition* (JSNTS 64; Sheffield: JSOT Press, 1991) 211-65.
- *Prophecy in early Christianity and the Ancient Mediterranean World* (Grand Rapids: Eerdmans, 1983).
- *Revelation 1-5* (WBC 52A; Dallas: Word, 1997).
- 'The Significance of the Delay of the Parousia for Early Christianity' in G. F. Hawthorne (ed.), *Current Issues in Biblical and Patristic Interpretation* (Grand Rapids: Eerdmans, 1975) 87-109.
Bailey, K. E., 'Informal Controlled Oral Tradition and the Synoptic Gospels' *Themelios* 20.2 (1995) 4-11.
Baird, J. A., *The Justice of God in the Teaching of Jesus* (London: SCM Press, 1963).
Baldwin, J. G., *Daniel* (TOTC; Leicester: IVP, 1978).
Barrett, C. K., 'The House of Prayer and the Den of Thieves' in E. E. Ellis and E. Grässer (eds) *Jesus und Paulus* (Göttingen: Vandenhoeck & Ruprecht, 1975) 13-20.
- *Jesus and the Gospel Tradition* (London: SPCK, 1967).
Bauckham, R. J., 'The Delay of the Parousia' *TynB* 31 (1980), 3-36.
- *The Gospel for All Christians* (Edinburgh: T&T Clark, 1998).
Bauer, D. A., *The Structure of Matthew's Gospel* (Sheffield: Almond, 1988).

Bauer, D. A. and M. A. Powell (eds), *Treasures Old and New* (Atlanta: Scholars Press, 1996).

Bayer, H. F., *Jesus Predictions of Vindication and Resurrection* (WUNT II, 20; Tübingen: Mohr, 1986).

Beale, G. K., *The Book of Revelation* (NIGTC; Grand Rapids: Eerdmans, 1999).

Beare, F. W., *The Gospel according to Matthew* (San Francisco, Harper and Row, 1981).

Beasley-Murray, G. R., *Jesus and the Kingdom of God* (Exeter: Paternoster Press, 1986).

- *Jesus and the Last Days* (Peabody: Hendrickson, 1993).

Beckwith, R. T., *The Old Testament Canon of the New Testament Church* (London: SPCK, 1985).

Betz, O., 'The Dichotomized Servant and the End of Judas Iscariot' *RevQ* (1964) 43-58.

Blenkinsopp, J., *Ezekiel* (IBC; Louisville, Westminster/John Knox Press, 1990).

Block, D. I., *The Book of Ezekiel* (2 vols; NICOT; Grand Rapids: Eerdmans, 1997).

Blomberg, C. L., *The Historical Reliability of the Gospels* (Leicester: IVP, 1987).

- *Interpreting the Parables* (Leicester: Apollos, 1990).

- *Matthew* (NAC 22; Nashville: Broadman, 1992).

Bockmuehl, M., *This Jesus* (Edinburgh: T&T Clark, 1994).

Borg, M. J., 'The Currency of the Term "Zealot"' *Journal of Theological Studies* 22 (1971) 504-12.

- *Conflict, Holiness and Politics in the Teachings of Jesus* (New York: Edwin Mellen Press, 1984).

- 'The Historical Jesus and Christian Preaching' *Christian Century* 102.26 (1985) 764-7.

- 'A Temperate Case for a Non-Eschatological Jesus' *Foundations and Facets Forum* 2.3 (1986) 81-102.

- 'An Orthodoxy Reconsidered: "The End-of-the-World Jesus"' in L. D. Hurst and N. T. Wright (eds), *The Glory of Christ in the New Testament* (Oxford: Clarendon Press, 1987) 207-17.

- *Jesus: A New Vision* (London: SPCK, 1993 [1987]).

- 'Reflections on a Discipline: A North American Perspective' in B. Chilton and C. A. Evans (eds), *Studying the Historical Jesus: Evaluations of the State of Current Research* (Leiden: Brill, 1994) 9-31.

Bornkamm, G., G. Barth and H. J. Held, *Tradition and Interpretation in Matthew* (London: SCM Press, 1963).

Boström, L., *The God of the Sages* CBOTS 29 (Stockholm: Almqvist and Wiksell, 1990).

Boyd, G. A., *Cynic Sage or Son of God?* (Wheaton: Bridgepoint, 1995).

Brown, C., 'The Parousia and Eschatology in the NT' *NIDNTT* 2:901-35.

Brown, R. E., *The Death of the Messiah* (ABRL; New York: Doubleday, 1994).

- *An Introduction to the New Testament* (ABRL; New York: Doubleday, 1997).
Brown, S., 'The Matthean Apocalypse' *JSNT* 4 (1979) 2-27.
Bryan, S., *Jesus and Israel's Traditions of Judgement and Restoration* (SNTSMS 117; Cambridge: Cambridge University Press, 2002).
Bultmann, R., *The History of the Synoptic Tradition* (Oxford: Blackwell, 1968).
- 'Is Exegesis Without Presuppositions Possible?' in S. Ogden (tr and ed) *New Testament and Mythology* (London: SCM Press, 1985) 145-53.
- *Jesus and the Word* (London, 1934).
- *Theology of the New Testament* (2 volumes; London: SCM Press, 1952).
Burnett, F. W., *The Testament of Jesus-Sophia: A Redaction-Critical Study of the Eschatological Discourse in Matthew* (Washington DC: University Press of America, 1979).
Burridge, R. A., *What Are the Gospels? A Comparison with Graeco-Roman Biography* (SNTSMS 70; Cambridge: Cambridge University Press, 1992)
Byrskog, S., *Jesus the Only Teacher* (CB NT 24; Stockholm: Almqvist & Wiksell, 1994).
- *Story as History, History as Story* (WUNT 123; Tübingen: Mohr, 2000).
Caird, G. B., 'Les eschatologies du Nouveau Testament' *RHPR* 49 (1969) 217-27.
- *Jesus and the Jewish Nation* (London: Athlone Press, 1965).
- *The Language and Imagery of the Bible* (London: Duckworth, 1980).
- and L. D. Hurst, *New Testament Theology* (Oxford: Clarendon Press, 1994).
Calvin, J., *Matthew, Mark and Luke, Vols I, II & III* (Grand Rapids: Eerdmans, 1972).
Caragounis, C. C., 'Kingdom of God, Son of Man and Jesus' Self-Understanding' *TynB* 40 (1989) Part I 3-23, Part II 223-238.
- *The Son of Man: Vision and Interpretation* (WUNT I 38; Tübingen: Mohr, 1986).
Carson, D. A., *Matthew* (EBC 8; Grand Rapids: Zondervan, 1984).
- 'Redaction Criticism: On the Legitimacy and Illegitimacy of a Literary Tool' in D. A. Carson and J. D. Woodbridge (eds) *Scripture and Truth* (Leicester: IVP, 1983) 119-42, 376-81.
Carter, W., *Matthew: Storyteller, Interpreter, Evangelist* (Peabody: Hendrickson, 1996).
Carver, E. I., *When Jesus Comes Again* (Phillipsburg: Presbyterian and Reformed Publishing Company, 1979).
Casey, M, *Son of Man: The Interpretation and Influence of Daniel 7* (London: SPCK, 1979).
- 'Where Wright is Wrong: A Critical Review of N. T. Wright's *Jesus and the Victory of God*' *JSNT* 69 (1998) 95-103.
Charette, B., *The Theme of Recompense in Matthew's Gospel* JSNTS 79 (Sheffield: JSOT Press, 1992).
Charlesworth, J. H., *Jesus Within Judaism* (London: SPCK, 1989).
- and C. A. Evans 'Jesus in the Agrapha and Apocryphal Gospels' in Chilton and Evans (eds) *Studying the Historical Jesus: Evaluations of the State of Current Research* (Leiden: Brill, 1994), 479-533.

Childs, B. S., *Introduction to the Old Testament as Scripture* (London: SCM Press, 1979).

Chilton, B. D., '[ὡς] φραγέλλιον ἐκ σχοινίων (John 2:15)' in W. Horbury (ed.) *Templum Amicitiae* (JSNTS 48; Sheffield: JSOT Press, 1991), 330-44.

- 'The Kingdom of God in Recent Discussion' in B. Chilton and C. A. Evans (eds) *Studying the Historical Jesus: Evaluations of the State of Current Research* (Leiden: Brill, 1994) 255-80.

- (ed.) *The Kingdom of God* (IRT 5; London: SPCK, 1984).

- 'Regnum Dei Deus Est' *SJT* 31 (1978) 261-270.

- and C. A. Evans (eds) *Studying the Historical Jesus: Evaluations of the State of Current Research* (Leiden: Brill, 1994).

Clarke, W. K. L., 'The Clouds of Heaven: An Exegetical Study' *Theology* 31 (1935) 63-72, 128-41.

Clines, D. J. A., *Job* (WBC 17; Dallas: Word, 1989).

Collins, J. J., (ed.), *Apocalypse: The Morphology of a Genre* (Semeia 14; Missoula MT: Scholars Press, 1979).

- *The Apocalyptic Imagination* (Grand Rapids: Eerdmans, [1984] 1998).

- *Apocalypticism in the Dead Sea Scrolls* (London: Routledge, 1997).

- *Jewish Wisdom in the Hellenistic Age* (Edinburgh: T&T Clark, 1997).

Cope, O. L., ' "To the Close of the Age": The Role of Apocalyptic Thought in the Gospel of Matthew' in J. Marcus and M. L. Soards (eds), *Apocalyptic in the New Testament: Essays in Honor of J. Louis Martyn* (JSNTS 24; Sheffield: JSOT Press, 1989) 113-24.

Cotterell, P. and M. Turner, *Linguistics and Biblical Interpretation* (London: SPCK, 1989).

Court, J. M., 'Right and Left: The Implications for Matthew 25.31-46' *NTS* 31 (1985) 223-33.

Crenshaw, J. L., *Ecclesiastes* (OTL; Philadelphia: Westminster, 1987).

- (ed.), *Old Testament Wisdom: An Introduction* (Atlanta: John Knox Press, 1981).

- *Theodicy in the Old Testament* (London: SPCK, 1983).

Crossan, J. D., *The Historical Jesus* (Edinburgh: T&T Clark, 1991).

Crown, R. W., *The Non-Literal Use of Eschatological Language in Jewish Apocalyptic and the New Testament*, Unpublished D. Phil. Thesis (Oxford, 1986).

Cullmann, O, *Christ and Time* (London: SCM Press, 1951).

- *The Christology of the New Testament* (London: SCM Press, [1959] 1963).

- 'Parusieverzögerung und Urchristentum: der gegenwärtige Stand der Diskussion' *TLZ* 83 (1958) 1-12.

- *Prayer in the New Testament* (London: SCM Press, 1995).

- *Salvation in History* (London: SCM Press, 1967).

Davies, W. D., *The Setting of the Sermon on the Mount* (Cambridge: Cambridge University Press, 1966).

- and D. C. Allison, *Matthew* (ICC 3 vols; Edinburgh: T&T CLark, 1988-97).

Dawes, G. W. (ed.), *The Historical Jesus Quest: Landmarks in the Search for the Jesus of History* (Louisville: Westminster/John Knox Press, 1999)

Day, J., R. P. Gordon and H. G. M. Williamson, *Wisdom in Ancient Israel* (Cambridge: Cambridge University Press, 1995).

Deutsch, C., *Hidden Wisdom and the Easy Yoke. Wisdom, Torah and Discipleship in Matthew 11.25-30* (Sheffield: JSOT Press, 1987).

- 'Wisdom in Matthew: Transformation of a Symbol' *NovT* 32.1 (1990) 13-47.

Dillard, R. B. and T. Longman, III, *An Introduction to the Old Testament* (Leicester: IVP, 1995).

Dodd, C. H., *According to the Scriptures: The Sub-Structure of New Testament Theology* (Digswell Place: James Nisbet, 1952).

- *The Parables of the Kingdom* (London: James Nisbet, 1936).

Dumbrell, W. J., *The Faith of Israel* (Leicester: Apollos, 1989).

Dunn, J. D. G., *Jesus and the Spirit* (London: SCM Press, 1975).

Eichrodt, W., *Theology of the Old Testament* (OTL; London: SCM Press, 1961).

Elliot, J. H., 'Review of *Conflict, Holiness and Politics in the Teachings of Jesus*' *Catholic Biblical Quarterly* 48 (1986) 736-7.

Erlemann, K., *Naherwartung und Parusieverzögerung im Neuen Testament* (TANZ 17; Tübingen/Basel: Francke, 1995).

Evans, C. A., 'Jesus' Action in the Temple: Cleansing or Portent of Destruction?' *CBQ* 51 (1989) 237-70.

- *Luke* (NIBC; Peabody: Hendrickson, 1990)

- *Noncanonical Writings and New Testament Interpretation* (Peabody: Hendrickson, 1992).

- 'Parables in Early Judaism' in R. N. Longenecker (ed.), *The Challenge of Jesus' Parables* (Grand Rapids: Eerdmans, 2000) 51-75.

Evans, C. S., *The Historical Christ and the Jesus of Faith* (Oxford: Oxford University Press, 1996).

Feuillet, A., 'Le Sens du Mot Parousie dans l'Évangile de Matthieu: Comparison entre Matt xxiv et Jac v, i-ii' in W. D. Davies and D. Daube (eds) *The Background of the New Testament and its Eschatology* (Cambridge: Cambridge University Press, 1956).

Finley, T. J., *Joel, Amos, Obadiah* (Chicago: Moody Press, 1990)

Fitzmyer, J. A., *The Acts of the Apostles* (AB; New York: Doubleday, 1998).

France, R. T., *Divine Government* (London: SPCK, 1990).

- *Jesus and the Old Testament* (London: Tyndale Press, 1971).

- *Matthew* (TNTC 1; Leicester: IVP, 1985).

- *Matthew: Evangelist and Teacher* (Exeter: Paternoster Press, 1989).

- 'On Being Ready (Matthew 25:1-46)' in R. N. Longenecker (ed) *The Challenge of Jesus' Parables* (Grand Rapids: Eerdmans, 2000) 177-95.

Friedrich, J., *Gott im Bruder?* (CTM; Stuttgart: Calwer Verlag, 1977).

Frost, S. B., *Old Testament Apocalyptic* (London, 1952).

Fuller, G. C., 'The Olivet Discourse: An Apocalyptic Timetable' *WTJ* 28 (1966) 157-63.

Gammie, J. G., and L. G. Perdue (eds) *The Sage in Israel and the Ancient Near East* (Winona Lake: Eisenbrauns, 1990).

Garland, D. E., *The Intention of Matthew 23* NovTSup 52 (Leiden: Brill, 1979).

- *Reading Matthew* (London: SPCK, 1993).
Gaston, L., *No Stone on Another: Studies in the Significance of the Fall of Jerusalem in the Synoptic Gospels* (NovTSup 23; Leiden: Brill, 1970).
Geddert, T. J., *Watchwords: Mark 13 in Markan Eschatology* (JSNTS 26; Sheffield: JSOT Press, 1989).
Gempf, C., 'Birth Pains in the New Testament' *TynB* 45 (1994) 119-135.
Gerhardsson, B., *The Gospel Tradition* (Lund: Gleerup, 1986).
- 'Illuminating the Kingdom: Narrative Meshalim in the Synoptic Gospels' in H. Wansbrough (ed.) *Jesus and the Oral Gospel Tradition* (JSNTS 64; Sheffield: JSOT Press, 1991) 266-309.
- *Memory and Manuscript with Tradition and Transmission in Early Christianity* (Grand Rapids/Livonia: Eerdmans/Dove, 1998).
- *The Origins of the Gospel Tradition* (London: SCM Press, 1979).
- *The Shema in the New Testament* (Lund: Novapress, 1996).
Gibbs, J. A., *'Let the Reader Understand': The Eschatological Discourse of Jesus in Matthew's Gospel* (Ann Arbor: UMI, 1987).
Glasson, T. F., 'The Ensign of the Son of Man (Matt. XXIV.30)' *JTS* 15 (1964) 299-300.
- 'Schweitzer's Influence - Blessing or Bane?' *JTS* 28 (1977) 289-302.
- *The Second Advent* (London: Epworth Press, 1945).
- 'What is Apocalyptic?' *NTS* 27 (1980) 98-105.
Goldingay, J., *Daniel* (WBC 30; Waco: Word, 1987).
Granger, J. W., *Matthew's Use of Apocalyptic* (ThD Diss, New Orleans Baptist Theological Seminary, 1990).
Gray, S. W., *The Least of My Brothers: Matthew 25:31-46: A History of Interpretation*, (SBLDS 114; Atlanta: Scholars, 1989).
Green, J. B. and M. Turner, *Jesus of Nazareth: Lord and Christ* (FS for I. H. Marshall; Exeter: Paternoster Press, 1994).
Greenberg, M., *Ezekiel 21-37* (AB; New York: Doubleday, 1997)
Gundry, R. H., *Matthew: A Commentary on his Handbook for a Mixed Church under Persecution* (Grand Rapids: Eerdmans, 1994).
- *The Use of the Old Testament in St Matthew's Gospel* (NovTSup 18; Leiden: Brill, 1967).
Haenchen, E., 'Mätthaus 23', *ZTK* 48 (1951) 38-63.
Hagner, D. A., 'Apocalyptic Motifs in the Gospel of Matthew: Continuity and Discontinuity' *HBT* 7 (1985) 53-82.
- *Matthew 1-13* (WBC 33A; Dallas: Word, 1993).
- *Matthew 14-28* (WBC 33B; Dallas: Word, 1995).
- 'Matthew's Eschatology' in T. E. Schmidt and M. Silva (eds) *To Tell the Mystery: Essays on New Testament Eschatology in Honor of Robert H. Gundry* (JSNTS 100; Sheffield: JSOT Press, 1994) 49-71.
- 'Matthew's Parables of the Kingdom (Matthew 13:1-52)' in R. N. Longenecker (ed.) *The Challenge of Jesus' Parables* (Grand Rapids: Eerdmans, 2000) 102-24.
Hare, D. R. A., *The Son of Man Tradition* (Minneapolis: Fortress, 1990).
Harrington, D. J., *Matthew* (SP1; Collegeville: Liturgical Press, 1991).

- *Wisdom Texts From Qumran* (London: Routledge, 1996).
Harrison, R. K., *Introduction to the Old Testament* (Leicester: IVP, 1969).
- *Jeremiah and Lamentations* (TOTC; Leicester: IVP, 1973).
Hartley, J. E., *Job* (NICOT; Grand Rapids, 1980).
Hatina, T. R., 'The Focus of Mark 13:24-27: The Parousia, or the Destruction of the Temple?' *BBR* 6 (1996) 43-66.
Hay, D. M., *Glory at the Right Hand: Psalm 110 in Early Christianity* (SBLMS 18; Nashville: Abingdon, 1973).
Hengel, M., *The Charismatic Leader and His Followers* (Edinburgh: T&T Clark, 1981).
- *Studies in Early Christology* (Edinburgh: T&T Clark, 1995).
Herzog, W. R., II, *Jesus, Justice and the Reign of God* (Louisville: Westminster/John Knox Press, 2000).
Hiers, R. H., *The Historical Jesus and the Kingdom of God* UFHM 38 (Gainesville: University of Florida Press, 1973).
- *Jesus and the Future* (Atlanta: John Knox Press, 1981).
- *The Kingdom of God in the Synoptic Tradition* UFHM 33 (Gainesville: University of Florida Press, 1970).
Higgins, A. J. B., 'The Sign of the Son of Man (Matt. XXIV.30)' *NTS* 9 (1962-63) 380-82.
Hooker, M. D., 'On Using the Wrong Tool', *Theology* 75 (1972).
- *The Signs of a Prophet* (London, SCM Press, 1997).
- 'Traditions About the Temple in the Sayings of Jesus' *BJRL* 70 (1988) 7-19.
Horsley, R. A., and J. S. Hanson, *Bandits, Prophets and Messiahs: Popular Movements at the Time of Jesus* (Minneapolis: Winston Press, 1985).
House, P. R., *Old Testament Theology* (Downers Grove: IVP, 1998).
Houston, W., 'What Did the Prophets Think They Were Doing?' *Bib Int* 1 (1993) 167-88.
Jeremias, J., *Jerusalem in the Time of Jesus* (London: SCM Press, 1969). J.
- *Jesus' Promise to the Nations* (London: SCM Press, 1959).
- *New Testament Theology* (London: SCM Press, 1971).
Kähler, M., *The So-called Historical Jesus and the Historic Biblical Christ* (Philadelphia: Fortress, 1964).
Käsemann, E., 'The Problem of the Historical Jesus', *ZTK* 51 (1954) 125-53. [Reprinted in *Essays on New Testament Themes* (SBT 41; London: SCM, 1964)].
- 'Sentences of Holy Law in the New Testament' in *New Testament Questions of Today* (London: SCM Press, 1969).
Keener, C., *A Commentary on the Gospel of Matthew* (Grand Rapids: Eerdmans, 1999).
Keown, G., P. J. Scalise, T. G. Smothers, *Jeremiah 26-52* (WBC; Dallas: Word, 1995).
Kidner, D., *Proverbs* (TOTC; Leicester: IVP, 1964).
Kik, J. M., *An Eschatology of Victory* (Phillipsburg: Presbyterian and Reformed Publishing Co, 1971).

Kim, K. K., *The Signs of the Parousia: A Diachronic and Comparative Study of the Apocalyptic Vocabulary of Matthew 24:27-31* (Ann Arbor: UMI, 1997).

Kingsbury, J. D., 'The Rhetoric of Comprehension in the Gospel of Matthew' *NTS* 41 (1995) 358-377.

- *Matthew: Structure, Christology, Kingdom* (Philadelphia: Fortress, 1975).

Knox, J., *The Death of Christ* (London, 1959).

Koch, K., 'Gibt es ein Vergeltungsdogma im AT?' *ZTK* 52 (1955) 1-42.

- *The Rediscovery of Apocalyptic* (London: SCM Press, 1972).

Kreitzer, L. J., *Jesus and God in Paul's Eschatology* (JSNTS 19; Sheffield: JSOT Press, 1987).

Kretzer, A., *Die Herrschaft der Himmel und die Söhne des Reiches* SBM 10 (Würzburg: Echter, 1971).

Kümmel, W. G., 'Eschatological Expectation in the Proclamation of Jesus' in B. D. Chilton (ed.) *The Kingdom of God* (IRT 5; London: SPCK, 1984).

- *Promise and Fulfilment* (SBT 23; London: SCM Press, 1957).

- *The Theology of the New Testament* (London: SCM Press, 1974).

Künzi, M., *Das Naherwartungslogion Matthäus 10,23: Geschichte Seiner Auslegung* BGBE 9 (Tübingen: Mohr, 1970).

Ladd, G. E., *A Theology of the New Testament* (Cambridge: Lutterworth, [1974] 1994).

- *The Presence of the Future* (London: SPCK, 1974).

- 'Why Not Prophetic-Apocalyptic?' *JBL* 76 (1957) 192-200.

Lagrange, M.-J., *Évangile Selon Saint Matthieu* (Paris: J. Gabalda et Cie, 1948).

Lambrecht, J., 'The Parousia Discourse: Composition and Content in Mt. XXIV-XXV', in *L'Évangile selon Matthieu: Redaction et théolgie*, ed. M Didier. BETL 29 (Paris: Gembloux, 1972) 309-42.

Lemcio, E. E., *The Past of Jesus* (SNTSMS 68; Cambridge: Cambridge University Press, 1992).

Lincoln, A. T., *Paradise Now and Not Yet* (Grand Rapids: Baker, 1991 [1981]).

Linnemann, E., *Is There a Synoptic Problem? Rethinking the Literary Dependence of the First Three Gospels* (Baker, 1992).

Longman, T., and D. G. Reid, *God is a Warrior* (SOTBT; Carlisle: Paternoster Press, 1995).

Luz, U., *Das Evangelium nach Matthäus 1-7* (EKK; Zürich: Benziger/ Neukirchen-Vluyn: Neukirchener, 1985).

- *Das Evangelium nach Matthäus 18-25* (EKK; Zürich: Benziger/ Neukirchen-Vluyn: Neukirchener, 1997).

- 'The Final Judgement (Matt 25:31-46): An Exercise in 'History of Influence' Exegesis' in Bauer, D. A. and M. A. Powell (eds), *Treasures Old and New* (Atlanta: Scholars Press, 1996) 271-310.

- 'The Son of Man in Matthew: Heavenly Judge or Human Christ' *JSNT* 48 (1992) 3-21.

- *The Theology of the Gospel of Matthew* (Cambridge: Cambridge University Press, 1995).

Maier, G., *Biblical Hermeneutics* (Wheaton: Crossway, 1994).

Manson, T. W., *The Teaching of Jesus* (Cambridge: Cambridge University Press, 1931).

Mare, W. H., 'A Study of the New Testament Concept of the Parousia' in G. F. Hawthorne (ed.) *Current Issues in Biblical and Patristic Interpretation* (Grand Rapids: Eerdmans, 1975) 336-345.

Marguerat, *Le Jugement dans L'Évangile de Matthieu* (Geneva: Labor et Fides, 1981).

Marsh, C., 'Theological History? N. T. Wright's *Jesus and the Victory of God*' *JSNT* 69 (1998) 77-94.

Marshall, I. H., *I Believe in the Historical Jesus* (London: Hodder, 1977).

- 'The Synoptic 'Son of Man' Sayings in the Light of Linguistic Research' in T. E. Schmidt and M. Silva (eds) *To Tell the Mystery* (JSNTS 100; Sheffield: JSOT Press, 1994) 72-94.

- 'Uncomfortable Words: VI. "Fear him who can destroy both soul and body in hell" (Mt 10.28 RSV).' *ExpT* 81 (1970) 276-80.

Martens, A. W., ' "Produce Fruit Worthy of Repentance": Parables of Judgment against the Jewish Religious Leaders and the Nation (Matt 21:28-22:14, par.; Luke 13:6-9)' in R. Longenecker (ed) *The Challenge of Jesus' Parables* (Grand Rapids: Eerdmans, 2000) 151-76.

McEleney, N. J., 'Authenticating Criteria and Mark 7:1-23' *CBQ* 34 (1972), 431-60

McKane, W., *Proverbs* (OTL; Philadelphia: Westminster, 1970).

McKim, D. K. (ed.), *Historical Handbook of Major Biblical Interpreters* (Leicester: IVP, 1998).

McKnight, E. V., 'Presuppositions in New Testament Study' in J. B. Green (ed.) *Hearing the New Testament* (Grand Rapids: Eerdmans/ Carlisle: Paternoster Press, 1995), 278-300.

McKnight, S., 'Jesus and the Endtime: Matthew 10.23', *SBL Seminar Papers 1986* (Atlanta: Scholars Press, 1986), 501-20.

- 'Jesus and Prophetic Actions' *BBR* 10.2 (2000) 197-232.

Meadors, E. P., *Jesus: the Messianic Herald of Salvation* (Peabody: Hendrickson, [1995] 1997).

Meier, J. P., *A Marginal Jew: Rethinking the Historical Jesus, Volume I* (New York: Doubleday, 1991).

- *A Marginal Jew: Rethinking the Historical Jesus, Volume II* (New York: Doubleday, 1994).

Merkel, H., 'Das Gleichnis von den "ungleichen Söhnen" (Matt XXI.28-32)', *NTS* 20 (1974) 254-61.

Meyer, B. F., *The Aims of Jesus* (London: SCM Press, 1979).

- 'Some Consequences of Birger Gerhardsson's Account of the Origins of the Gospel Tradition' in H. Wansbrough (ed.) *Jesus and the Oral Gospel Tradition* (JSNTS 64; Sheffield: JSOT Press, 1991) 424-40.

- 'Jesus' Ministry and Self-Understanding' in B. Chilton and C. A. Evans (eds) *Studying the Historical Jesus: Evaluations of the State of Current Research* (Leiden: Brill, 1994) 337-52.

Michaels, J. R., 'Apostolic Hardships and Righteous Gentiles' *JBL* 34 (1965) 30-37.

Michel, O., 'The Conclusion of Matthew's Gospel' in G. N. Stanton (ed.) *The Interpretation of Matthew* (Edinburgh: T&T Clark, [1983] 1995) 39-51.

Milik, J. T., *The Books of Enoch: Aramaic Fragments from Qumran Cave 4* (Oxford: Clarendon, 1976).

Milikowski, C., 'Which Gehenna? Retribution and Eschatology in the Synoptic Gospels and in Early Jewish Texts' *NTS* 34 (1988) 238-49.

Moore, A. L., *The Parousia in the New Testament* (NovTSup XIII; Leiden: Brill, 1966).

Moore, G. F., *Judaism in the First Centuries of the Christian Era: The Age of the Tannaim* (3 volumes in 2; Peabody: Hendrickson, 1997 [1927, 1930]).

Moore, S. D., *Literary Criticism and the Gospels* (New Haven: Yale, 1989).

Morris, L. L., *Apocalyptic* (London: IVP, 1972).

- *The Biblical Doctrine of Judgment* (London: Tyndale Press, 1960).

- *The Gospel According to Matthew* (Leicester: IVP, 1992).

Moule, C. F. D., 'The Function of the Synoptic Gospels' in E. Grässer and O. Merk (eds), *Glaube und Eschatologie: Festschrift für Werner Georg Kümmel zum 80 Geburtstag* (Tübingen: JCB Mohr, 1985) 199-208. Reprinted with minor additions to notes in C. F. D. Moule, *Forgiveness and Reconciliation* (London: SPCK, 1998) 179-89.

- *The Origin of Christology* (Cambridge: Cambridge University Press, 1977).

- ''The Son of Man': Some of the Facts' *NTS* 41 (1995) 277-279.

Mowinckel, S, *He That Cometh* (Oxford: Basil Blackwell, 1956).

Murphy, R., *Ecclesiastes* (WBC; Waco: Word, 1992).

- *Wisdom Literature* (FOTL 13; Grand Rapids: Eerdmans, 1981).

Neale, D. A., *None But the Sinners* (JSNTS 58; Sheffield: JSOT Press, 1991).

Neill, S. and Wright, N. T., *The Interpretation of the New Testament 1861-1986* (Oxford: Oxford University Press, 1988).

Newman, C. C. (ed.), *Jesus and the Restoration of Israel* (Downers Grove: IVPUSA, 1999).

Newport, K. G. C., *The Sources and Sitz im Leben of Matthew 23* (JSNTS 117; Sheffield: Sheffield Academic Press, 1995).

O'Connor, K. M., *The Wisdom Literature* (MBS 5; Collegeville: Liturgical Press, 1988).

Olmstead, W. G., *Matthew's Trilogy of Parables* (SNTSMS 127; Cambridge: Cambridge University Press, 2003).

Ortlund, R. C., Jr., *Whoredom* (NSBT 2; Leicester: IVP, 1996).

Orton, D. E., *The Understanding Scribe* (JSNTS 25; Sheffield: JSOT Press, 1989).

Overholt, T. W., 'Seeing is Believing: The Social Setting of Prophetic Acts of Power' *JSOT* 23 (1982) 3-31.

Pate, C. M., *Communities of the Last Days* (Leicester: Apollos, 2000).

Perrin, N., *The Kingdom of God in the Teaching of Jesus* (London: SCM Press, 1963).

Plevnik, J., *Paul and the Parousia: An Exegetical and Theological Investigation* (Peabody: Hendrickson, 1997).

Porter, S. E., *The Criteria for Authenticity in Historical-Jesus Research* (JSNTS 191; Sheffield: Sheffield Academic Press, 2000).

- *Idioms of the Greek New Testament* (BLG 2; Sheffield: Sheffield Academic Press, 1992).

Powell, M. A., *The Jesus Debate* (Oxford: Lion, 1998).

- and D. R. Bauer (eds) *Who Do You Say That I Am?* (FS for J. D. Kingsbury; Louisville: Westminster/John Knox Press, 1999).

Pregeant, R., 'The Wisdom Passages in Matthew's Story' in Bauer, D. A. and M. A. Powell (eds), *Treasures Old and New* (Atlanta: Scholars Press, 1996), 197-232.

Reddish, M., *Apocalyptic Literature: A Reader* (Peabody: Hendrickson, 1993).

Redditt, P. L., *Haggai, Zechariah, Malachi* (NCBC; Grand Rapids: Eerdmans, 1995).

Reiser, M., *Jesus and Judgment* (Minneapolis: Fortress, 1997). German edition: *Die Gerichtspredigt Jesu: Eine Untersuchung zur eschatologischen Verkündigung Jesu und ihren frühjüdischen Hintergrund* (NANF 23; Münster: Aschendorff, 1990).

Riches, J., *A Century of New Testament Study* (Cambridge: Lutterworth, 1993).

- *Matthew* (NTG; Sheffield: JSOT Press, 1996).

Ridderbos, H. N, *The Coming of the Kingdom* (Phillipsburg: Presbyterian and Reformed Publishing Co., 1962).

Riesner, R., *Jesus als Lehrer* (WUNT II, 7; Tübingen: Mohr, 1981).

- 'Jesus as Preacher and Teacher' in H. Wansbrough (ed.) *Jesus and the Oral Gospel Tradition* (JSNTS 64; Sheffield: JSOT Press, 1991) 185-210.

Robinson, J. A. T., *Jesus and His Coming: The Emergence of a Doctrine* (London, 1957).

Ross, A. P., *Proverbs* (EBC 5; Grand Rapids: Zondervan, 1991).

Rowland, C., *Christian Origins* (London: SPCK, 1985).

- *The Open Heaven* (London: SPCK, 1982).

Russell, D. S., *The Method and Message of Jewish Apocalyptic* (London: SCM Press, 1964).

Sabourin, L., 'Traits apocalyptiques dans l'Évangile de Matthieu', *Science et Esprit* 33 (1981) 357-72. (Translation in *RelStBul* 3 (1983) 19-36.)

Sand, A., 'Zur Frage nach dem "Sitz im Leben" der Apokalyptischen Texte des Neuen Testaments' *NTS* 18 (1972) 167-177.

Saldarini, 'Comparing the Traditions: New Testament and Rabbinic Literature' *BBR* 7 (1997) 195-204.

Sanders, E. P., *Jesus and Judaism* (London: SCM Press, 1985).

- *Judaism: Practice and Belief 63BCE-66CE* (London: SCM Press, 1992).

- *Paul and Palestinian Judaism* (London: SCM Press, 1977)

Sanders, J. A., 'A New Testament Hermeneutic Fabric: Psalm 118 in the Entrance Narrative,' in C. A. Evans and W. F. Stinespring (eds) *Early Jewish and Christian Exegesis: Studies in Memory of William Hugh Brownlee* (Atlanta: Scholars Press, 1987) 177-90.

Sandy, D. B., *Plowshares and Pruning Hooks: Rethinking the Language of Biblical Prophecy and Apocalyptic* (Leicester: IVP, 2002).

Schiffman, L. H., *The Eschatological Community of the Dead Sea Scrolls* SBLMS (Atlanta: Scholars Press, 1989).

Schlatter, 'Die Bedeutung der Method für die theologische Arbeit,' *Theologischer Literaturbericht* 31 (1908) 5-8. ET by R. W. Yarbrough: 'Adolf Schlatter's "The Significance of Method for Theological Work": Translation and Commentary,' *SBJT* 1.2 (1997) 64-76.

Schürmann, H., 'Die vorösterliche Anfage der Logientradition,' in *Der historische Jesus und der kerygmatische Christus* , H. Ristow and K. Matthiae (eds) (Berlin: Evangelische Verlaganstalt, 1960) 342-70.

Schweitzer, A., *The Quest of the Historical Jesus* (London: A&C Black, ³1954). German original: *Vom Reimarus zu Wrede* (1906).

Schweizer, E., *The Good News according to Matthew* (London: SPCK, 1975).

- *Jesus* (London: SCM, 1971).

Scobie, C. H. H., 'Israel and the Nations: An Essay in Biblical Theology' *TynB* 43 (1992) 283-305.

Scott, B. B., 'The Gospel of Matthew: A Sapiential Performance of an Apocalyptic Discourse' in L. G. Perdue, B. B. Scott and W. J. Wiseman (eds) *In Search of Wisdom* (Louisville: Westminster/John Knox Press, 1993).

Scott, R. B. Y., *Proverbs, Ecclesiastes* (AB 18; New York: Doubleday, 1965).

Selman, M. J., 'The Kingdom of God in the Old Testament' *TynB* 40 (1989) 161-183.

Sim, D. C., *Apocalyptic Eschatology in the Gospel of Matthew* (SNTSMS 88; Cambridge: Cambridge University Press, 1996).

- 'The Meaning of παλιγγενεσία in Matthew 19:28' *JSNT* 50 (1993) 3-12.

Slater, T. B., 'One Like a Son of Man in First-Century CE Judaism' *NTS 41* (1995) 183-198.

Smith, R., *Micah-Malachi* (WBC; Waco: Word, 1984).

Snodgrass, K. R., 'Recent Research on the Parable of the Wicked Tenants: An Assessment' *BBR* 8 (1998) 187-216.

Stacey, W. D., *Prophetic Drama in the Old Testament* (London: Epworth Press, 1990).

Stadelmann, H., *Ben Sira als Schriftgelehrter* (WUNT 6; Tübingen: JCB Mohr, 1980).

Stanton, G. N., *A Gospel for a New People* (Edinburgh: T&T Clark, 1992).

- *The Interpretation of Matthew* (Edinburgh: T&T Clark, [1983] 1995).

Stauffer, E., *New Testament Theology* (London: SCM Press, 1955).

Stein, R. H., 'The "Criteria" for Authenticity,' in R. T. France and D. Wenham (eds) *Gospel Perspectives: Studies in History and Tradition in the Four Gospels* 1 (Sheffield: JSOT Press, 1980), reprinted in *idem, Gospels and Tradition* (Grand Rapids: Baker, 1991) 153-87.

- 'An Early Recension of the Gospel Traditions?', *JETS* 30 (1987).

- 'The Genre of the Parables' in R. N. Longenecker (ed.) *The Challenge of Jesus' Parables* (Grand Rapids: Eerdmans, 2000) 30-50.

- *Jesus the Messiah* (Leicester: IVP, 1996).

Stone, M. E., *Fourth Ezra* (Philadelphia: Fortress, 1990).

Stott, J. R. W., *The Message of Acts* (Leicester: IVP, 1990).

Strecker, G., *The Sermon on the Mount* (Nashville: Abingdon Press, 1988).

Stuart, D., *Hosea-Jonah* (WBC; Waco: Word, 1987)

Stuhlmacher, P., *Jesus of Nazareth - Christ of Faith* (Peabody: Hendrickson, 1993).

Suggs, M. J., *Wisdom, Christology and Law in Matthew's Gospel* (Cambridge MA, Harvard University Press, 1970).

Talbert, C. H., 'The Myth of a Descending-Ascending Redeemer in Mediterranean Antiquity' *NTS 22* (1976) 418-40.

Tasker, R. V. G., *The Gospel according to St. Matthew* (TNTC; London: Tyndale Press, 1961).

Telford, W., *The Barren Temple and the Withered Tree* (JSNTS 1; Sheffield: JSOT Press, 1980).

Theissen, G. and A. Merz, *The Historical Jesus* (London: SCM Press, 1998).

Thompson, J. A., *The Book of Jeremiah* (NICOT; Grand Rapids: Eerdmans, 1980).

Travis, S. H., *Christ and the Judgment of God* (Basingstoke: Marshall, Pickering, 1986).

- *Christian Hope and the Future of Man* (Leicester: IVP, 1980).

- 'The Value of Apocalyptic' *TynB* 30 (1979).

Trilling, W., *The Gospel according to St. Matthew* (London: Burns and Oates, 1969).

Tully, M., *Lives of Jesus* (London: BBC Books, 1996).

Twelftree, G., *Jesus the Miracle Worker* (Downers Grove: IVP, 1999).

Vandakumpadar, S., *The Parousia Discourse Mt 24-25: Tradition and Redaction* (PhD Diss, Pontifical Biblical Institute, 1976).

VanGemeren, W. A., *Interpreting the Prophetic Word* (Grand Rapids: Zondervan, 1990).

Vanhoozer, 'The Reader in New Testament Interpretation' in J. B. Green (ed.) *Hearing the New Testament* (Grand Rapids: Eerdmans/ Carlisle: Paternoster Press, 1995), 301-28.

Vermes, G., *Jesus the Jew* (London: SCM Press, 1974).

- 'The Use of *bar nash/bar nasha* in Jewish Aramaic' in M. Black, *An Aramaic Approach to the Gospels and Acts* (3rd edition; Oxford: Clarendon, 1967) 310-28.

Volz, P., *Die Eschatologie der jüdischen Gemeinde* (2nd edition; Tübingen: Mohr [Siebeck], 1934)

Wallace, D. B., *Greek Grammar Beyond the Basics* (Grand Rapids: Zondervan, 1996).

Watson, F., *Text and Truth: Redefining Biblical Theology* (Edinburgh: T&T Clark, 1997).

Watts, J. D. W., *Isaiah 1-33* (WBC; Waco: Word, 1985).

Watty, W. W., 'Jesus and the Temple – Cleansing or Cursing?' *ExpT* 93 (1981-82) 235-39.

Webb, R. L., *John the Baptizer and Prophet* (JSNTS 62; Sheffield: Sheffield Academic Press, 1991).

Weber, K., *The Events of the End of the Age in Matthew* (Ann Arbor: UMI, 1997)

Weiss, J., *Jesus' Proclamation of the Kingdom of God* Translated and Edited with an Introduction by R. H. Hiers and D. L. Holland (London: SCM Press, 1971). German original: *Die Predigt Jesu vom Reiche Gottes* (Göttingen: Vandenhoeck & Ruprecht, 1892).

Wenham, D., *The Rediscovery of Jesus' Eschatological Discourse* GP 4 (Sheffield: JSOT Press, 1984).

- ' "This Generation Will Not Pass...": A Study of Jesus' Future Expectation in Mark 13' in H. H. Rowdon (ed.) *Christ the Lord* FS for Donald Guthrie (Leicester: IVP, 1982) 127-50.

Wenham, J. W., *Christ and the Bible* (Downers Grove: IVP, 1973).

Whybray, R. N., *Ecclesiastes*, (NCBC; Grand Rapids: Eerdmans, 1989).

Wilder, A. N., *Eschatology and Ethics in the Teaching of Jesus* (2nd edition; Westport: Greenwood Press, 1950).

- 'Eschatological Imagery and Earthly Circumstances' *NTS* 5 (1959) 229-45.

Willett, T. W., *Eschatology in the Theodicies of 2 Baruch and 4 Ezra* (Sheffield: JSOT Press, 1989).

Witherington, B., *The Christology of Jesus* (Minneapolis: Fortress, 1990).

- *The Jesus Quest* (Carlisle: Paternoster Press, 1995).

- *Jesus, Paul and the End of the World* (Exeter: Paternoster Press, 1992).

- *Jesus the Sage* (Edinburgh: T&T Clark, 1994).

- *Jesus the Seer* (Peabody: Hendrickson, 1999).

Wood H. G., 'Interpreting This Time' *NTS* 2 (1956) 262-6.

Wright, N. T., *Jesus and the Victory of God* (London: SPCK, 1996).

- *The New Testament and the People of God* (London: SPCK, 1992).

- 'Theology, History and Jesus: A response to Maurice Casey and Clive Marsh' *JSNT* 69 (1998) 105-112.

- *Who Was Jesus?* (London: SPCK, 1992).

Zager, W., *Gottesherrschaft und Endgericht in der Verkündigung Jesu* (BZNW 82; Berlin: de Gruyter, 1996).

Zuck, R. B., *Sitting with Job: Selected Studies on the Book of Job* (Grand Rapids: Baker, 1992).

Index of Authors

Paternoster Biblical Monographs

(All titles uniform with this volume)
Dates in bold are of projected publication

Joseph Abraham
Eve: Accused or Acquitted?
A Reconsideration of Feminist Readings of the Creation Narrative Texts in Genesis 1–3
Two contrary views dominate contemporary feminist biblical scholarship. One finds in the Bible an unequivocal equality between the sexes from the very creation of humanity, whilst the other sees the biblical text as irredeemably patriarchal and androcentric. Dr Abraham enters into dialogue with both camps as well as introducing his own method of approach. An invaluable tool for any one who is interested in this contemporary debate.
2002 / 0-85364-971-5 / xxiv + 272pp

Octavian D. Baban
Mimesis and Luke's on the Road Encounters in Luke-Acts
Luke's Theology of the Way and its Literary Representation
The book argues on theological and literary (mimetic) grounds that Luke's on-the-road encounters, especially those belonging to the post-Easter period, are part of his complex theology of the Way. Jesus' teaching and that of the apostles is presented by Luke as a challenging answer to the Hellenistic reader's thirst for adventure, good literature, and existential paradigms.
2005 */ 1-84227-253-5 / approx. 374pp*

Paul Barker
The Triumph of Grace in Deuteronomy
This book is a textual and theological analysis of the interaction between the sin and faithlessness of Israel and the grace of Yahweh in response, looking especially at Deuteronomy chapters 1–3, 8–10 and 29–30. The author argues that the grace of Yahweh is determinative for the ongoing relationship between Yahweh and Israel and that Deuteronomy anticipates and fully expects Israel to be faithless.
2004 / 1-84227-226-8 / xxii + 270pp

Jonathan F. Bayes
The Weakness of the Law
God's Law and the Christian in New Testament Perspective
A study of the four New Testament books which refer to the law as weak (Acts, Romans, Galatians, Hebrews) leads to a defence of the third use in the Reformed debate about the law in the life of the believer.
2000 / 0-85364-957-X / xii + 244pp

Mark Bonnington
**The Antioch Episode of Galatians 2:11-14 in Historical and Cultural
Context**
The Galatians 2 'incident' in Antioch over table-fellowship suggests significant
disagreement between the leading apostles. This book analyses the background
to the disagreement by locating the incident within the dynamics of social
interaction between Jews and Gentiles. It proposes a new way of understanding
the relationship between the individuals and issues involved.
2005 / 1-84227-050-8 / approx. 350pp

David Bostock
A Portrayal of Trust
The Theme of Faith in the Hezekiah Narratives
This study provides detailed and sensitive readings of the Hezekiah narratives (2
Kings 18–20 and Isaiah 36–39) from a theological perspective. It concentrates
on the theme of faith, using narrative criticism as its methodology. Attention is
paid especially to setting, plot, point of view and characterization within the
narratives. A largely positive portrayal of Hezekiah emerges that underlines the
importance and relevance of scripture.
2005 / 1-84227-314-0 / approx. 300pp

Mark Bredin
Jesus, Revolutionary of Peace
A Non-violent Christology in the Book of Revelation
This book aims to demonstrate that the figure of Jesus in the Book of Revelation
can best be understood as an active non-violent revolutionary.
2003 / 1-84227-153-9 / xviii + 262pp

Robinson Butarbutar
Paul and Conflict Resolution
An Exegetical Study of Paul's Apostolic Paradigm in 1 Corinthians 9
The author sees the apostolic paradigm in 1 Corinthians 9 as part of Paul's
unified arguments in 1 Corinthians 8–10 in which he seeks to mediate in the
dispute over the issue of food offered to idols. The book also sees its relevance
for dispute-resolution today, taking the conflict within the author's church as an
example.
2006 / 1-84227-315-9 / approx. 280pp

Daniel J-S Chae
Paul as Apostle to the Gentiles
His Apostolic Self-awareness and its Influence on the Soteriological Argument
in Romans
Opposing 'the post-Holocaust interpretation of Romans', Daniel Chae competently demonstrates that Paul argues for the equality of Jew and Gentile in Romans. Chae's fresh exegetical interpretation is academically outstanding and spiritually encouraging.
1997 / 0-85364-829-8 / xiv + 378pp

Luke L. Cheung
The Genre, Composition and Hermeneutics of the Epistle of James
The present work examines the employment of the wisdom genre with a certain compositional structure and the interpretation of the law through the Jesus tradition of the double love command by the author of the Epistle of James to serve his purpose in promoting perfection and warning against doubleness among the eschatologically renewed people of God in the Diaspora.
2003 / 1-84227-062-1 / xvi + 372pp

Youngmo Cho
Spirit and Kingdom in the Writings of Luke and Paul
The relationship between Spirit and Kingdom is a relatively unexplored area in Lukan and Pauline studies. This book offers a fresh perspective of two biblical writers on the subject. It explores the difference between Luke's and Paul's understanding of the Spirit by examining the specific question of the relationship of the concept of the Spirit to the concept of the Kingdom of God in each writer.
2005 / 1-84227-316-7 / approx. 270pp

Andrew C. Clark
Parallel Lives
The Relation of Paul to the Apostles in the Lucan Perspective
This study of the Peter-Paul parallels in Acts argues that their purpose was to emphasize the themes of continuity in salvation history and the unity of the Jewish and Gentile missions. New light is shed on Luke's literary techniques, partly through a comparison with Plutarch.
2001 / 1-84227-035-4 / xviii + 386pp

Andrew D. Clarke
Secular and Christian Leadership in Corinth
A Socio-Historical and Exegetical Study of 1 Corinthians 1–6
This volume is an investigation into the leadership structures and dynamics of first-century Roman Corinth. These are compared with the practice of leadership in the Corinthian Christian community which are reflected in 1 Corinthians 1–6, and contrasted with Paul's own principles of Christian leadership.
2005 / 1-84227-229-2 / 200pp

Stephen Finamore
God, Order and Chaos
René Girard and the Apocalypse
Readers are often disturbed by the images of destruction in the book of Revelation and unsure why they are unleashed after the exaltation of Jesus. This book examines past approaches to these texts and uses René Girard's theories to revive some old ideas and propose some new ones.
2005 / 1-84227-197-0 / approx. 344pp

David G. Firth
Surrendering Retribution in the Psalms
Responses to Violence in the Individual Complaints
In *Surrendering Retribution in the Psalms*, David Firth examines the ways in which the book of Psalms inculcates a model response to violence through the repetition of standard patterns of prayer. Rather than seeking justification for retributive violence, Psalms encourages not only a surrender of the right of retribution to Yahweh, but also sets limits on the retribution that can be sought in imprecations. Arising initially from the author's experience in South Africa, the possibilities of this model to a particular context of violence is then briefly explored.
2005 / 1-84227-337-X / xviii + 154pp

Scott J. Hafemann
Suffering and Ministry in the Spirit
Paul's Defence of His Ministry in II Corinthians 2:14–3:3
Shedding new light on the way Paul defended his apostleship, the author offers a careful, detailed study of 2 Corinthians 2:14–3:3 linked with other key passages throughout 1 and 2 Corinthians. Demonstrating the unity and coherence of Paul's argument in this passage, the author shows that Paul's suffering served as the vehicle for revealing God's power and glory through the Spirit.
2000 / 0-85364-967-7 / xiv + 262pp

Scott J. Hafemann
Paul, Moses and the History of Israel
The Letter/Spirit Contrast and the Argument from Scripture in 2 Corinthians 3
An exegetical study of the call of Moses, the second giving of the Law (Exodus 32–34), the new covenant, and the prophetic understanding of the history of Israel in 2 Corinthians 3. Hafemann's work demonstrates Paul's contextual use of the Old Testament and the essential unity between the Law and the Gospel within the context of the distinctive ministries of Moses and Paul.
2005 / 1-84227-317-5 / xii + 498pp

Douglas S. McComiskey
Lukan Theology in the Light of the Gospel's Literary Structure
Luke's Gospel was purposefully written with theology embedded in its patterned literary structure. A critical analysis of this cyclical structure provides new windows into Luke's interpretation of the individual pericopes comprising the Gospel and illuminates several of his theological interests.
2004 / 1-84227-148-2 / xviii + 388pp

Stephen Motyer
Your Father the Devil?
A New Approach to John and 'The Jews'
Who are 'the Jews' in John's Gospel? Defending John against the charge of antisemitism, Motyer argues that, far from demonising the Jews, the Gospel seeks to present Jesus as 'Good News for Jews' in a late first century setting.
1997 / 0-85364-832-8 / xiv + 260pp

Esther Ng
Reconstructing Christian Origins?
The Feminist Theology of Elizabeth Schüssler Fiorenza: An Evaluation
In a detailed evaluation, the author challenges Elizabeth Schüssler Fiorenza's reconstruction of early Christian origins and her underlying presuppositions. The author also presents her own views on women's roles both then and now.
2002 / 1-84227-055-9 / xxiv + 468pp

Robin Parry
Old Testament Story and Christian Ethics
The Rape of Dinah as a Case Study
What is the role of story in ethics and, more particularly, what is the role of Old Testament story in Christian ethics? This book, drawing on the work of contemporary philosophers, argues that narrative is crucial in the ethical shaping of people and, drawing on the work of contemporary Old Testament scholars, that story plays a key role in Old Testament ethics. Parry then argues that when situated in canonical context Old Testament stories can be reappropriated by Christian readers in their own ethical formation. The shocking story of the rape of Dinah and the massacre of the Shechemites provides a fascinating case study for exploring the parameters within which Christian ethical appropriations of Old Testament stories can live.
2004 / 1-84227-210-1 / xx + 350pp

Ian Paul
Power to See the World Anew
The Value of Paul Ricoeur's Hermeneutic of Metaphor in Interpreting the Symbolism of Revelation 12 and 13
This book is a study of the hermeneutics of metaphor of Paul Ricoeur, one of the most important writers on hermeneutics and metaphor of the last century. It sets out the key points of his theory, important criticisms of his work, and how his approach, modified in the light of these criticisms, offers a methodological framework for reading apocalyptic texts.
2006 / 1-84227-056-7 / approx. 350pp

Robert L. Plummer
Paul's Understanding of the Church's Mission
Did the Apostle Paul Expect the Early Christian Communities to Evangelize?
This book engages in a careful study of Paul's letters to determine if the apostle expected the communities to which he wrote to engage in missionary activity. It helpfully summarizes the discussion on this debated issue, judiciously handling contested texts, and provides a way forward in addressing this critical question. While admitting that Paul rarely explicitly commands the communities he founded to evangelize, Plummer amasses significant incidental data to provide a convincing case that Paul did indeed expect his churches to engage in mission activity. Throughout the study, Plummer progressively builds a theological basis for the church's mission that is both distinctively Pauline and compelling.
2006 / 1-84227-333-7 / approx. 324pp

David Powys
'Hell': A Hard Look at a Hard Question
The Fate of the Unrighteous in New Testament Thought
This comprehensive treatment seeks to unlock the original meaning of terms and phrases long thought to support the traditional doctrine of hell. It concludes that there is an alternative—one which is more biblical, and which can positively revive the rationale for Christian mission.
1997 / 0-85364-831-X / xxii + 478pp

Sorin Sabou
Between Horror and Hope
Paul's Metaphorical Language of Death in Romans 6.1-11
This book argues that Paul's metaphorical language of death in Romans 6.1-11 conveys two aspects: horror and hope. The 'horror' aspect is conveyed by the 'crucifixion' language, and the 'hope' aspect by 'burial' language. The life of the Christian believer is understood, as relationship with sin is concerned ('death to sin'), between these two realities: horror and hope.
2005 / 1-84227-322-1 / approx. 224pp

Rosalind Selby
The Comical Doctrine
The Epistemology of New Testament Hermeneutics
This book argues that the gospel breaks through postmodernity's critique of truth and the referential possibilities of textuality with its gift of grace. With a rigorous, philosophical challenge to modernist and postmodernist assumptions, Selby offers an alternative epistemology to all who would still read with faith *and* with academic credibility.
2005 / 1-84227-212-8 / approx. 350pp

Kiwoong Son
Zion Symbolism in Hebrews
Hebrews 12.18-24 as a Hermeneutical Key to the Epistle
This book challenges the general tendency of understanding the Epistle to the Hebrews against a Hellenistic background and suggests that the Epistle should be understood in the light of the Jewish apocalyptic tradition. The author especially argues for the importance of the theological symbolism of Sinai and Zion (Heb. 12:18-24) as it provides the Epistle's theological background as well as the rhetorical basis of the superiority motif of Jesus throughout the Epistle.
2005 / 1-84227-368-X / approx. 280pp

Kevin Walton
Thou Traveller Unknown
The Presence and Absence of God in the Jacob Narrative
The author offers a fresh reading of the story of Jacob in the book of Genesis through the paradox of divine presence and absence. The work also seeks to make a contribution to Pentateuchal studies by bringing together a close reading of the final text with historical critical insights, doing justice to the text's historical depth, final form and canonical status.
2003 / 1-84227-059-1 / xvi + 238pp

George M. Wieland
The Significance of Salvation
A Study of Salvation Language in the Pastoral Epistles
The language and ideas of salvation pervade the three Pastoral Epistles. This study offers a close examination of their soteriological statements. In all three letters the idea of salvation is found to play a vital paraenetic role, but each also exhibits distinctive soteriological emphases. The results challenge common assumptions about the Pastoral Epistles as a corpus.
2005 / 1-84227-257-8 / approx. 324pp

Alistair Wilson
When Will These Things Happen?
A Study of Jesus as Judge in Matthew 21–25
This study seeks to allow Matthew's carefully constructed presentation of Jesus to be given full weight in the modern evaluation of Jesus' eschatology. Careful analysis of the text of Matthew 21–25 reveals Jesus to be standing firmly in the Jewish prophetic and wisdom traditions as he proclaims and enacts imminent judgement on the Jewish authorities then boldly claims the central role in the final and universal judgement.
2004 / 1-84227-146-6 / xxii + 272pp

Lindsay Wilson
Joseph Wise and Otherwise
The Intersection of Covenant and Wisdom in Genesis 37–50
This book offers a careful literary reading of Genesis 37–50 that argues that the Joseph story contains both strong covenant themes and many wisdom-like elements. The connections between the two helps to explore how covenant and wisdom might intersect in an integrated biblical theology.
2004 / 1-84227-140-7 / xvi + 340pp

Stephen I. Wright
The Voice of Jesus
Studies in the Interpretation of Six Gospel Parables
This literary study considers how the 'voice' of Jesus has been heard in different
periods of parable interpretation, and how the categories of figure and trope may
help us towards a sensitive reading of the parables today.
2000 / 0-85364-975-8 / xiv + 280pp

Paternoster
9 Holdom Avenue,
Bletchley,
Milton Keynes MK1 1QR,
United Kingdom
Web: www.authenticmedia.co.uk/paternoster

July 2005

Paternoster Theological Monographs
(All titles uniform with this volume)
Dates in bold are of projected publication

Emil Bartos
Deification in Eastern Orthodox Theology
An Evaluation and Critique of the Theology of Dumitru Staniloae
Bartos studies a fundamental yet neglected aspect of Orthodox theology:
deification. By examining the doctrines of anthropology, christology, soteriology and ecclesiology as they relate to deification, he provides an important
contribution to contemporary dialogue between Eastern and Western
theologians.
1999 / 0-85364-956-1 / xii + 370pp

Graham Buxton
The Trinity, Creation and Pastoral Ministry
Imaging the Perichoretic God
In this book the author proposes a three-way conversation between theology,
science and pastoral ministry. His approach draws on a Trinitarian
understanding of God as a relational being of love, whose life 'spills over' into
all created reality, human and non-human. By locating human meaning and
purpose within God's 'creation-community' this book offers the possibility of a
transforming engagement between those in pastoral ministry and the scientific
community.
2005 */ 1-84227-369-8 / approx. 380 pp*

Iain D. Campbell
Fixing the Indemnity
The Life and Work of George Adam Smith
When Old Testament scholar George Adam Smith (1856–1942) delivered the
Lyman Beecher lectures at Yale University in 1899, he confidently declared that
'modern criticism has won its war against traditional theories. It only remains to
fix the amount of the indemnity.' In this biography, Iain D. Campbell assesses
Smith's critical approach to the Old Testament and evaluates its consequences,
showing that Smith's life and work still raises questions about the relationship
between biblical scholarship and evangelical faith.
2004 / 1-84227-228-4 / xx + 256pp

Tim Chester
Mission and the Coming of God
Eschatology, the Trinity and Mission in the Theology of Jürgen Moltmann
This book explores the theology and missiology of the influential contemporary theologian, Jürgen Moltmann. It highlights the important contribution Moltmann has made while offering a critique of his thought from an evangelical perspective. In so doing, it touches on pertinent issues for evangelical missiology. The conclusion takes Calvin as a starting point, proposing 'an eschatology of the cross' which offers a critique of the over-realised eschatologies in liberation theology and certain forms of evangelicalism.
2006 / 1-84227-320-5 / approx. 224pp

Sylvia Wilkey Collinson
Making Disciples
The Significance of Jesus' Educational Strategy for Today's Church
This study examines the biblical practice of discipling, formulates a definition, and makes comparisons with modern models of education. A recommendation is made for greater attention to its practice today.
2004 / 1-84227-116-4 / xiv + 278pp

Darrell Cosden
A Theology of Work
Work and the New Creation
Through dialogue with Moltmann, Pope John Paul II and others, this book develops a genitive 'theology of work', presenting a theological definition of work and a model for a theological ethics of work that shows work's nature, value and meaning now and eschatologically. Work is shown to be a transformative activity consisting of three dynamically inter-related dimensions: the instrumental, relational and ontological.
2005 / 1-84227-332-9 / xvi + 208pp

Stephen M. Dunning
The Crisis and the Quest
A Kierkegaardian Reading of Charles Williams
Employing Kierkegaardian categories and analysis, this study investigates both the central crisis in Charles Williams's authorship between hermetism and Christianity (Kierkegaard's Religions A and B), and the quest to resolve this crisis, a quest that ultimately presses the bounds of orthodoxy.
2000 / 0-85364-985-5 / xxiv + 254pp

Keith Ferdinando
The Triumph of Christ in African Perspective
A Study of Demonology and Redemption in the African Context
The book explores the implications of the gospel for traditional African fears of occult aggression. It analyses such traditional approaches to suffering and biblical responses to fears of demonic evil, concluding with an evaluation of African beliefs from the perspective of the gospel.
1999 / 0-85364-830-1 / xviii + 450pp

Andrew Goddard
Living the Word, Resisting the World
The Life and Thought of Jacques Ellul
This work offers a definitive study of both the life and thought of the French Reformed thinker Jacques Ellul (1912-1994). It will prove an indispensable resource for those interested in this influential theologian and sociologist and for Christian ethics and political thought generally.
2002 / 1-84227-053-2 / xxiv + 378pp

David Hilborn
The Words of our Lips
Language-Use in Free Church Worship
Studies of liturgical language have tended to focus on the written canons of Roman Catholic and Anglican communities. By contrast, David Hilborn analyses the more extemporary approach of English Nonconformity. Drawing on recent developments in linguistic pragmatics, he explores similarities and differences between 'fixed' and 'free' worship, and argues for the interdependence of each.
2006 / 0-85364-977-4 / approx. 350pp

Roger Hitching
The Church and Deaf People
A Study of Identity, Communication and Relationships with Special Reference to the Ecclesiology of Jürgen Moltmann
In *The Church and Deaf People* Roger Hitching sensitively examines the history and present experience of deaf people and finds similarities between aspects of sign language and Moltmann's theological method that 'open up' new ways of understanding theological concepts.
2003 / 1-84227-222-5 / xxii + 236pp

John G. Kelly
One God, One People
The Differentiated Unity of the People of God in the Theology of
Jürgen Moltmann
The author expounds and critiques Moltmann's doctrine of God and highlights the systematic connections between it and Moltmann's influential discussion of Israel. He then proposes a fresh approach to Jewish–Christian relations building on Moltmann's work using insights from Habermas and Rawls.
2005 / 0-85346-969-3 / approx. 350pp

Mark F.W. Lovatt
Confronting the Will-to-Power
A Reconsideration of the Theology of Reinhold Niebuhr
Confronting the Will-to-Power is an analysis of the theology of Reinhold Niebuhr, arguing that his work is an attempt to identify, and provide a practical theological answer to, the existence and nature of human evil.
2001 / 1-84227-054-0 / xviii + 216pp

Neil B. MacDonald
Karl Barth and the Strange New World within the Bible
Barth, Wittgenstein, and the Metadilemmas of the Enlightenment
Barth's discovery of the strange new world within the Bible is examined in the context of Kant, Hume, Overbeck, and, most importantly, Wittgenstein. MacDonald covers some fundamental issues in theology today: epistemology, the final form of the text and biblical truth-claims.
2000 / 0-85364-970-7 / xxvi + 374pp

Keith A. Mascord
Alvin Plantinga and Christian Apologetics
This book draws together the contributions of the philosopher Alvin Plantinga to the major contemporary challenges to Christian belief, highlighting in particular his ground-breaking work in epistemology and the problem of evil. Plantinga's theory that both theistic and Christian belief is warrantedly basic is explored and critiqued, and an assessment offered as to the significance of his work for apologetic theory and practice.
2005 / 1-84227-256-X / approx. 304pp

Gillian McCulloch
The Deconstruction of Dualism in Theology
With Reference to Ecofeminist Theology and New Age Spirituality
This book challenges eco-theological anti-dualism in Christian theology, arguing that dualism has a twofold function in Christian religious discourse. Firstly, it enables us to express the discontinuities and divisions that are part of the process of reality. Secondly, dualistic language allows us to express the mysteries of divine transcendence/immanence and the survival of the soul without collapsing into monism and materialism, both of which are problematic for Christian epistemology.
2002 / 1-84227-044-3 / xii + 282pp

Leslie McCurdy
Attributes and Atonement
The Holy Love of God in the Theology of P.T. Forsyth
Attributes and Atonement is an intriguing full-length study of P.T. Forsyth's doctrine of the cross as it relates particularly to God's holy love. It includes an unparalleled bibliography of both primary and secondary material relating to Forsyth.
1999 / 0-85364-833-6 / xiv + 328pp

Nozomu Miyahira
Towards a Theology of the Concord of God
A Japanese Perspective on the Trinity
This book introduces a new Japanese theology and a unique Trinitarian formula based on the Japanese intellectual climate: three betweennesses and one concord. It also presents a new interpretation of the Trinity, a co-subordinationism, which is in line with orthodox Trinitarianism; each single person of the Trinity is eternally and equally subordinate (or serviceable) to the other persons, so that they retain the mutual dynamic equality.
2000 / 0-85364-863-8 / xiv + 256pp

Eddy José Muskus
The Origins and Early Development of Liberation Theology in Latin America
With Particular Reference to Gustavo Gutiérrez
This work challenges the fundamental premise of Liberation Theology, 'opting for the poor', and its claim that Christ is found in them. It also argues that Liberation Theology emerged as a direct result of the failure of the Roman Catholic Church in Latin America.
2002 / 0-85364-974-X / xiv + 296pp

Jim Purves
The Triune God and the Charismatic Movement
A Critical Appraisal from a Scottish Perspective
All emotion and no theology? Or a fundamental challenge to reappraise and realign our trinitarian theology in the light of Christian experience? This study of charismatic renewal as it found expression within Scotland at the end of the twentieth century evaluates the use of Patristic, Reformed and contemporary models of the Trinity in explaining the workings of the Holy Spirit.
2004 / 1-84227-321-3 / xxiv + 246pp

Anna Robbins
Methods in the Madness
Diversity in Twentieth-Century Christian Social Ethics
The author compares the ethical methods of Walter Rauschenbusch, Reinhold Niebuhr and others. She argues that unless Christians are clear about the ways that theology and philosophy are expressed practically they may lose the ability to discuss social ethics across contexts, let alone reach effective agreements.
2004 / 1-84227-211-X / xx + 294pp

Ed Rybarczyk
Beyond Salvation
Eastern Orthodoxy and Classical Pentecostalism on Becoming Like Christ
At first glance eastern Orthodoxy and classical Pentecostalism seem quite distinct. This ground-breaking study shows they share much in common, especially as it concerns the experiential elements of following Christ. Both traditions assert that authentic Christianity transcends the wooden categories of modernism.
2004 / 1-84227-144-X / xii + 356pp

Signe Sandsmark
Is World View Neutral Education Possible and Desirable?
A Christian Response to Liberal Arguments
(Published jointly with The Stapleford Centre)
This book discusses reasons for belief in world view neutrality, and argues that 'neutral' education will have a hidden, but strong world view influence. It discusses the place for Christian education in the common school.
2000 / 0-85364-973-1 / xiv + 182pp

Hazel Sherman
Reading Zechariah
The Allegorical Tradition of Biblical Interpretation through the Commentary of Didymus the Blind and Theodore of Mopsuestia
A close reading of the commentary on Zechariah by Didymus the Blind alongside that of Theodore of Mopsuestia suggests that popular categorising of Antiochene and Alexandrian biblical exegesis as 'historical' or 'allegorical' is inadequate and misleading.
2005 / 1-84227-213-6 / approx. 280pp

Andrew Sloane
On Being a Christian in the Academy
Nicholas Wolterstorff and the Practice of Christian Scholarship
An exposition and critical appraisal of Nicholas Wolterstorff's epistemology in the light of the philosophy of science, and an application of his thought to the practice of Christian scholarship.
2003 / 1-84227-058-3 / xvi + 274pp

Damon W.K. So
Jesus' Revelation of His Father
A Narrative-Conceptual Study of the Trinity with Special Reference to Karl Barth
This book explores the trinitarian dynamics in the context of Jesus' revelation of his Father in his earthly ministry with references to key passages in Matthew's Gospel. It develops from the exegeses of these passages a non-linear concept of revelation which links Jesus' communion with his Father to his revelatory words and actions through a nuanced understanding of the Holy Spirit, with references to K. Barth, G.W.H. Lampe, J.D.G. Dunn and E. Irving.
2005 / 1-84227-323-X / approx. 380pp

Daniel Strange
The Possibility of Salvation Among the Unevangelised
An Analysis of Inclusivism in Recent Evangelical Theology
For evangelical theologians the 'fate of the unevangelised' impinges upon fundamental tenets of evangelical identity. The position known as 'inclusivism', defined by the belief that the unevangelised can be ontologically saved by Christ whilst being epistemologically unaware of him, has been defended most vigorously by the Canadian evangelical Clark H. Pinnock. Through a detailed analysis and critique of Pinnock's work, this book examines a cluster of issues surrounding the unevangelised and its implications for christology, soteriology and the doctrine of revelation.
2002 / 1-84227-047-8 / xviii + 362pp

Scott Swain
God According to the Gospel
Biblical Narrative and the Identity of God in the Theology of Robert W. Jenson
Robert W. Jenson is one of the leading voices in contemporary Trinitarian theology. His boldest contribution in this area concerns his use of biblical narrative both to ground and explicate the Christian doctrine of God. *God According to the Gospel* critically examines Jenson's proposal and suggests an alternative way of reading the biblical portrayal of the triune God.
2006 / 1-84227-258-6 / approx. 180pp

Justyn Terry
The Justifying Judgement of God
A Reassessment of the Place of Judgement in the Saving Work of Christ
The argument of this book is that judgement, understood as the whole process of bringing justice, is the primary metaphor of atonement, with others, such as victory, redemption and sacrifice, subordinate to it. Judgement also provides the proper context for understanding penal substitution and the call to repentance, baptism, eucharist and holiness.
2005 / 1-84227-370-1 / approx. 274 pp

Graham Tomlin
The Power of the Cross
Theology and the Death of Christ in Paul, Luther and Pascal
This book explores the theology of the cross in St Paul, Luther and Pascal. It offers new perspectives on the theology of each, and some implications for the nature of power, apologetics, theology and church life in a postmodern context.
1999 / 0-85364-984-7 / xiv + 344pp

Adonis Vidu
Postliberal Theological Method
A Critical Study
The postliberal theology of Hans Frei, George Lindbeck, Ronald Thiemann, John Milbank and others is one of the more influential contemporary options. This book focuses on several aspects pertaining to its theological method, specifically its understanding of background, hermeneutics, epistemic justification, ontology, the nature of doctrine and, finally, Christological method.
2005 / 1-84227-395-7 / approx. 324pp

Graham J. Watts
Revelation and the Spirit
A Comparative Study of the Relationship between the Doctrine of Revelation
and Pneumatology in the Theology of Eberhard Jüngel and of
Wolfhart Pannenberg
The relationship between revelation and pneumatology is relatively unexplored.
This approach offers a fresh angle on two important twentieth century
theologians and raises pneumatological questions which are theologically crucial
and relevant to mission in a postmodern culture.
2005 / 1-84227-104-0 / xxii + 232pp

Nigel G. Wright
Disavowing Constantine
Mission, Church and the Social Order in the Theologies of John Howard Yoder
and Jürgen Moltmann
This book is a timely restatement of a radical theology of church and state in the
Anabaptist and Baptist tradition. Dr Wright constructs his argument in dialogue
and debate with Yoder and Moltmann, major contributors to a free church
perspective.
2000 / 0-85364-978-2 / xvi + 252pp

Paternoster
9 Holdom Avenue,
Bletchley,
Milton Keynes MK1 1QR,
United Kingdom
Web: www.authenticmedia.co.uk/paternoster

July 2005

Made in the USA
Monee, IL
17 September 2022

14149203R00174